4-91
20.00
B&T
VER

☞ **W9-CEB-554**

GV      John, Tommy.       26,146
865
.J58 TJ
A3
1991

**DATE DUE**

TJ: My Twenty-Six Years In Baseball
GV865.J58A3 1991          26146

John, Tommy
      VRJC/WRIGHT LIBRARY

DEMCO

# TJ: MY TWENTY-SIX YEARS IN BASEBALL

# TJ

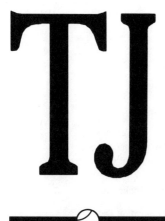

## My Twenty-six Years in Baseball

## TOMMY JOHN

*with Dan Valenti*

BANTAM BOOKS
NEW YORK · TORONTO · LONDON · SYDNEY · AUCKLAND

T.J.

A Bantam Book / April 1991

The Major League Baseball trademarks depicted in this book were reproduced with
permission from Major League Baseball Properties, Inc.

All rights reserved.
Copyright © 1991 by Tommy John.

No part of this book may be reproduced or transmitted
in any form or by any means, electronic or mechanical,
including photocopying, recording, or by any information
storage and retrieval system, without permission in writing from
the publisher.
For information address: Bantam Books.

**Library of Congress Cataloging-in-Publication Data**

John, Tommy.
TJ : my 26 years in baseball / by Tommy John with Dan Valenti.
p.    cm.
ISBN 0-553-07184-X
1. John, Tommy.   2. Baseball players—United States—Biography.
I. Valenti, Dan.   II. Title.   III. Title: T.J.
GV865.J58A3   1991
796.357'092—dc20
[B]     90-47873     CIP

*Published simultaneously in the United States and Canada*

Bantam Books are published by Bantam Books, a division of Bantam Doubleday Dell
Publishing Group, Inc. Its trademark, consisting of the words "Bantam Books" and the
portrayal of a rooster, is Registered in U.S. Patent and Trademark Office and in other
countries. Marca Registrada. Bantam Books, 666 Fifth Avenue, New York, New York
10103.

PRINTED IN THE UNITED STATES OF AMERICA
RRH   0 9 8 7 6 5 4 3 2 1

*To my dad, who provided me
with the motivation to succeed in baseball.*

*To my family—my wife Sally,
daughter Tami, and sons Tommy, Travis, and Taylor—
for allowing me the time away from home
to pursue my career in baseball.*

*—T.J.*

*To Paula and to my family, for their support.*

*—D.V.*

# ACKNOWLEDGMENTS

Various baseball people played key roles in this story, and they must get the biggest thanks, for without them, there would be no story to tell. These include, from Tommy's Cleveland years: Jerry Kindall, Hoot Evers, Bob Kennedy, and Gabe Paul. From the White Sox: Al Lopez, Eddie Stanky, and Ray Berres. From the Dodgers: Walter and Peter O'Malley, Al Campanis, Ben Wade, Red Adams, Tom Lasorda, Dr. Frank John, and Bill Buhler. From the Yankees: George Steinbrenner, Al Rosen, Sammy Ellis, Mark Connor, Dick Howser, Clyde King, Lou Piniella, and Dr. Charles P. Melore. From the Angels: Gene Autry, Buzzie Bavasi, Gene Mauch, and Tom Morgan. From the A's: Sandy Alderson.

Others helped by giving generously of their time. These include Jeff Mangold, Bill Pennington, Dave Nightingale, Bill Madden, Moss Klein, Murray Chass, Ken Coleman, Randolph Taylor, Howard Cosell, Dave Righetti, Don Mattingly, Don Baylor, Bob McClelland, Howie Kaplan, Bill Fugazy, Dr. O. S. Hawkins, Fred Claire, and Rev. Lareau Lindquist. Special recognition goes to His Eminence Terence Cardinal Cooke, and Sally's mom, Opal Simmons. We would also like to thank the research department of the National Baseball Hall of Fame in Cooperstown, New York, John Foster and Karen Rufo of the Media Services Group in Pittsfield, Massachusetts, Michael L. Valenti: the P.R. staff of the New York Yankees, and the Williams College library.

## Acknowledgments

Finally, from the book side, we thank our agents, Scott Siegel of Siegel & Siegel, Ltd. and Angela Miller of the Miller Agency, and our editors at Bantam, Tom Dyja and Greg Tobin. Their contributions were invaluable.

—Tommy John and Dan Valenti

". . . perfect hope is achieved on the brink of despair
when, instead of falling over the ledge,
we find ourselves walking on air.
Hope is always just about to turn into despair,
but never does so."

—Thomas Merton
*No Man Is an Island*

# TJ: MY TWENTY-SIX YEARS IN BASEBALL

# 1.

# DARKHORSE

Y ou never really expect it will end. You know it's going to be over one day, but when that day comes, you're still a little surprised.

You do not stop being who you are, though, just because you've taken off the uniform for the last time. When an athlete's career is over, the looking back is all part of the same process—a life that's still being lived, by the same person. Remembrance can be as alive, as vivid, and as instructive as the events upon which it reflects. That's how I feel when I look back on my twenty-nine years in baseball, twenty-six of them in the major leagues.

I pitched my first big league game while John F. Kennedy was still in the White House, and my last with the presidency occupied by another baseball fan, George Bush. I was the last active pitcher to give up a home run to Mickey Mantle. In my twenty-six years in the major leagues, more than 49,000 ball games were played: about one third of all the games in history. No one plays that long without developing an ability to overcome obstacles and bounce back from defeat. To make comebacks.

I've been coming back, it seems, most of my professional life. It's not that I lacked people who believed in me or in my abilities to play baseball. They've been there all along the way—family, friends, fans— and their support has been invaluable. But circumstance breeds challenge

3

and creates obstacles, whether it's injury, personal tragedy, or being judged "too old" to play baseball anymore. Survival rests on the ability to prove yourself, over and over again.

After a ball player turns forty, this challenge intensifies; it seems that for every person who's pulling for you, there are two who say you can't make it.

When Casey Stengel was fired after losing the 1960 World Series to the Pittsburgh Pirates, he told the writers: "I'll never make the mistake of being seventy again." A younger man might have been forgiven for losing, but not Casey in 1960 . . . nor me, it seemed, for the last five years of my career.

Each year from 1985 to 1989, I had to "make the team," had to prove that I could still pitch. An older player doesn't have the luxury of nursing an injury, or having two bad outings in a row. And no struggle was tougher than my bid to make the New York Yankees as a walk-on in 1989.

The 1988 season had ended on a note of uncertainty. That year, and the year before, had been successful ones for me: 22 wins and a .611 winning percentage, both second best on the staff for those two years. But '88 had a Jekyll and Hyde quality about it. In my first 23 games, 20 of them starts, I went 8–3, but in my final 12 starts the record slipped to 1–5. It was a combination of poor pitching and lack of support.

Late in September, with the pennant race decided and the Yankees out of it, I went in to see club owner George Steinbrenner at Yankee Stadium, to ask him where I stood for next year. The end of the season usually wasn't a good time for a veteran ballplayer to talk to George, because he had other things on his mind—the free agent market, trades, contract situations. But I didn't want to wait. Waiting is another thing a forty-five-year-old ballplayer can't do.

George's office was something every Yankee player was aware of, as much for its physical presence as for the intrusive character of its inhabitant. The office overlooked the field, which meant when George was in town, he saw everything that happened during the game. You knew he was up there, watching. Looking up from the field, George's lair was just to the right of the last luxury box on the third base side.

The office had taken on George's personality. It was huge, centered by a big desk. Not flashy, but commanding; not ostentatious, but dripping with power. The walls were lined with photos of key players and events from his years as owner. But the most startling piece of furniture—the one that always stood out, no matter how many times you'd been in there—was The Chair.

The Chair was a gigantic baseball-glove chair. It stood about six feet high and four feet across, filled with Styrofoam balls. That's where you sat when you talked to George: in the pocket of the glove, so he had you in the palm of his hand.

I went inside. There was George, dressed in a blue blazer, gray slacks, and a club tie, his virtual "uniform" when at Yankee Stadium. He sometimes wore suits, but usually it was a blazer and slacks, and never, ever, without a tie. In fact, the only time you'd ever see George without a tie was in Florida at spring training, when he'd dress in a golf shirt, slacks, and windbreaker.

After we talked in general about my season, I asked George a simple question:

"Am I in the team's plans for 1989?"

George sat back in his chair, fiddling with the Yankee world's championship ring on his finger. He looked me directly in the eye.

"Tommy," he said, "you don't have anything to worry about."

He talked about loyalty and how the organization felt about me. He praised the job I had done for him over the years, but he wouldn't be more specific about his intentions, not spelling out if he meant there was a spot for me as a player, or perhaps a coaching job. The reason, as it turned out, was that he was less than two weeks away from changing managers. Lou Piniella was out. A new manager would be coming in, with a new philosophy on how the Yankees should be run.

On October 7, 1988, George made the sixteenth managerial change in the sixteen years of his reign as owner, naming Dallas Green as his new field boss. George decided he wanted to go another route when the 1988 season ended—to change the direction of the organization by bringing in a disciplinarian. He felt Lou had lost control of the ball club.

The Yankees set a club record with 16 wins in April of '88, and had been in first place all but two days in May, where they stayed for the first nineteen days of June. From late June through August, we hung close, but we dropped three of four in a crucial series against the Red Sox at Fenway Park in the middle of September. On September 15 we beat Sox ace Roger Clemens to climb within three and a half games of Boston, but they went on to take the next three, erasing hopes for a repeat of 1978 and all but ending our flag hopes.

5

George got tired of seeing the club fold late in the year, and felt that the players needed a heavier hand, someone to come in and lay down the law. Someone who would have it done his way . . . or the highway. Dallas certainly had that reputation. He had dragged the Philadelphia Phillies, kicking and screaming, into a World Series victory in 1980.

The change didn't faze me. I'd been around long enough and had gone through enough managerial changes not to be overly concerned. Managers come in and bring their own people with them, their own ideas. That's baseball. Besides, Dallas was a winner. True, he had only two full years as a big league field boss, but he won both times, a world championship in 1980, and a divisional title in 1981. I had no idea how Dallas felt about me, either personally or as a pitcher.

If anything, I thought he liked my style of pitching. In 1985, when I was with the Angels and he was general manager of the Cubs, Dallas tried to trade for me, even up, for Dick Ruthven. The Angels nixed that deal, though, because Ruthven had a $400,000 payout in deferred money. California didn't want to assume that debt. But Dallas wanted me, and I heard he was disappointed when the deal fell through. That's the first thing that crossed my mind when I heard that he was coming in to manage the Yankees. The guy wanted me once, so he probably would have some use for me for 1989. I felt good about it.

On Halloween the Yankees held a press conference to introduce Dallas to the New York media. Halloween's a big day in our house. My wife Sally and I dress up along with our children, a tradition we carried over from our own childhoods. The kids' school throws a big party, and we were running around, getting everybody ready in costume and makeup. We were literally going out the door when the phone rang. It was Moss Klein, who covered the Yankees for the Newark *Star-Ledger.*

"Did you hear what Dallas said about you today?" he asked me.

"No. What did he say?"

"Are you sitting?"

Moss related that the topic of Tommy John and Ron Guidry came up, and Dallas said he had absolutely no plans for me. He left the door open a little bit for Guidry, but as for John, there wasn't even "the remotest chance" of him pitching, either as a starter or out of the bullpen. Dallas said I had had a great career, but a guy who's forty-five years old should be doing something else with his life, and not playing baseball.

He added that it was time to make way for some of the younger pitchers, and that I didn't fit in with his plans for the 1989 Yankees. As far as he was concerned, I was finished. As I came to learn, Dallas isn't the most tactful person in the world. He says things then closes his mind. End of discussion.

I hung up the phone and quickly filled Sally in before we left for the party. Our reactions were different. I was more surprised than hurt. She was upset. I wasn't that troubled, having been written off by managers and teams before. A new boss comes in with his fixed ideas about me, but I end up making the ball club. Now, if George Steinbrenner had been the one to say I was finished, I *would* have been worried. Sally said she assumed that Dallas simply reflected George's thinking, but I disagreed. I knew of Dallas's pride in being his own man. His thoughts were his own. He wanted to come in with some perceived distance between George and himself.

"Let's wait and talk to George first before we assume too much or do anything hasty," I advised her.

Sally agreed, but I could tell she was still upset. Despite my reassurances, and even my attempts to push Dallas's remarks out of my mind, the situation haunted us during the party. The press conference had been splashed all over the news, and everybody kept asking us about it. Sally feared that if Dallas meant what he said, it might spell an inglorious end to my career. She feared the humiliation of having twenty-five years in baseball ended by a new manager coming in and simply saying I was all done. She took it hard.

At the party, I did my usual joking around with the schoolchildren. We ran one of the booths, a dart toss game. From time to time, when a kid would toss one of the darts, it reminded me of pitching a baseball. Was Sally right? Would my career end this way? Doubt was creeping slowly into my mind.

What bothered me was that I knew in my heart I could still pitch. But would Dallas give me a chance? That's all I needed, or wanted: a chance. That's all I've ever wanted when faced with an uphill battle. When I blew my arm out in 1974, people gave up on me. But I knew in my mind that if I could just get that one chance in a hundred, I could take care of the rest. When my son Travis fell out a third-story window in 1981, all I wanted to hear from the doctor was that he had a chance. Just a chance.

Dallas's remarks had come out of the blue. I didn't have any idea he would categorically say "That's it. It's all over." For each of the last four years, I had to come into spring training riding the line of making the team or being released. I needed to win a job, true. I was willing to do that. But I wasn't willing to hear the words "no chance." *No chance* means literally that: it's impossible. The more I thought about what Dallas had said, the more it got to me and the more I started to boil.

When we got home, Sally and I didn't talk about it anymore. But the phone didn't stop ringing. The writers wanted to know my reaction, what my plans were, and if I was going to quit and look for something else. I answered diplomatically, just telling the truth. I said I wasn't done as a pitcher, but couldn't really say anything definitive until I spoke to George and to Dallas.

Steinbrenner tried to call me a couple of days later, but I missed the call. I ended up calling him, wanting to know just where I stood in the light of Dallas's comments. George was honest.

"This is what Dallas wants to do," he told me. "I've given him complete control of this team. He wants to go with some of the young pitchers, and his staff agrees. It's his team, Tommy. I don't want to step on him."

George was absolutely right. He then added a little reassurance.

"We'll talk at some point about doing something within the organization: coaching, minor league managing, front office, TV work, whatever. You've been a good Yankee. I won't forget that."

"Okay, George," I answered. "You know how I feel about you and the Yankees. You've been great to me and my family. Whatever you have in mind is fine. But I know I can still pitch."

George and I didn't talk after that. I couldn't declare for free agency. I had done so in 1986 and 1987 as a favor to the team to free up space on the forty-man roster, and repeater rights in baseball's Basic Agreement prevented me from doing so again. In early December, just before the big league draft at the winter meetings, I got a call from New York's general manager, Bob Quinn, who talked on his speaker phone, explaining my options in his typical soft-spoken manner. He put it this way: I could take an assignment to Columbus of the International League, or the Yankees would have to release me. By agreeing to a Columbus contract, the team could take me off the forty-man roster, protect one of the young pitchers from the draft, and not have to let me go.

I told Bob I could agree to a minor league contract with certain stipulations: first, that they pay my major league salary. Second, that the contract specify that after x number of days I would either be called up to the Yankees or released from my contract and paid an agreed-upon buyout figure. Quinn, however, said the Yankees wouldn't agree to that.

"If you accept the Columbus contract, Tommy, you'd be going down to the minors as a minor leaguer."

"I have no intention of doing that," I answered, explaining that pitching down in the minor leagues wasn't going to help me, unless I was desperate to hang on, which I wasn't. If I couldn't pitch for a big league ball club, then I was through playing ball.

I asked Bob point-blank: "Do you have any plans with me for the Yankees?"

"No, we don't," he said.

"You mean you don't want me to pitch at all? Not even come to spring training on a trial basis?"

"No. We won't have anything like that for you."

So it was just a matter of time, apparently, before my Yankee career ended with a whimper . . . December 20, to be exact. That's the last day a team can offer you a contract. If they don't, you become an unrestricted free agent.

No offer came. Without so much as an i being dotted, I was on free float, baseball's equivalent to zero gravity: being released without a ball club.

We got a Christmas card from George. In his immaculate and delicate penmanship, George expressed regret. He said that the last two months had been the most uncomfortable he could remember. He was particularly pained, he said, at approving the decision not to offer contracts to me or Willie Randolph, but that he had to do so, to "exert new leadership" for the Yankees. He ended with a softener, expressing his feelings toward me.

". . . remember where my office is," he concluded.

It was a heartfelt note; George through and through.

Sally and I faced the uncertain future as we had throughout our marriage: together. We prayed, not for God to remove our difficulties, but for courage. I pray daily, taking the things that are going on in my life and bringing them before God.

The Bible says that God will never put more of a burden on you than what you're able to bear. That's the basis of my faith, and what I kept coming back to in my mind. Job was like that. He was hit with everything: affliction after affliction. But he never lost his faith. The other biblical notion in all of this was that adversity breeds strength. Being a Christian doesn't mean an easy life; a Christian has just as many problems as the next guy. But it does mean having a method of dealing with what's thrown your way.

Well, the worst thing you can do when things aren't going your way is to sit around moping and feeling sorry for yourself. I had just begun a winter workout program to get myself in shape. After my release, I dove into my workouts even harder and with elevated intensity. For one thing, it became an emotional outlet, a safety valve. But I believed that somehow I'd get a chance to pitch again; when that chance came, I had to be physically ready, so I wouldn't embarrass myself or the club.

Shortly after my workouts began, Chicago White Sox owner Jerry Reinsdorf called me. I had pleasant talks with Jerry and with White Sox manager Jeff Torborg. Jeff and I had been good friends since his days as the Yankees bullpen coach. Reinsdorf told me the White Sox might want to bring me into spring training, more or less as a player coach— a player advisor, really—to help their young pitching staff. Whatever pitching I could give them would be a bonus, Jerry said. An added attraction for me was Sammy Ellis, Chicago's pitching coach, who had helped me so much when he was with the Yankees a few years earlier. Chicago's interest sparked my workouts even more.

Jeff Mangold, former strength coach with the Yankees, developed a fitness program for me. Jeff had been fired when Dallas came aboard. The team wanted a complete change, and that included the strength program. Jeff landed on his feet, however, and started a company called Phase 4 Fitness, where he worked as a personal trainer, a sports trainer, and as a corporate fitness consultant. I liked Jeff's work when he was with the Yankees. He's a good coach, very intense, and an excellent motivator.

My winter workout program wasn't an ordinary one. I never trained harder in my life. We worked out Monday, Wednesday, and Friday each week at a health club in Paramus, New Jersey, not far from my home in Cresskill. For the first three weeks we performed a general strength program to tone the muscles and lay a foundation for the heavier work to come. Jeff taught me proper lifting techniques on the free weights, correcting my form. I had never been big on free weights, but I did it this time to build up my strength.

After the third week, Jeff increased the intensity. He developed a circuit of a dozen exercises. The circuit alternated two or three strength exercises such as barbell squats, lat pull-downs, and shoulder press, with an aerobic activity such as running or climbing a Stairmaster. He'd throw in some light abdominal work and stretching also. For each exercise, I'd have a minute to do a certain amount of repetitions, say fifteen reps at x number of pounds. Between stations, Jeff would let me rest for about thirty seconds while he set up the next exercise.

Jeff's strategy was lighter weights, but with many repetitions performed at great speed. The idea was to overload my body, the muscular and cardiovascular systems, so that I would get used to performing under fatigue. The workouts elevated my heart rate into the 160s. We kept my heart rate in my target zone for ten minutes of a twenty-minute workout. After such strenuous work, pitching would hardly seem taxing.

On Mondays and Wednesdays Jeff put me through the circuit, increasing the weights and also the duration. After completing a full circuit, I'd get a two-minute rest, then go through the gauntlet again. When I got done, I was absolutely exhausted. My heart rate would be exploding, and my metabolism would stay high for hours after, burning up calories. It was grueling, but fun. I had never worked out with such intensity before, and very quickly I started to feel the difference. In fact, I soon got into amazing shape.

To augment our work at the gym, I bought a treadmill and a "Versaclimber." These went in our bedroom, where I would work out and do things on my own, things you could do at eleven o'clock at night, when you couldn't go down to the health club. Including running, stretching, shooting hoops, and the circuit work, I'd spend four hours at the gym. On my off days I'd work out for about four hours at home, on the treadmill and climber, and with outside jogging. On workout days I'd cut down my home sessions, but still did something each night.

People who saw me working out at the time told Sally that I was like a man on a mission. It's funny. Sally started coming to the health club with me, and she started enjoying her own workouts. So, over the weeks, we built up relationships with the regulars at the spa. Every day they'd ask me, "Tommy, did you hear anything yet? Did a ball club call you? What's George going to do?"

They were behind me, really pulling for me. This support had an energizing effect on my workouts, but more important, it made me feel great that there were people out there who still cared about me and my career. When people are behind you like that, it makes the mental struggle less exhausting. You get added drive to continue, because you don't want to let down your supporters.

The workouts continued with no further word from the ball club. Then the unexpected happened. On February 3, thirteen days before pitchers and catchers were to report to camp, George Steinbrenner flew into New York on business and made a surprising announcement. He reversed the team's recent policy on older players, offering Ron Guidry a deal to come down to spring training: $250,000 guaranteed for coming to Fort Lauderdale, with another $250,000 if he made the club.

During the announcement, Murray Chass of the *New York Times* asked George about me. George didn't tip his hand categorically, but he said he might offer me the same deal. The writers jumped on that, saying words to the effect of: "Wait a minute. Dallas Green said Tommy was all done. Are you overruling Dallas?"

I could see what they were doing: trying to stir something up between Dallas and George. That's part of playing baseball in New York. George sells papers. But that didn't concern me; there was a glimmer of hope that I might remain a Yankee, which is what I really wanted.

Joe Durso of the *Times* called me up and asked me how I felt.

"I'm one of the few players who didn't want to leave," I told him. "If I had my druthers, I'd want to stay in New York and pitch for the Yankees. Everybody says George said this and George said that. I haven't talked to George in two, maybe two and a half months. Ever since they said they were going with the younger guys, I've been calling other clubs to find a job . . . But I was surprised to read over the weekend that George seemed interested . . . I want to pitch. But George and I have to sit down and talk."

George didn't surprise me by what he did for Guidry. He was very good to guys who have played well for him, guys who have won for him. Gator was part of a World Series winner. We never won a world's title when I was on the ball club, but we won a divisional title and the American League pennant in 1981, and I pitched well both times. George remembers things like that. He's loyal. He likes people to be loyal in return.

Guidry and I were "good Yankees." It was as simple as that. We pitched well, kept our noses clean, and provided good images. We had the "Yankee look," what George called "Yankee tradition." In the back of my mind was my chat with George back in September, when he told me: "Tommy, you don't have anything to worry about." He was a man of his word.

I tried to call him at his offices in Tampa, but he wasn't around. His secretary put me on his call list, and when he got back to me, George invited me and Sally down to Tampa to have lunch with him and discuss the future. This was right in the middle of my talks with the White Sox.

We jumped on a plane and flew down to Tampa on Wednesday, February 8. George had his limo and driver there to meet us at the airport and drive us to the hotel. George came in, dressed in a dark, conservative business suit. We had a nice lunch and talked. All this took place at the Bay Harbour Inn in Tampa, a luxury beachfront hotel which George owned. I guess George favored the hotel over his office at his company headquarters because he would not be interrupted or distracted.

After the amenities were over, we got down to business.

"What are you thinking? What do you want to do?" he asked me.

I told him I'd been working out and that I was in great shape.

"I know I can pitch for somebody. I'd love to pitch for you."

We discussed my performance in 1988. George knew that I led the club in starts and was second in innings pitched (176 ⅓). He even brought my statistics up. He was leading up to something.

George agreed that my 9–8 could have been improved if I'd had better defense behind me, and said that some of the losses weren't my fault. I appreciated that, and then brought up the topic of Dallas Green.

"Dallas says that I don't have a chance to make the team."

George came back quickly.

"Dallas is my manager, but I control who goes to spring training. You can come down; you'll be given a chance. I can offer you the same deal that I gave to Ron. A guaranteed $250,000 for coming to camp. Another $250,000 if you make the team."

George's words washed over me with a sense of relief. Sally then asked the hard question that needed to be asked.

"George, do you think we can take the offer without Dallas's approval? Because he made such a point about this being *his* team, and that he'd run it *his* way. Tommy might go down there and get blackballed."

George didn't say anything. His mouth tightened. Sally then asked George if he would call Dallas, to ask his new manager what his plans were for Tommy.

"I'm serious," Sally said. "Can you call him? We read in the paper—"

George interrupted: "What's been in the paper about it?"

"George, you know what's been in the paper on how Dallas feels about Tommy," Sally replied. "He says he's finished."

"No," George said. "I don't believe that. He didn't say that."

"Well," Sally answered, "it's a direct quote."

I then asked George if he thought I should call Dallas and tell him about the offer.

"I don't want to do anything that will cause problems for the team," I told George. "Dallas obviously doesn't want me. If I have *any* chance to make the ball club, I'll go. But if he's absolutely adamant about me not making it, I don't know. Because if a manager says you've got no chance, it's hard to persuade him otherwise. But if Dallas says, 'Hey, Tommy, if George wants you to come down, I'll give you a look, a fair evaluation,' that's all I'd want to hear."

George said Dallas would give me a fair chance.

"Yeah," I said, "he probably will. But I would feel better if I called him and heard it straight from his mouth."

George then looked at us and said: "I'm not going to call Dallas. Look, when you and Sally get back home, think about my offer. I heard you're negotiating with another team. See what they can do, and compare that with my offer. Then you call Dallas. That's a good idea and I advise it. Talk about it with him and see where you stand. But I think he'll give you the same shot Guidry has."

George then tried to convince us: "You guys come down to spring training. I think it's hard at forty-five years old, but if you think you can still pitch, Tommy, that's good enough for me. I think you'll get your shot at it."

I told George I'd let him know by Monday or Tuesday. We flew back home to New Jersey on Friday, talking things over, weighing the pros and cons of each situation. The White Sox were close to making me an offer—a good one—but we were leaning toward George and the Yankees. Much depended on what we heard from Dallas.

We got back and I called Jerry Reinsdorf, filling him in on my meeting with George.

The press, in the meantime, got on the story. The New York *Post* led with it this way: "George Steinbrenner continues to do it his way

—with or without the blessings of Dallas Green." It went on to say, accurately, that "John . . . did not immediately jump at the offer."

Some of the talk shows got on me for that. I remember a broadcaster on WFAN in New York raking me over the coals for not taking Steinbrenner's offer immediately. He blasted me for trying to hold George up for more money. I went on a show myself as a guest and answered those charges.

"You want to really know what's going on? First, I told George I'd have an answer for him by Tuesday. Second, I want to get to Jerry Reinsdorf first and tell him what had transpired. It's only courtesy. It's common decency." I was not holding out for more money.

And I did owe that much to the White Sox. They had been extremely cordial and fair with me, and I had to let them know about George's guaranteed offer. When I got through to Reinsdorf, he asked me what I was going to do. He said George's offer to me made the Chicago papers.

"I honestly don't know, Jerry. What do you think I should do?"

"As much as we'd love to have you down in Sarasota with the White Sox, I think I'd have to have you committed if you didn't take the guaranteed money. In your right mind, you can't turn George down. The worst thing that's going to happen is that you won't make the Yankees, but you'll get your $250,000. We'll keep tabs on you in spring training, and if you're released, you might make our ball club anyway."

He was right, of course, and hearing him say that made our decision easier. Then we asked the kids how they felt. When you come down to a decision of this magnitude, you can't be selfish. You don't just lay down the law and say, "We're going here." I've seen a lot of ball players take the iron-fisted approach when it comes to the family, and the kids ended up hating baseball. It disrupted their lives, their fathers were never home, and they didn't have any say in the matter.

So we asked the children: Would you rather go to the White Sox, or should we stay with the Yankees? We told them I might not make either team. The kids—Tami, Tommy, Travis, and Taylor—all wanted to stay in New York. They were doing well in school, and that's where their friends were. They liked the team, the Stadium, and the players, especially Don Mattingly and Dave Righetti.

But there was one more call to make before making my decision.

Saturday morning, February 11, I tried calling Dallas. I got his answering machine. I made three calls to him that day, and left messages each time. Finally, Saturday night, Dallas returned my call. I was in the kitchen. Sally was upstairs, straightening out some drawers in the boys' room.

We both picked up at the same time. Sally said later that she was going to hang up, but when she heard "This is Dallas," she decided to listen, because it might get interesting.

Did it ever.

Dallas was blunt and gruff. If you took out all the four-letter words, his conversation was very short. But that's Dallas. I asked him what his plans were. He did most of the talking; I did most of the listening.

Dallas said he was angry that I went to George without getting his permission, but said sarcastically, "I'm only the manager.

"I don't know what you've got on the old man," he bellowed, "but apparently it's something big. Because I don't want you down here [at training camp], but the old man does. It's his money. I can't keep him from spending it, and I can't stop him from bringing you down. All I can tell you is you'll be wasting your time and my time. I said it before: a guy your age should quit baseball. You should be doing other things."

"Like managing," I said.

"We don't have the goddamn time to spend with an old, bleeping fart like you. Guidry's only thirty-eight. I can understand inviting Guidry to camp. But you're forty-five bleeping years old. You've had a great career, but dammit, you should be doing something else. A forty-five-year-old man has no bleeping business playing baseball! We're going to try to get our ball club ready to go. If you do come, don't expect my coaches to spend any time with you. They're going to be busy. I don't want you bothering them or expecting any special privileges. Come on down and take the old man's blankety-blank money. I don't blame you for that. I probably would too. I don't know how much you'll pitch or get to do if you come down here. But if you feel you need to do this, you do it."

"Well, thank you, Dallas," I answered, trying to stay calm and contained. "I just want to ask you one thing. Do I have a chance? If I come down, will I get even a *remote* chance?"

Dallas hedged: "I'm telling you. You really shouldn't be playing baseball."

I pressed him: "Are you saying I won't get any look, any evaluation?"

16

"No," he answered. "I'm not saying that. All I'm saying is we won't have time for you."

"Just tell me: do I have a chance?"

He paused: "You don't have a chance in hell of making my ball club."

I thanked him for his time. Before I hung up, I said: "I'll tell you one thing, Dallas. You will never see a ball player work harder than I will."

That's how the conversation ended. Sally came flying down the stairs, screaming her head off. She was livid.

"We've been married almost nineteen years," Sally said. "I've never heard anybody in baseball talk to you the way that man just did."

Nor had I, to be honest. I later learned, from talking with him and watching him in action, that Dallas routinely dealt with people that way. But I've played for tougher managers, guys who were difficult and hard-nosed, so I tried to take what Dallas said in that context.

I had held my tongue during our phone call because I respected Dallas. I may not have liked him, but I respected him as a baseball man, and I respected his title as manager of the New York Yankees.

Sally asked me if I had ever had a run-in with Dallas to possibly explain his manner on the phone. The answer was no. I explained that, if you thought about it rationally, you could understand his being upset with George's intervention. He was getting his first taste of how George likes to run his ball club. Dallas wasn't used to that, and I don't think he wanted to believe that George would cross him. He was, in his own mind, the intimidator. But as Dave Nightingale of *The Sporting News* observed, Dallas's idea of intimidation is to be six feet, five inches tall and scream a lot.

The phone call had a curious effect on me. Instead of spurring me into the waiting arms of the Chicago White Sox, it upset me to the point where I couldn't wait to get down to spring training with the Yankees. Courtesy of Dallas, I had an added incentive for going to Fort Lauderdale instead of Sarasota with Chicago. I wanted to go down and prove that Dallas was wrong. He expected some broken-down wreck to be wheeled onto the field with an oxygen mask over his mouth. He expected some geezer hanging on for a quick quarter of a million dollars. I was determined he would never see that. Sally backed me 110 percent.

I dove into my workouts with the added incentive. On Monday, with word of my meeting with George all over New York, we walked into the spa for one of our last workouts. The usual noise that one hears in a spa—the clanging of the weight machines, the silvery, lubricated sound of the exercise bikes, the huffing and puffing of people—quieted down. People stopped what they were doing, many of them in mid-exercise, and burst into cheers. It was as if I had just graduated from high school and had been signed as a rookie. The spontaneous show of affection touched Sally and me deeply.

From then on, whenever someone would see me working out, they'd yell encouragement. People would see me running in the streets of Cresskill and clap. They'd hold up their fists and say: "Go for it, Tommy." It meant a great deal to me as I prepared for the challenge of spring training.

By the time we left for Florida, I was in top shape. Dallas didn't know that. I would educate him. I might not make the team, but at least I would rip the door to his closed mind right off its hinges. That was the underlying factor in my decision to take George's offer.

Logically, another man in the same situation might have used what Dallas said as a reason to rush to the White Sox. They had a good package if I made the team. The base was around $350,000 with strong incentives. I was comfortable with the organization. But after talking with Dallas, I was what other people were calling me: a man on a mission. I don't know what it is about me that responds that way to challenges; I just do. I've always been that way.

Now, I was ready to really start going. The first team workout was less than a week away, on February 17. Sally and I went out to dinner that night, Saturday night of Valentine's Day weekend. We felt that George had confidence in me, and we hung on to that. We decided to take that confidence, my heart and determination, wrap it up in a ball, and go for it.

We celebrated with a quiet, romantic dinner at a restaurant in Cresskill. Sally and I sat by the fireplace, both feeling giddy, a little like newlyweds. We talked all evening of the challenge that lay ahead and how we'd attack it.

# 2.
# BEGINNINGS

T he phone conversation with Dallas had been motivating but unnerving. If I wanted to play baseball in New York, it would be a colossal struggle. Baseball was never meant to be that way. Everyone who's played the game as a kid, for the love of it, feels that way. Baseball's not just another business run by owners and agents, driven by contracts and politics. It's a game first played on a sandlot field or a playground diamond with your friends. Somehow, you always want it to stay that way; the way it was in the beginning.

I was born on May 22, 1943, in Terre Haute, Indiana. We were a family of four: my dad, Thomas E. John Sr.; my mom Ruth; and my sister Marilyn, who was six years older than me. My dad was a full-blooded Welshman. Mom's folks were from southern Indiana, a mix of English, Irish, Scotch, and some Indian. I think a lot of my personality comes from the Welsh influence. The Welsh are a tough, hard-nosed people, and that's probably where my determination, even stubbornness, derives.

My parents were warm and open, and their love affected me profoundly as I grew up. I realized that more and more, the older I got. If anything else from my parents stayed with me the rest of my life, it was the need to respect authority. I was taught to respect coaches, teachers,

VERNON REGIONAL
JUNIOR COLLEGE LIBRARY

parents, adults. You addressed them as "Yes, ma'am; no, ma'am. Yes, sir; no, sir." Whatever they said, that's the way it was.

It was a comfortable, lower-middle-class upbringing. My dad worked for the Public Service Company of Indiana as a lineman. I never had a clue as to what he made, but at his highest, he probably never got more than $15,000 a year. He'd supplement that by taking on odd jobs. I remember one summer, he and some friends put in smoke alarms in houses. One guy would get the contracts on them, and my dad would come in on a Saturday and install them. He took me with him whenever he could. I happily tagged along like a shadow.

My mom stayed home. She didn't go to work until my sister went off to college. She raised her family. That was her job. After that, she worked off and on, but when I was growing up, she was always home. There was no such thing as a latchkey child back then.

We lived about two blocks from school. When school got out, I'd race home, jump into my play clothes, and go outside to play with my friends. If it was fall, we'd play football. In the winter, the sport was basketball.

We had a basketball hoop set up in the backyard, and we used that until we were old enough to play organized basketball in a gymnasium. Until then, we played basketball outside, with snow on the ground. We'd go out, shoot baskets, and after a while the snow would pack down pretty good. It got slick, but you could still shoot. As I got older, I'd bike all over the city, playing basketball in different driveways and back-yards. There were three or four homes that had real good driveways, with poured concrete half-courts.

Indiana lives for basketball. The movie *Hoosiers* accurately captured Indiana's basketball atmosphere, especially the shots of the barns, with the hoops nailed up on them. That's how it is in Indiana. Basketball is part of your cultural heritage.

One memory in particular exemplifies how my parents cared about me, and it involves basketball. When I was a little boy, my mom and dad got me a basketball for Christmas. I had no idea what they paid for it, but it was much better than the cheap, rubber one I had. This one was leather, regulation size and weight, my first really good one. Boy, that was special, because back then we'd get one big gift for Christmas and that was it. The rest of our gifts would consist of clothes, maybe underwear or pajamas. That basketball was my pride and joy. Our basketball hoop was outside on the garage, in Dad's garden. It was a garden during the spring and summer, a basketball court in the fall and winter.

Not too long after getting the ball, I was playing with it, put a shot up, and it hit a shard of glass in one of the garage windows. The ball ripped open. I was crushed. Normally, I'd take the ball down to the filling station and have it patched, but this ball couldn't be saved. I was afraid to tell my dad, because I knew it cost him a lot, so I went in and told my mother. When Dad came home, she told him what happened and smoothed it over.

Dad didn't get mad at all. He knew it was an accident. He and Mom went down to the sporting goods store the next day and bought me another ball just like the first one. I never forgot that; it was a tangible expression of my parent's care. It was a little thing, but it's the ordinary actions that become the best measures of extraordinary love.

When basketball season ended, baseball took over. We lived a mile outside town, at 3133 North Sixteenth Street, and the atmosphere was city and rural at the same time. Terre Haute had a population of about 75,000 people—not a metropolis, but not small either. There were always fields and parks to play in; Spencer Field on the north side of town, Woodrow Wilson to the south.

Spencer Field was three blocks square with about ten baseball diamonds. We played at Spencer constantly. Summers were best. You could find games going on all the time. I'd ride my bike down to Spencer in the morning and get in a game. Even if my team wasn't scheduled to play, I'd hang around, because somebody would invariably come up short. You'd always be in a game. You may not be playing the position you'd normally play, but you were playing baseball. To me, that was all that mattered.

I found myself attracted to pitching right away. I enjoyed the feeling of being in the middle of the diamond, holding the ball, in charge of the game, attention focused on me. You felt important, like no other position on the field. The game doesn't start until the pitcher puts the ball in play. The other appeal was pitching's cat-and-mouse aspect. That game-within-a-game takes place on every pitch, on every batter; it keeps the game fresh.

Dad didn't push me, but he did encourage me, simply because I enjoyed sports. He made sure that I had plenty of equipment growing up: gloves, baseball shoes, football gear. Mom and Dad never minded us playing in our backyard, no matter how much we tore it up. They'd rather have us there than somewhere else out of sight, where you could get into trouble. When my dad built the house, he bought two lots and put the house in the middle. So we had a side yard and a big back-yard, big enough to punt footballs in. We did everything back there: football, basketball, baseball, driving golf balls. Whatever the sport re-quired, that's what our yard became. It could be Wrigley Field, Soldier's Field, or Sportsman's Park, transformed instantly by the imagination.

Dad had been a good semipro baseball player himself, and he had a lot to teach me about the game. One day, he was sitting in the kitchen, drinking a cup of coffee, when he discovered just how serious I was about pitching. He looked out the window to see his eight-year-old son in the backyard, struggling with a wheelbarrow full of dirt, spilling most of it. The wheelbarrow was too much for me. I almost fell under its weight, but I wouldn't give up. Dad watched me for quite a while.

"What's Tommy doing?" Mom asked.

"I'm not sure, but I think he's trying to build himself a pitcher's mound," Dad answered. He quickly finished his coffee and came out to help me. Together, we fashioned a pretty nice mound. We then mea-sured off a distance and dug out a spot for home plate.

One of the most important early lessons he taught me was to throw strikes. When I was about eight, I sent off for a book on how to pitch by Bob Feller. It cost me three dollars, which was a lot for a kid back then. I eagerly read the book from cover to cover and got hooked on pitching. In the back of the book, Feller showed how to build a strike zone using stakes and string to outline where the knees and shoulders would be on an imaginary batter. I showed it to Dad. He went out, got some stakes, and built it for me. Then he told me something that I never forgot. He said that no matter how hard a pitcher could throw, it didn't mean a thing unless he could throw strikes. Location, not speed, was the most important thing for a young pitcher to learn.

I'd take a bucket of balls and, throwing off my mound, spend hours pitching to the stake-and-string strike zone, with my dad catching behind the strings. The strings made me aware of the strike zone. Every year, Dad would set up the strike zone in the spring, drive the stakes down, and I'd work on my control, throwing a hundred pitches a day all spring. By the time I was ready for high school, I had better than average control, even though I was a left-hander.

I grew up as a dyed-in-the-wool Cubs fan. I followed them religiously, in the papers and on the radio. My favorite players were Dee Fondy and Hank Sauer. I'd listen to broadcasters Bert Wilson and Jack Quinlan do the play-by-play, following the game in my mind. At night I'd listen to Harry Caray, Jack Buck, and Joe Garagiola broadcast the St. Louis Cardinals games. We'd get the *Game of the Week* on television, but all they seemed to show back then were the Yankees, and I didn't care for them, though I did like Whitey Ford. My dad told me Ford was a good one to watch. He had a nice, easy motion, and never seemed to be working hard when he pitched. He pitched with his head, Dad said.

Dad also taught me not to be afraid to throw a lot. Kids often hear a lot of cautionary advice, but Dad said the only way to develop a fastball is to try to throw one. Dad said a person didn't have to be born with a natural fastball. If you weren't blessed with one, you could develop one by throwing a lot and throwing hard. By throwing often and hard, he said, you build up arm strength, and that's what happened with me.

Besides organized ball and pickup games, we'd spend hours at a time playing stoop ball, where you throw a rubber ball against the steps. If you catch the ball, it's an out. Certain distances mark single, double, and so on. My best friend, Mickey Kulinski, was a Cardinal fan, and when we played stoop ball, it was always the Cubs versus the Cardinals, complete with our own play-by-play:

"Dee Fondy digging in for the Cubs. Here's the pitch. There's a drive hit deep. It's rolling to the alley. Here comes Miksis in to score, and Fondy pulls up with a stand-up double."

Mick would do a similar play-by-play, but with names like Joe Cunningham, Red Schoendienst, and Stan Musial. Mickey and I were inseparable. Not only was he my stoop-ball mate, but he was also the only catcher I had all through Little League, Babe Ruth League, and Legion ball. I think that continuity helped me develop the consistency a young pitcher needs if he is to someday elevate his game to the professional level.

Over the course of the spring, we'd go to a couple of big league games, usually on a Sunday in April or May, before my Little League season started. During the season, our team's sponsor, Art Compton Cleaners, would take us to a doubleheader in Cincinnati. We'd go in a five-car caravan, with the parents driving. Mr. Compton was a great sportsman, and he'd buy thirty tickets to the game. We'd catch the twin bill at Crosley Field, then after the game drive to Coney Island, a big amusement park.

The mothers would make fried chicken, potato salad, and cole slaw, the men would haul the beverages, and we'd have a tailgate party in the Coney Island parking lot. We'd spend the rest of the day and early evening at Coney, riding the rides, playing the games on the midway, then drive back home. Looking back on it now, I don't know how our parents had the energy to put in a day like that.

In my Little League years I first got the "feel" for baseball, learning to appreciate its subtleties, and I fell in love with the game. Dad coached my team, and he believed his boys should enjoy the game. He never yelled and screamed, but gave each of us coaching according to the individual's abilities. I learned early on that the real joy of baseball is, above anything, the *fun* of playing. I felt that way from Little League through Legion ball and even when I made it to the major leagues. The day it wasn't fun anymore was the day I would have quit.

My father spent hours with me, working on my pitching motion, my mechanics. He advised me not to throw curves when I was real young, but then, when he thought I was strong enough, he took me to my first real professional coach: Arley Andrews.

Arley and his twin brother Harley had been legendary high school basketball players at Gerstmeyer High School in Terre Haute, but Arley, an excellent pitcher as well, opted for baseball. He signed with the Philadelphia Phillies in the mid-1950s under the bonus rule and played for several years in their organization before hurting his arm. In fact, at one point he played with Dallas Green. I used to kid Dallas about that in spring training, 1989. I told him anybody who played with Arley Andrews couldn't be all bad.

After Arley's arm went bad, he returned to Terre Haute a failed pitcher. But he had the gift of gab, which he used to land an outstanding job as sales manager with a local oil company. He had no college degree and no relevant experience, but he went in and talked his way into the job. Arley could talk Eskimos into buying snowballs.

Dad came into my room one day and said to me: "Tommy, how would you like to go visit Arley Andrews? Arley can show you the proper way to throw a curveball, the way the Phillies taught him."

My heart jumped: "Arley Andrews; a real pro!"

Arley lived about a mile north of our house. We drove to Arley's house and pulled up in his driveway. He came out of the house to meet us. Arley was six feet, two inches tall, about 200 pounds. He towered over me, and seemed almost regal in his bearing. I kept thinking, this man has pitched in the pros.

He took us behind the house, where he had a mound. Arley explained to me in his quiet Indiana drawl how to throw the breaking ball. He insisted that the curve be thrown overhand.

He put a ball in my hand and had me go through my motion.

"Pull down, Tommy," he told me. "Pull it right down, as if you're yanking a window shade. And keep your fingers closer together."

Arley then demonstrated, with Dad catching. I can still hear the "whomp" of the ball as it whooshed its way into my father's mitt. His ball *sounded* different. Sore arm or no, he could still make the ball talk. Arley flipped me the ball and patiently corrected my first efforts. Before long I was throwing curves. It took me a while to get the hang of pulling down with the wrist to get the spin that makes the ball break, something that takes strength. My pitches weren't exactly falling off the end of the table, but to me they looked pretty good. When we drove home, I thanked Dad for taking me to see Arley. He just smiled.

Dad was there for my sister Marilyn too. Her gift was singing. My folks managed to save enough money to send her to college, and she attended the Conservatory of Music in Cincinnati. He'd drive her to and from school, whenever she needed it. I remember once she had a recital in Terre Haute. Dad drove down to Cincinnati, which in those days was about a four-and-a-half-hour drive, picked her up and drove her home that night; nine hours in the car.

The next night, Marilyn gave her recital. After it was over, Dad drove her back to school. He let me go with him. We must have left at nine that night. He dropped her off at school at one-thirty in the morning, got back to Terre Haute at six-thirty, then went right in to work to put in an eight-hour day. But he never thought anything of it; one of his kids needed him.

It was in high school that I first started to attract attention for my pitching; but ironically, I was known more for my basketball playing. That was the mentality in Indiana. You played basketball first. Anything else was a poor relative.

I grew into my basketball role. When I left eighth grade, I stood five feet, six inches tall. In September of my sophomore year I was six-two, an eight-inch spurt in just fourteen months.

I played both sports at Gerstmeyer High School. I liked basketball.

25

By the time I was a senior, thirty-five colleges had offered me full scholarships, but my debut was less than smashing.

Gerstmeyer had a tradition of fine basketball teams, and you had to be superior just to make the team as the twelfth player. As a freshman, I made the junior varsity, but found myself buried at the end of the bench; my coach, Bill Welch, had nothing to judge me on other than what he had seen in practice—and I was lousy in practice.

Coach Welch was an extremely good basketball coach, a disciplinarian. If you bounced a ball after he blew his whistle, you had to take laps up and down the gymnasium stairs. When he blew that whistle, there was no last shot, no last bounce, no last word. You just stopped, stood, and listened to what he had to say.

We'd warm up, then do skill and agility exercises. Then we'd sit down and go over the day's plans, what we wanted to accomplish offensively and defensively. When we'd start practice again, my knees would be killing me, and I could never get started until I had been playing hard for fifteen minutes or so. Every time we stopped practice, the knees would hurt again, because of the huge growth spurts I was going through at the time. Even as a freshman I knew I could play, but I wasn't a board-banger; other kids would knock people around in practice, chatter, yell . . . that's never been one of my traits, and it's another reason why I didn't seem to be making much of an impression on Coach Welch.

Our first game that year was against Greencastle. Talk about debuts: I never got my fanny off the bench, not even in garbage time. I just sat there and told myself: "I'll get my chance. I'll get my chance."

Our second game was against the powerhouse Crispus Attucks High School in Indianapolis, an all-black team that was coming off a state championship in 1956–57. They were outstanding, and raced in front, 22–1. It was annihilation. Nobody on Gerstmeyer was playing well. Coach Welch just kept putting guys in there, and finally, the slaughter was so bloody, he sent me in, just before half-time. He must have been desperate.

But I felt good, got a few baskets and rebounds, and surprised the coach. He kept me in there the second half, and I played excellent ball. I started to pop from all over the floor. I grabbed rebounds and pushed the ball up the floor as if we were trailing in a one-point game with five seconds left. We lost the game but I won my status. I played feverishly

26

because this was a chance. I might not get another, and had to make the most of this opportunity. My work impressed Coach Welch, and I shot up the depth chart overnight. My playing time increased. Coach Welch used me as first or second substitute off the bench for a while, then I cracked the starting lineup. From that point on I played well enough to become a local star, and I attracted the attention of college recruiters from across the country.

Running parallel to my high school basketball prowess, however, was my baseball career. I enjoyed basketball, but I *loved* baseball, pitching for a Babe Ruth team that went to the state championships. The honors started piling up. In my first two years of Legion ball, I threw two no-hitters, one on July 2, 1960, against a team from Marshall, Illinois, and the other three weeks later, on July 22, against Linton, Indiana. That got me some notice, as did my four-year high school–Legion average of 16 strikeouts per seven-inning game.

My pitching career almost ended before it ever began. My Babe Ruth team played an exhibition game against the Wayne Newton Post #346 Legion team, coached by Bill Welch. In the first inning the second batter hit a line drive right at me. Instinctively, I put my hand up to protect my face, and the ball smashed into my pitching hand. I went down. Coach Welch ran over from the third base coaching box. The bone stuck through the skin of my thumb, with the thumb dangling backward. It was a compound dislocation fracture. The only thing that held it there was skin and tendon. I healed fast, but by the time I was ready to play, our team had been eliminated in the regional finals at Middleboro, Kentucky.

My first major career choice would be basketball or baseball. Despite my success on the court, I could see the handwriting on the wall even in my sophomore year. First, I thought I was much better in baseball than in basketball. Second, I would never get real big, and I wasn't that fast. Even back in the early sixties, basketball was changing from the slow, bumbling, half-court style to a bigger and quicker up-tempo style, dominated by guys much bigger than six-two. I realized that I might do well in college, but the pro game would pass me by. The third factor was simply this: I loved to play baseball. All this added up to a decision, only half realized at first, that if I were to make it as a professional athlete, it would be on the diamond and not on the hardwood.

The baseball scouts weren't around in droves as were the college recruiters, but fourteen teams eventually checked me out. I had a good, live fastball, the main pitch in my arsenal, plus a finely developed curveball, thanks to Arley Andrews.

My first audition for the scouts came because they were there to see the *other* guy pitch. When I was a sophomore at Gerstmeyer, our baseball team was going to play a team from Danville, Illinois. They had a hot-shot stud pitcher by the name of Steve Kelly, who later signed with the Kansas City A's. I begged my coach, Howard Sharpe, to let me pitch against him. My ulterior motive was that Kelly had thrown four or five no-hit games, and scouts were following him in droves wherever he pitched. I got beat that game, but pitched well in front of about fifteen scouts. It was a productive loss.

During my senior year in high school I got calls just about every day from college basketball coaches and such schools as Indiana, Louisville, LSU, Vanderbilt, North Carolina State, Georgia Tech, Florida, and Davidson. With each call, the pressure intensified to make a decision.

I wanted to go to college, because I loved math and thought I might be able to do well as an engineer or in business. The people in Terre Haute were expecting me to choose basketball, not only because basketball was like a religion to them, but also because they probably had Arley Andrews's baseball failure in the back of their minds. Some people feared the same would happen to me and didn't mind telling me so.

To help me make up my mind, my parents took me on a spring vacation to Florida. Bruce Connatser, a scout for the Phillies from Terre Haute, had followed me during high school and knew of my looming career decision. He arranged it so that we could go to the Phillies spring training camp in Clearwater, meet some of the coaches and players, and work out to give me a taste of what big league baseball was like.

We left for Florida on a Friday night in mid-March, 1961, and arrived in Clearwater the next night. Mom, Dad, and I checked into the Jack Tar Hotel, then one of the classiest hotels on Florida's west coast. A bellman showed us up to the room, and I'll never forget the look my parents had when they walked inside. They seemed awestruck. The room was nicer than any room we ever stayed in on vacation. Typically, we'd stay in tourist homes, equivalent to today's bed-and-breakfasts, where rooms cost maybe eight dollars a night. That was a far cry from the Jack Tar's fifty-dollars-a-night elegance.

At camp, Philadelphia's traveling secretary greeted us and introduced me to some of the players, including Paul Brown, a young phenom pitcher from Holdenville, Oklahoma. Paul and I became friends. We worked out and ate together. He was an outstanding pitcher and a nice young man.

On the day of my first workout, I reported to the stadium, too naive, really, to be properly intimidated. The biggest thrill was when they gave me a uniform and let me work out with the team for two days. I also met Dallas Green for the first time. He was on the Phillies and went on to have an illustrious record in the majors. People don't know that the first major league uniform I ever wore was the red pinstripes of the 1961 Phillies.

I watched how Robin Roberts got dressed. When you're in high school, you just take off your jeans and put your baseball pants on, over your regular underwear. But the Phillies had long underwear, cut off at the thighs. We had white socks. They had sanitary hose over which went the baseball stocking. The trick was to keep the socks from falling down. This may not sound like much, but when you've never done it before, you don't know what you're doing. And I didn't want to go out there with major leaguers and have my socks fall down.

So I studied Roberts. He pulled his pants down, pulled the bottoms up to where the socks were rolled down, then bloused the pants over the socks. Look at any photo of a big leaguer in the early 1960s or prior, and you'll see the puffy, bloused-down pants. Guys don't do that today, but I bloused my pants for the rest of my career in baseball.

I worked out with the pitchers. My group included Chris Short, Frank Sullivan, Jack Baldschun, Art Mahaffey, John Buzhardt, and Robin Roberts, one of my pitching idols. The team was managed by Gene Mauch, and I took no end of delight kidding Mauch about it years afterward, when I pitched for him in 1982 and 1985.

"You had your chance for me back in 1961," I would kid Gene, "but you blew it."

I felt great. Here I was, a seventeen-year-old kid from Indiana, in a major league uniform—probably with a number like 77 or 89—standing alongside real major league pitchers. We worked out two days, throwing, running, hitting. I never took my eyes off Roberts as he warmed up, ran, horsed around, batted. He moved with an economy of motion, as if every little thing he did had a larger purpose behind it. One of the coaches, Sibby Sisti, the old infielder for the Boston Braves, also worked with me a little. The experience didn't overwhelm me, and I got the feeling that I might be good enough to become a major league pitcher.

When it was time to leave, the Phillies graciously "comped" our $500 hotel bill, and the family drove ecstatically home on Saturday.

In the last half of my senior year, I tried to sort through all the offers. One coach actually made up my mind for me. That was the legendary Adolph Rupp from the University of Kentucky. I was having a great senior year, averaging 20 points and 16 rebounds a game. Rupp was romancing the Van Arsdale twins at the time, Tom and Dick. But when they signed a letter of intent to go to Indiana, Adolph went looking for me.

He came to the house one day with his assistant, Harry Lancaster. I was out playing golf, so he talked to my dad. Dad had never been a great admirer of Rupp's coaching philosophy. We had some kids from Terre Haute go down to Kentucky and play for him, and they'd come back after their first year and tell stories about Adolph throwing tirades, physically kicking players in the butt, abusing them. Couldn't you see that happening now in the 90s! Not all tough coaches are bad, of course. The high school coaches we had were dominators. That's part of sports. But you need to be tough within a framework. Adolph went beyond the limits, and that turned my mom and dad off.

Rupp went quickly downhill from a bad start. After Adolph made his pitch, Dad was honest and said his son was thinking about skipping college to give professional baseball a shot.

"There have been a lot of major league ball clubs scouting Tommy, and we've got some pretty keen interest," Dad said.

Rupp then said the wrong thing in reply.

"We've got some really good baseball players ourselves down at Kentucky. Scouts are there all the time. Your son might not even be able to make our baseball team down there."

That set my father off, and he just lit into Adolph.

"I've never liked your act from when you had Howard Dardeen [Howard was one of the Terre Haute players who went to Kentucky to play for Rupp]. I've heard stories about you, about your physical abuse. I've never cared for that style of coaching or your personal style."

Dad was just getting going. He cited my stats, and then started emphasizing his points with his hands, as he did whenever he became excited or angry.

"You were after the Van Arsdale twins like a dog in heat, and after that deal falls through, you come to Terre Haute for Tommy John, your consolation prize. Well, Mr. Rupp, he's not available."

He ended with his best line.

"There's the door. Don't let it hit you in the rear end on your way out."

"Nobody talks to me like that," Adolph huffed.

"There's the door," Dad repeated, louder. Rupp stormed out, followed by Lancaster. A few minutes later Lancaster came back in to apologize. He said Coach Rupp had been on the road a long time, was having a bad trip, and wasn't getting much sleep.

"Don't think we don't want your son, Mr. John, because we do," Lancaster added.

"I appreciate you coming back and apologizing, but Kentucky would be the last place I send my son."

I finished my high school baseball career with a 28–2 mark—both losses to Danville. After the season was over in my senior year, Bruce Connatser, the Phillies scout, told my parents:

"There's going to be a lot of teams that are going to be after Tommy. I can't tell you what to do. Listen to all the offers. But do me one favor. Give me the last chance to try and sign him."

My mom and dad agreed. That was only fair.

There was one other notable trip made late in my senior year that helped me make my decision: a weekend visit to the University of Illinois. The university was offering me the chance to play basketball and baseball. I met with their baseball coach, Lee Eilbracht, and he gave some great advice.

"Tommy," he said, "I'd love to have you play baseball for me, but ask yourself what a college education is worth in hard cash. If you want to play pro ball, you've got to look at it as a business proposition. Four years of school would cost your mom and dad about $20,000 if they paid for it themselves. So when these ball clubs come to you, that's what they'll have to come up with . . . more than $20,000. If they offer less, it's a wash. You'd be better off going to college. But if they offer more than $20,000, the balance swings in favor of pro baseball."

Coach Eilbracht's advice clinched my decision. It would be baseball—if a team would offer me more than $20,000. Making my choice took the psychological weight from my shoulders.

Dad and I now had a perspective, a financial framework, to help us when the scouts came around to talk about signing. There were no such things as agents back then. Dad was my agent, a man who had never talked money before with a major league team.

The Washington Senators, the Chicago Cubs, the Phillies, the Los Angeles Angels, and the Cleveland Indians all made bids. The Senators, Cubs, and Angels, however, weren't offering anything near the $20,000-plus line, so it came down to the Indians and the Phillies. Cleveland scout John Schulte had been watching me pitch for a couple of years, and knew my abilities pretty well. He was the first to come by the house to talk turkey.

Schulte said he was very high on me and thought I had a good chance to make it to the majors with the Indians.

"A 28–2 record is something your son can be extremely proud of," Schulte told Dad. "It's convinced the Indians. We want to make an offer."

Even though Dad and I knew it was coming, actually hearing the words was an altogether different experience.

"What?" Dad asked, almost in surprise. "You mean you want to give Tommy a contract?"

Schulte smiled. "That's exactly what I mean."

Dad took a deep breath and told him we wouldn't listen to any offer under $20,000. Schulte said he had no problem with that, but any offer over $20,000 would require the approval of his bosses in Cleveland, who would have to see me work out in person. We agreed.

But if I had known then what I know now, I would have spent that summer trying out and showcasing myself for every team that was interested, and not just the Indians. We could have gotten into a bidding situation. But this was 1961, and we had no idea of such dealings. Besides, that wasn't in Dad's nature.

I graduated on June 8, 1961, and the week after that, my dad and I were on a train, bound for Municipal Stadium in Cleveland, facing the unknown. The club had rooms for us at the Auditorium Hotel. We went to the ball park the next day, both feeling a little jittery. I didn't know what to expect; it was a little like being put on trial. But the Indians did all they could to make me feel welcome. Bob Kennedy, the assistant farm director, greeted us and introduced us to the front office staff: General Manager Gabe Paul, scouting chief Paul O'Day, and all the secretaries. Kennedy then took us into his office. Covering up an entire wall was the Big Board listing the rosters for all of Cleveland's teams: the Indians, Salt Lake City, Reading, Burlington, Selma, Dubuque, and so on. The effect was impressive, almost overwhelming.

Man, I thought, this is an organization.

Kennedy took me to the dressing room, gave me a uniform, and—

having learned my lesson from Robin Roberts—I put it on like a veteran. The Cleveland uniform had one thing I had never seen. The outside stirrups had built-in heavy elastic at the top that kept your socks up. It struck me as high-tech and state-of-the-art.

We went outside in cavernous Municipal Stadium, 74,000 empty seats surrounding us. God, it was huge—one of the biggest in all of baseball. Long linear rows of dark empty seats cascaded down to field level in an almost hypnotic pattern. The stands looked distant and unreal, like a painted backdrop or part of a movie set. I tried to imagine what this stadium would be like full of people—so did the Cleveland front office, for many years after, when attendance was so bad. The fragrant, newly mown grass was a deep green.

Al Jones, the bullpen catcher, came over and with a big smile introduced himself to me and my dad. He treated me like a kid brother, asking me about home, my family, where I went to school, trying to relax me.

"I got a glove here that's a good popper," Al said. "So if you can throw the ball pretty good, it'll pop loud, especially in this empty park. It'll make you sound like you're really throwing hard. So just relax."

I threw a bit on the sidelines until I was warmed up, trying not to show how scared I felt. I was just hoping my first twenty balls wouldn't be in the dirt or sail to the screen. When I finished my last warm-up toss, I stopped to wipe my brow. My left foot was shaking.

"Are you ready, Tommy?" Kennedy asked.

"As ready as I'll ever be," I answered as I walked to the pitcher's mound.

My first four pitches were all over the place. Jones just told me to relax. I thought about throwing strikes. My next pitch came in good, popping the mitt loudly for a strike. I felt good after that, and threw for about twenty minutes, mostly fastballs with some curves. After I showered, Kennedy told me he liked what he saw, then asked me if I minded coming back tomorrow to throw again for the farm director, Hoot Evers, who was in Mobile, Alabama, signing an outfielder named Tommie Agee. I was going to pitch for Hoot Evers! At that time, it was like the general manager of the major league club coming to evaluate you.

In the office after my first workout, we met with Paul, Kennedy, and O'Day. They said they liked my throwing and Paul offered us $35,000 to sign.

"Boy, that's nice," my dad said, trying to contain his excitement.

"But there's just one thing. I promised Bruce Connatser the last crack at Tommy. I promised him that, and I got to hold true."

I gulped, hoping they wouldn't hardball us. Much to my relief, Gabe Paul smiled and agreed, saying that was the only fair thing. When we got back to the hotel Dad called Connatser and told him about Cleveland's offer. Bruce called his bosses in Philadelphia, phoned us back, and said they couldn't top it.

The next day we went back to the stadium, where I threw again, this time for the benefit of Mel Harder, the big league pitching coach, and Hoot Evers. I was scared to death of Evers. Some of the prospects who were working out that day had asked me: "Have you met Evers yet?" When I said no, they just rolled their eyes. "Boy, he's a real so-and-so. You can't do anything right as far as he's concerned. He carries a lot of weight. One wrong word from him and you can kiss it good-bye."

I filed that away, hoping my meeting with Evers would be put off as long as possible. He sounded like a terror. Hoot had been a career .278 hitter with Detroit, Boston, Cleveland, and several other clubs, and when he stood in the box for my warm-up, I felt as if the Grim Reaper himself had climbed in. Fortunately, I threw well for the second straight day.

After the workout, we went back to the office to see Gabe Paul.

"Well, Mr. John, what do you think? Can we sign your boy?"

"We've talked it over," Dad said, "and we'll sign if you'll give us $40,000."

As soon as dad got the words out of his mouth, Gabe pounced. He stuck his hand out, they shook, and he had the signed contract. My dad knew then that we had sold ourselves short. We probably could have gotten between $50,000 and $60,000 without too much trouble. But $40,000 was more money than any of us ever thought of having, and we took it.

Paul and Kennedy then went through all the pitchers in the organization. They said Sam McDowell and I were the system's best left-handed pitching prospects. They then projected how they saw my progress, if things went well. After signing, I would play out the year in Class D ball at Dubuque, Iowa. They wanted me to get my feet wet there rather than struggle at a higher classification. In 1962 they projected me in B ball, followed by Single A and Triple A. With that schedule, I'd be pitching in the big leagues somewhere between 1965 and 1966.

After the signing, we didn't really celebrate. We got back on the train to Terre Haute, where I had to get my things together for Dubuque. I was happy at the bonus I got, but I simply felt that this was something I always wanted to do, and now I was getting my chance. I believed what the Indians had told me: if everything went right and I didn't get hurt, I would be pitching in the big leagues in 1965 or '66. In fact, immediately after the signing I experienced buyer's remorse. I wondered if I had made the right decision in selecting professional baseball over college basketball.

Fortunately, my doubts didn't last long.

Cleveland pitched me in a couple of exhibition games against the International League All-Stars and the Cincinnati Reds. We got on a bus from the train station to take us to the park, and who but the dreaded Hoot Evers should walk down the aisle in my direction, absolutely erect, the way he always walked.

Hoot was nattily dressed in a coat and tie, the kind of guy you couldn't imagine wearing jeans and sneakers. He appeared older and more imposing to my young eyes than his actual forty years. He sat his tall, well-muscled frame in the seat next to me. Hoot had the outdoor complexion you'd expect of a man who had spent so many years playing baseball under the sun.

"Tommy, I want to talk to you," he said in a low-pitched, midwestern accent.

My knees were knocking. Uh-oh, here it comes, I thought. He's going to blast me for something. I held my breath.

Well, I couldn't have met a more pleasant man.

We had a long, friendly talk, a fatherly talk. Hoot spoke in soothing tones, and as I sat there listening, I wondered why the guys would paint such an ugly picture of Hoot. Their portrait of the man and the flesh-and-blood version now sitting in the seat next to me were two different people.

Hoot gave me a rundown on the Dubuque club and told me what I might expect when I got there.

"You're going to see guys do a lot of things that you just won't believe. You'll see guys play hungover or maybe steal a drink or a beer between innings. You'll see guys stay out all night and chase girls all day. Just remember how your mom and dad brought you up and you'll be okay."

Hoot also urged me not to try to save money on food. He said too many young ballplayers try to get by on their dollar and a half in daily meal money.

"They buy a loaf of bread and some lunch meat and try to make it last all week. You're single and don't have a family to support. Take some of your own money with you and eat right. Above all, try to have at least one salad a day. Eat plenty of vegetables and greens; in the summer, that's the best thing for you."

He then talked about expectations.

"We want you to go down to Dubuque and learn. Don't get upset if you get hit hard in the beginning. You saw some good baseball teams in high school, didn't you?"

"Yeah," I said, quickly warming up to the man.

"How many good hitters did they have?"

"One, maybe two."

"Well," Hoot said, "every team that you play from here on out will have those one or two hitters all through their lineup. So don't get too concerned if you start getting cuffed around. The Indians won't be worried about that. The main thing is learn something each time you pitch. If you do that, you'll be fine."

We talked on the bus, before and after the game. I thought about how wrong those other guys were about Hoot. Then it hit me: they were just trying to rattle me so I wouldn't do well, or maybe even give up. That's typical of baseball, something I experienced time and time again throughout my career. Unless you know a guy well, you can't trust what he says about anyone else. I learned a lot from Hoot and still talk to him often. I'll never forget how helpful he was.

When Eddie Stanky took over as manager of the White Sox in 1966, people would tell me what an absolute tyrant he was, an S.O.B., a slave driver. Yet I probably learned more baseball under Eddie than any manager I ever played for. I wish I could have played for him ten years. He was just that good.

But guys attempt to get a psychological edge by trying to spook you out. Baseball is extremely competitive, and some guys respond with a dog-eat-dog mentality. They don't see you as a teammate but as the guy who might take their meal ticket away by making the team.

In the exhibition game against the International League All-Stars, I pitched three innings for the Indians, giving up an unearned run. Later, in August, Cleveland called me up from Dubuque—with my 3–3 record—to pitch in an exhibition game against the Cincinnati Reds, the

National League pennant winner that year. I went five innings, giving up one run. After the game, one of the Tribe's pitchers, Frank Funk, congratulated me and said if I could pitch like that against the Reds, I ought to be able to burn up the Midwest League. I went 7–1 the rest of the season.

The added benefit of pitching in the exhibitions was a chance to meet Jim Piersall, who sat next to me on a train ride from Cleveland to Buffalo.

Jim had almond-shaped eyes and dark good looks, really a striking figure. He was a star by then, one of the top center fielders in baseball. Jim was a high-strung man, always fidgeting, exuding a nervous excitement that could pass for charisma. On the field Jim was able to channel that quality; he could hit and run, and made fantastic catches appear routine. Off the field he had the hurried demeanor of a man who thought he had to be someplace else. He couldn't seem to relax. I was surprised when he sat next to me on the train and stuck out his hand.

"Hi. My name is Jim Piersall."

I was too scared to say much. I told him my name, and then Jim asked me a lot of questions: where I was from, did I just sign, what kind of pitches did I have, that sort of thing. As he sat there, I just kept seeing Tony Perkins, the actor who starred in the movie *Fear Strikes Out,* a film that documented Jim's nervous breakdown and recovery when he was playing with the Red Sox.

"I'm going to give you one piece of advice," Jim said. He was a star, so I listened. "Always get to the ball park as early as you can, because it looks like you really want to play. Get there early, even if it's just to sit there and do nothing or oil your glove. You'll make an impression."

I put that in the back of my mind, and the habit of arriving early stayed with me my entire career.

When we got off the train in Buffalo, Jim asked me where I was going to eat. I said I didn't know, so he invited me to dine with him and a couple other players in the coffee shop of our hotel. We went there, sat down, and a waitress brought us menus and water.

"We're in a hurry," Jim said. As he sat there, he kept getting more impatient and nervous. I couldn't figure it out. All of a sudden he bolted from the table.

"If you don't mind, I have to leave. I can't stand to sit in a restaurant and wait. I can't stand it. I'm sorry. I've got to go someplace else and eat."

With that, he rushed out of the restaurant. I thought it was something I did. He came back about an hour later as we were finishing up our meal. He apologized. He said he ate at a cafeteria. I just assumed that his behavior was part of his emotional problems, but it certainly impressed upon me that he marched to a different drummer.

A few years later, in 1964, Jim provided a perspective on his bizarre behavior.

"Look at me," he said. "I'm way past my prime, but I'm making forty grand a year. You know why? Because people come out to the ball park and expect to see me go crazy. So every once in a while I'll give them a thrill and do something nuts, like sit on the outfield fence or argue with an umpire. Just enough for people to enjoy. It's keeps me in the money. Besides, I have nine kids to feed."

Dubuque of the Class D Midwest League would be equivalent to today's A leagues. In 1963 the B, C, and D minor leagues were all combined onto the A level. The Indians paid me $750 a month, pretty good minor league money in those days; in fact, probably more than three times what most other guys on the team were making. Hoot Evers warned me not to let anybody see my paycheck because it would only lead to resentment.

"The guy making two hundred and fifty dollars will want what you're getting," Hoot told me. That's how it was in 1961 and that's how it is now. The guy who's making a million a year feels gypped compared to his teammate who's pulling down $3 million.

The Indians had D teams in Dubuque, Iowa, and in Selma, Alabama. They sent me to Dubuque because it was fairly close to home—an important factor for a kid who just turned eighteen—and also because of Merrill "Pinky" May, the manager of the Dubuque Packers.

Pinky was a short man with glasses, a ruddy face, and a sunny disposition. He was a kind man and a good teacher, and he had a knack of working with teenagers trying to adjust to professional baseball. He also was from Indiana, which made me feel more at home in my new surroundings.

Pinky, so called because of his reddish hair, had played third base for Philadelphia in the late thirties and early forties. He knew the game. Pinky was a good field manager, and could scream and yell at the umps with the best of them. But he never blasted his players. He could get into a player when the situation called for it, but he never did so vindictively. He was a family man who knew how to handle young men.

**Beginnings**

One of his sons, Milt, was the bat boy for Dubuque. Milt later went on to a fine career of his own as a big league catcher.

The Selma team, on the other hand, was managed by Walter Novick, who was Pinky's opposite. Walt was tough and crusty, a tobacco chewer, a drinker, and also a man who was known for making bets with his players. He was a competent manager but a lousy role model. The organization had a big investment in me and some of its other prospects and wasn't about to entrust our fates to the streetwise Novick.

Dubuque is a small river town, back then about 98 percent Catholic. The first thing to hit me on my new team was the cold shoulder. Here was a ball club that had trained together since March in Daytona Beach, Florida, and by June the cliques were well established. Everytime a young player joins a team midseason, it means that somebody had to leave. That's just the way baseball is. Naturally, the newcomer gets viewed with hostility. Besides, most of my teammates were older than me. The answers were short and the eyes threw darts.

Cleveland had just signed a bunch of high schoolers—myself, Agee, Frank DeCastris, and Larry Patterson, a talented one-eyed pitcher who I always thought would make it. We came in together, and we took refuge in each other. That helped my adjustment greatly.

Art Siefert—a short, stocky left-handed pitcher—came over and warned me that a lot of my teammates wouldn't have anything to do with me. He advised me to just keep my mouth shut and my ears open. He said that after a while, when my newness wore off, they'd accept me as a ball player. That always struck me, since Art had been mired in the Class A level for three years, still waiting for his chance to advance in the organization. And here I was, a young, hot-shot bonus pitcher who was probably going to take his chance away.

My first day in town I stayed at a run-down hotel. How bad was it? The fire escape consisted of a knotted rope tied to the end of a spike. I guess they figured that if there was a fire, the rope wouldn't burn. Cleveland got me out of there fast, arranging a room for me in the home of Mr. and Mrs. Matt Olansky, a gentle couple in their sixties. He was a Polish Jew in the real estate business, the kind of guy who, an hour after you meet him, makes you feel like you've known him all your life. She was an outgoing, grandmotherly type.

Their own children had left home, and they liked the idea of having a teenager in the house again. They gave me a key to the front door and told me to use their home as if it were my own. After night games

**39**

I'd let myself in, go upstairs to my room, and go to sleep. They were only paid to give me a room, but they'd often throw in meals on the house. Matt would make me fried-egg sandwiches, which I politely gagged down, since I don't like eggs. He also made latkes—pancakes fried in oil—that were delicious. Arranging a place for me with the Olanskys was one way Cleveland made sure they could protect their investment in me.

My best buddies on the Packers were Siefert and Agee. Siefert, who always had a smile on his face, helped me the most by showing me what to do, and when. He'd tell me when it was time to shag balls in the outfield, or to run. He showed me around town, tipping me off about restaurants, introducing me to people.

Agee was a ruggedly built but shy man, a few months older than me. He had as much raw talent as anybody I've ever seen in baseball. Tommie quietly shared the rookie's life with me: sweeping out the clubhouse, washing the uniforms, polishing the spikes. In D ball there were no clubhouse attendants.

Dubuque was the epitome of small-town life. The people were friendly, everyone knew everybody else, and there wasn't a thing to do: no excitement, few restaurants or recreation choices, a decaying slum section. So we spent as much time as we could at the ball park. The closest thing we had to a hangout was the Hollywood Grill, run by a man named John Thomas. The first time I walked in, he came up to me and said:

"Thomas John, I'm John Thomas. Get it? Nice to know you."

We'd breakfast at the Hollywood, sit around, chew the fat, have lunch later, then leave for the ball park around two-thirty in the afternoon.

Siefert pitched the first game I saw upon joining the team. He looked so polished to me, throwing a forkball, change-up, slider, curveball, fastball. Art had more pitches than I ever dreamed about. He'd throw his breaking ball, even when he was behind on the count. I just sat up there in the stands, my heart sinking. I don't know if I can pitch up here, I thought.

To make matters worse, Pinky May gave me a stack of pitching charts to study for my first start the next night against Quincy, a farm team of the San Francisco Giants. I had never seen a pitching chart before in my life, and couldn't make head or tail of them.

The charts are kept by the next night's pitcher. A chart indicates the count, where the ball was pitched, and where it was hit. Next to each batter's name is a square, in which you record the sequence of that particular at bat for the given inning.

At the top there would be little boxes for balls. On the bottom you'd find the boxes for strikes. So if a strike came in on the first pitch, you'd fill in the first box on the bottom. You would also record pitch location. If the ball came in low and away, you would put a dot in the proper location on the schematic of the strike zone. If it was a fastball, you would put a 1 by the dot. If it was a curve, you'd put in a 2, and so on; 3 for a slider, 4 for a change-up, and 5 for "other," such as a knuckler. Then, in the same square, you'd have a configuration of a baseball diamond, where you showed where the ball was hit. A squiggly line meant a grounder. A straight line was a fly ball.

I sat there with the Quincy charts, baffled by the dots and lines. I went to bed that night confused and overwhelmed. With those hieroglyphics in front of me I didn't feel like a pitcher, but more like a student studying for a trig test. I broke out in a cold sweat, my head swimming in a whirlpool of numbers.

What am I doing here? How can I memorize all this? I thought, and threw the charts down. To this day I still can't understand a pitching chart.

When I got to the park my heart was pounding like a bass drum. Pinky tried to calm me down, telling me it was no different than high school ball.

"If you just go out there and pitch the same way," he said, putting his arm on my shoulder, "you'll do fine."

What saved me, however, was my catcher, Jackie Hernandez, who couldn't speak English. That forced us to keep things simple. Before we warmed up, he asked me: "What you throw?"

"Fastball, curveball," I answered.

Jackie smiled. "Don't worry. We get it. Watch me."

That's all I did. I threw what Jackie called, lasted 5⅓ innings, and got the win. For the record, the first man I faced in my professional career was Hal Lanier, who later went on to play for the Giants and manage in Houston. By the sixth inning I was missing the plate badly. All my pitches were high, a sure sign that I was tiring.

After the game Pinky told me I had to build up my stamina. I was used to seven-inning high school games. Up here, he told me, it's a nine-inning game. He put me on a program of more running and more throwing between starts, and it slowly built up both my arm and legs.

41

I got into 14 games for Dubuque, all but one of them starts, and finished at 10–4, with a 3.17 earned run average and four complete games. It was a fine year, and on the whole an enjoyable personal experience.

But in Dubuque you never forgot you were in the *lower* minors. Even the enthusiastic fans couldn't make you forget the lumpy infields, the rickety wooden parks, the numbing bus rides that would get you into a town like Kokomo with just enough time to rush into your uniform and get on the field with no practice. We even had a game called on account of fish flies. Dubuque's on the river, and at certain times of the year the fish flies fester in hordes like a biblical plague. One night they all swarmed up to the lights, which weren't that good to begin with. The field got dimmer and dimmer until they had to call the game.

It was a year of paying my dues. I needed to make an impression so that better things would come my way . . . much the same position I found myself in twenty-eight years later, trying to make an impression on Dallas Green with the Yankees in Fort Lauderdale, Florida.

# 3.

# UP (AND DOWN)
# THE ORGANIZATION

O n Monday, February 13, 1989, I
sat in the kitchen at home, sip-
ping orange juice. I picked up the
phone and called George Steinbrenner's direct line at his office in Tampa.

George got on the phone and jumped right in with his question:
"Well, what do you think? Do you still want to be a Yankee?"

"George, I sure do. The offer sounds good."

"Tommy," he said, "you've made the Yankees proud of you before,
and I know you'll do it again. Glad to have you back."

He wished me the best. I hung up the phone and sat in the kitchen.
Sally smiled at me. I felt a stillness inside, the kind of quiet that comes
after you formalize a decision you knew deep down you'd make all along.

George was genuinely pleased that I accepted his offer. He was
pleased on two levels: on a personal level, because we were friends;
and on a professional level, because he thought it would help the team.
As much as people liked to say George was bad for the Yankees, they
forget one thing—no one wanted to win more than he did. He just had
a hard time going about it the correct way; his will to win sometimes
clouded his better judgment, as was seen by the events in the summer
of 1990, when he was removed by the commissioner from his involvement in the team's on-field activities. If the team was on the right track,
George was happy—though not necessarily satisfied. But if there was
a down spell, George reached for the trigger. Impatience has been his

biggest downfall. He blasted his manager, his coaches, his players, often with negative results.

George was unique among baseball owners. He operated from what I call the Military Syndrome. If you follow military history, which is one of my hobbies, you see that generals often and casually fire their subordinate officers. If you couldn't take a town or a bridge, you got fired and the general brought in someone who could. General Patton, one of George's idols, did that all the time; that's the way George is. He sees the game of baseball as a set of objectives that can be met by adherence to a series of rigid strategies . . . strategies that he alone ultimately determines and for which he alone must be ultimately responsible.

But the other component of that personality is appreciation when the job is well done and the effort is there. For all his faults, George is loyal. Loyalty to George is like a code, an honor-bound quality that goes beyond money or other mundane considerations. It is his saving grace. He was loyal to Billy Martin. He brought me back. He brought Guidry back, and also Goose Gossage, Gene Michael, Clyde King, Billy Martin (a few times), and Lou Piniella, to name a few.

After talking to George, I called Jerry Reinsdorf and told him of my decision. I thanked him for his interest, and he said the White Sox would keep a close eye on me during spring training. If I didn't get a chance to pitch for Dallas Green and the Yankees cut me, the White Sox might pick me up, giving me a safety net. Then Jerry told me something that struck me as odd.

"I've never had a player call me back like that," he said.

I thought he was kidding me, but no, he said it had never happened that a player he was negotiating with signed with someone else then called him to let him know about it. To me, it's only courtesy. That's how I was brought up. I did the same thing in 1979, when I signed as a free agent with the Yankees. We got back to every general manager who had drafted me with a call or a letter telling them of my decision and thanking them for their interest.

Now Sally and I had to scramble. I was due in camp on Thursday, February 16, with the first workout on Friday. We had less than four days, with no place to stay in Fort Lauderdale and a ton of logistics to arrange. Usually we start hunting for a spring-training home in November or December. It's more difficult for us to find something nice because when we go, we take the whole family.

Realtors think every ball player makes $3 million a year and assume you can rent a house for $8000 a month. They think you have gold buried in your backyard, and they want to get their share. We had no place to stay when we got to Florida, and for the first four days Sally, the three boys, and I lived in two rooms in a hotel. We then lucked out into a house through a friend, who heard it was for rent. For five weeks we lived on the Intercoastal Waterway in the Coral Ridge section, one of Fort Lauderdale's better areas.

We've always put the kids in school down there so they can be with me and Sally during spring training. People have accused us of messing up their education, but Sally and I believe you've got to keep the family intact or you're going to mess up more than their education. Besides, there's a wonderful tutor school down there, the Fort Lauderdale School for Winter Visitors. The teachers back home in Cresskill photocopy the lesson plans for the coming week and express mail it to us on Friday so we get it Monday morning in Fort Lauderdale. The kids take their textbooks down with them, and the teachers in Florida teach from the Cresskill lesson plan. The kids are then on the same schedule as their classmates back home.

The boys accompanied us to Florida. Tami, a freshman in high school, was in the school play and was playing softball. She had a lot of activities, and it was tough for her to leave, so we made arrangements for her to stay with friends. Tami didn't miss out on spring training totally, however; she came down twice for visits. It is rewarding and relaxing to have the family with me. The love and support I got from them is immeasurable.

I don't think there was a soul down there who thought I had a snowball's chance in hell of making the club. Dallas's feelings about me were well publicized, and no one dreamed I'd get a fair chance. I was leery myself. I had been in tenuous situations before, for example in 1986, when I came to Fort Lauderdale as a walk-on, with *no* guarantees, *no* money. But at least manager Lou Piniella had an open mind. He said he was going to give me some chances to pitch. I couldn't count on that from Dallas.

But I put such thoughts out of my mind. I had asked Dallas during our phone conversation on Saturday for one favor. If he didn't think I could pitch, I asked him not to wait until the last day of camp to let me go. Because if a manager wants to be a real horse's hind end, he cuts you a day before the season starts and there's nowhere for you to go. Everyone's rosters are set for the first month and a half, and you're left out in the cold, scrambling to find a team. I asked Dallas to tell me ten days or two weeks before camp broke. But he wouldn't even give me an answer on that.

We arrived at Fort Lauderdale Stadium on Friday morning, February 17, feeling determined and positive, ready for the first day of workouts. Actually seeing the stadium again gave the experience a new "reality." Coming down to win a job was no longer just an idea or an abstraction for me. It was now as real as the dirt and grass of the ball park.

One of the guards at the gate, a senior citizen who had been there awhile and was normally very outgoing, told us that things were different this year. He seemed cold and distant. We didn't park in the players lot, but in the fans parking area. I wasn't going to step on anyone's toes. I'd let my pitching do the talking for me. Sally, who has a good sixth sense about such things, said she felt unwelcome. She felt the tension and stayed in the car, because everybody in the world knew Dallas didn't want me anywhere around. The stadium workers, clubhouse people, staff—they all seemed to be treading very lightly around me, as if walking on eggshells. They didn't want to get too friendly with me in case Dallas were to see it and get mad.

Following Jim Piersall's advice from almost twenty-eight years earlier, I arrived at the ballpark at seven-fifteen A.M., the first player there. Dallas and his staff were milling around. I asked Nick Priore, the clubhouse attendant, where he had my locker (the locker was back where all the no-chancers changed, not in the usual spot with the regulars), sat down, got changed, then went out and jogged for about forty minutes.

It was eight-fifteen when I came back in. After a shower, I started putting equipment in my locker, getting it organized. Dave Righetti came in and we exchanged warm greetings. We had been very close since he first came up in 1981, when I saw him pitch so impressively as a rookie. All of a sudden Dallas bounced out of his office, came over, thrust out his hand and said in his booming voice:

"Dave! Dallas Green. Good to see you. Good to see that you're the first guy here. I like that."

"No, Dallas," Dave said. "I wasn't the first guy here. T. J. was." Dallas looked at me, shrugged, and walked away. He didn't acknowledge me, as if I were Cosmo Topper. Righetti looked at me.

"Doesn't give one a great feeling of confidence, does it?" I cracked rhetorically.

## Up (and Down) the Organization

The coaches started filtering over: pitching coach Billy Connors, hitting/outfield coach Frank Howard, first base coach Pat Corrales, third base coach Lee Elia, dugout coach Charlie Fox, and bullpen coach John Stearns. They said hello to me. Connors and Howard made small talk, and then finally Dallas came over.

"Hi, Tommy," he trumpeted in his volcanic voice. "Did you get settled? Good. What I said before still goes. Don't expect a lot down here."

Welcome to Day One.

At the first team meeting, everyone was introduced. The trainer, the strength coach, the field coaches, everyone spoke briefly on what they expected out of the guys. That's standard operating procedure for the first day of spring training. Then Dallas got up and spoke of his "new program."

"We're going to separate you guys out," he blared. "My program's going to find out what you guys are made out of. It's going to tell me who wants to play and who doesn't. No one else in baseball has this program. It's mine, and I'm going to make it ours. It is a structured program, designed for a purpose, and you will carry it out without bitching. We will learn it as a team. You will not question it. And you pitchers. You don't run enough. I'm going to have you guys running, and I don't want to hear any bleeping complaints. I'm a ninety-foot guy. When a guy doesn't bust it for ninety feet, it hurts the team. You guys got your bleeping guaranteed contracts. Okay. Just don't think you've got a bleeping guaranteed job."

Righetti looked at me, puzzled, and I returned an equally baffled look. What was Dallas talking about with his "new program"? I'd been to twenty-eight spring trainings and seen them run every which way, including loose. But the truth is, there's only so much variation you can employ in baseball. It's a simple game: you can run, throw, field, or hit. And that's it. The book of Ecclesiastes was right: there's nothing new under the sun. Sure enough, Dallas's program wasn't different, at least in a baseball sense. What he wanted wasn't so much a training camp but a boot camp, with constant running and discipline. This was part of his overall plan, blessed by George Steinbrenner, to turn around what was perceived as a lax Yankee attitude.

Dallas started us running full tilt from the first day. That was his idea of being "different." Normally, the manager takes a week or so to build up to fever pace. Not Dallas. He wanted us to suck it up for the first five or six days, kind of like the Marine Corps, where they give you a pointless exercise just to show you who's boss. It's called attitude readjustment.

There was one drill in particular, which Dallas called the circle jerk. The pitchers were divided into two groups. Cones were placed in back of second base, on the shortstop side of second base, and in the two outfield corners and power alleys, so what you had were two large triangles, one each in left and right fields. Two coaches hit fungoes to you as you ran one of the triangular courses. If the ball was there, you caught it and flipped it to one of the other coaches. Halfway through the drill Dallas blew his whistle and you ran back the other way.

He'd stand there, arms crossed, yelling: "Okay, you guys. Bust it. Pick it up. Come on, move it. This isn't the Girl Scouts."

The exercise strained everyone; not their muscles as much as their credulity. It was unnecessarily involved. You could get the same effect simply by having players do a dozen hard laps around the field, before or after practice, timing them. You'd then save actual practice time for more productive activities and drills.

But the aptly named circle jerk was just part of Dallas's schtick. Dallas had the whistle. He was the boss. You did it his way because he told you to do it, not because it made sense or didn't make sense. His camp wasn't about training; it was about control.

We started out running the circle jerk for twelve minutes, and built up in a few days to twenty minutes. It wasn't hard; we just went out and did it because we had to do it. After that we had five minutes to go in, change into a dry uniform, and get back on the field for more drills.

I don't know if Dallas realized it but I'd been jogging six miles a day, so running the circle jerk hardly taxed me. But my heels were hurting. One day I was out there running the exercise. Dallas came up to me, started jogging with me.

"I understand you have problems with your legs," he said.

"No, Dallas. The problem's with my heels. I have a hard time running on grass. If you ran this drill out in the parking lot, it wouldn't bother me a bit. But in the soft grass, my heels sink down too far and I have a problem with it."

"Well, Tommy," he said with condescension, "if it gets too tough on you, you just drop out."

"Dallas," I said, "let me tell you something. I'll die out here before

I'll quit. You can take that to the bank, because that's gold. I'm not the fastest guy out here, but I will not quit running this drill, and you can run us a-l-l d-a-y l-o-n-g. I won't quit. I'll die first."

He said nothing, dropped out and went back to his coaches. I went on running. But Dallas was hoping I'd drop out, that I'd jump at the offer to quit the drill, so he could turn around and tell the press: "See, I told you guys he's too old."

As it was, Dallas couched his early public statements about me with ambiguity.

"I'm not trying to make a big deal out of it," Green told Bill Pennington of the New Jersey *Record.* "I told George and Tommy John how I felt about the situation. I told them all that I'd handle it professionally. [Tommy] will have the opportunity to be seen and evaluated. Then we'll let the chips fall where they may."

Every time Dallas tried to stick me like that, it just gave me added incentive. After our full workout I'd go out for more work on my own . . . making sure he knew about it. I'd make it a point to have Righetti, Don Mattingly, or Mike Pagliarulo ask me, as I was passing Dallas:

"Tommy, don't you get enough running during workouts?"

"That stuff," I'd say loud enough for Dallas to hear, "that's wimpy. I want to get out and run some distance. I'm going out to run for ninety minutes."

I'd jog around the ball park, but only for about twenty minutes or so. I just wanted to gig Dallas a little. He'd just look at me and say nothing.

I told strength and conditioning coach Gary Weil that I'd do however many sprints he called for, but at my speed. He said that was fine. But I made sure that I did more than anybody else: more running, more lifting, more stationary bicycling. I had to. Generally, I always worked that way in camp, even after coming off a twenty-win season. My two rules were: (1) be the first to show up at the ball park, and (2) be the hardest worker in camp. It was like that in 1989, and also my very first spring training, with the Cleveland Indians in 1962.

My first spring training camp took place in Tucson, Arizona. Much the same as in 1989, I went in not knowing what to expect. It was awesome being in the big league camp. I didn't know that many guys, but I tried to pick out those players who were similar to me in background and temperament. Hoot Evers told me that. In that first camp, Steve Hamilton, the tall lefty reliever, and Jerry Kindall, the team's regular second baseman, took an interest in me.

Hamilton was six-seven, and had been quite a basketball player at Morehead State. His basketball background gave us something in common. He had two prominent physical characteristics, other than his height: a protruding Adam's apple that bobbed as he spoke, and a Nellie Fox–sized wad of chewing tobacco in his cheek. Hamilton's claim to fame in baseball is the Folly Floater, an improbably arcing ephus pitch he developed late in his career.

Hamilton, who knew a nervous rookie when he saw one, told me to just be myself.

"You're going to get a lot of guys who will tell you a lot of things about pitching," Steve said. "Most of it will be conflicting advice. Listen to everybody. Be reasonable, be polite, be attentive. Don't shut anybody out. Try what they say. If you can use it, fine. If you can't, throw it out. But I'm telling you from experience, Tommy. Don't let the so-called experts tell you what to do if it doesn't work for you, because they'll send you right down the tubes. Just be yourself." Boy, was that true!

Kindall, a quiet, fair-skinned man with a thin, infielder's build, would take me to Fellowship of Christian Athletes meetings, Youth for Christ meetings, and to church. I used to follow him when he played for the Cubs. He was a great-field, no-hit second baseman whose glove kept him in the lineup. Jerry signed with the Cubs after a great career with the University of Minnesota, where he led the Gophers to Big Ten and NCAA championships in 1956. He always played hard and got the most out of his abilities, the kind of worker a youngster should emulate.

Jerry was a godly man and he'd talk about his faith with a low, nasal quality in his voice, as if he had a cold all the time. He saw the scared rookie and befriended me, which was totally out of character for the time. Veterans didn't give rookies the time of day in the early 1960s. But that didn't make a difference to Jerry. He introduced me to a lot of good people, and was a strong influence on my early career.

"I see you're palling around with Kindall," Hoot told me. "That's good. He's the kind of guy you want to be around. You'll be much better off for it."

My mom and dad used to tell me the same thing: you can tell good from bad, people you want to be like and those you don't want to emulate. Pick out the good ones. They were talking about guys like Kindall, Bobby Richardson, Albie Pearson. Of course, I had friends in other walks, non-Christians, nonbelievers, radicals, conservatives, you name it.

But I stayed away from the bad apples. They were easy to spot. All you'd have to do was listen to their conversations in the clubhouse, or on the field during batting practice. Guys would talk about what they did the night before, how much they caroused, what bars they hit, what girls they picked up. If you keep your ears open, you find out who the bad apples are; they expose themselves through their own lips.

But just because a guy mixed it up at night didn't mean we couldn't be friends. For example, one of my friends was Gary Bell, a free-spirited, happy-go-lucky righthanded starter and one of the biggest drinkers on the team. He chummed around with the other Indian "rounders," a group that included Woodie Held, Barry Latman, and Bob Allen. They had all come up through the minor leagues together.

Gary was very nice to me, and was a great guy to have on a ball club. He had a great sense of humor. He's the kind of guy who would give up a three-run homer and find something funny to say about it. It's not that Bell wasn't a serious competitor. He was. It's just that he let everything roll off his back. In 1964 we roomed together one road trip in California, and he went out of his way to put me at ease.

"Tommy," Bell said, "we run kind of hard and drink more than we should. You've got a lot of talent. You probably shouldn't do what we're doing. So don't think you have to go out with us."

Gary was honest with me, and I respected him for that.

We're all creatures of our early environment, products of our childhood. I was just fortunate to have come from a family-oriented background, brought up in a typically conservative, midwestern town, a Christian background. Look at a guy like Billy Martin. Billy had a tough childhood. He grew up fighting on the streets of Oakland's toughest section. His life reflected that, and he battled all his life. But between the white lines, a Tommy John and a Billy Martin could both play with the same intensity for the same purpose. That's one of the beauties of baseball.

My faith was a great source of strength early in my career, when I was away from home and before I married Sally. They could have been lonely, doubtful years, but they weren't. People sometimes have a misconception that when you become a Christian, bells and whistles go off, lights flash, your problems disappear, and you stop having fun. Nothing's further from the truth.

Christianity simply means making a decision to put your life in Christ's hands. You want your life to follow the example of Christ. You can make that decision publicly or alone in your bathroom, in a stadium with 40,000 people or in the silence of your own heart. Your problems will still be there; you'll still have car payments to make, disputes to resolve. The difference is that you now have help in handling the difficulties of daily life. You have a source of strength to overcome adversity. With that help, you bend but don't break.

I had a good spring that year. Kindall and Hamilton broke the ice for me and saved me from the usual rookie ostracization. The bottom of the pecking order wasn't as bad as it could have been. Manager Mel McGaha treated the rookies indifferently, giving out assignments without a lot of embellishment, acting as if we automatically knew what he wanted. That's where Jerry and Steve helped me out: they showed me what to do in drills, introduced me to guys on the team, and helped me feel more comfortable. McGaha pitched me a few times, and I was pleased with my performances. The Indians were serious about developing young pitching. If the organization had a philosophy back then, it was to try to stack up on young arms, like myself, Gary Bell, Mudcat Grant, Sam McDowell, Sonny Siebert, Steve Hargan, and Luis Tiant.

Because of my good year at Dubuque and my showing at Tucson, the Indians thought I was ready for Class A ball, at Charleston, West Virginia, of the Eastern League. That represented a huge jump, since I would bypass D, C, and B levels.

At Charleston I learned how much I needed to learn about pitching.

For the first time in my young life, I realized that *I didn't know how to pitch.* Up until then, I got by simply rearing back on every pitch and firing the ball as hard as I could. That's how I was pitching at the beginning of the year at Charleston. As a result, I was always pitching from behind, then would have to lay the fastball in to get a strike. But these hitters would just lose the ball on me. I'd be fine one game, then get absolutely hammered. My control was shot; the harder I threw, the wilder I got, and it shook my confidence. I don't know what would have happened to me if Steve Jankowski hadn't saved me from myself.

Jankowski, a player coach on the team, lived with me at a rooming house in Charleston. He was nine years older than me. Steve had been injured in Triple A, and he no longer entertained dreams of making the big leagues. He was a career minor leaguer in the best sense of that term, an organization man who filled in wherever they needed him. Jankowski was a veteran, and I asked him what my problem was. He leveled with me.

"You're overthrowing," he said. "You don't have to throw every pitch at one hundred percent. You're a typical young pitcher, used to striking guys out. You struck guys out in high school, in Legion ball. You come up here and try to throw every pitch through a brick wall. But on this level you won't get by too long doing that. These guys mean business. You get hitters out on ground balls, fly balls, line drives. Put the ball in play. Let your fielders make the plays behind you. You've got eight guys waiting to help you out."

"Yeah," I asked, "but how do I do that?"

"Here's what you do. The next time you pitch, try not to strike anybody out. I mean it. Throw at about eighty percent, almost as though you're throwing batting practice. Let the batters hit it."

Jankowski's advice sounded dubious at first, but in my next start it became a revelation, and it created the pattern of pitching I would adopt for the rest of my career.

The next game came against York, Pennsylvania. Following Jankowski's advice—reluctantly at first—I pitched a complete game, three-hit shutout, with 12 strikeouts and only one walk. From that game on I was a totally different Tommy John. I won my next three starts pitching this way.

My control improved after that: 1962 at Charleston and Jacksonville, 162 innings, 87 walks; 1963 at Charleston, Jacksonville, and Cleveland, 207 innings, 57 walks. I became the Tommy John people would come to know over the next twenty-seven years, a pitcher whose style could be described as: "Here it is. Hit it."

The simplest yet most elegant explanation of pitching I ever heard came from Warren Spahn, the great left-hander for the Boston and Milwaukee Braves. Spahn said hitting is timing. Pitching is upsetting timing. He was exactly right. He's one guy in baseball I never met but wished I had. I'd love to talk pitching with him.

A pitcher wants to upset the batter's timing. That's why the off-speed pitch is so effective. If you can change speeds, the batter's already got his bat going, he's out there on that front foot, and you really mess him up. You can throw a change-up off a fastball, a curve, and even a slider. It's the arm motion that fools the batter. On your change-up, the windup stays the same and your arm speed stays the same. But your grip on the ball changes. I threw my change-up off my pinky and ring fingers. With the other fingers off the ball, it comes out of your hand slowly. It baffles hitters because they swing off your arm motion. From watching the arm, the batter's expecting a fastball or a curve. But the ball comes in slower, and he's caught in no-man's land.

Hitters have changed enormously over the years. When I first broke in, batters by and large looked for a fastball to hit hard, out of the ball park, especially on a 2–0 or 3–1 count. The prototypical power hitters of the day hit that way, guys like Rocky Colavito, Mickey Mantle, Boog Powell, Norm Cash, Joe Adcock, Harmon Killebrew, Dick Stuart, and Don Lock. Even contact hitters like Tony Kubek, Billy Moran, Ed Bressoud, and Jerry Lumpe tended to jack it up when they were ahead on the count. When you got a guy 2–0, he'd try to hit the next pitch on the roof. The most effective pitchers of that time—Whitey Ford comes to mind—were the guys who could change speeds on 2–0 and catch the batter overswinging. He'd usually pop the ball up or hit a little ground ball.

Today, when hitters get ahead of the count, they hit the same way as they do when they're down 0–2. You'll see that as much with power hitters such as Bo Jackson, Kirby Puckett, and Dwight Evans as you do with contact men like Wade Boggs, Tony Gwynn, and Steve Sax. They try to go up the middle with everything, which is what the Charley Lau–Walt Hriniak theory preaches. Don't try for homers; just make contact. Look at the decline in home runs since the peak years of the 1960s. The 1980s, in fact, were the first decade since the dead-ball era in which no batter reached the fifty-home-run plateau, though Cecil Fielder hit 51 in 1990 for the Tigers.

Another difference is the inside pitch. In earlier years you could brush a hitter off the plate with a ball up and in; you'd intimidate the batter so he wouldn't look for anything on and over the plate. As a result, he'd be a little gun shy. But today the rules have taken away the brush-back from pitchers. As a consequence, you can't knock anybody off the plate. Hitters go up looking for the ball out over the plate and dive in after it. That's why the change-up is so important.

Back then, if you wanted to get the hitter "thinking," you just buzzed a heater in under his chin—the old Sal Maglie "how are you fixed for blades?" ball. Maglie, in fact, made a 22-game winner out of Jim Lonborg in 1967 when Jim was pitching for the Boston Red Sox. He taught Lonborg to "shave" batters, which is exactly what Jim did. He won the Cy Young award that year and led the league in strikeouts and hit batsmen.

Today you can't do that, so you use a change-up. You could say today's change-up is equivalent to yesterday's brush-back or "message" pitch. I didn't stay on the inside of the plate often, and that was one knock against me early in my career: I was too much a gentleman, too "nice." But every now and then I'd bust a fastball in on the hands or up under the chin to keep the hitter honest. Pitchers don't have that option today. At the first tight pitch upstairs the batter is ready to charge the mound, with the umpire backing him up.

I didn't throw the change-up until the last two years of my career, when I needed something extra in the arsenal. Until then all I ever threw was the fastball and curve. I was a two-pitch pitcher. My fastball moved and my curveball broke down and in to right-handed hitters. I'd change the break of my curve depending on how fast I threw it, and so I had a variety of curveballs. I could also cut a fastball when I needed to move it inside to a right-handed batter. These "off" pitches served the same function for me as a change-up.

I was blessed in that my ball naturally broke down. The sinkerball was my meal ticket. But I also learned the mechanics that added to my natural ball movement. I learned them when I was with the White Sox. Ray Berres, the pitching coach there, taught me to throw with my hand position going from straight up to straight down. It takes effort and a lot of practice to throw a ball that way, since the uncorrected tendency is to keep your hand positioned at an angle. It's called throwing high-to-low, and that's the way I pitched, driving the ball down with my hand and fingers.

What I discovered when I took Steve Jankowski's advice is that my ball moved more when I didn't overthrow. And ball movement is critical. The plate is seventeen inches wide. If your ball moves, your plate is wider than the guy who throws straight, even if he can throw to spots, which most pitchers can't do.

Here's what I mean by saying you have a "wider" plate. If you've got good ball movement coupled with control, you can start your pitch four or five baseball widths off the plate and it will zip in for a strike. To the batter, it starts out looking like a ball, so he holds up. When the ball comes in he has a hard time generating enough bat speed to handle the pitch. Or, if you start the ball right down the middle of the plate, the ball ends up tailing outside. In that case, the batter sees it coming in fast, then has to hastily adjust at the last minute to an outside pitch. You have so many options if you can get your ball to move. And an umpire who knows your pitching style will understand that and give you more of the black on the plate.

A pitcher with a straight fastball, on the other hand, must pitch to locations. If his control is off just a hair, he'll be ineffective. A straight-baller starts on the plate and stays on the plate. About the only pitchers who have success that way are the pure flamethrowers. It's a tough way to pitch, since you must always have your best stuff. That's why a Sandy Koufax or a Nolan Ryan could be so inconsistent early in their careers.

The million-dollar question, of course, is, "Can you learn how to move the ball?" I honestly don't know. Johnny Sain, who was my pitching coach after Ray Berres in Chicago, said he could never get his ball to move just by throwing it. He had to artificially—mechanically—"move" it; that is, snap the wrist for a curve or screwball. Usually, left-handers, for whatever reason, throw balls that naturally tail or drop, and I don't think that's ever been explained.

A sinkerball sinks because of spin, pure and simple. You release the ball with a backward, off-center spin. If the ball leaves your hand with a backspin coming directly vertical to the ground, the ball won't drop. You need a backspin of between ten and fifteen degrees off center, throwing the ball from high to low, trying to get the ball on a downward plane as it comes to the plate.

It's not an overstatement to say that if it weren't for the sinker, I'd have never made the big leagues, or if I did, I wouldn't have stuck. I never threw the ball hard enough for that. For me, the sinkerball was literally my career.

Jankowski helped me realize that. I wasn't going to do it with a fastball, so I'd better learn another way. My adjustment showed up in my performances for Charleston, and the front office noticed. At the end of July I got a call from Hoot Evers. My record was 6–5 with a 3.87 ERA. This doesn't look dazzling, but the figures represented a great improvement after Jankowski talked to me. Hoot asked me if I thought I could pitch in the Triple A level, at Jacksonville in the International League. I said I didn't know, but maybe.

"They've had some injuries up there and need a pitcher. We're going to send you up. You've been pitching well. You can throw strikes. Jacksonville has a fine ball club. I think you'll be all right."

Small world. I got the call because of Al Jones, the bullpen catcher who caught me the year before during my tryout at Cleveland. When Jacksonville was looking for a pitcher to promote, Al told someone in the front office about me. He said he caught this kid last year who had good stuff and could throw strikes.

Triple A is one step below the majors, and I really felt out of my league. The players were five, six years older than me. The Jacksonville ball club was a solid, mostly veteran team, with guys like Harry Chiti, Larry Brown, Jones, and Vic Davalillo. But the biggest problem was with my manager, Ben Geraghty.

Geraghty was a soft-spoken Irishman with a deeply wrinkled face who couldn't stand young players. Actually, he was a good manager for that particular ball club, one full of veterans to whom he could relate. But he was murder on young players. I found that out when Jones first introduced me to him.

I walked into the clubhouse, which was an exceptionally nice one, with carpeting, wide lockers, and a trainer's room complete with a whirlpool. In the lower minors the clubhouses were small, dark, stifling rooms that were sometimes so bad we'd suit up for games at the hotel. After the game you'd go back to the hotel to undress and shower. If you did shower at the park, you'd have to do it early to get any hot water. There was no air-conditioning—just a single exhaust fan that usually didn't work. But in Jacksonville the locker room was luxurious and seemed to welcome me—more than I could say for my new manager.

Al Jones took me into Geraghty's office, which smelled like cigarettes and beer.

"Ben, this is Tommy John, the pitcher we called up from Charleston."

"Hi," Ben growled, short and clipped, as if he had bitten off a plug of rancid chewing tobacco. His greeting rattled me, and I searched for something to say.

"Is there anything you w-w-want me to do?" I nervously asked, stammering.

"Get dressed."

It was like a bucket of cold water thrown in my face. I trudged out of the office to my locker and put my uniform on.

Managers weren't supposed to be like this. Pinky May at Dubuque and Johnny Lipon at Charleston were both good with young men, good teachers. They knew how to prod, pad, push, cajole, nurture, encourage, and motivate young talent. Ben wasn't like that. He was an old-timer who liked veterans because he didn't have to say anything to them or teach them anything. He just made out his lineup card and let them go out and play. To Geraghty, young guys such as myself didn't know squat and hadn't yet paid their dues.

After a game, Ben wouldn't give a young player the time of day, no matter if you did well or not. He'd sit with his coaches and some of the older players and polish off a case and a half of beer. He wouldn't leave the locker room until the beer was all gone.

I later found out that Ben was once an excellent instructor, but had been emotionally scarred by a horrific bus accident that occurred when he was managing years earlier in the Milwaukee Braves organization. His team was on a bus ride and the driver fell asleep. The bus went off the side of a mountain; several of his players died and more were seriously injured. Ben was never the same after that.

That also explained an odd bit of behavior that puzzled me after joining Jacksonville. I noticed that Ben never slept on long bus trips. He'd sit in his seat all night, wide awake, just staring out the window. Or when the club was at home, he'd go into his office, which was directly opposite my locker, and sit there silently chain-smoking cigarettes and swigging his beer. He'd stare at nothing, as if trying to remember something . . . or maybe trying to forget.

I got into eight games for Jacksonville in 1962, seven of them starts, ending up at 2–2, 4.76. Geraghty had no choice but to use me, since he had only three starting pitchers. I joined the club in Jacksonville as they were just getting ready to go on the road. We jumped a DC-6 to LaGuardia Airport in New York City, got in at four in the morning, waited a few hours for the plane to Syracuse, where we arrived late that morning.

I pitched that night because there was no one else available. As usual, I got to the park early. I sat in front of my locker, got undressed, and tried to quiet myself down. That was easier to do in the locker rooms of old, since there weren't any of today's high-tech distractions: boom boxes, TVs, VCR machines, stereos, weight rooms, and the like. There might be one radio, which the manager controlled. Outside of the usual horseplay and talk of late-night exploits, the atmosphere was almost entirely baseball. There would typically be eight to ten copies of *The Sporting News* lying around, which you read to check up on guys ahead of you in the organization.

Harry Chiti, who had played in the big leagues for about ten years, caught me that night in Syracuse against the Chiefs, then a Detroit Tiger farm team. Chiti called a game more suited for a veteran pitcher. He called for a ton of curveballs. My control was all over the place. Chiti, however, wouldn't back off the curve, and I was too new and too green to shake off a catcher who had almost 500 big league games under his belt.

My next game was in Rochester, and Jones caught me. That made the difference. He wouldn't call for a breaking ball until I was ahead in the count. I stuck mostly with my fastball, went seven innings and got a win. My biggest thrill from that game was striking out pinch hitter Luke Easter, the big power-hitting first baseman for the Indians in the early fifties.

Jacksonville won the championship, and in the playoffs I started two games, again because Geraghty had no one else. I won two games in the seven-game series, but we lost four games to three.

During the off-season in the winter of '62, I took courses at Indiana State University, but I also worked hard to stay in shape. My exercise regimen included running, playing basketball, and refereeing Indiana high school basketball games. For fun, I even did some play-by-play for basketball games. When spring training opened up in 1963, I was in Tucson again, with the forty-man roster. I knew I had no chance of making the Indians; my goal was cracking the rotation at Jacksonville.

Well, I made Jacksonville, but I never got the chance to pitch. Geraghty buried me. He wouldn't use me. Rex Edmundson of the Jacksonville *Times-Union*—a considerate man who would take me out to eat, or hook me up with rides to the ball park—kept asking Geraghty: "What about Tommy John?"

"He's a young kid," Ben would answer. "He's going to have to wait his turn."

For the first six weeks of the season I pitched twice, winning my only decision. Disappointment, anger, and bewilderment welled up inside me as, game after game, I rode the bench, totally ignored by Geraghty. If he had to say anything to me, it would be in curt half whispers or grunts. When you're in that situation, your mind starts to get away from you a little. Was I all done? Would my career end this way, wasting away on a minor league bench? This wasn't a completely unrealistic scenario. If a young pitcher doesn't pitch, if he can't make his impression, he becomes a forgotten man. Many careers have ended in such an ignominious way.

Finally, on May 1, reprieve came in the form of a call from Cleveland. They were going to send me back down to Charleston, Hoot Evers said. The organization knew what was going on, and realized I had to be pitching. I was too valuable an investment to be riding the bench. Hoot tried to console me and rationalize the move; it wasn't to be viewed as a demotion. He didn't have to say a word in the club's defense. I was delighted to be leaving the gloom of Jacksonville and Geraghty. If I had been left there, I might have rotted on the vine.

I packed my car and took off. On my way to Charleston, I stopped to visit my sister Marilyn, who was now living in Cincinnati. I stayed two days and drove on to Charleston. When I got to the ball park, the team wasn't there. They had left for a road trip. The brass was angry at me and I got chewed out. They were looking for me two days ago, they said. No one had mentioned anything to me about a specific reporting date, but that didn't matter. As I would find out over the years, that type of miscommunication was typical of professional baseball. The players are always the last to know.

I hopped a flight into Utica, New York, and joined the ball club in Elmira, where I was scheduled to pitch. When manager Johnny Lipon saw me, he smiled broadly and said: "Welcome back, biggie. We've got a good ball club here. Let's have some fun!"

I felt as if a two-ton load had been taken from my shoulders. A young lefty has enough problems without having to carry the weight of the world as well.

Unlike last year at Charleston, when I was still the "new guy," I knew most of my teammates well, having played together in D ball or the year before. My good friends included Luis Tiant, Don Schaefer, and Pete Olson.

The 1963 Charleston club was an outstanding team. We had Duke Sims and Buddy Booker catching, Bob Chance at first, Tony Antanazzio at second, Jackie Hernandez (who caught my first professional game at Dubuque) at short, and Antulio Martinez at third. The outfield, left to right, consisted of Tony Curry, who had been with the Phillies in 1961; Tommie Agee in center; and Auggie Garrido in right. It was a great defensive team that also could score runs, exactly what a sinkerballer needed.

I won my first game against Elmira, and not much went wrong after that. For the first time in my professional career, I was dominant. Johnny Lipon used me in 12 games, all of them starts. I went 9–2, 1.61, eight complete games, with only 12 walks in 95 innings.

I had my friends, my niche on the team, and started having fun again in the Eastern League, home of the endless bus ride. The shortest trip we had—Charleston to York, Pennsylvania—was twelve hours long. Our longest trip was about twenty-four hours, to Springfield, Massachusetts. The floating bridge game, plus my high spirits, made the rides tolerable. Even Luis Tiant's cigars didn't bother me.

Luis would smoke these horrendous, long, Cuban cigars. We'd be on the bus all night, and wake up to a thick blue haze from Tiant's ropes. Tiant had an almost supernatural ability for keeping a cigar lit. Luis would cut up in his high-pitched voice, joking, cackling, and the eternal flame held true. He could even take a shower and keep his stogie going. In the confined space of a bus, the smoke would gag you. He'd fall asleep on the bus, but the cigar would somehow stay alive all night.

One particular road trip drove home in a strange way Steve Jankowski's advice about not overthrowing. After a night game in Binghamton, New York, we drove to Springfield, checking into the Sheraton Motor Lodge there at five-thirty A.M. I was scheduled to pitch that night at seven-thirty. But it just so happened that the U.S. Open was in its second day at Brookline, just outside of Boston, about eighty miles away from Springfield. Arnold Palmer, Julios Boros, and other great golfers of the day would be playing on one of the country's outstanding courses. Now the sensible thing to do after getting into Springfield would have been to have breakfast, then try to rest up for the night's game. But the Open beckoned.

I was a golf addict as it was, and so were Don Schaefer and Pete Olson. We'd try to play as much golf as we could, sneaking our clubs onto the back of the bus and piling up suitcases all around to hide them. Schaefer had an American Express card. He and Olson were talking of renting a car and driving in to see the tournament. Don and Pete knew I wanted to go, but since I had to pitch that night, they said they would understand it if I stayed at the hotel and tried to rest.

"No way," I answered. "I'll have another game to pitch in five days, but I might not ever get a chance to see another U.S. Open."

Within the hour we were in a Hertz car zipping across the state on the Massachusetts Turnpike. We tramped around the Open all day long, following the leaders, wolfing down hot dogs and chugging Cokes. We got back to Springfield just in time to hurry to the ball park. We were physically exhausted from the long day, yet I still had a game to pitch. I put my uniform on like an eighty-year-old man and dragged myself to the mound.

I shut out Springfield 5–0.

I was overtired and couldn't overthrow. It was a classic validation of Jankowski's advice.

Back in the clubhouse, I just sat sort of dazed in front of my locker. Fatigue started to bury me like an avalanche. Johnny Lipon came over, congratulating me for my masterpiece.

"You won't be pitching tomorrow, Tommy. Why don't you get out to Brookline tomorrow and see the Open."

"No thanks, skip," I said. "I'll just watch it on TV."

After my twelve games in Charleston, the organization sent me back up to Jacksonville. Hoot Evers said I'd accomplished everything I needed to get done in Charleston.

"You wanted to pitch, and it's obvious you're better than this league," Evers said. "It's to your benefit that you go back up to Jacksonville and learn how to pitch in Triple A ball. It will accelerate your rise to the big leagues."

I wasn't sure about that after my disastrous experience at Jacksonville early in the year. But the team was totally different my second time there in '63.

Ben Geraghty had passed away in June. Word filtered down to Charleston that he died of cirrhosis of the liver. Many of the old-timers said that the beginning of the end was that tragic bus accident. After that crash, he wouldn't allow himself to get close to his players again, especially his young players. Apparently, alcohol was the way he insulated himself. Despite my experiences with Ben, his death saddened me.

The team was now managed by thirty-one-year-old Casey Wise, who had played as recently as 1960 with the Detroit Tigers. Casey was a player's manager, an easygoing fellow who had good rapport with the kids.

Casey used to bring his German shepherd dog to the park once in a while. The dog shadowed Casey on the field before game-time, but when the game began, he stayed out in the bullpen with the pitchers. He was a huge dog that scared us to death by his very size. He'd lay down in the bullpen—anywhere he wanted, as the joke goes—and not take his eyes off Casey the entire game. Every time Casey went from the dugout to the third base coaching box, the dog's ears would perk up. When Casey went to the mound to take a pitcher out, he'd signal to the bullpen and the dog would jump up and down, wagging his tail. We all thought the dog would be the next pitcher in the game.

Under Casey, a lot of the veteran ball players were jettisoned to make way for youth: players like myself, Mike Cuellar, Tiant, Sam McDowell, and Sonny Siebert. Some of the veterans hated Casey for that.

The '63 Jacksonville team had the makings of an outstanding staff —on paper. The truth is, we were still learning about pitching, the defense was shaky, and we had absolutely no offense. The ball club was so bad that at one time six of the nine hitters in the batting order were hitting below .200. We finished so far out of first place that we may have ended in the Sally League instead of the International League.

I learned a valuable lesson in clubhouse politics that summer, just another in a series of events that helped me shed some of my innocent illusions about professional baseball.

Wise, being mild-mannered and young, had trouble with some of the veterans on that team. The vets were feeling nervous, given the organization's dedication to its youth movement. Casey was just too nice a guy to be effective as a manager.

Casey could be hard-nosed if he had to, but it was forced. It just wasn't part of his makeup, and in the long run it would have eaten away at him too much for his own good. He would give an order and a veteran would just look at him and say to his face, "Who the hell are you to tell me that?"

One game we were getting blown out, 12–2. Wise ordered Ed Donnelly to mop up in relief. Donnelly had been a star on the team in 1962, but in '63 he was having a bad year and on his way out. Donnelly refused to go into the game. Wise, seeking to avoid a confrontation, then asked me if I wanted to pitch. I said sure. Then Donnelly got all over the manager.

"You aren't going to throw the bleeping kid into this game, you blankety-blank. He's got a future ahead of him." The raging pitcher then turned to me.

"Don't you warm up," he screamed.

"Ed, I have to." Actually, I didn't mind at all, welcoming the chance to tune up.

Wise and Donnelly then started shouting in each other's faces, eyeball to eyeball, outside the dugout in front of the fans.

"Donnelly, you're through with this ball club. Get upstairs. I've had enough of you," Wise barked.

After the game, the team started filing into the locker room. Donnelly was there waiting for Wise.

"I thought I told you to leave," Casey said.

"I'm not leaving until I have it out with you. Let's go."

They started fistfighting, really duking it out. Nobody broke it up. Finally, when it ended, Wise stormed into his office and Donnelly slammed the door on his way out of the clubhouse. The veteran pitcher was released that day. It made me realize two things: that players as well as managers operate from hidden agendas, and that you butt heads with a manager—rightly or wrongly—only at great peril to your career.

My stats for Jacksonville, 6–8 and 3.53, were actually pretty good for that terrible team, but surely not good enough to impress anyone upstairs. Or so I thought.

Certain moments you don't forget: events such as the purchase of your first car, the delight of your first real kiss, your wedding day, the birth of a child. For a ball player, it's something else.

We were playing in Little Rock, Arkansas. I was in my hotel room when the phone rang. It was Casey.

"Tommy, would you come over to my room, now?"

I was wondering what it could be. Had I done something to anger him? Why did he want me immediately? Couldn't be anything good.

I knocked on his door, and Casey answered, a hint of a smile on his face.

"Come on in, Tommy. Sit down."

I walked over to the green, vinyl-upholstered sofa and took a seat. Casey did the same.

"Tommy, I just got a call from Cleveland . . ."

Uh-oh, I thought.

"You're going up when they expand the roster on September first."

I sat there stunned. Me? Called up? The big leagues?

Casey shook me out of my reverie with a word of advice: "You're going to see guys with better fastballs, better curveballs. Just remember one thing. You've got a *Tommy John* fastball and a *Tommy John* curveball. Go up there and just be Tommy John. You've got enough stuff. You can pitch up there and win."

He then went through the roster of Cleveland's pitching staff, as if he were ticking off a mail call.

"Grant, Donovan, Ramos, Perry, Bell, Kralick, Latman. Don't worry about them. You just be *John*. Give yourself a chance."

"Thanks, Casey."

"Don't thank me, Tommy. You earned it."

We shook hands. I ran back to my room on air, packed in fifteen minutes, and left immediately for Cleveland. On my arrival, manager Birdie Tebbetts called me into his office. He said he'd try to use me when he could, maybe out of the bullpen. He said he just wanted me to get my feet on the ground and try to get comfortable pitching in the big leagues.

"Hopefully," he said, "you'll take advantage of this opportunity."

"Yes, sir," I bubbled.

Everything about Municipal Stadium looked magical: the cavernous stands; the crowds; the large, air-conditioned locker room; the meticulously manicured grass; the smooth infield; the clubhouse kids who took care of all your errands. I wasn't even twenty-one and I was in The Show!

My first major league appearance came on the road against the Washington Senators at D.C. Stadium on September 6, 1963, with the Indians at 68–76, buried in a sixth-place tie with Boston, 25 games behind the Yankees. Dick Donovan started for us against Bennie Daniels of the Senators before a crowd of 12,054. Donovan struggled, giving up ten hits and six runs in his six-plus innings. We were trailing in the game, 6–2. In the top of the seventh the phone in the bullpen rang.

"Get John warmed up."

My heart fluttered and I felt lightheaded. I was probably hyperventilating. I got loose, snatching anxious glances at the field. When Donovan gave up a hit to the first Senator batter in the bottom of the seventh, Birdie popped out of the dugout. He made his way toward the mound, said a few words to Donovan, took the ball and made the motion to the bullpen, flicking his left hand.

Oh, my God, I thought frantically. He's going to make a move. He wants the lefty. He wants *me*!

"Tommy, you're in there," said the bullpen coach matter-of-factly.

The guys in the bullpen started patting me on the back, telling me to "go get 'em." I grabbed my jacket, all fired up and ready to mow the Senators down, but there was one slight hitch. I couldn't get the bullpen gate open! It wasn't a normal latch, and I didn't know how to work it.

"Where the hell is T.J.?" the squawk box blared behind me.

I started to panic, thinking I might have to climb the gate, and have the two bullpens plus twelve thousand people laughing at this rube left-hander who couldn't get out of his own way. Not knowing what else to do, I started shaking the gate. Somehow, it popped open. It had to be divine intervention. Walking toward the mound, I thanked God that the gate opened.

My next dilemma was precisely how to come in. There was no bullpen cart, and I didn't know if I was supposed to jog in and look like an anxious rookie, or saunter in with my jacket slung over my shoulder like a veteran. I compromised with a slow trot.

I got to the mound, feeling like it was all a dream. Birdie explained the game situation and put the ball in my hand.

"There it is, kid. Throw strikes. Let's see what you've got."

Hank Soar, the home plate ump, declared the game back in play. The first batter I faced was Don Zimmer. My knees were shaking as I went into the stretch. My left foot sided the rubber and I stared in for the sign. Zimmer looked like Popeye in the batter's box: a big chaw of tobacco, squinty eyes, crew cut, and large forearms.

My first pitch was a fastball for a called strike. Zim let go a stream of tobacco juice, which he aimed outside the box, toward the third base dugout. Zimmer took a big cut at the next pitch, a sinking fastball, but just got over it, topping a slow grounder to third. Max Alvis charged the ball, scooped it up, and threw to Fred Whitfield at first for the out. The runner moved to second on the play. I don't remember too much about the rest of the inning, except that there were a couple of hits—I think by Ken Retzer and Don Blasingame—and that my legs didn't stop shaking until I got back to the dugout after getting the third out. I recall getting out of the inning on a sinker to Minnie Minoso, which he beat into the ground to Alvis at third.

It wasn't a bad debut: one inning, two hits, one unearned run. An interesting footnote to the contest was reported in the *Washington*

*Post*'s game story: it was the 100,000th game played in the major leagues since May 4, 1871.

In all, Birdie got me into six games, two of them starts. Both starts were against the Angels and both facing Dean Chance, their tough right-hander. That second start came in Cleveland on the Saturday afternoon *Game of the Week*.

Albie Pearson led off for the Angels, and on the first pitch, on national TV, I slipped. What had been intended as a curveball came in as a blooping ephus pitch. After the game Pearson asked me if I was trying to embarrass him.

"Albie, I slipped. I almost fell on my can on national TV. Would I do that on purpose?"

"Yeah," he laughed. "I didn't think you were the kind of guy who'd show somebody up."

I pitched well that game, losing to Chance 3–2. Overall, I finished at 0–2, but my ERA was a confidence-boosting 2.21 in 20⅓ innings. That first taste of the big leagues stayed with me all winter. It had been quite an experience. The guys on the team basically ignored rookies, especially those who were around only for the last three and a half weeks. But that didn't matter. I enjoyed my stay, got my feet wet, adjusted well, and knew I belonged in the majors.

When the season was over, Birdie called me into his office and told me to think of all the things that had happened to me during the season. He said a good pitcher learns as much during the off-season as he does during the season. The good ones will sit back and reflect on what they did right and what they did wrong. They'll study what they tried to do and what they will need to do next year to make themselves better, more competitive pitchers. It was sage advice from the old catcher. Catchers make excellent managers because they call the game, and pitching is seventy percent of baseball. The great managers have been the ones who knew how to handle a pitching staff.

"What are your plans for the off-season?" Birdie asked me.

"I'm going back to Indiana State and take some courses."

Birdie shook his head and said the team wanted me to play winter ball. Some guys look at that as an insult, but not me. It meant three things: steady paychecks during the off-season, a chance to work on my pitching during the "extra" season, and a reunion with Johnny Lipon, my manager at Charleston. Johnny was managing in Ponce, Puerto Rico, and that's where I'd be playing. Puerto Rico's the only place I'd consider playing winter ball, since you don't need a visa to go there and the playing conditions are better.

In places like the Dominican Republic and Venezuela, if you don't pitch well, you coincidentally end up with visa problems when you try to get out of the country. The fans are fanatic and they take it personally if you have a bad season.

Birdie told me I'd like Puerto Rico. I did—the ambience, that is. The tropical weather in winter had its own charm. Normally in November I'd be back in Indiana with winter closing in; here, I was in the sun every day. Ponce itself was a quiet little town on the southern end of the island. It had a town square with a fountain in the center, and a certain run-down, sleepy appeal. But like most of Puerto Rico, it was economically stratified: there were the very wealthy and the abject poor, and nothing in between.

I got paid $500 twice a month for playing six games a week. The Puerto Rican fans take the winter season seriously. This is their regular season, their "big leagues." Each team would be stocked with local talent, augmented—under arrangements with U.S. major league clubs —by eight to ten American ballplayers. The native Puerto Rican players played intensely, but there were problems with the U.S. players. These guys played in the States from late February to early October. The winter season in Puerto Rico went from November to mid-January. So the U.S. guys were essentially playing year-round. They tended not to play hard in the winter, and understandably so. Why risk an injury in winter ball? But the Puerto Rican fans didn't like that and would get on you.

At games, armed cops would roam the stands. It was wild. No one cared if fans stole gloves, bats, and equipment from the American players. They were the rich gringos who could easily buy replacements. Fans would steal you blind, and the cops would look the other way. But if there was any kind of trouble or fighting in the stands, the police would go in with clubs swinging, no questions asked. They'd beat people senseless at the slightest provocation, dragging people out of the stands, while the game was going on.

I found all of this exciting, but I didn't like what was happening to my arm. After my first five games my arm started feeling tender. I shut out Mayaguez, but the next morning my arm was killing me. I couldn't bend my elbow. There was severe pain and I couldn't even lift my arm high enough to brush my teeth or eat properly. The only way I could eat was bring my arm to the table and lower my head to the spoon. I was shaving, washing up, brushing my teeth, eating right-handed.

I told Lipon, and he skipped over my next start, hoping the rest would help. I went to a local physical therapist, who diagnosed tendonitis and treated me with lukewarm water and ultrasound. She told me not to throw for two weeks. I followed that advice, but there was no improvement in the arm. The Indians ordered me back home.

I flew to Cleveland on Saturday, November 16. That flight back was burdened by gloomy flights of imagination about my arm. What if it didn't heal? What if I couldn't pitch again? Bob Kennedy, Cleveland's assistant farm director, met me at the airport and suggested that I see Bob Bauman, the trainer for the St. Louis Cardinals. Bauman was considered to be the best man in baseball for restoring lame arms back to health.

The next day, back home in Terre Haute, I called Bauman, and made an appointment for Friday, November 22. I flew into St. Louis on Thursday, got a room at the George Washington Hotel, close to Bauman's office, and spent the night trying not to think the worst. The next day Bauman carefully examined the arm and said I probably had a small tear in the muscle fiber. He made an appointment for me early that afternoon with team orthopedist Dr. I. C. Middleman.

Middleman thoroughly examined the arm and confirmed Bauman's diagnosis of torn fibers. But while waiting for an injection of cortisone, the radio announced that President John F. Kennedy had been shot and killed in a motorcade in Dallas. I was dumbfounded. It gave me instant perspective. Here I was, fretting over a torn muscle, while the President of the United States had just had his head blown away.

We couldn't believe—we didn't want to believe—the awful news from Dallas. But we had to put it aside. Dr. Middleman concluded his exam and told me to rest the arm until spring training. He said there was no structural damage, no cause for concern, and that simple rest and exercise would do the trick. Bauman gave me some hand and arm exercises to do, and I practiced them religiously all winter. By the time spring training came around in 1964, my elbow was fine.

# 4.

# THE OPENING DOOR

Dallas sought to drive home his message about the "new" Yankee philosophy in every way he could. The clubhouse itself became an advertising medium for the Cultural Revolution he was fomenting. Dallas papered the walls of the clubhouse in Fort Lauderdale with a bunch of motivational signs. One stood out in particular. It read:

THE WILL TO WIN

IS NOT WORTH A NICKEL

UNLESS YOU HAVE THE WILL TO PRACTICE

As I sat in front of my locker the first week of spring training, dressing each day in the classic Yankee uniform, I'd look at that sign with a mixture of hope and trepidation. For me, it could have read:

THE WILL TO WIN

IS NOT WORTH A NICKEL

UNLESS YOU HAVE THE CHANCE TO PRACTICE

Would I get that chance? A fair chance? I honestly didn't know.

But it felt great simply to be in the clubhouse again. The clubhouse occupies a unique spot in the tenor of the game. Things on the field can be going good or bad, but you'll always find a thousand little intrigues, minidramas, and quiet boredoms being played out in the typical baseball locker room.

Clubhouses today are noisier, busier, roomier, and better equipped and ventilated than their counterparts from the early 1960s. You walk in, and it doesn't smell like a locker room anymore. There's no perfume of sweat, liniment, and pine tar, no pungent sting of rubbing alcohol to assault your nostrils, no dampness—only the antiseptic smell of any modern, clean, well-lighted place. But one thing's the same: the clubhouse still pulsates with baseball life, that odd blend of character and caricature that occurs when you take a couple dozen men from separate backgrounds and different parts of the country and put them together from mid-February to early October.

You enter any clubhouse and some guys are talking baseball, another is trying to round up tickets for some friends, three others are telling jokes, and a few more are needling each other or engaging in horseplay. Several sit on stools in front of their lockers and quietly read: paperback novels, the financial pages, the box scores from yesterday's games. The slumping and recently benched cleanup hitter broods darkly on his stool. Someone else is on the pay phone to his agent. A coach tells of playing in an exhibition game in the 1940s and hitting against Satchel Paige.

At a table, three players sit and autograph baseballs. Another tries to catch up on his mounting fan mail. One guy is stretched out on the carpet, sleeping. In the trainer's room, a pitcher with a sore arm glumly gets a rubdown, while an outfielder is in the whirlpool trying to loosen up a tight hamstring. A catcher hobbles to the bathroom with five pounds of ice wrapped around his throbbing ankle. The superstar is in front of the VCR, watching tapes of his swing.

In the exercise room a utility infielder is riding the stationary bike, singing a tune from the fifties. Six boom boxes blare music from separate corners of the clubhouse, everything from rock to rap, classical to country. The beat writers wander in and out, checking on the latest gossip. Four guys surround a color TV, watching a golf match. One does a humorous play-by-play. There's a table near the middle of the room with boxes of free sunflower seeds, gum, chewing tobacco, and snuff.

It's a player's second home, a refuge. At Fort Lauderdale we were in a minor league clubhouse, and that's typical of spring training. But you still find a big league atmosphere. After a game or a workout, for example, players are treated to lavish spreads with cold cuts, meats, salads, vegetables, desserts, which they eat in climate-controlled comfort. In the old days you got potato chips, soda, and salted nuts.

In 1989 I was more conscious than ever of the clubhouse charm, I guess because I came so close to not getting an offer. Now, if only the Yankees would give me my chance on the field.

I knew Dallas's coaching staff couldn't give me a lot of help: not because they were bad guys, but because they had their orders. The coaches were hard workers, but they couldn't risk giving me too much attention, as far Dallas was concerned. They were in an awkward position, and I told pitching coach Billy Connors I understood that.

I caught him alone in the clubhouse early one morning.

"Billy, I know where you guys stand," I told him. "You've got about as much time for me as you have for a bad case of the flu."

"Tommy," Connors said, "you know how I feel about you. There aren't many guys who have done as much as you've done in the game and for the game. If there's anything I can do to help, let me know."

His words warmed me.

"I know you can't work with me here," I said, "because Dallas has already told me you won't have time for me. But if I need help, I know of parks away from the stadium where we can go. I'll get high school kids to catch me. If you see that I need help and it's going to be too much for you to do it here, we'll do it that way. I don't want to do anything that will alienate you with Dallas. That's not why I'm here. I'm here to make this ball club. I just want the same chance as anybody else."

Connors looked at me and smiled: "Pal, you know me better than that. We won't have to sneak off and hide our sessions. If you need help, we'll do it here. Let's just wait until things thin out."

Dallas had 22 pitchers in camp on the first day. I was listed number 21 on the depth chart, barely above Luis Sanchez. That's probably because I could speak English. Only ten pitchers would go north with the Yankees. That's what Connors meant by "thinning out." As more pitchers are sent down and released, he'd have more time for the ones who remained. That, we both hoped, would include me.

I didn't feel buried by the twenty pitchers listed ahead of me, having long ago learned to pay no attention to spring training depth charts. Such charts were abstractions, early best-guesses on the part of the coaching staff. The only depth chart that ever mattered to me in spring training

VERNON REGIONAL
JUNIOR COLLEGE LIBRARY

was the one that hadn't been invented, the one that measures how much a guy has to give.

I wasn't really a "story" yet around camp. Dave Winfield, our big offensive gun, was having serious trouble with his back—he eventually sat out the whole season—and Rickey Henderson arrived late in camp. Both situations sold enough papers in New York to fell forests.

With Rickey, Dallas painted himself into a corner. Rickey had a history of reporting late to camp, but Dallas had told the press that he and Rickey had good communication, and that his recalcitrant outfielder would show up on time. Camp, however, opened with no Rickey. The press milked it for all they could. Dallas blasted Rickey, saying he had no patience for prima donnas and throwing out little digs.

"Maybe he's with Margo," Dallas said of Henderson, referring to the Wade Boggs–Margo Adams sex scandal that had just exploded in Boston's Winter Haven camp.

Steinbrenner gave Green carte blanche when it came to naming the coaching staff. George said if Dallas were to turn the team around, he'd have to have his guys in there. It was no secret around camp that George didn't like a couple of Dallas's coaches, but he kept Dallas off balance by never telling him which ones they were.

Underneath a facade of cooperation, George and Dallas were engaged in psychological warfare. Dallas was really upset at the "old man," as he used to contemptuously call him (He's only about five years older.) He saw my presence in camp as George's attempt to interfere. He was miffed at me because I had talked to George first without getting his clearance. But why did I have to get Dallas Green's permission? I was a free agent. I had no contract with the Yankees. Why couldn't I call a man with whom I'd had a business and a personal relationship for almost ten years? I asked Dallas that. He gruffed it off and never did answer me.

Dallas's problem with me was simple—he had to save face. He came in as field boss of the Yankees with the attitude that he would be different from previous Yankee managers, that he would not put up with meddling from the top, that he would run the team his way and not back down from the owner.

But after that fine show of bravado, George shoved Tommy John down his throat. With that, Dallas soon found himself dealing with exactly what his predecessors had faced: the irresistible tidal pull of the owner's influence. How do you handle an owner who's no shrinking violet, who's not going to hesitate to tell you how to run the show? Dallas had no easy answers, and that bothered him.

For my part, I didn't want to be the catalyst of a fight between George and Dallas. That's why I kept my mouth shut. Dallas treated me like an unwanted house guest, but I made sure I did my own dirty laundry and bought my own meals.

Lee Elia and Connors were the only two coaches who went out of their way to make me feel welcome. The others weren't bad to me, just indifferent. They had their orders from Dallas and had to protect their new positions. But that's life in baseball. It gets very political. I'd seen it all before, and it didn't bother me. I was a big boy.

Elia would take me aside. We had played together for the White Sox in 1966 and were friends. That's one thing about baseball—when you play with a guy on the same team, you have a bond, a brotherhood that can last a lifetime.

"You've got a tough road ahead of you," he'd say. "Just keep your chin up and your mouth shut. Let the chips fall where they may. I'm pulling for you, T.J."

The coaches, all of them hard workers, reflected Dallas's personality and were the perfect foils for him. Dallas himself was a big man, an intimidating six-five, 260-pound presence, and his coaches were cut from a mold just as imposing.

Charlie Fox had a black belt in karate, and I think Pat Corrales did also. Elia was a tough, hard-nose guy; John Stearns played defensive back at Colorado; Frank "Hondo" Howard stood six-eight and weighed 275 pounds. The team perceived them as Dallas's enforcers, and that created tension, especially with the younger players. Dallas was like the new kid in the neighborhood who knows that some guys might like to take a shot at him, so he surrounds himself with the toughest guys on the block.

My first concern was getting my arm in shape. In spring training, especially before the Grapefruit League schedule begins, you need to pitch every day to build up your arm and to work on your mechanics: the step back, windup, pivot, and arm extension that goes into a pitcher's motion.

For a pitcher, spring training is just what the name implies—you are training your arm in the spring for the 162-game regular season. How does a pitcher do that? By throwing every day.

Your workdays are days 1, 3, 5, and 7. That's when you do your heavy load work: warm up in the bullpen with the pitching coach watching you, throw hard on the side, and throw batting practice. On your off days—days 2, 4, and 6—you just throw the ball a little bit, lightly. It might involve no more than throwing ten minutes at half speed to a catcher who's wearing a fielder's mitt. All you're doing is throwing strikes and practicing proper mechanics to throw proper pitches. Everytime you throw, even that lightly, you're building up your arm.

Dallas and Billy Connors also were big on long throwing in the outfield. The Yankee pitchers threw that way every day for ten minutes. That was an excellent arm exercise.

Every pitcher's arm will "go dead" early in spring training. That's a routine part of getting the arm in shape to pitch. In baseball parlance, a "dead arm" is not the same as a "sore arm." The latter is a true cause for concern; it means your arm is damaged, usually in the shoulder or elbow. A dead arm, however, is a normal condition, something you simply work your way through. You feel it in the bicep. In my first spring training, at Tucson in 1962, I experienced a dead arm. I went in to the trainer, all worried, and he just laughed at me. He said I'd be over it in four or five days, and that's just what happened.

You keep throwing, and all of a sudden your bicep doesn't hurt anymore. That's the sign that your arm is built up. And that's the stage you want to be at by the time the exhibition season begins. At that point you should be able to throw hard for twenty-five minutes without undue fatigue or pain.

I threw whenever the coaches would let me, or whenever there was an extra catcher around who would catch me. Catchers Bob Geren, Jamie Quirk, Joel Skinner, Don Slaught, Brian Dorsett, and Dave Sax each had their turns with me, and they couldn't have been more cooperative. I could sense that, while the coaches had to be couched in their dealings with me, the players were on my side.

After practice I would throw some more. I had plenty of throwing time, and in that regard Dallas did not treat me differently than any other pitcher. That was the first slight ray of hope.

I think I had surprised Dallas by coming to camp in such good shape. He didn't talk to me those first few days so I don't know what was going on in his mind, but I believe my physical condition caused him to think something like: "Maybe Tommy wasn't conning me when he said he could still do it." At the very minimum, I had proved to him that I was in top shape and could still work hard.

One day at the end of the first week of workouts, the team trotted off the field after practicing rundown and cutoff plays. The pitchers, who are used as the runners in those drills, were all dripping with sweat, including me. I ducked into the dugout, got a quick drink from the water cooler, and was heading to the locker room when Dallas spoke.

"Tommy. Got a second?"

Dallas was standing on the upper step of the dugout, leaning on one leg, surveying the empty field. His baseball cap was pushed back on his head, the way he often wore it, and his thick white hair fluffed out under the bill. The rest of the guys filed into the clubhouse to change uniforms or get something to drink.

I picked up a white towel from the bench, mopped my brow, climbed the three steps of the dugout and stood facing Dallas. I didn't know what to expect. Was he going to blast me? Tell me I had been released? What?

"I want to ask you a question," he said in a normal tone of voice.

"Shoot."

"You've been here a long time, right?"

"Yeah, since 1979, off and on," I answered.

"Are these guys as badly trained in the fundamentals as they're showing? Or is it just me?"

I couldn't believe it. He was asking my opinion, genuinely interested in learning something from me.

"They're the worst bunch I've ever seen," he stated.

"Yeah," I said, "You're right, Dallas. They are bad."

I told him that in my years with the club, the Yankees never worked on fundamentals as hard as they could have. I explained my theory for that. It was a result of those great teams in the 1976–77–78 seasons.

Look at that lineup. In the infield they had Chris Chambliss at first, Willie Randolph at second, Bucky Dent at short, Graig Nettles at third, and Thurman Munson behind the plate. The outfield consisted of Roy White, Lou Piniella, Mickey Rivers, and Reggie Jackson. The bench had guys like Cliff Johnson and Paul Blair. The pitching staff included Catfish Hunter, Ed Figueroa, Ron Guidry, Goose Gossage, Sparky Lyle, and Dick Tidrow. That was an awesome core of a team, with older ballplayers and established stars who didn't need to work on fundamentals.

Then a changeover happened in the early to mid-eighties. The nucleus of that great club was gone. In its place were young players and journeymen types from other teams, often last-place teams, guys who *did* need work. But that work went undone. When I first came over from the Dodgers in 1979, it struck me too: the team couldn't play fundamentally sound baseball. It surprised me. These were, after all, the Yankees. Or the pseudo-Yankees, you could say, a mishmash of players from other organizations who each learned to do things differently.

These Yankees never took fundamentals seriously. When they had to practice bunting or fielding, the players griped and treated it as torture, or something that was beneath them as major leaguers. Yet plays like that—rundowns, bunts, cutoffs—get screwed up in the regular season and it costs you games. I was with the Angels for the last month of the 1982 season, and we made more good cutoff plays in four weeks than the Yankees made the whole season. Winners take pride in executing the fundamentals.

Dallas listened intently to all this.

"That's interesting. I think you're right about that. They looked bad in the drills. We'd need three months of spring training to get the plays down," Dallas said, shaking his head. "Thanks a lot, Tommy."

Dallas walked into the clubhouse, leaving me there in the dugout, almost dumbfounded. The sweat trickled down into my eyes. I rubbed my face again with the towel. I thought at least the guy respects me enough as a professional to ask for my opinion and trusted he'd get a straight answer. Here he was, trying to learn the makeup of a new team, a new organization, and part of that learning was to turn to me for an opinion. That was the first inkling that Dallas Green was going to treat me halfway human.

The writers were wondering: Can Tommy John pitch? They debated publicly if I had a chance to make the ball club—the 1964 Indians ball club. My elbow had fully recovered from the tendonitis suffered over the winter while playing in Ponce. I did my exercises and the arm was strong. The media felt I had a shot at going north with the Tribe if I pitched well. I came to camp optimistic and eager to prove myself.

Perhaps it's my genes; perhaps it was my upbringing; maybe it's the fact that faith hasn't been an irrelevant exercise performed once a week on Sunday, but an actual part of my day-to-day life. Or maybe it's a combination of all these things. Whatever the reason, I've been blessed with an essentially optimistic nature.

Optimism isn't some rosy, unrealistic attitude one puts on during difficulties. It's not a mask. For me, optimism means performance in the face of trouble, a doubling of efforts in times of adversity, the persistence to keep coming back. Problems are opportunities and obstacles are challenges. For true Christians, a door closing simply means that another one is opening up elsewhere. Somewhere down the line the "way" gets revealed; that, if I had to sum it up in one sentence, has been the secret to all my comebacks, both in baseball and in my personal life.

Cleveland manager Birdie Tebbetts had suffered a heart attack and was sick all spring of 1964 in an Arizona hospital. George Strickland, the third base coach, took over as interim manager. Early Wynn, who the year before hung on long enough to win his 300th game for Kansas City, was the pitching coach.

Strickland had enough headaches of his own to pay me much mind, and Wynn, the man of whom it was said "he'd knock down his own grandmother," wasn't very informative or helpful. He was from the Ben Geraghty school: young guys had to pay their dues. The abrasive Wynn was quite a change from the fatherly Mel Harder, his predecessor. Fortunately, Dick Donovan, the veteran right-hander and the man I relieved in my first big league game, took an interest in me and took up some of the slack, working with me a little bit on the side.

Not having Birdie around early in the season hurt me, however. He liked the way I pitched, but Wynn didn't. He thought I needed more than a fastball and curve and insisted I develop a slider, the "nickel curve," a pitch just coming into wide favor throughout baseball. Early taught the pitch to me, I worked on it all spring, and I fell in love with it.

I could throw the slider for strikes. However, I relied on it too heavily, to the point where I neglected my fastball. As I did that, I lost my control and started pitching behind batters, putting pressure on myself. In gaining the slider, I had lost the sinking fastball, my best pitch.

Back then, teams could carry 28 men on the roster for the early part of the year. Cleveland carried two extra pitchers, both rookies: me and Sonny Siebert. I didn't play much. Strickland used me in a mop-up role for a couple of April games. When I did pitch, I had no control. My confidence was shot. The slider was killing me, and I didn't even know it.

Wynn couldn't tell me; after all, he was the one who wanted me throwing the pitch. At that time, a ball club didn't have all the coaches they have today. You had your two base coaches and the pitching coach. That was it. So there were fewer knowledgeable eyes who might have been able to sit me down, à la Steve Jankowski, and tell me what I was doing wrong. As it was, I spent day after day in the bullpen, lost in a mental funk. April turned into May, Strickland wasn't using me, and I had never felt lower.

People used to say Strickland would make a good manager. He read a great deal, and not comic books. He read a lot of Thomas Aquinas, the great Catholic saint and mystic, and many books on philosophy and psychology—Nietzsche, Sartre, and the like. He also understood formal logic. But the thing was, when he talked, you couldn't understand what he was saying. He'd get very deep, and you'd lose his point. Or he'd be enigmatic. He had a favorite saying: "Don't get careless. Don't get gay. Just get your rest." No one ever figured out what that meant.

Ten days before cutdown day, the Indians played a doubleheader against the Orioles. Strickland ran out of starters, and penciled me in for the second game. He was in a no-lose position. If the utterly improbable happened and I pitched well, fine. But if, as expected, I got shelled, then the brass would have a convenient excuse to send me down. With cutdown day approaching and twelve pitchers on the staff, someone had to go. Why not me? Lead the lamb to the slaughter in Game Two against the Orioles and solve your roster problem.

We lost the first game on May 3 by the score of 5–2, Baltimore's Dave McNally getting the win over Jim "Mudcat" Grant. In the nightcap I was matched against Robin Roberts, one of my childhood pitching idols, and role model during my brief workout with the Phillies in the spring of 1961.

Strickland and Wynn thought I'd go out there and get bombed, which would justify their decision to send me down. I just went out there figuring the worst that could happen is I'd get hit hard, which is what everyone was expecting anyway. That relieved the pressure. I wasn't nervous.

Joe Azcue caught me for my pregame warmups, and I felt pretty good—nothing out of the ordinary. As I sat in the dugout, during the first half of the inning, I reminded myself not to overthrow.

After the anthem Dick Howser, our shortstop, came over to me. He patted me on the back and told me to relax, have some fun, and that the team would be behind me.

Dick was out of Florida State University and came up with the Athletics in 1961. He was an aggressive, sparkplug type who'd lead both on and off the field.

"Just let 'em hit it, T.J.," Dick said. "We'll make the plays. You'll be okay."

You could tell even then that Dick would make a fine manager.

From the start I felt comfortable. During the first-inning warm-ups I noticed a change in my arm: it felt extremely loose and relaxed, almost lubricated, as if there were ball bearings in my left shoulder.

Jackie Brandt, Luis Aparacio, and Brooks Robinson went down 1–2–3 in the Oriole first. I was placing the ball wherever I wanted. Roberts was equally sharp, and through five innings we were hooked up in a scoreless tie.

In the top of the sixth I led off and slapped a single to the right side, past the dive of second baseman Jerry Adair. I rode to third on Howser's double, and when Sam Bowens dropped Vic Davalillo's long fly to right, I trotted home with the game's first run. Later in the inning Fred Whitfield plated Davalillo with a sacrifice fly, putting us up 2–0.

In the top of the seventh Max Alvis upped our lead to 3–0, jacking a Roberts fastball into the left field seats. It was his first home run of the year. When he got back into the noisy dugout, I went up to him and shook his hand.

"Max, you couldn't have picked a better time for that first one."

"Tell me about it," he answered, laughing.

With two outs in the bottom of the ninth, the game still at 3–0, Orioles manager Hank Bauer sent up righty Joe Gaines to pinch hit for Roberts. Roberts, incidentally, had one of his team's three singles, the only hits I had allowed—Adair and Dick Brown had the other two.

I toed the rubber and peered in to Azcue for the sign. I told myself to finish it off. On a 2–2 count, I came in with a sinking fastball which Gaines swung right over. Strike three! I had my first major league win, a complete-game, three-hit shutout over my idol, Robin Roberts.

The game was over in 94 minutes. I faced only 29 batters, struck out six, and made just 73 pitches, the lowest pitch total I would ever record. From a purist's point of view, it was probably the best game of my career.

To this day I cannot fully account for or explain what I did that was so right. It was just one of those days where everything worked. I was pitching in another zone, making great pitch after great pitch. I got away with one mistake, to Jackie Brandt. Brandt had some pop in his bat. He was a good low-ball hitter who gave me trouble. In one sequence of pitches around mid-game I got a fastball up too high. I winced. Brandt's eyes lit up, but he got under it and popped out.

That game turned a few heads. Home plate umpire Joe Paparella, dean of American League umps at the time, called it the finest pitching performance he had ever seen. First base umpire Frank Umont dittoed Paparella's remarks. Gordon Cobbledick of the Cleveland *Plain Dealer* wrote: ". . . he's always going to be a pleasure to watch because, to a degree that's nearly unique among present-day practitioners of the art, he gets the job done with neatness and dispatch." Reg McAuley wrote in the *Sporting News:* "Not since Bob Feller's first start . . . when he fanned 15 and beat the St. Louis Browns, 4–1, August 23, 1936, has a young Indian made such an impression."

My first big league win meant surviving the cut, and Strickland started to use me. I lost my next start to the Yankees at Yankee Stadium. In 1964 the pennant-bound Yankees were in the last year of that incredible stretch going back to 1949, when they had failed to win the pennant only twice. The first three batters of that game are in my memory as if it were yesterday.

Tony Kubek led off and beat out a grounder between short and third. The ball was just out of Max Alvis's reach; Howser gloved it in the hole but had no play. Bobby Richardson, the next man, smoked a low line drive up the middle; I deflected it partially with my glove, and the ball hit me in the groin area. It tore my jock off, literally stripped it off. If I hadn't gotten a glove on that ball, I wouldn't have had children.

I looked down and felt my jock sitting on my hip. I walked behind the mound, straightened myself out as best and with as much decorum as I could, and got back on the pitching rubber. Catcher John Romano had his head down, his feet pawing the dirt, trying to stifle a laugh. Mickey Mantle was standing in the right-side batter's box, lumber resting on his shoulder, grinning at the rube lefty and saying something to Romano.

Mantle then gave me a demonstration of his awesome power. I got a quick strike on him, then threw a fastball away, a good pitch. I thought I had it by him. Mick flicked his wrists. He hit what looked like a little fly ball to right field, but it just kept sailing and sailing. Leon Wagner drifted back, back, and ran out of room. The ball carried several rows into the right field stands. Three batters into the game, and we were down 3–0.

As he jogged around the bases, Mantle gave me a sly grin that meant: "Welcome to the big leagues, kid." I nodded.

I beat Boston in my next start, upping my record to 2–1. That was the last game I won all year.

Most of my losses were tough ones. One in particular illustrates a key difference between then and today over the way pitchers are used. Back then, the pitcher's job was to go nine innings. There were no setup men in middle relief, and Boston's Dick Radatz was just establishing the mold for what would become the century's greatest change in the game as far as pitching was concerned: the closer.

I was beating the Red Sox 2–1 going into the last frame at Fenway Park. With two outs in the bottom of the ninth, Dalton Jones reached on an infield error. Red Sox manager Johnny Pesky sent up left-handed-hitting Russ Nixon as a pinch hitter. Nixon fought off a tough curve and punched a fly ball down the right field line. It curved around the foul pole—Pesky's Pole as they call it in Boston. The ball plopped into the first row of seats, about 303 feet away, giving the Sox a 3–2 win. I couldn't believe it. As I walked off the mound, Nixon circled the bases. I could hear him say to third base coach Billy Herman as he rounded the bag: "I'll take it. I'll take it."

Had that game been played today, the closer, not Tommy John, would have been out there for the ninth inning. Today, a manager might be fired for leaving his twenty-one-year-old rookie starter in the game to face the winning run in the bottom of the ninth; or if not fired, then ripped apart in the press.

The team wasn't playing well, and we bounced around fifth, sixth, and seventh place all year. The bats were silent, with no .300 hitter in the lineup. Only Leon "Daddy Wags" Wagner was a consistent power threat, finishing with 31 homers and 100 RBIs, though Romano, Alvis, and Woodie Held could pop one out once in a while. The Indians also had no stopper. We ended the year with no pitcher going more than 200 innings—remarkable back then, in the era of the nine-inning start—and our top winner was Jack Kralick, who went 12–7.

My own losses mounted as well, and I got sent down to the Triple A Portland (Oregon) Beavers right after the All-Star break. Losing games bothered me, and I still hadn't found my consistent stuff. The team had arrived in New York for a late July series with the Yankees; I was supposed to pitch on Sunday. Instead, General Manager Gabe Paul called me into the manager's office at Yankee Stadium.

"You're going down, Tommy," Gabe said, explaining that the only way to build my confidence back up was to win some ball games, and that I'd have a better chance of doing that at Portland. Besides, the Indians had to make room for Luis Tiant, who was smoking the Pacific Coast League with a sizzling 15–1 record. Gabe told me not to get discouraged, but to go down, work on throwing strikes and getting ahead of hitters. The sidebar to my demotion is Tiant's performance in the Sunday game. He outdueled Whitey Ford, blanking the powerful Yankees 1–0 while fanning an even dozen.

Johnny Lipon, who had managed me at Charleston and at Ponce, was now the field boss at Portland. After watching me pitch in my first start on a Sunday in San Diego, he sat me down in his office.

"That wasn't you out there pitching, not the Tommy John I know. It's that darn slider. That's not a good pitch for you," he said. Johnny told me to concentrate on my control, and "go back to what got you there," my fastball and curveball. "Forget the slider."

That's all it took, one set of experienced eyes. Lipon saw right away that the slider was pitching me out of the big leagues. It took me a while to get back into my groove, but with Lipon's guidance, I came around, and in my last three or four games, pitched once more with authority.

Lipon was an excellent manager. He treated players like adults. When we'd go to Hawaii, he'd tell us to have fun, enjoy the sights, the ocean, the beaches. He encouraged us to be ourselves. He was an excellent handler of men, and I never understood why he didn't get the chance to manage in the big leagues.

On September 1, when the rosters expanded, I got called back up to Cleveland. Tommie Agee got the call as well, and he asked me to ride to Cleveland in his '64 Chevy. We'd share the driving. I eagerly accepted, since it solved my transportation problem, and also because I liked Tommie. We came to Dubuque at the same time, and had formed a bond. Pitcher Steve Hargan also signed up for the trip. He was heading home to Fort Wayne, Indiana, and asked if he could ride with us. As far as we were concerned, the more the merrier.

Agee was from Mobile, Alabama, a city that has produced such great players as Willie Mays, Hank Aaron, Billy Williams, and Willie McCovey. Tommie had blinding speed and was built like a linebacker. Once, in a game at Dubuque, he got picked off of first base intentionally. The pitcher threw to first base, Agee broke for second, and beat the first baseman's throw. That's how fast he was. He could outrun just about any ball hit in the general vicinity of center field. Tommie was also a vicious slider. He'd take you out in a second if you hung around the bag too long. Off the field, however, he was a quiet, polite man who wouldn't say boo.

The local Kentucky Fried Chicken outlet had been awarding free buckets of chicken for home runs hit during the season. Agee had a bunch of his award tickets still unused, I had three, and Hargan had one. Agee suggested we cash in all the tickets, so we wouldn't have to stop to eat. We'd just chow down on the chicken.

We went to the Kentucky Fried Chicken store, loaded up with about ten barrels of chicken, plus several six-packs of soda, and started driving. We drove without incident day and night for two days, with a pile of chicken bones in the car that made it look like a piranha had been there.

Somewhere that second night, with Agee at the wheel, the Chevy cruised along in the quiet of a black night on a deserted Idaho road. Hargan and I were sleeping—Steve in the front seat, me in the back— to the hypnotic sound of the engine and the wheels on the road.

Suddenly the car stopped, jolting us awake. I roused myself from sleep, disoriented, trying to figure out what was happening. I heard voices, yelling and cursing, plus the sound of horses. The first thing I saw were two rifles pointed at my head.

There were a dozen men on horseback, with shotguns and rifles, shining flashlights on us.

"Step out of the car with your hands up," one of them shouted.

We climbed out, and they flashed sheriff's ID badges. But they didn't have uniforms on; they looked like cowboys. I thought we were going to get blasted away. Here we are, two whites and a black, looking like convicts. We hadn't shaved or showered in two days. Our clothes were all rumpled, and the car was littered with bones and buckets of cold chicken that were obviously purchased a couple days earlier. We *looked* guilty. My heart was pounding.

They frisked us and searched the car. I asked what was wrong. They said that three men had just robbed a motel of $300 in Twin Falls, Idaho. They were the sheriff's posse, checking out the back roads.

"We're ballplayers," I said. "We're on our way to Cleveland to play for the Indians."

They gave us this look that said: Do you think we were born yesterday? I went to go to the car, and one of them yelled: "Freeze! Now!" I heard a rifle cock. He didn't have to tell me twice.

I explained that I wanted to get my equipment bag out of the trunk, to prove who we were. Hargan and Agee were still there with their hands up, looking like men trapped in a bad dream. The guy let me get the equipment bags. I moved gingerly, with no sudden movements, since their fingers were resting on the triggers. Fortunately, the bags had the team logos of the Beavers and the Indians on them. Finally, after what seemed an eternity, they were satisfied as to who we were and they let us go.

About a mile down the road another posse stopped us and we went through the same routine. There was actually nothing to read into the posse's actions: they were only doing their job. They didn't stop us because a black man was driving, but because we needed checking out.

As we hit the road again, I took over the driving, figuring Agee's luck had run its course. We nervously kidded about the experience.

"It was something right out of *Gunsmoke,* man," Agee said.

"Yeah," Hargan replied. "When they told us to get out, I was waiting for guns to go off."

"That's when I wished Tommie was a little better-looking," I cracked, Agee and Hargan laughing.

At the first truck stop we hit, in Rock Springs, Wyoming, we pulled in there with all the truckers, threw the cold water on our faces, and shaved off our scraggly beards. Back in the car, I told Agee: "At least now, Tommie, we don't look like armed robbers."

The rest of the trip took place without a hitch, and we pulled into Cleveland in one piece.

Birdie—who was now back as manager—used me quite a lot out of the bullpen, almost every other day, for the rest of the season. I pitched well.

One of my games was memorable in a way that I could have gladly done without.

One night against New York in Cleveland, the Yankees were rallying late in the game, hammering Gary Bell. I didn't know it at the time, but I later found out from our trainer that Birdie was taking heart medicine that produced side effects. Birdie was normally easygoing, but the medication made him agitated and also occasionally clouded his thinking.

With Bell running out of gas, Tebbetts signaled down to the bullpen for Don McMahon, a right-handed relief specialist, to warm up. Birdie never used the dugout phone. He always gave arm signals to the bullpen. To signal for McMahon, Birdie would flex his arms like a muscleman. Don started warming up.

A few pitches later Birdie signaled "Is the lefthander ready?" by lifting his cap in his left hand and moving it around in circles. I had warmed up earlier in the game four times, in the second, third, fourth, and fifth innings—something that's unheard of today. Bob Allen was the other left-hander in the bullpen. In Birdie's signaling system, I was the "tall lefty," indicated by holding the left arm straight up over his head, and Allen was the "sidearm lefty," called when Birdie held his left arm straight out and parallel to the ground. Which lefty did Birdie want? We didn't know, since he held his left arm at the three-quarter position, halfway between me and Allen.

Early Wynn told Allen to start warming. Having warmed up four times already, I was in no position to do so again, and so everyone assumed Birdie wanted Allen. After stalling for as much time as possible, George Strickland came out to the mound to yank Bell. He signaled for me, the "tall lefty," with his left arm straight over his head.

"What?" McMahon asked incredulously. "The kid isn't even warmed up."

Early rushed over to me with this strange look on his face, sort of a cross between bewilderment and helplessness: "Kid, hurry up and get some tosses in. They want you in there, now."

"What kind of crap is that?" McMahon asked Wynn, who ignored the question.

I hurriedly tossed six warm-up pitches, grabbed my jacket, and went in to pitch. I had no choice. The manager had called. On the mound, Strickland asked me if I was ready.

"As ready as I can be on six pitches," I answered.

Lou Dimuro, the home plate umpire, told me to throw my eight warm-up pitches, and then throw over to first base as many times as I needed to get my arm ready. It didn't help. I gave up consecutive hits to Tom Tresh, Joe Pepitone, Elston Howard, Clete Boyer, and Phil Linz. Each one was a ringing shot.

It got so bad, fans started booing: "Get that bum out of there."

When I finally got the side out and came into the dugout with the game now hopelessly out of hand, Birdie was hopping mad.

"What the hell are you doing out there in the bullpen, sitting on your butt? You blankety-blank, I'm going to fine you and suspend you! What do you think you're pulling, not warming up when I tell you to?"

He didn't give me the chance to explain that he had called first for McMahon, then Allen, and not me, to warm up. Birdie's threat scared me, and later in the clubhouse I went to Wynn for help. That was no easy thing in itself, since Early never had much to say to me.

Wynn was burly, bordering on fat. No one could outeat or outdrink Early Wynn. An army couldn't. After my first big league appearance, in Washington, I'd gone back to the hotel with the team. At about one A.M., past midnight curfew, my roommate Mike de la Hoz came into the room, frantic.

"Tommy, I've just come from the hospital. Azcue's dying."

"Dying? What's wrong?"

"I don't know," Mike answered. "But they say he's dying."

The next day, we got to the park and found out what happened. Azcue made the mistake of going out to dinner with Early, and he tried to keep up with him. Azcue ended up eating and drinking so much, they had to rush him to the hospital to get his stomach pumped. That next morning, there was Early, out on the field in a rubber suit, running in the outfield, sweating it all out of his system.

Wynn was a heavy drinker with a mean, surly personality. I didn't relish going to him for help, but I had to turn to someone. I couldn't let Birdie think I had screwed up so badly.

"Early," I pleaded, "Birdie's mad. He's going to suspend me. Will you talk to him for me?"

"Let me see what I can do."

Wynn went into Tebbetts's office and came out a few minutes later, shaking his head.

"Kid, sometimes the best thing to do about these things is to ride them out."

McMahon—a nail-tough, confident-bordering-on-cocky, Brooklyn-born veteran—overheard that and exploded. He lit into Wynn, calling him everything in the book.

"You're the blankin' pitching coach. You no good blank, have some balls! Go in and stand up for the kid!"

Wynn didn't move.

"Well, if you won't, I will!"

Mac marched straight into the manager's office, slamming the door behind him. I could hear him yelling, screaming, and cursing. When he came out, McMahon walked over to me with an ironic grin on his face.

"I think we just got it straightened out."

As I was leaving the park, Birdie called me in; he asked me what happened. I told him that no one had given me the signal to warm up. Birdie said he believed me, and that the incident would be considered forgotten.

I was ticked, though, at Wynn. In my quiet, rookie way, I let him know. I didn't throw chairs, but he got the message.

"Thanks a whole lot for standing up for me, Early," I told him the next day. He just sneered.

From that time on I never cared much for Early Wynn. Here I was, this green kid, a rookie still learning how to pitch, and he let me go down the tubes without a word of protest. I lost respect for him. A pitching coach must stand up for his pitchers. Don McMahon, on the other hand, couldn't have looked bigger in my eyes. It took guts to do what he did.

The season ended with the team in a sixth-place tie, 20 games behind the Yankees. The Tribe had been mired in a string of five consecutive losing seasons, and inside, we wondered if we were ever going to come out of it. I finished with a lousy 2–9 record, with 25 appearances and 14 starts. My 3.93 ERA, though, bordered on respectability. Birdie told me I had just become a member of the pitcher's union. I had paid my dues.

Back in Terre Haute I enrolled again at Indiana State University, taking four courses. On January 20, 1965, after one of my calculus classes, the professor gave me a message to call my father at home. I was worried that something had happened, an accident maybe.

"Pop, what's the matter?"

"You've just been traded," he told me.

"Traded? Who?"

"To the White Sox. You'll be playing ball in Chicago next year, Tommy."

# 5.

# WINDY CITY

B eing traded from the only organization you've ever known is a little like leaving home for good. Part of you doesn't want to go. I had some of those feelings, but was looking forward to my new baseball home. The White Sox had a fine team, finishing second in 1964, a scant game behind the Yankees. The Indians were not improving, and with Chicago I might make my mark on a winning team.

The trade was a complicated three-way deal involving the White Sox, the Indians, and the Kansas City Athletics. Cleveland sent me, Tommie Agee, and catcher John Romano to the White Sox for catcher Camilo Carreon and slugging outfielder Rocky Colavito. Chicago had obtained Colavito from Kansas City earlier that same day for outfielders Jim Landis, Mike Hershberger, and pitcher Fred Talbot. Moving together with Agee softened the initial shock of meeting a whole new set of teammates.

Colavito was the linchpin of the deal. The Indians had been desperate to get Rocky back to Cleveland, where years before he had been such a gate attraction. His trade from Cleveland to Detroit even-up for Harvey Kuenn after the 1959 season nearly caused riots among Indian baseball boosters. Now the Rock was back.

Hoot Evers told me later that the Indians agonized over letting me go. You never like to give away promising home-grown talent. It's funny.

Much later, I asked Ray Berres, the White Sox pitching coach, why Chicago wanted me. My big league record to that point was a pathetic 2–11. Berres said he had marked down in his scorebook a game I lost 2–1 to Chicago, where Al Weis beat me with a home run.

Berres said I had made a half dozen outstanding pitches, and after that game he told White Sox manager Al Lopez that "when that kid out there had his arm in the proper position, he was unhittable. Keep an eye on him."

Lopez told General Manager Ed Short to make the trade. Lopez was the manager, but he also ran the organization. He'd give Short the parameters of a particular deal, and Short would try to execute it. Contrary to popular opinion, the great trades the White Sox made were engineered by Lopez, not the general manager. Lopez was an acknowledged dugout mastermind, a man with a superb grasp of the game. He had the distinction of being the only manager to beat the Yankees to the pennant between 1949 and 1964. Lopez turned the trick twice, with the 1954 Indians, and with the 1959 Go-Go White Sox.

Lopez had a better handle on all the facets of the game than any manager I ever played for. He knew about hitting, offense, defense, pitching, catching, and strategy. The Senior, as he was dubbed, also understood player psychology, and knew how to communicate with his players. He was tough to play for in that he demanded so much out of you, but that just made you a better performer. Al was the type of manager who was smart enough, and secure enough, not to overmanage. He threw the bats and balls out on the field and simply let you play.

Lopez never pulled bed checks or spied on his players. His requirements were simple and easy to understand: he demanded that you be at the ball park on time, that you hustle, and that you keep your nose clean. He had very few signs, and fewer rules. But he did have one, which a lot of managers had back then. On the road, the hotel bar was *his* bar. Al wasn't big for meetings, but at the beginning of the year, he'd give his annual lecture.

"The hotel bar is for me, my coaches, the front office, and the sports writers," he would say. "I don't want to come in and see you guys sitting there, drinking all night. That's my bar and it's off limits to you."

That's a good rule, because after road games, that's when you see guys fooling around, drinking too much, or married guys putting the moves on girls at the bar. The press sees it, rumors start circulating, and there's trouble.

"I can't stop you guys from going out and playing the big time," Lopez would lecture. "But if you do, don't bring girls back to this hotel. I don't want to hear from my general manager or from the press 'Did you see so-and-so walking in the lobby at three o'clock in the morning with that blonde on his arm?' Have some class. If you have to do that, then go someplace else, because I don't want to see it, and I don't want to hear about it. And don't come in at three in the morning. Come in at seven or eight and make them think that you've been to early mass."

The players listened, because Al commanded that kind of respect. I only saw him get ripped at the players one time. We used to barnstorm out of spring training, leaving Sarasota and playing our way north— "barnstorm" is a word kids today probably don't even know. We'd suit up at the local hotel and bus to the ballpark.

That spring, 1965, we played a game in Charlotte, North Carolina. To save time making the eleven o'clock bus to the park, we ate breakfast in the hotel snack shop—in our uniforms. Well, Al was in there, too, having coffee with his coaches. They were dressed in their civvies: coats, ties. Lopez didn't say a word. But when we got to the park, he called a team meeting, which he *never* did.

He lit into us.

"What the hell were you guys doing in the coffee shop with your uniforms on? Do you know how bush that looks? Are you that lazy? The next time, get up a little earlier, come down and have breakfast, then go back up and dress in your room. You're in the major leagues. Wake up and start acting that way."

Lopez found out beyond a doubt that I was a team man, and that if he gave an order, I followed it.

If you goofed up on the field, especially a mental error, Lopez would make you run. In spring training, 1965, I was pitching in the third inning against the Twins at Sarasota. With old friend Jerry Kindall on first, Bob Allison grounded a ball to the right side. I broke toward first to cover, but the seeing-eye job scooted between first baseman Moose Skowron and second baseman Don Buford into right field. Kindall broke for third. Floyd Robinson fielded the ball and came up throwing. I failed to get back across the diamond to back up third on the throw, and sure enough, Robinson's throw sailed over third baseman Pete Ward's head. The ball rolled into the dugout and Kindall scored. Well, I got my three innings in, and my pitching was over. But Al told me to go to the outfield "and run until I tell you to stop. We'll see if you can pick up a little speed on your sprints."

So I started running . . . from the fourth inning to the ninth inning. No one came out to tell me to stop. To make it worse, the game went into extra innings. When the game was finally over, I trudged into the locker room wringing wet, dripping with sweat, face scarlet red, exhausted.

"What are you doing here?" Lopez asked. "Why are you in uniform? You were done pitching seven innings ago."

"You told me to run until you gave me the word to stop."

He started laughing: "Did I tell you that?"

"Yeah," I answered.

"Oh God! I forgot all about it, didn't I?"

"Yeah."

Lopez then started laughing until tears came down his cheeks. He was howling with laughter.

"That's good," he said. "At least I know you follow orders." He walked away, still giggling to himself.

With the White Sox, I became a pitcher. The key to my success was pitching coach Ray Berres. I just didn't know what I was doing as a pitcher until he got me. Berres didn't teach pitches. He didn't show you how to throw the slider, forkball, screwball, or split-fingered fastball. But he had a tremendous understanding of pitching.

My problem with the Indians was that I threw the ball from different arm angles, without a clue to proper positioning. That's why, prior to 1965, I had trouble with consistency. Ray, a catcher with the Pirates in his playing days, was an absolute master of pitching mechanics. He liked his pitchers throwing basically the same way: get your arm up and throw down, mostly overhand.

All spring he'd tell me things like "Stay back, get your arm up, retain your weight" . . . all this baseball jargon that I didn't grasp. One day, as I was leaving Payne Park in Sarasota, Ray was out in foul territory, hitting golf balls with a sand wedge. He asked me to come over. He knew I was an avid golfer and he asked me for some help.

"I've just been terrible," Ray said. "Tell me what I'm doing wrong here."

He took the wedge back in a quick backswing, brought it forward in a quick, choppy down motion, sending his shots all over the place.

"Ray," I said. "Slow your backswing down until you get to the top. Take it back nice and easy, then explode into the ball."

He took my advice and hit some pretty good-looking balls.

"Yeah, that was perfect," I said.

Ray looked at me: "That's what I've been trying to tell you about pitching. Stay back, get your arm up. In other words, ease into your motion, then explode with your release."

"Slow . . . slow . . . slow . . . explode!" I said, repeating one of his favorite expressions. "I'll be a son of a gun."

From that time, I understood his theory, that the slower and more easy your motion, the more of an optical illusion it becomes to the batter when the ball gets released. Ray had me work on getting my arm up, getting the elbow up high in my motion, and throwing from high to low in a gentle, almost hypnotic windup. I tried to pitch that way the rest of my career.

Ray was my pitching coach for two years, but those two years were enough to have lasting impact. Before Ray Berres, I didn't know how to pitch. After Ray Berres, I did. Look at the Chicago staff's stats for the Ray Berres years: respective team ERAs were a brilliant 2.99 and 2.68 in 1965 and '66.

Ray also made me more aware of the art of pitching; for example, he stressed the importance of staying ahead of hitters. You can't overstate the significance of pitching ahead in the count. That's the name of pitching. He also taught me that on certain hitters, and in particular spots, you're better working from behind in the count, a practically blasphemous statement for a pitcher to hear or make.

The only time you can get away with pitching from behind is if you can throw the off-speed pitch with control. A slip pitch negates the need to stay ahead in the count because certain batters are so eager for the off-speed stuff. I used to purposely pitch from behind occasionally to some hitters, especially the free-swinging power hitters, for that very reason.

I had success pitching to Johnny Bench that way, especially with runners on base. I'd go to 2–0 deliberately to Bench, and then come in with a slow curve or sinking fastball that starts down the middle of the plate then drops. He'd try to hit it 520 feet and become unglued. But if I was up 0–2 or 1–2 with Bench, he'd shorten his swing for more bat control. With his power, that's all he needed to drive a ball out of the park or up an alley. For me, Bench was more dangerous when I was *up* on the count.

I had luck pitching that way to the Milwaukee Brewers when they had those great "Brew Crew" teams in the early 1980s, and sluggers like Ben Ogilvie, Gorman Thomas, Cecil Cooper, Robin Yount, and Paul Molitor. When their power hitters were up on the count, they'd be looking to unload and were ripe for a slow curve or a sinking fastball. But hitters don't hit like that anymore. The pure power hitter is becoming a dinosaur. The days of Mantle-Sievers-Cerv-Gentile-Mays-Killebrew-Jensen-Snider-McCovey are over.

People used to say that I pitched more with my head than my arm, and I took that as a compliment. A pitcher needs to be aware of everything as he stands on the mound, and know how to pitch strategically. Take, for example, the 0–2 pitch. Dallas Green had a good theory on that, and I agreed with it.

"On 0–2, go after the guy. Get the S.O.B. out," Dallas would say. "You've got him down, so go after him. Blow him away."

He'd say that, and I'd think: Boy, this is a pitcher talking.

But most of the managers I played for were hitters, not pitchers, and they went by the book, which says: "Don't let a batter get a hit on an 0–2 count." Managers have an obsession about that, and will even fine you for giving up a hit on 0–2.

On 0–2 most managers want you to waste a pitch, then come in with something good. But if you miss with that one, now you're 2–2. The batter's even. Now what do you throw? You're going to throw your best pitch, and a smart hitter will know that. You see it happen so often on a 2–2 count. The batter starts guessing correctly and begins fouling off pitches. You end up throwing him eight or nine pitches, when you could have got him out on three. Over the course of the game you'll end up throwing 15 to 20 extra pitches that way, which might make the difference between tiring in the sixth or seventh inning. Also, the more pitches you throw a batter in any given at bat, the greater the chance of making a mistake. They don't call it a "waste" pitch for nothing.

Why not throw your best pitch on 0–2? Go after the hitter. You don't groove the ball, of course, but you go after him with your best pitch. The hitter's not looking for your best pitch then. John Candelaria was like that. He'd get up on a hitter 0–2 and go right after him. He gave up some 0–2 hits, but got more 0–2 outs, and saved his arm some pitches.

# Windy City

I got my chance to pitch in 1965 because our left-handed ace, Gary Peters, went down with a bad back. He stayed at my apartment before his wife and kids came up from Florida, and he had to sleep on a mattress on the floor because of his back. His back hurt so bad he would have to literally crawl to the bathroom in the morning. He could not straighten up, and Peters was probably the strongest ballplayer I've ever seen in my life. He was raised in the woods of western Pennsylvania and lived a Rambo lifestyle, going into the woods, living off the land, hunting, trapping, fishing, eating berries.

Peters was also one of the funniest men in baseball, infamous for his practical jokes. One time, the White Sox came into Anaheim early one evening to play the Angels the next day. The Yankees had just finished a series with the Angels and were flying out at midnight. Somehow, Peters got his hands on Joe Pepitone's room key. At about nine P.M. he snuck into Pepi's room. Pepi was out like a light, snoring. Peters crept in, got up on the bed, and started jumping up and down, screaming like a madman. Pepi shot up like a bolt of lighting, frightened out of his wits. He finally got the light on and saw Peters jump off the bed, who laughed as he ran out of the room ahead of Pepitone's curses.

We had a reserve outfielder on the White Sox named Ed Stroud, nicknamed the Creeper because of his blazing speed. One day in Sarasota, Creeper came into the locker room and started taking his clothes off to get into uniform. Peters had been skindiving the day before and had caught a baby octopus. He kept it alive in a tank of seawater. Everybody in the locker room knew what Peters was planning, and as we sat there watching Creeper undress, we were trying not to laugh. When Stroud stripped down to his shorts, Peters grabbed the octopus out of the tank with both hands.

"Creeper!" he yelled.

"Yeah?" Stroud said, looking up.

Peters immediately fired the octopus at him. The eight tentacles attached themselves to Stroud's body. He started to scream, pulling the tentacles off with these loud, suction-cup noises. But as soon as he pulled one tentacle off, another reattached itself. Stroud panicked, running out of the clubhouse in his shorts, shrieking. The guys had to catch him, hold him down, and pull the octopus off. When they did, he had suction marks all over his chest.

Peters was pulling stuff like that all the time. On the mound, however, he was a deadly serious competitor, one of the top lefties in baseball. When we lost him to his bad back, it really hurt the team. Our other left-hander, Juan Pizarro, also was hurt in 1965. Al Lopez turned to me to step into the rotation.

If it hadn't been for the injuries to Peters and Pizarro, I would have been in the bullpen, most likely to stay. That's what Lopez planned. My first appearance for the White Sox, in fact, came on opening day in 1965 in Baltimore. I struck out Boog Powell to end the game, and picked up a save.

Chicago turned in a fine 95–67 record in 1965, good for second place, seven games behind the Minnesota Twins. It was my first experience with a winning team in the majors. The White Sox were in the race long enough to keep the season interesting, but we just couldn't catch the Twins, who were led by Most Valuable Player Zoilo Versalles and the pitching of my ex-teammate, Jim "Mudcat" Grant. Our starting lineup was consistent, with all the regulars at double figures in home runs—led by Skowron and John Romano at 18 apiece. But the injuries to the pitching staff caught up to us.

The trade that brought me to the Windy City worked out well for Chicago. Romano hit 18 homers, Agee had a great year down at Indianapolis, and I went 14–7, 3.09 in 183⅔ innings, with 27 of my 39 appearances as a starter. The 14 wins led all Chicago starters. For the record, Rocky Colavito put up some fine numbers in Cleveland: .287, 26 HRs, 108 RBIs.

For my 14 wins the White Sox paid me the big league minimum, $7000, and I was happier than a pig in slop to get it. The big-money guys on the team, guys like Romano and Skowron, were making around $40,000.

During the off-season the White Sox wanted me to go down to play winter ball in Puerto Rico again. I wanted nothing of it; I yearned to get back to Indiana State University at Terre Haute, where I was in my fourth semester as a math major. Lopez called me into his office near the end of the season.

"What are you going to do, sit on your ass all winter and do nothing?"

No, I told him, I was going to college. General Manager Ed Short said the team wanted me in winter ball to work on my pickoff move, of all things. I balked, and kept saying I didn't want to go. Then I got a lesson in old-school "hardball," the way it was played before the players won their right to be free agents.

"Let me put it to you another way," Short told me. "If you won't go, we can bury you in the minor leagues, and you'll never see the light of day. I don't care if you're 14–7. You'll never be heard from again. I guarantee it."

"Ed," I said, "I'm stubborn, but not dumb. When do I leave?"

Short's "persuasion" worked. Jerome Holtzman, writing about the incident in *The Sporting News,* put it this way: "Southpaw Tommy John, like the good soldier he is, did as the White Sox ordered him."

I played in a golf tournament in Palm Springs and reported, "like the good soldier," to San Juan, playing for Charlie Metro, one of the White Sox coaches, and later Less Moss, when Charlie was fired.

The fans down there were excitable. Jay Alou went 3-for-3 one day. The fourth time he came up, he struck out with men on base. The fans went crazy, throwing stuff all over the field, booing. It didn't matter that he had three hits. I used to tell Jay they wanted the Chi-Chi Rodriguez treatment on every at bat.

The winter season ran from November to mid-January. By the first week of December I had been pitching extremely well, had worked on my pickoff move, and felt there was no point in me being in Puerto Rico any longer. It was time to go home, time to come up with a "convenient" sore arm. I told Moss my elbow was bothering me. Short ordered me back to the States to see Dr. Coyle in Chicago, the team physician.

"What's wrong here?" Dr. Coyle asked me during my visit.

"Well, Doc, I think it's terminal. I've got a case of Terre Haute elbow."

"Terre Haute elbow? What's that?"

"When I was down in Puerto Rico pitching, it hurt like crazy. But the minute I got off the place and got back to Terre Haute, the soreness went away."

Dr. Coyle started laughing: "I take it you didn't want to pitch down there?"

He performed a token exam.

"I'll tell them you have epicondalitis, a fancy term for a sore elbow. That will satisfy everybody."

Right about that time, around December 1965, Lopez resigned as manager. He was having health problems, and he wanted to spend more time at home with his family. I was driving in Terre Haute, and over the car radio came a report that the White Sox had named Eddie Stanky as the new manager. I didn't know a thing about Eddie, except that he had once managed the Cardinals and had the reputation of being a hard-nosed guy.

I golfed that winter with some of my teammates, and guys would tell me what a tyrant, what a no-good S.O.B. Stanky was, saying how he was hell on his players.

"He'll bleeping run you into the ground, Tommy. You wait and see."

Eddie and I met on the club's hot-stove press tour that winter, in January 1966. The hot-stove circuit would take the manager and a dozen players to various Illinois cities. At a typical stop there's a press conference with the manager, cocktails and dinner, and interviews with the ball players so the local media can get their quotes and stories before spring training begins.

After the affair in Rockford, Eddie sat down next to me and asked me all about myself as a ball player: What are your pitches? Are you a good hitter? Can you bunt? How's your fielding? Can you throw your curve for a strike? What are your strengths? What do you have trouble with? He then told me what we were going to work on in spring training, both as a team and individually.

He talked that way with all the players on the tour. I had never seen a big league manager do that. Eddie came up to his players, like he was a college coach, and asked concerned questions. That really impressed me, that he would take the time. Most new managers come in thinking they have all the answers, or they assume that because you're in the big leagues, you automatically know what to do and what the manager wants.

So much for the "tyrant," who proved to be a knowledgeable, astute baseball man, a man who would listen to what you had to say. I can say this without qualification: I learned more baseball under Eddie than anybody else in my career. He was without doubt the best teaching manager I ever had. I would have loved playing ten years for Eddie, instead of the two and a half I actually did.

Stanky got his reputation as a monster, I suppose, from his toughness. He'd drive his players and was inflexible. If you played for Stanky and you busted your butt, if you hustled all-out, if you ran hard on every ground ball, he was the easiest guy in the world to play for. But ball players who didn't give him 110 percent effort all the time had a battle. These were the same ball players who would end up knocking the man.

Eddie's demanding attitude came from the fact that he wasn't a big man and didn't have great natural talent. But he nonetheless enjoyed a ten-year big league career with the Dodgers, Braves, and Giants . . . because of sheer determination. He squeezed every drop of feisty ability out of himself, and he expected his players to do the same.

"You don't need talent to hustle," he would say.

And if he didn't see the kind of hold-nothing-back effort he wanted, he'd fine you. Once Lee Elia hit a ball he thought was going out of the park, so he gave it a home run trot. The ball hit off the wall and Elia coasted into second base with a double. After the inning was over Elia came into the dugout to get his glove.

"You thought that ball was out of the park, didn't you? You started that Cadillac trot early, didn't you? You're a little guy!" Stanky said, his voice rising. "You don't hit home runs! When you hit the ball, I want you to run all out, all the time! Have fifty dollars on my desk after the game."

Eddie hated to see guys like Mantle, Killebrew, or Yastrzemski hit a ball back to the pitcher and not even take five steps down the line. That drove him absolutely nuts.

In 1989 everybody talked about how hard Dallas Green ran the Yankees camp. That was nothing compared to Stanky's, which was grueling. You ran everywhere, all the time. But the difference was that Eddie knew how to pace a team. He'd work you hard, then know when to give you a breather. Eddie wanted you totally into the practices, both body and mind. For example, he had the pitchers throw batting practice without a protective screen, because he said the screen "breeds complacency."

I had to hold out and threaten not to sign in 1966 to earn a raise from the minimum to the princely sum of $11,000. Back then, just about no players had agents. If I had come in with an agent, Ed Short would have tossed the both of us out on our ears. The negotiations were totally one-sided in favor of the team. Players were like indentured servants. It was like Short told me: "If you don't do what we say, we'll bury you."

The team slipped to fourth place in 1966, at 83–79, 15 games off the pace set by Baltimore. Frank Robinson had come over to the American League, and led the Orioles all year. Robby ended up winning the Triple Crown. The White Sox were hurt by injuries to Hoyt Wilhelm, J. C. Martin, Ron Hansen, and Pete Ward, and we never got untracked. Our main problem, however, was at the plate. The team hit an anemic .231, with only one man above 20 homers—Agee, with 22; Tommie also led the regulars with a .273 batting average. Six of our eight regulars were below .250. Only our pitching kept us competitive, with a glittering staff ERA of 2.68, led by Gary Peters and his league-leading 1.98.

As a pitcher, I continued growing, learning. I again led the staff in wins, going 14–11, and lowered my ERA to 2.62 in 223 innings. All but one of my 34 appearances were starts, and my five shutouts tied for the league lead. Much of that I owe to Eddie.

All year Eddie would call me into his office or talk to me on the bench, not so much to go over hitters, but to say which man he didn't want to get a hit in a crucial situation. If it were the Orioles, it might be Frank or Brooks Robinson, or it could be Andy Etchebarren, their number-eight hitter, if he was hot. Stanky expected you to follow the opposing teams.

In that way, Eddie made you more aware of what was going on, not just within the limited sphere of your own team, but in the league, and that made me a better pitcher. He'd come up and say: "You're pitching next against Boston, right? Who's their leading hitter?"

"Conigliaro."

"Who leads them in stolen bases?"

"Tartabull."

"Who's the leading RBI guy?"

"Scott."

When Eddie asked you these questions, you'd better have the answers or he'd get mad. When his ball players were at the park, he wanted their total attention to be focused on the game. It would drive him nuts to see a guy come into the park with the *Wall Street Journal* or the financial section of the *Chicago Tribune*.

"Guys today are more worried about their investments than they are about their batting averages," he'd lament.

Eddie was also secure enough to let his pitching coach handle the pitchers. Some managers won't do that. I was sad to see Berres let go after the 1966 season, but felt I had absorbed enough of his "slow delivery" philosophy not to flounder as I had before.

A sinkerball pitcher relies much more on a pitching coach than a power pitcher does. The guy with the heater just rears back and throws. But the sinkerball is a "position" pitch. If the backward spin is off-angle just a little, the ball won't sink. Then you're in trouble, especially if you're like me and don't throw very hard. Hand and arm position are crucial; the slightest difference in position can kill you. That's why my best years came when I had pitching coaches who spotted those slight changes.

Berres's successor, Marv Grissom, was a hard-nosed guy, but he didn't try to change me, except for having me throw more inside pitches.

In 1967 we got into a four-team pennant race with the Red Sox, the Tigers, and the Twins. It was an incredible experience to be involved in a race like that, the closest in baseball since 1908.

The White Sox, with an offense held together by paper clips and rubber bands, led most of the year. We had to fight and scratch for every win. One look at our bats will tell you why: first base, Tom McCraw, .236; second base, Wayne Causey, .226; shortstop, Ron Hansen, .233; third base, Don Buford, .241; outfield, Ken Berry, .241; outfield, Agee, .234; outfield, Pete Ward, .233; catcher, J. C. Martin, .234. The bench wasn't much better, as the team batting average of .225 indicates. The typical White Sox rally was a walk, a stolen base, move to third on an infield out, and score on a sacrifice fly. We won a lot of 1–0, 2–1, and 3–2 games that way.

Our pitching kept us in it. The Big Three of Horlen, Peters, and myself chipped in with 45 wins and ERAs of 2.06, 2.28, and 2.48 respectively. Bob Locker got in 77 games, saved 20 of them, and had a 2.09 ERA. We were in first place for something like 67 straight days. Going into the final week of the season, all four teams had a chance to win it.

Carl Yastrzemski had an unbelievable year, one of the greatest all-around seasons in the history of the game. He won the Triple Crown, and after the All-Star break you couldn't get him out. He was a fielding demon in left field, making circus catches and throwing out runners. If Boston needed a big hit or a big defensive play, Yaz was there.

Oddly enough, Eddie Stanky may have been partly responsible for Yaz's heroics since he helped light a bonfire under the Boston superstar. At least the Boston press thought so.

Eddie loved talent and he hated to see players waste it, either through lack of hustle or by not using their heads. He put Yaz in this latter category, especially in the years before '67. Stanky was discussing the 1967 All-Star team with Doug Gilbert of the *Chicago American*, giving quick impressions of each man. When Yaz's name came up, Eddie tossed out his now famous line:

"Yastrzemski's an All-Star from the neck down."

The Boston papers picked up on it, and when we came into Fenway

Park, it was like a combination World Series game, circus, zoo, stag party, and barroom brawl. The Boston fans got on us and all over Eddie, booing his every move. It sure made those Boston games exciting.

Two games from 1967 stand out in my mind, both against the Red Sox. Both were pivotal.

The first was played at Fenway Park on June 15. We were in first place, five games ahead of Boston. For ten innings the game was scoreless, with starters Bruce Howard and Boston's Gary Waslewski dominant. But in the top of the eleventh we broke through. Walt "No Neck" Williams doubled into the left field corner off John Wyatt. Williams took third on Don Buford's infield out, and later scored on Ken Berry's clutch, two-out single. The bench erupted.

John Buzhardt came on for his second inning of relief in the bottom of the eleventh, and got Yaz on a pop out and George Scott on a soft line drive. The fans were quiet. But Joe Foy kept Boston's hopes alive with a single to left, bringing up power-hitting Tony Conigliaro, who was having an All-Star year. Tony was always a dangerous hitter, but just devastating in Fenway. You had to pitch him inside to be effective.

Buzhardt came in with two unhittable curveballs and got up on the count 0–2. But then he tried to be cute and started nibbling. At 2–2 Tony fouled a few pitches off, and soon the count was full. It's a perfect example of what I said earlier about the 0–2 count. If you don't go right after the guy, the next thing you know, he's back even.

Buzhardt wanted the 3–2 pitch back the minute he threw it, a fastball up and over the plate. Tony lost it fifteen feet up into the screen atop the Green Monster in left, handing us a crushing 2–1 loss. The fans went crazy, and our failure to put the Red Sox away gave them a huge lift.

The second game that stands out from the 1967 season was played at Comiskey Park in Chicago. It was the first game of a Sunday doubleheader on August 27. The Red Sox had won the day before to tie us for first place, beating Joe Horlen, 6–2. The Sunday twin bill was our second in three days, and Stanky had to start twenty-three-year-old Fred Klages in the opener.

Boston cuffed Klages for three runs in five innings. Going into the bottom of the seventh, the Red Sox led 4–1 on Yaz's two solo home runs and George Scott's two-run single. We answered with two runs of our own in the bottom of the seventh off Boston starter (and my ex-mate) Gary Bell. We caught a huge break in the inning when Mike

Andrews botched a perfect double-play ball at second. The score stayed 4–3 going into the bottom of the ninth.

Berry led off the ninth against Bell and drilled a two-bagger down the left field line. Yaz cut the ball off quickly, but Berry cruised in with an easy double. The fans were up on their feet. This game, after all, meant first place.

The managerial wheels started turning. Stanky put on the bunt play and Ron Hansen laid down a beauty, forcing first baseman George Scott to field the ball for a 3–4 putout. With Berry on third, ninety feet away from tying the game, Stanky sent up Duane Josephson to hit for Hoyt Wilhelm. Boston manager Dick Williams countered by going to his closer, righty John Wyatt.

Wyatt came in with a fastball on the first pitch, and Josephson sent a line drive to medium right field. Normally, Conigliaro would have been in right for the Red Sox. Tony had a great arm, and it's doubtful Berry would have tried to score. But Tony had been knocked out of action nine days earlier in a near-fatal beaning suffered at the hands of the Angels' Jack Hamilton. That put José Tartabull in right. Tartabull had great speed but no throwing arm.

Berry tagged. Here was the race: the speedy Berry against the weak-armed Tartabull. At stake: first place.

Berry broke, tearing down the line, and Tartabull uncorked the ball with all his strength. The ball came in high, and it looked certain Berry would score. But Boston catcher Elston Howard made an unbelievable play. He leaped in the air, caught Tartabull's throw one-handed, landed, blocked Berry off the plate with his left foot, and swooped the glove down, catching Berry with a tag on the hand.

It was an extremely close play. Everyone held their breath as home plate umpire Marty Springstead waited on the call, to see if Howard held onto the ball. Springstead's right arm came up. Berry was out. The double-play ended the game. The bench let out screams of protest.

I've never seen a manager tear out of a dugout like Eddie Stanky did after the call on Berry. He circled Springstead like a swarm of angry bees. Eddie protested, shouted, screamed, ranted, raged, raved, fumed, spit, and stomped. But when it was all over, Boston was in first place, a game in front of us.

Springstead was umping third base in the second game. A fan came running out of the stands in the top of the first inning. He rushed Springstead, trying to throw a punch, but Pete Ward, our third baseman, tackled the guy and pinned him to the ground until the security guards got there.

The nightcap was a real "gut check" for the team, and somehow we found enough inside to grind out a 1–0, eleven-inning win. Gary Peters pitched a brilliant four-hitter, going the route. But I know the team felt it should have taken two. That would have put us in first by two games and might have put a wet blanket on Boston's fire.

Eddie took the loss hard. The next night, in fact, he was still hot, and got thrown out of the game bringing the lineup cards to home plate. He could be tough on umps.

My best game in '67 came at Fenway Park on September 3, where I shut out Boston 4–0. That's the game where I won a suit from Stanky, who gave a new suit to any pitcher who threw a complete game and gave up 20 or more ground balls. I threw 27 grounders that game, the most of my career. The total included ground outs and also ground singles. More important than the new suit, however, were the standings. The win left us in third place, trailing the second-place Red Sox by a half game, the front-running Twins by a game, and ahead of the fourth-place Tigers by a half game.

We spent the month of September never more than a game out. It was nerve-wracking, pulsating fun. Truth is, we lost the pennant by not winning the games we should have down the stretch. We lost a crucial doubleheader to the last-place Kansas City club on September 28, leaving us one and a half games behind the pace. Peters and Horlen lost to Chuck Dobson and Catfish Hunter. A sweep would have put us in first. Even a split would have given us a share of the lead. We were devastated. There was a wire story which quoted Yastrzemski about that double loss:

"When I heard that Chicago lost twice to Kansas City, I couldn't believe it. We've got to be the luckiest team in baseball, really. Maybe we are destined to win this thing, like some people say."

The official end for the White Sox came the following night when the Washington Senators, another doormat team, beat me in a 1–0 heartbreaker. They scored their only run with two outs in the fifth on a single by Fred Valentine. I would have been out of the inning when he popped a ball in foul territory, off the first base line. But the ball drifted into the first row of some special boxes that had been temporarily put there. First baseman Tom McCraw reached in, but the ball landed inches from his glove. That kept Valentine alive, and he singled to left on the next pitch for the winning run.

Normally, the clubhouse was a happy place. After each win, or before the game for good luck, we'd play Merle Haggard's "Branded Man," which became the team's unofficial anthem. Stanky liked that esprit de corps. But after those last three losses—games we should have won, games that would have meant the pennant—we were crushed. The place was like a morgue, and we were blaming ourselves for dropping those games to bad teams. Stanky came out of his office and addressed the team:

"Boys, I want to tell you one thing. I'm proud of you. The mouse had the elephants standing up on chairs, holding their skirts up, squeaking 'Eeek, a mouse!' Boys, we were the mouse. We played the best we possibly could. Don't feel bad about anything. Be proud. Hold your head up and be proud of your season . . ."

Eddie started choking up, his eyes welled, and he hurried back into his office and closed the door. He came out later, red-eyed.

The race came down to the Twins and the Red Sox at Fenway on the final two days of the season. Boston swept, with Yastrzemski going 7-for-8 and Jim Lonborg getting the clincher for his 22nd win. The Red Sox, skippered by rookie manager Dick Williams, had come from a ninth-place finish in 1966 to win their Impossible Dream championship.

In 1967 I lowered my ERA to 2.48, but my record slipped to 10–13 in 178 innings. I pitched in some hard luck, but my biggest problem was a debilitating gastrointestinal virus that weakened me during the second half. In a ten-day period, while doing a stint with the Air National Guard, my weight dropped from 198 to 170 pounds. Stanky used to say that my virus cost us the pennant.

We started 1968 by losing our first ten games. Ed Short, with Lopez not around, made a terrible trade, sending Al Weis, J. C. Martin, and Tommie Agee to the Mets for Jack Fisher and Tommy Davis. Fisher was a good, not great, journeyman pitcher, most noted for giving up a home run to Ted Williams on his last big league at bat. He could give you 200 to 250 innings, and pitch around .500 ball. Davis, however, wasn't a White Sox type player at all. He could hit, but couldn't run or field, and we were a team based on pitching, speed, and defense, especially in the outfield.

The trade was disastrous. Short gave away our best outfielder—Agee, a guy who could catch up to anything that stayed in the park and who could hit with power—and it weakened us tremendously. Weis, Martin, and Agee all were to play key roles in 1969 when the Mets shocked the baseball world by beating the Orioles in the World Series.

Behind the trade was an ill-advised philosophical change instituted by the Chicago front office, a plan that ran the team into the ground. The White Sox became worried about scoring more runs. They moved completely away from speed, defense, and good pitching. That's why they made the Davis trade, to get an RBI man. But Davis wasn't the same man he was in 1962, when he hit .346 and drove in 153 runs with the Dodgers. He broke his ankle in 1965, and it never fully healed.

As it turned out, Davis only drove in 50 runs in 1968, and over the next few years the overhaul withered the White Sox on the vine. The team's winning percentages—or should I say, losing percentages—from '68 to '71 (my last year in Chicago) were .414, .420, .346, and .488.

But as bad as things were going for the team in 1968, they were going good for me. 'Sixty-eight was the Year of the Pitcher, the year Yastrzemski won the batting crown with a .301 average, the year Bob Gibson pitched 306 innings with a 1.12 ERA. By the All-Star game I was 7–0 with a 1.68 ERA. I made the American League squad and got into the game at the Astrodome, pitching two thirds of an inning. I lost a few heartbreakers over the next month, but I was still 10–5, 1.98 by the third week of August.

On August 22, however, my career almost came to an end in a game against the Tigers.

To properly explain what happened, let me say first that the Detroit Tigers had a fine hitting coach, Wally Moses, who taught his hitters to be aggressive and lean over the plate. Stanky and his pitching coach Marv Grissom were telling us to throw inside more. The combination of these two opposing teachings resulted in an accident waiting to happen.

In an earlier series against the Tigers that year, White Sox pitchers had hit eight Detroit batters. The press speculated that Stanky was telling us to throw at hitters. He never did; he told us to pitch inside. There's a big difference. All this left an undertow of bad blood between the two teams.

In the third inning of the August 22 game at Tiger Stadium, the Tigers were leading 1–0. Dick McAuliffe led off and worked me for a 3–2 count. He fouled off a couple of pitches, and my next pitch just slipped out of my hand. I was trying to get the ball up, because Dick was a low-ball hitter, but it got away from me and sailed over everybody's head to the backstop. I certainly wasn't throwing at Dick, but he didn't see it that way. McAuliffe started down to first base.

"What kind of bleep is that?" he yelled to the mound. Then he lost his head and charged me.

All I was thinking about was trying not to get hurt, so I lowered my body to tackle him. My plan was to wrestle him to the ground and then wait for help. In a baseball fight, if you survive the first ten seconds, you won't get hurt. McAuliffe, however, drove his knee deep into my pitching shoulder, ripping ligaments and causing a separation. The benches emptied, but I didn't see any of it. I was on the ground, writhing in pain. God, I was hurting. Think about it—a separated shoulder means having your shoulder torn from its socket.

I had thrown my last pitch of the year; the papers were wondering if it was the last pitch of my career.

I flew with the team back to Chicago, my shoulder heavily taped and iced. At the hospital the next morning team doctor Jerry Loftis confirmed the extent of the injury and advised an operation. He wanted to put a pin in the shoulder to hold it in place, then surgically reattach the ligaments.

I was extremely leery about surgery. At the time, operations on arms and shoulders not only weren't that effective, but were dangerous. The surgical procedures were practically prehistoric compared to the medical science of today. The White Sox had a phenom pitcher, Greg Bollo. He was a young man with great stuff, but he developed bone chips in the elbow. They operated on his arm, and Bollo was never heard from again. That wasn't going to happen to me. I wanted a second opinion. Ed Short, however, wouldn't let me get one.

"Second opinions aren't in your contract," Short told me. "You can't have one. We have a doctor. That's why we pay him, and that's the doctor you use."

We went back and forth on this until the end of the season without resolving the issue. I decided to act on my own, surreptitiously. I went home to Terre Haute, had my own doctor take X rays, then brought the film to Dr. Danny Levinthal in Palm Springs. Dr. Levinthal was a seventy-five-year-old orthopedist who had been recommended by Bill Sampson, an attorney friend of mine. I did all this on the sly, never telling Short.

Dr. Levinthal had seen a thousand separated shoulders and was an expert. He checked my X rays, examined me, and then asked me a question.

"What are you going to do out here this week, Tommy?"

"I'm going to play golf. It doesn't hurt me to swing."

"Fine," Dr. Levinthal said. "If your shoulder *does* start hurting, stop playing. Now, let me ask you this. Do you have a pretty big golf bag?"

His question puzzled me. Why would he want to know that?

"Yeah, it's good-sized."

"Excellent. I want you to carry that bag on your left shoulder as much as you can, to keep pressure on the shoulder bone and force it down. You'd be surprised how much that can help. But I wouldn't advise cutting into that shoulder . . . not if you want to pitch again."

That's all I needed to hear. I carried the bag on my shoulder and it did help. In November, about six weeks after the injury, I went down to the instructional league in Florida and cautiously worked my arm back into shape. I successfully stalled the team about getting the operation.

My arm killed me at first, so I just played light catch and some pepper. By December, however, it came around. That next spring the team doctor examined the shoulder again.

"This thing is really solid," Dr. Loftis said with surprise. "You know, it really looks great. It's a good thing we didn't operate on it, now isn't it?"

That statement amazed me. The only reason I didn't get the operation in the first place is because I didn't take Loftis's advice to do so and snuck behind the team's back for a second opinion. But like the "good soldier," I went along with the charade.

"Yeah, Jerry. Sometimes the conservative approach is better. Besides, I'm allergic to operations."

He laughed. The writers and fans followed my progress closely that spring. Arthur Daley wrote in the *New York Times* on March 19, 1969: "There was no way the pitch [to McAuliffe] could have been interpreted as a beanball. The count on the batter was 3 and 2, and beanballs never are thrown on such a count . . ."

The prevailing theme was that my injury was unnecessary and it would be tragic if I couldn't come back and pitch effectively. Some wondered how I'd hold up when the season began.

I had to prove all over again that I could still throw. Just as I had to do with the Yankees twenty years later.

# 6.
# FOLLOWING
# THROUGH

As the 1989 grapefruit schedule was about to begin, only a handful of people believed I had a chance to make the team: Sally, the kids, my dad, and O. S. Hawkins and his wife. O.S. is pastor of the First Baptist Church in Fort Lauderdale, and we became friends when I first came to the Yankees in 1979. O.S. would have dinner with us on Sunday nights, and we'd golf together. He told me before the games started that the stage was set for something good to happen.

"God wants us to succeed, Tommy. So go for it," he told me. "Shove it down their throats. Whatever happens, you know that we love you."

With that kind of support, with Sally and the boys and our daughter encouraging me, I was psychologically ready for the marathon. Biblically speaking, that's the only way an athlete can come back: to put all the things in the past behind you and put all your energies into what lies ahead.

The family settled nicely into our house at Coral Ridge. It had a pool for the kids and was only six blocks from the ocean, across the street from the Coral Ridge Country Club. The club is owned by the Robert Trent Jones family, and we got a month's membership. We'd golf, dance, and play bingo with the older people. Coral Ridge became my refuge, where I could get away from the park.

Maybe I should have said that thousands of people believed in me, because the fans were tremendous. They identified with me. I was the guy with the beer belly, the guy who had to struggle. New York fans love an underdog. I think that's one of the reasons why Billy Martin was successful in New York and why George brought him back five times —because the fans believed he was an underdog.

Every time I popped my head out on the field the fans would applaud and there'd be shouts of "Go get 'em, Tommy," "We love you, T.J.," or "Show that Green." The fans have been a tremendous source of strength ever since my son Travis's accident.

After the first couple of weeks of workouts and Dallas's daily pontifications in the locker room, the guys were wondering, "Can he believe this stuff?" Dallas would talk about how we weren't working hard enough as a team, about how we had to "suck it up," about how his changes were going to lead us to the pennant. After one such meeting, I was talking with Dave Righetti and Mike Pagliarulo, and Rags said: "He sounds like Moses, going to lead his children out of the land of pharaoh and into the Promised Land. He even looks like Moses, with that white hair."

The movie *The Ten Commandments* played on TV the night before, and Rags said Charlton Heston as Moses reminded him of Dallas, with the hair, the booming voice, and the overall bearing. Pagliarulo and Richard Dotson, both in Dallas's doghouse, picked up on it, and before long the team had a nickname for their manager. You'd come into the locker room in the morning, and Dotson would ask: "I wonder what Moses has planned today?"

As a baseball man, Dallas was very good. That wasn't his problem. He had won as a manager in Philadelphia and had built a winner as general manager of the Cubs. But it was just the way he approached things—pompous, always talking down to players. Chuck Tanner once told me he never forgot the fact that he was a player. When he became a manager, he remembered how he wanted his manager to treat him. With Dallas, it was different.

Dallas announced his projected exhibition starters: Andy Hawkins, Dave LaPoint John Candelaria, Charlie Hudson, and Jimmy Jones. He said these guys would get a lot of work, but that everyone would get a look. That included the fringe kids—Dave Eiland, Darrin Chapin—as well as the fringe veterans—me, Guidry, Dickie Noles, Clay Parker, Luis Sanchez, Dotson, Chuck Cary.

# Following Through

He lived up to his word. As much as you can in six short weeks, Dallas gave everyone a look. Including me, and that was encouraging. I'd be pitching. For my life.

My first outing came on March 4, in a B game. B games are reserved mainly for rookies and minor league prospects, plus warm bodies to fill out the roster. Clubs use B games to weed people out: to give someone a quick look before he gets sent down or released. The only time you'll see a regular in a B game is if the player needs the work.

We played at Bobby Maduro Stadium, an anachronistic ball park you'd expect to see in the lower minor leagues or in a Norman Rockwell painting, with wooden stands and the curved roof in back. The sun blazed into the low nineties and the stadium was virtually deserted, with about twenty-five people in the stands. The Yankee regulars would play before the crowd in the cool of the night at new Joe Robbie Stadium.

Richard Dotson started, going the first four. Ron Guidry, also pitching for his survival, came on for two innings of relief. Gator pitched well and I picked him up to start the sixth inning.

My fastball was sinking, a good sign. Butch Davis led off with a ground single, but that was erased on another grounder, this one converted into a double-play. A third ground ball ended the inning. As I came into the bench, I got a drink at the water cooler. Billy Connors was there.

"Billy, if I walk Larry Sheets on four pitches, or if I hit him, don't think I'm wild. I'm *trying* to hit him."

Dallas was within earshot. He looked at me and raised his eyebrows.

"What did Sheets do to you?"

I told Dallas the story. Sheets, who was due up the next inning, showed me up in a game in 1986. We were getting killed, 15–2. Lou Piniella ran out of pitchers, so I volunteered to mop up.

The first time up against me, Sheets homered, which didn't bother me. But his next time up, with the score now 18–2, he pulled a major no-no: he bunted on me. A batter never shows up a pitcher that way, late in a lopsided game. I vowed then and there that Sheets would go down the next time I faced him. But 1987 and 1988 went by, and I never got the chance to face Sheets in a situation where the game wasn't on the line. Now, in the next inning of this exhibition game, I'd get my chance.

After I told my story, Dallas just smiled. As a former pitcher, he understood.

"Well, if you're looking for a reason to make a guy eat some dirt, that would do it."

"Do what you've got to do," Connors chimed in.

Bob Horner led off the bottom of the seventh, and I struck him out. I got the next batter on a grounder to second. Sheets came up. My first three pitches were tight, but I couldn't get the ball inside far enough to hit him. After I fell behind 3–0, he gave me a look. At least I got him thinking. But payback notwithstanding, I didn't want to put him on base. I came in with a strike, and he hit an easy ground ball to second for the third out. My first stint was over: two shutout innings, one hit, no walks, one strikeout, and seven ground balls.

When I came into the dugout, Dallas didn't say a word. He didn't say "good job, bad job." Nothing. Billy Connors, with Dallas there on the bench, said three words.

"Do your running."

Which I did.

Dallas was guarded in his postgame comments about me.

"He knew exactly what he was doing, as he always does. He looks like he knows he's in a dogfight."

In 1969 I was not in a dogfight, but my position on the team was just as questionable. The White Sox anxiously held their breath as I reported to spring training. How would I throw? Would I bounce back from the torn shoulder ligaments and separation suffered in the melee with Dick McAuliffe?

Someone asked me if I was going to go after McAuliffe the first time he faced me. I had no intention to retaliate, I said, but I left some doubt in my public remarks.

"Someday I will [retaliate], and he'll always wonder what pitch it's going to be. Will it be the first pitch that I throw him, or the second, or the tenth? Will it be the first game or the third?"

McAuliffe was a good, aggressive hitter. He had an awkward, open stance from the left side, with his bat held oddly, well out in front of the body. He'd battle you on every pitch. But after my comments, he didn't dig in against me as before. He laid back now to see where the ball was going. He became a defensive hitter, and wasn't effective against me the rest of his career. I had McAuliffe thinking, which is the worst possible thing a batter can do. It was as Yogi said: "You can't hit and think at the same time." Sometimes psychology is the best form of revenge.

The club was 34–46 in 1968 when they fired Eddie Stanky and brought back Al Lopez, hoping he could resurrect the White Sox of old. But even Lopez couldn't make a silk purse out of a sow's ear, not in light of the team's disastrous "rebuilding." The Senior's record was as bad as Stanky's: 33–48.

The White Sox had brought Luis Aparacio back at shortstop in a trade with the Orioles for Don Buford. Luis had a solid year but had lost a step defensively. We missed Buford's 27 stolen bases and 15 home runs. Tommy Davis flopped at the plate, hitting eight home runs and driving in just 50 runs. For the second straight year our team batting average was below .230—.228, to be exact. No starter won more than 12 games (Horlen), and Gary Peters and Jack Fisher combined to go 12–26. All of which was a formula for an eighth-place tie with the Angels, a whopping 36 games behind the Detroit Tigers.

In 1969, my comeback year and baseball's first year for divisional play, the decline continued. Lopez quit 17 games into the season, and Don Gutteridge took over the rest of the way. The results were the same: a 68–94 mark, 29 games behind Billy Martin's Western Division champs, the Minnesota Twins. In one short year the team ERA jumped from 2.75 to 4.21. We were hitting more but had no pitching, speed, or defense.

To make a bad situation worse, Ed Short put in an Astroturf infield at Comiskey Park. Our infield was capable, but not swift, with Gail Hopkins, Bobby Knopp, Aparacio, Bill Melton, and Pete Ward. The turf killed us. We couldn't catch up to balls; otherwise routine grounders were shooting by for base hits. Short defended the Astroturf, saying it was a proven fact that there are more double-plays on plastic infields. Of course, I told him, and the reason is that you have more runners on base. As it was, the club's attempt to redefine itself, to change from Hitless Wonders to Windy City Bashers, proved totally unsuccessful.

I had losing years in both 1969 and 1970. In '69 I was 9–11, 3.25, but I turned in 232⅓ innings, the most of my career, putting to rest any doubts about the status of my arm. In 1970 I led the staff in wins (12), innings (269), starts (37), complete games (10), walks (101), and strikeouts (138). There was no Big Three. Wilbur Wood was a year away from stardom. Only Jerry Janeski and myself went over thirty starts.

113

The rest of the staff was a collection of journeyman talent, guys like Bob Miller, Jerry Crider, Danny Murphy, Lee Stange, Floyd Weaver, and Steve Hamilton. My ERA of 3.26 led the starters, but the 12–17 record bothered me.

I learned how much I loved baseball that summer by learning how much I hated losing. It was an important discovery. Losing would have bothered me more if I found that I didn't care. And believe me, it was a real test, since the team bottomed out at 56–106, the worst record in baseball.

Having the worst record in baseball is an embarrassment. You hate playing before the home crowd because you know you'll end up disappointing them. And you hate going on the road because in each new town you come in as whipping boys, even laughing-stocks. Like Rodney Dangerfield, you get no respect.

Before he left, Eddie Stanky told me one thing I never forgot. He told me to always work out "as if you're going to be traded, or that you want to be traded." He said scouts often come to the ball park early to watch batting practice and snoop around. Maybe you're having a so-so year or the club is getting tired of the way you're pitching. But if you work out hard every day, bust your butt on every play, hustle whenever you're out on the field, people will notice and word will get around.

If there's a trade that might be made in the off-season, the scouts will remember you as a guy who's good for a team. Eddie told me I'd be surprised by the number of times clubs would turn down good ball players, not because of their on-the-field performance, but because they are not good team men. That all changed with free agency. Today, teams look only at performance. They don't care if a player's a bad influence, if he doesn't like to take infield, if he misses a plane now and then, if he's late for practice, if he has an attitude problem, or if he's an ax murderer. If a team can rent your bat or your arm for a year or two, they'll do it and be happy about it. That's also why it's becoming rarer these days to find teams with—what do you call it?—character, identity, heart.

Stanky's advice stayed with me in 1970. I didn't want to stay in Chicago. I was sick of losing. The clubhouse atmosphere was terrible. We'd file into the ball park expecting to lose. Players were bickering at each other, and the pitching staff was unsettled. Three managers— Gutteridge (49–89), Bill Adair (4–4), and Chuck Tanner (3–13)—went through twenty-two pitchers without much luck. Nothing went right, even in the off-season, when one of our promising young pitchers, Paul Edmundson, died in an explosive car crash. This team was snakebit.

My biggest win in 1970 came off the field, when I married Sally Simmons on the night of July 13 in Plainfield, Indiana, one of the hottest nights in what had been a typically hot Indiana summer. Prior to that, I had been the happy bachelor, rooming in Chicago with Cubs coach Joe Amalfitano, enjoying dating, golfing, and having fun without responsibility. But a part of me longed for stability, a good woman by my side who would share in the joys, and the sorrows, of my life.

Then I met Sally.

The first time I laid eyes on her was in October 1968, during Homecoming Weekend at Indiana State University in Terre Haute, where Sally was a coed. I was a guest of the football coach at the homecoming game, and she was a member of the Blue Berets, the student group charged with giving campus tours and with escorting visiting VIPs. My own education, as I've mentioned, was interrupted by a series of off-season events: in 1966 the White Sox forced me to go to Puerto Rico; in 1967 I recuperated from my viral illness; in 1968 I spent all winter getting my shoulder back in shape after my collision with Dick McAuliffe.

At half-time of the football game I saw this attractive young lady in a bright blue uniform escorting Senator Birch Bayh's father to the microphone on the field. She caught my eye right away, and from the sidelines I made sure I read her name tag.

"Sally Simmons." I filed the name away. I didn't get the chance to meet her, and soon after, I left for California, then the Bahamas, to play in golf tournaments. I didn't see Sally again until January 1969, at an Indiana State basketball game. We had a mutual friend, John Knox, the captain of the football team. The football players served as ushers at basketball games, and when I saw John, he asked me if I had ever made contact with Sally after seeing her at homecoming. I said no.

"Well," he said, with a devilish smile on his face. "She's at the game tonight."

He then went running up the stands and shouted down to Sally: "Hey, Space"—her nickname—"come here. I want you to meet Tommy John! Tommy John of the White Sox! Come on! Come down and meet him, now's your chance!"

Sally's friends were all laughing and teasing. She was with a date, and she cringed with embarrassment. She wouldn't come over. When

Knox got back to me, I asked him for Sally's phone number. The next morning I called her. She didn't believe it was me. She thought Knox was playing a practical joke on her.

"Is this Sally Simmons?"

"Yes."

"Hi. This is Tommy John."

"Knock it off. I know it's you, John Knox."

"No. It's Tommy John."

"Who is this, really?" she asked.

"I'm telling you. It's Tommy John. I want to apologize for last night. I didn't know Knox would do that. I was as embarrassed as you were. Would you join me for a cup of coffee?"

She accepted. I was at Marshall Hall in fifteen minutes. We went to a place called the Big Wheel, a coffee shop on U.S. 41 in Terre Haute. Sally had never had coffee in her life, and she was afraid to order anything. When I ordered my coffee black, she did the same thing. She tried not to cringe when swallowing the hot, bitter liquid. We talked about our families, our backgrounds, and hardly mentioned baseball. I could tell right there we had a . . . well, the best minds of the ages have tried to explain love and haven't totally succeeded, so I won't try. But we had a rapport, a chemistry, and I suppose I knew, deep down, that Sally Simmons would end up as Mrs. Tommy John.

On our first date she went with me to a sports banquet in Worthington where I was the featured speaker. Before Sally left home that night, her dad gave her a dime to put in her shoe, to use for an emergency phone call, "In case he tries anything." Mr. Simmons had heard about those notorious single ball players.

The "banquet" was hardly that: there was no food served, so when it was over, we were both famished. We were looking for a place to have a quick bite, so I pulled into the Albert Pick Motel, which had a nice little coffee shop. But it also had the reputation among Indiana State coeds for being *the* place for one-night stands. A girl seen coming out of there in the morning might just as well take out an ad in the newspaper advertising her indiscretion.

Sally told me later she was afraid I was going to try to put the moves on her, and that her dad was right about "them ballplayers." But when we walked past the registration desk to the coffee shop, she let out a deep sigh of relief. She said that incident wiped out the last remaining doubts she had about me.

We continued dating and kept in contact during the year. I wasn't sure about marriage. It scared me. I was twenty-five, and when you've been a bachelor for so long, you don't hastily make changes. I had seen too many ball players hook up with girls who had ulterior motives, who wanted to be around big league money and the big league lifestyle. These women looked on baseball as a ticket to easy money and glamour. I had dated a lot and was petrified of such women.

Sally was different. First, she knew nothing about baseball. She didn't even know who, or what, the Chicago White Sox were. Second, she was an Indiana girl from Plainfield, a town of about five thousand. To me, that meant a midwestern upbringing, and a solid, conservative nature.

She was nineteen; her dad thought I was too old for her, and at first Sally felt the same way. At that time, six years was a big age difference. She also didn't know me, and lumped me in with "those Terre Haute guys." Terre Haute's townies had a bad reputation on campus, as guys always on the make. She also was a little in awe, even wary, of my career as a ball player, the fact that I knew famous people, that my circles and spheres seemed so much larger and worldly than hers.

But over time, and with a good word about me from school president Dr. Alan Rankin, Sally overcame her doubts. I popped the question to her in December 1969, in front of her dormitory. She said yes, a joyful, leaping, dancing yes. We then went home and had a celebratory dinner with my mom and dad.

We initially planned an October wedding, but then moved it up to July, during the 1970 All-Star break. Sally graduated in June. Then, we drove her home to tell her mom and dad. Why not? I was fed up with the losing atmosphere of the ball club, and thought it'd be great to have Sally with me for the long second half of the season. We were both eager to get on with it anyway. I guarantee that 95 percent of the people in Terre Haute thought we moved the date up because Sally was pregnant. People would say: "So, your moving it up. Oooooh."

I pitched Sunday afternoon in Kansas City on a sweltering day. My concentration was shot, of course, and I don't even remember if I won or lost the game. All I remember is how hot I was. I flew home, got in Sunday night for the rehearsal at the church, played eighteen holes of golf the next day and that night we got married, July 13, 1970.

It seemed like half the town was there. A bunch of my teammates came down in a convoy of rented cars, and our relatives were flying in and driving in from all around the state. There probably hasn't been a wedding in history where *everything* went according to plan, and ours was no exception. On this blistering night the air-conditioning at Plainfield's United Methodist Church broke down. As the ceremony went on I could hear the guests rustling and fidgeting in the heat, and I was hoping the ceremony would end soon. At last the minister pronounced us man and wife. After greeting everyone in the reception line, we walked out of the church. There was just one thing missing: the car. Someone had forgotten to make arrangements for our transportation from the church. Bob McClelland, my best friend—who ran the Chrysler dealership in Terre Haute—came to the rescue and loaned us a station wagon.

We drove all night, unloaded the gifts in Chicago, then took off for a one-day honeymoon at a resort called The Abbey at Lake Geneva, Wisconsin. We spent the day boating on the lake, had dinner, visited the Jack Childers family, and later saw Joan Rivers perform at the Playboy Club, where we endured a series of newlywed jokes. The next morning we left to drive back to Chicago. I was pitching Thursday, and had to be at the team workout Wednesday.

Sally didn't understand how we could just leave our honeymoon like that. I said that baseball was my job. I'm not a romantic in that sense, I guess. Most people would have taken the time off and reported the next day, right before game-time. But I didn't want to miss my running and throwing. As the years went on, Sally got used to the often chaotic and nomadic baseball lifestyle. So much for the glamour of a baseball wife.

We rented a place at a singles village in Lisle, just east of Aurora, about thirty-five miles out of Chicago. The day of that first workout after the honeymoon, Sally went to the park with me and watched from the stands. She's been with me ever since, and has been, without doubt, the main driving force in my life.

Our marriage has been a good one; we've had our share of problems. Every couple has. The key is how you deal with them. The secret for our happiness is that we were both brought up to believe in the sanctity of marriage. It is *holy* matrimony. When you go into that church, you are going before God and making a commitment of fidelity before Him. The only exclusive contract in my life was the one I signed with Sally Simmons on July 13, 1970.

We also communicate. When I'm on the road, we talk everyday and sometimes twice a day by phone. We share the good times, and the problems also. I think many marriages end because, at the first sign of a disagreement, the two sides stop talking. That's what the cliché means—that you've got to "work on a marriage." Marital success doesn't happen by itself. It takes conscious effort, whether you've been married 51 days, or 51 years, as my mom and dad were.

Sally's an extremely strong person and that helps me incredibly. More than once she has been the rock that held steady when everything else was falling apart. I'm strong to a point, but having her support has made the difference many times in my life.

At the end of the '70 season the White Sox sent Gary Peters to the Red Sox, leaving me and Joe Horlen as the staff's elder statesmen. By then I was in the big money. Big money. I have to laugh when I compare our salaries back then to today's multimillion-dollar ball players. In '69 and '70 I cracked the $30,000 mark, and in 1971 I signed for $47,000.

Wilbur Wood had a phenomenal year for us in 1971. The year before, he appeared in 77 games, all in relief. In '71 Chuck Tanner and his pitching coach Johnny Sain converted Wood to a starter, and he pitched 334 innings, going 22–13 with a 1.91 ERA. Tanner never liked to use a knuckleballer in relief, because of the way the knuckler danced and moved all over. He solved that by making Wood a starter.

The knuckler puts very little strain on your arm, and Wood could pitch and pitch and pitch. That was Johnny Sain's theory. You pitch the guy who's hot until he drops.

Sain was the opposite of Ray Berres; Sain could show you how to throw any pitch in the book, but he couldn't look at your motion and tell if your mechanics were off. For a sinkerballer, that spells trouble. Johnny believed in the slider, and, like Early Wynn had in Cleveland, he wanted me to add the slider to my repertoire. I never got the hang of that pitch, meaning I couldn't throw it without it affecting my fastball.

But Sain kept after me to throw slider, slider, slider. I worked on it for six weeks in the spring and six weeks during the regular season. And just as in 1964, my fastball stopped sinking; it got as straight as a taut string. The situation reached the point where I couldn't throw two consecutive pitches over home plate. I had no idea why I had lost my control, and neither did Sain. I tried everything to get myself straightened out but nothing worked. I remember Horlen saying to me: "God, I've never seen you throw like this. You look as if you've never pitched before."

It took an opposing player to find out what I was doing wrong. Gail Hopkins, who had been with the White Sox the year before and was now playing first base for the Royals, saw me warming up on the side one day in Kansas City. He came over to me.

"T.J., you're throwing terrible," Hopkins said. "What's the matter?"

"Don't have a clue, Hoppy."

He then grabbed a bat and stood in, watching my pitches.

"Your ball doesn't have good spin on it, Tommy."

He took off his baseball cap, then looked at me with one eye through an air hole on the top of the cap. Ballplayers will do that to study a pitcher; the hole blocks everything out and you see only the guy throwing the ball.

"When you throw the ball, your hand is out of position," he said.

"It is? What do you think I should do?"

"Just get your hand in back of the ball. Position the hand straighter when the ball comes out of your hand, the way you used to throw."

I tried it and threw a screwball, and the ball had a good spin on it.

"Wow!" Hoppy said. "That's a whole lot better than it was."

I experimented for the next two days, working on my hand position. Sain was in the bullpen in Anaheim watching me warm up and he remarked how well my fastball was moving. It was the first time all year my ball showed any kind of darting movement. I knew what was coming next.

"T. J., let me see your slider," Sain requested. I had already told the bullpen catcher, Chuck Brinkman, that if Sain asked me to throw the slider, I would just throw my curveball harder and cut the break down on the ball. Both the curveball and the slider are breaking pitches, but a curveball is slower, and a slider is harder. So all I did was throw my curveball harder than I normally would, and it fooled Sain.

Don't get me wrong about Sain—he had a lot of good pitching ideas. For example, he would tell us to get batters out with pitches that aren't physically taxing to throw. With Wilbur Wood, it was his knuckler. With me, it was my slow curve. He would tell me, "You don't have to grunt when you pitch." He'd say just throw that "here-it-is, hit-it" curve.

It was great advice, but then he'd start in again on the slider. He did it with Tom Bradley too. Bradley began the 1971 season on fire. He was awesome for the first eight weeks, relying on his fastball and curveball. But after Sain got him to go to the slider more and more, he lost his fastball. He might have won 22 or 23 games that year, but finished at 16–16.

My pitching problems had landed me in the bullpen. Tanner lost confidence in me, and rightly so. He would not use me with the game on the line. I only pitched in mop-up situations.

The game that saved me was an emergency start against the Orioles. Tanner ran out of pitchers because of doubleheaders, and had to start me. Paul Blair, the leadoff batter, started the game by lining a ball inside the third base bag. Our left fielder, Rick Reichardt, was not known for his defense. But Reichardt hustled over, made a beautiful backhand pickup, and threw a perfect strike to Mike Andrews at second base, cutting Blair down. Reichardt's play shook me out of my doldrums. It wiped the slate clean. They never came close to scoring the rest of the game, and we won.

After that I got into a good groove, and as bad as I was before, that's how good I got after. My experiments with hand positioning were successful, and not only did I regain my sinker, but my control and confidence as well. I pitched a two-hit shutout against Jim Palmer and the Orioles in my next appearance. I was back.

It was Sain's theory that when a guy got hot you pitched him as often as you could, and he pitched me on two days rest four times. He even pitched Wilbur Wood, our ace, in both games of a doubleheader. Wilbur pitched 44 games, 42 starts, won 22, and threw 334 innings, an incredible total. He pitched on two days rest most of the second half. The Big Three of the staff—Wood, Tom Bradley, and John—totaled 849 innings. Today, in the age of specialization, it's common for a staff's Big Three to pitch less than 600 innings.

The Chicago offense at least provided a little more punch. We finally had a true power hitter, third baseman Bill Melton, who registered 33 circuit clouts. We crawled to within four games of .500 in 1971. That was good for third place, but we trailed Dick Williams and the A's (101 wins) by 22 ½ games. That was the year twenty-one-year-old lefty Vida Blue owned baseball for the A's, winning 24 games, striking out 301, and registering a league leading ERA of 1.81.

I checked in at 13–16 with a 3.62 ERA in 229 innings, not bad when you throw in my early season difficulties. But I had the gut feeling my Chicago days were over. I got the first hint I had worn out my welcome when General Manager Roland Hemond cut back on my allowance for serving in the National Guard. The money covered travel, room and board, and expenses. It came to about $4000, and Roland wanted to cut it to $1800.

"Roland," I said, "I know you're going to try to move me."

"Oh no. No, Tommy. We won't trade you," he said.

"I tell you what. The winter meetings are in Scottsdale this year," I said, reaching into my pocket. "Here's a dime, Roland. It's a local call, because I live in Scottsdale. When the trade is made, you can make the call on me. This is my treat."

He again denied that there would be any trade, but I shook his hand.

"Thanks for everything," I said. "I appreciate what the White Sox have done for me, and I honestly mean that. I tried my best, but things just did not work out."

On December 2, 1971, I was working out in the yard in Scottsdale, digging a trench around the pool. My driveway was loaded with twenty-two tons of river rock that I was hauling into the trench from a wheel-barrow. Sally came out and said Hemond was calling for me. My stomach turned butterflies. My only question was: Where would I be going? There were rumors in the papers about a deal either to Atlanta or Pittsburgh.

"Tommy, I just want to let you know before the press does that we've traded you."

"Where?"

"The Dodgers. We traded you for Richie Allen." The White Sox also threw in minor league infielder Steve Huntz, who was assigned to Spokane.

Los Angeles! Stanky's advice paid off. The Dodgers heard good things about my attitude and my work habits, and took a calculated risk in giving up a slugger like Allen.

I couldn't contain my excitement. I told Sally, and she asked if the Dodgers were any good.

"Yeah," I said, "they have a good team, good pitching, and I hear it's an outstanding organization."

We both hugged. The Dodgers called soon after that. General manager Al Campanis introduced himself and welcomed me to the team. I didn't get a lick of work done the rest of the day, because the L.A. papers and the Chicago papers were calling me for my reactions. I didn't want to have this taken the wrong way, I told them, but for me, the trade was like going from a Chevrolet to a Cadillac.

But we found it hard to say good-bye. I loved Chicago as a place to play and live. We had made a lot of friends there, and the fans were wonderful: intensely loyal and knowledgeable. They don't give up on you. Comiskey Park was a great park to pitch in, with deep lines. I had the privilege of playing for two great managers in Lopez and Stanky. Chicago was a midwestern city, with which I identified, and Terre Haute was only three hours away by car. It was a lot to give up. Still, the last four years had been losing ones, and I was excited about a chance to join an organization like the Dodgers.

Sally and I talked about it, and our only real concern was being so far from Indiana. But we decided that was the price we'd have to pay. My dad felt great about the trade because he knew the Dodgers were one of baseball's class outfits.

After my first press conference with the Los Angeles media, Campanis and I went back to his office to talk about my contract. I was making $47,000 with the White Sox, and it's an unwritten rule in baseball that when you're traded, you're supposed to get an obligatory raise. But Campanis wanted to cut my salary. I was hesitant, so we finally agreed to the same amount I had made with Chicago. I didn't like it, but I didn't want to start off on the wrong foot. Back then, before agents became popular and before free agency, you pretty much had to take what they offered. The Ed Short "we'll bury you" mentality took a long time to die out.

Some of the L.A. media questioned the deal, trading a slugger of Allen's reputation for a lefthanded pitcher with a career 84–91 record. Tom Lasorda, who at that time was the team's Triple A manager, kidded me, saying the Dodgers wanted Steve Huntz, and that *I* was the throw-in. But we paid no attention to the media's second-guessing, and jumped into L.A. feet first.

Before the Dodgers leave for spring training each year, they play an exhibition game against the University of Southern California at Dodger Stadium. It's a nice gesture to the fans, who can attend free. In the 1972 game I pitched for the first time in the classic Dodger-blue home whites. Sally sat up in the wives' section, and no one knew her from Eve. She said when I came into the game, the wives were asking questions like: "He's a reliever, isn't he?" "Isn't he from the American League?" "The White Sox? Where are they?"

I hadn't made much of an impression. Campanis wanted to cut my salary, the press questioned the trade, and the wives had no idea of who the White Sox were. And yet, I was happy and excited.

The Dodgers wrote the book on how to treat ball players. When I came over, everyone from chairman of the board Walter O'Malley to Al Campanis to director of press relations Red Patterson stressed that the Dodgers were a family. If you had any problems, you could come to the team for help.

Peter O'Malley, the club president, told me: "We want you and your wife to be happy. We feel if a man is happy here and wants to be a Dodger, he'll perform better on the field. A contented cow gives sweeter milk."

Many teams think families have nothing to do with baseball, and actually look at wives and children as a nuisance. Teams like that alienate the player's family, and all of a sudden he's taking flak from both sides, from the club and from the family. Soon he finds his marriage in trouble. The Dodgers, on the other hand, cared about the men who played for them, and also their families. They did everything they could to help you keep a decent home life going. To a family-oriented man such as myself, that was very important. The Dodgers allow wives and families on *any* road trip, which is different from any team in baseball as long as they asked permission.

The Dodgers had their own plane, so you flew charter all the time. All the seats were first-class, with extra leg room. The food was not "airline chow." On a Dodger flight you wouldn't get raw chicken with two inches of skin on it. You got delicious meals. On one flight Sally and I asked for skim milk. There wasn't any. But on the next trip they had skim milk on the plane. I started to understand what this talk about "bleeding Dodger blue" was all about.

Before I married Sally, while she was still my girlfriend, some of my Chicago teammates didn't mind her being at the discos and clubs, where she would see married ballplayers out with girlfriends or trying to hustle girls. But the minute we said "I do," these teammates said "You can't"—can't bring Sally into three specific Chicago clubs anymore, because they were off limits to wives. These clubs were meat markets, notorious for "scoring," pickups, and action. I was infuriated.

"First of all, don't tell me where I can and can't go. Second, I wouldn't take my wife into places like that, so don't worry about keeping your affairs secret. Third, I couldn't care less what you do, or how many bimbos you pick up."

That confrontation had really soured me on the White Sox, and was one of the reasons that I played so hard to be traded. The Dodgers, both the front office and the players, wanted the wives along, even on the road. I had been on the road long enough to know what happens. Whether you're a ball player, a writer, a traveling salesman, a mechanic, or a teacher, certain men will cheat on their wives and others won't. But being on the road—with good money, good hotels, and a transient lifestyle—increases the chances for that happening. Girls will follow ball clubs around, and each team has its groupies. It's a little like being a rock star. If you want cheap sex, it's yours for the asking. That aspect of baseball will probably never change.

Down in Vero Beach at spring training, 1972, I met the Dodgers pitching coach Red Adams and liked him immediately. He didn't come on strong, didn't act like a man with all the answers. He loved my sinking fastball and told me to throw it as much as I wanted.

Red was positive and upbeat, with a fine sense of humor. To make a certain point about pitching, he would spin these self-deprecating yarns about his days as a pitcher. For example, to make the point that a pitcher needs to be able to bounce back quickly in a game when he gets hit hard, he'd say something like: "I always started out trying to throw a no-hitter. Then after the first batter, I worked on the one-hitter. After I faced the second hitter, I wanted to keep it down to a nice two-hit shutout. After the third batter, I wanted to pitch a three-hit, one-run game."

Red Dog, as we called him, was a superb teacher. His ability to poke fun at himself put me completely at ease. He was in the Ray Berres class when it came to diagnosing motion and mechanics. But unlike Ray, who wanted his pitchers to throw overhand, Red told us we could throw the ball any way we wanted as long as we followed certain basics. Red preached the importance of retaining your weight over the rubber, staying back on the back leg, and not overstriding with the front leg. This was the same thing Berres taught about gliding into your motion slowly, only told in different words.

Red told me that in the National League, I would do better relying on my fastball more than my curve. Red was exactly right, and under his coaching I prospered in Los Angeles. If you look over my career, you'll see I had my best years for pitching coaches who understood technique—guys like Ray Berres, Red, Mark Connor, and Sam Ellis—as opposed to those who were pitch coaches, such as Johnny Sain, Marcel Lachemann, and Art Fowler.

I'll tell you when I knew Red Adams was brilliant. In the early days of camp he tried to get me to change my motion. I had always pitched stepping out sideways from the rubber. Red wanted me to square up my delivery. The experiment didn't work out, and when I went back to throwing my normal way, I threw the ball extremely well. He came up to me and admitted he was wrong. He told me my way was much better. It takes an extremely strong and intelligent person to do that, especially in baseball, where so many people will not admit to their mistakes. From then on I knew I was in good hands with Red.

In spring training in '72 even Walter O'Malley went out of his way to make me feel at home. Mr. O'Malley threw his annual St. Patrick's Day party for the players, families, friends, staff, sponsors, and the press. The festivities included a golf tournament. Mr. O'Malley—a friendly, wonderful man—selected me for his team, and I had one of the rounds of my life, finishing two under par at 70. We won the tournament and he said with a big laugh: "Tommy, now you know why I wanted you on the Dodgers." We went into the pro shop to select our prizes, and Mr. O'Malley was like a kid in a candy shop. He kept asking me: "What should I get, Tommy? Huh? What should I get?"

Mr. O'Malley was probably the only owner in baseball to give more than the time of day to Marvin Miller, head of the players' union. Miller met with the Dodgers that St. Pat's day, going over union matters, and after the meeting was over, Mr. O'Malley invited him to the party. He may not have agreed with Miller on the issues, but he respected the man and his title.

The Dodgers ran spring training in their own unique, P.R.-conscious way. The complex consisted of Holman Stadium and four practice fields, and there was no such thing as roping the fans off or keeping them behind fences. When you came out of the clubhouse at Vero Beach, the fans were right there, a few feet from the door. You had to sign autographs and pose for pictures. That's the way the ball club wanted it. There's no way of calculating what that kind of goodwill means to the box office, but it's no coincidence that the Dodgers draw upward of three million fans each year. That in turn has an effect on the players. A packed ball park really psychs you up.

My new manager was Walt Alston, a quiet, intelligent man out of the University of Miami. He was an easy man to play for, with a reserved, steady manner. Walt was a virtual unknown when he succeeded Charlie Dressen as Dodger manager in 1954, but he guided Brooklyn to its only world title in 1955. He won world titles in L.A. in 1963 and '65. Walt managed conservatively, rarely stealing or using the hit and run. He wouldn't give any kind of offensive signs and played things close to the vest.

To this day I don't know why, but Walt wouldn't let me complete many games; he'd give me the quick hook. I'd pitch six innings, and if I gave up a base hit in the seventh, I was gone. For me to pitch a complete game for Alston, it had to be a "no-brainer," where we were up by a dozen runs, or I had to be pitching so well that the other team never came close to scoring. Walt managed me from 1972 to 1976. In that time I started 84 ball games and completed just 19—and eight of those were shutouts. Walt never told me why he used me that way and I never asked him. That was just the way he handled me.

There was a player's strike in 1972 and the Dodgers voted to go along, 27–3. One of the dissenters was Frank Robinson, in my opinion one of baseball's all-time greats. Frank's on-field performance speaks for itself, but that strike vote taught me something about the man. After the vote was announced, Robinson addressed the team.

"I don't believe in the strike," he told us, "and I voted against it. But I was voted down, so now I'm on your side. I'm with you guys."

It takes an extremely perceptive and generous man to say something like that. The other reason I respected Frank so much is that he'd answer any questions you had for him on the bench. I'd often ask him: "What would you be looking for in this situation as a hitter?" And he'd tell me what and why.

Frank was extremely intelligent, and also one of the game's legendary hard-nosed players. Frank didn't have a great year in 1972 (.251, 19 HRs, 51 RBIs), but he played hard all year. I can still remember his vicious slides into second base to break up double-plays. That says a lot about a player. As Eddie Stanky used to say, it doesn't take ability to play hard. All it takes is an extra bit of heart that enables you to dig down and play the game with intensity, whether you're going good or bad. That's how I tried to play the game, and I respected Frank tremendously for the way he did it. He set a positive role model for the team.

When the strike ended about nine games into the season, many teams had trouble staying united. There were residual bad feelings. The Dodgers prevented that, mostly because of Mr. O'Malley. Before the job action, he came in and talked to us.

"I don't agree with the strike. I think you guys are wrong. But you have every right to strike. In America, that's one of your options as workers, and I support that. Just remember—the Dodgers are a family. When the strike ends, we're going to have to start playing baseball again. I want you guys to be in this strike united, as one. Work out, keep in shape. When the strike's over, be ready to play together, united, as one."

The strike meant the end of the great Maury Wills as a player. Wills had come out of nine years of obscurity as a shortstop in the Dodger chain. The Dodgers actually gave up on him in 1959, selling him conditionally to the Tigers for $35,000. Detroit returned Maury that spring, deeming him unworthy of the price. Three years later he stole 102 bases, and baseball was never the same.

Almost single-handedly Maury turned baseball from its love affair with plodding, one-dimensional sluggers and got the game to consider pure speed as serious offensive and defensive weapons. But in 1972 Wills was thirty-nine, and he didn't keep in shape during the layoff. When he came back, his reflexes and timing were shot; he couldn't make contact at the plate, hitting an anemic .129 in 132 at bats.

There was a late April game against the Expos. Wills was leading off against Carl Morton, a journeyman pitcher who would end the year with an ERA near 4.00. Maury was hopelessly overmatched. After his last at bat, he came back to the dugout with a dazed look on his face. He took a seat on the bench, nodded over to Alston, and said with a quiet dignity: "He's certainly justified if he takes me out."

That marked Maury's swan song as a player. On April 29 Alston inserted a young, red-haired shortstop named Bill Russell into the lineup. Russell drove in our only run that game in a 7–1 loss to the New York Mets. The Dodger shortstop position was secure for the next dozen years.

When I came to Los Angeles, I didn't know a soul. But during the year I became good friends with Russell, Claude Osteen, and Joe Ferguson; Russell in particular. Bill was a quiet midwesterner from Pittsburg, Kansas. He wasn't a flashy dresser, didn't have a fancy house or car. Those things weren't important to him. But he could play shortstop.

Bill made plays other shortstops wished they could make. But he did it all in his steady, unassuming way, and never got the credit he deserved. He was without doubt the best shortstop that ever played behind me.

We got off to a fast 10–3 start in '72. It took me only into my first game to realize the Dodgers were different from the White Sox. I pitched the second game of the season against the Braves in Atlanta, being moved up a day when the scheduled starter, Claude Osteen, came down with a stomach flu. In the fourth inning the Braves had runners on first and second with one out. Earl Williams hit a soft ground ball to Steve Garvey at third. Garvey threw to second baseman Jim Lefebvre. Jim straddled the bag and took the throw as the runner barreled in. Lefebvre, a feisty player, hung tight, not giving an inch. The runner hit him, but Jim got off a perfect throw to Wes Parker at first for the inning-ending double-play.

I watched in amazement. In the last three years in Chicago, that play wouldn't have been made. Our second baseman would have pulled the ripcord and bailed out, satisfied with the one out. I walked off the field, congratulated Lefebvre, and thought: Man, I'm into something good here. I'm on a higher plane.

I became a totally different pitcher in the National League. In the Junior Circuit, an off-speed hitting league, I threw my curve about half the time. But the National League had mostly fastball hitters. Red Adams told me that if I kept my fastball down and away, I could make a living off it. It goes back to the notion of pitching "bad" to a guy's strength. A fastball hitter, because he *wants* the fastball, will chase a "bad" fastball—that is, one purposely placed low and on the black, or just outside the strike zone. In a nine-inning game for the Dodgers, I would throw just six or seven curves, in total contrast to the way I pitched in Chicago.

Another difference in the leagues was umpiring. National League umps had a low strike zone. They gave you the low pitch. In the American League, a ball at the waist or above was a strike. In the National, it was a ball. In general, National League umps had a strike zone at the belt and below. One reason for this difference was the American League's use of the balloon chest protectors, which forced umps to stand up higher behind the catcher. They saw the balls better that were up in the strike zone. But with the National League's low strike zone, it made sense to rely on my sinking fastball.

You don't find these differences between the two leagues today. No one uses balloon chest protectors, and the umpires are better and more uniformly trained. As a result, hitters over the years have become pretty much the same in both leagues.

Despite the fast start, the club never seriously threatened for the division, finishing third at 85–70, behind the Reds and the Astros, 10½ games out. We were knocked out of first on April 28, and looked up at the leaders the rest of the way.

I pitched with soreness in my pitching elbow for all of 1972. In May, Dr. Frank Jobe, the team's orthopedic physician, checked my elbow. X rays showed a couple of floating bone fragments. He injected it to get the inflammation down, and I pitched that way for the rest of the year. The elbow would get sore, and I'd get cortisone and novocaine injections that would be good for about five games.

But in a game at Dodger Stadium against the Giants on September 23, I was involved in a play that led to my first arm surgery. I was on second base and tried to score on a hard single to center. When I slid into the plate, I jammed my left elbow into the ground. I felt a shooting pain up and down my arm. I tried to shake it off, but in the bottom of the inning I couldn't throw with any velocity and couldn't get the ball over the plate. The elbow started hurting bad and my fingers tingled.

Dr. Jobe took another set of X rays and found that my slide had dislodged the bone chips from the surrounding muscle and into the joint itself. Dr. Jobe said there was no way around surgery. My season, a decent one (11–5, 2.89), was over.

Arm surgery. Those are the scariest two words a pitcher can hear. You never want to be operated on, especially on your pitching arm. I had seen too many fine careers end under the surgeon's knife. The main fear is that you won't be able to come back. Arms are tricky things, and there's never a guarantee you will bounce back from surgery. But Dr. Bob Curlan, one of the finest orthopedic surgeons on the West Coast, agreed with Dr. Jobe, and the two men performed the operation. We wanted to get it done right away, so I could begin my comeback as soon as possible and be ready the following spring. Five days after my slide into home plate, they cut into my arm.

When I woke up in the recovery room, Dr. Jobe was there with Sally. He had me squeeze his fingers and performed a few tests. He said things looked fine. I was starving, and the first thing I asked Sally was to get me a Big Mac and fries from a McDonald's near the hospital.

I was out of the hospital in two days, and we went back home to Scottsdale with my arm in a cast. Ten days later they took the cast off and I started building the arm back up. My mom and dad came out to visit for Thanksgiving, and that's when I first tested my arm. Dad and I went out in the yard and played catch, just as we had done so many years ago in our backyard in Terre Haute.

The writers called me up, asking about the operation.

"I asked Dr. Jobe if he could put a Koufax fastball in my elbow. Well, he did, but it was a Mrs. Koufax fastball."

The rest of the winter I continued with my throwing, and as spring training got closer, the Dodgers sent me a contract, calling for the same salary, $47,000. I immediately sent it back to Campanis with a note.

"Obviously, Al, you made a mistake. Maybe your secretary mistyped. I think that first figure should be 6 and not 4."

Campanis wrote back saying it wasn't a mistake. He said, "We don't know if you can pitch after the operation." Al kept calling me, telling me I had to report. I told him the best way for that to happen was to give me what I wanted, $65,000.

The next day, three days after camp opened, Al called.

"Tommy, if you're here by tomorrow, you've got your money."

That meant scrambling like mad to close the house, close bank accounts, get plane tickets, and do a hundred other errands. The best way to fly to Vero Beach from Phoenix is to fly to L.A. first, then catch a direct flight. I didn't know that at the time, so we had a dreadful Phoenix-Dallas-New Orleans-Miami itinerary. We flew all night, got into Miami at eight A.M., then drove up Florida's east coast to Vero. Sally checked us into the Holiday Inn, and I drove immediately to Dodgertown. What happened next is typical of how baseball operates.

I went straight into Campanis's office, eyes bloodshot, exhausted from the all-night trip.

"You look terrible," he said. "What's wrong?"

"I flew all night."

"Why did you do that?" he asked.

"Didn't you tell me yesterday I'd have my money if I got down here by today?"

"Yeah, but you didn't have to fly all night. You could have left this morning. Just so you left Phoenix by today, that's what I meant."

That's so characteristic of baseball, not telling you what you need to know. I let out an exasperated laugh.

"Where do I sign?"

"Welcome aboard," Al said, beaming. I settled for $63,000.

That spring I learned something about coming back from an injury, and the psychological barrier you have to overcome.

There was no pain in my arm, but I threw the ball just so-so. I pitched in a Grapefruit League game against the Twins, gave up five runs in three innings, and everybody starting asking me about my arm. I mean everybody, from Red Adams to the wives to the beer vendor to the parking lot attendant. This went on for three days, and it was starting to drive me nuts.

Dr. Jobe was the only one who realized what was wrong. He confirmed that physically my arm was fine. He said I could throw as hard as I wanted, and I would not hurt the arm. My problem, he said, was a mental one; I was subconsciously holding back. That night, I lay in bed thinking about that. Finally I made up my mind. Tomorrow I would crash through that barrier, or die trying.

As I left for the park the next morning, I told Sally: "When I come back today, I'm either going to be packing it in and my arm's going to be broken, or I'm going to get these people off my back, hounding me, asking what's wrong with my arm."

I threw on the side for an hour and fifteen minutes, as hard as I could. I couldn't call it pitching. It was just blind throwing. I'd get the ball back from the catcher, rear back, and hurl it with all my might, not even looking where I was throwing. After forty minutes of fastballs, I threw all curves, as hard as I could. When the workout ended, my elbow killed me. I went into the clubhouse, iced it down, then did my running.

The next day the elbow felt much better, so I tried the same thing, but not as long: blind throwing for forty minutes. The arm improved further; it was tender, but not as bad as the day before. The following day there was no pain at all. In my mind, I was back. The next time I pitched, against a Triple A ball club, I went five shutout innings. The ball moved and my sinker was really dropping. I was over the psychological hump.

When players call me now about coming back from arm injuries, I tell them about that barrier. It may take two weeks, six months, or a year to break through it. The doctors can't tell you how long, the trainers can't tell you, the pitching coach can't tell you. You are the only one in the world who knows.

In 1973 the Dodgers started the changeover from the old Wills-Davis-Lefebvre-Gilliam teams to the new one, with Steve Garvey, Dave Lopes, Bill Russell, Ron Cey, Bill Buckner, Tom Paciorek, Joe Ferguson, Lee Lacy, Von Joshua, and Steve Yeager. In all, they brought up eleven players from Triple A.

On most teams such a wholesale turnover means a couple or more losing seasons, as with the rebuilding efforts of the White Sox. But on the Dodgers the restructuring wasn't traumatic at all. The main reason was, by the time the new guys were ready to step in, they felt fully integrated into the team. When these guys were in Triple A, for example, the Dodgers would have them mix with the big league players. They'd eat together, stand in line together, dress together, so that by 1973 the younger players didn't feel intimidated by coming up to the big leagues.

The second factor in the seamless transition was Tommy Lasorda, who managed those guys in Ogden, Utah, in the Pioneer League, up through Albuquerque in Triple A—and later in the majors. His players took on Lasorda's cocky and confident manner. When he managed at Ogden, Tommy actually had his players write a letter to each Dodger at their respective positions. In this letter the young players told who they were and that eventually they would take the veteran's spot on the team.

A perfect example of Lasorda's influence was Dave Lopes. Lasorda not only converted Lopes from an outfielder into a fine second baseman, he converted his personality as well. Before Lasorda, Dave was shy and introverted. Tommy kept telling him to assert himself. And as his confidence grew, Dave did just that, becoming outspoken, a catalyst, a leader. He was a guy whose blazing speed made things happen on the field and whose personality made things happen in the clubhouse. When something needed to be said to a teammate, even if it was critical, Lopes would be the guy to say it.

The 1973 Dodgers started out on fire. We were in first place most of the first half, but on July 1 we lost a crucial doubleheader to the Reds that turned everything around.

We were sitting pretty, the Reds trailing us by eleven games as we went into Riverfront Stadium in Cincinnati to begin a three-game series. Don Sutton had a 3–1 lead in the ninth inning of the first game. In the top of the ninth Ron Cey singled home Willie Davis with what looked to be a vital insurance run. In the bottom of the ninth Tony Perez led off with a fly ball to deep center. Davis, normally an excellent fielder, broke the wrong way. The ball hit his glove but popped out. The scorer initially ruled an error, but changed it to a double.

Sutton buckled down to get Bobby Tolan on a pop out to Lopes, and then busted a fastball by Larry Stahl for strike three. With two outs manager Sparky Anderson went to work. Sparky sent up Johnny Bench to bat for Dave Concepcion. Bench, who wasn't starting because of a pulled muscle in his right leg, represented the tying run. Sutton had started pawing the dirt on the mound, tugging at the bill of his cap, fidgeting. Bench was a tough out for him.

I was sitting on the bench next to Roy Hartsfield, Alston's bench coach.

"Uh-oh," Roy said. "I don't like what I see. He doesn't want to pitch to Bench."

With first base open, Sutton walked Bench on four straight pitches. Darrel Chaney ran for Bench and left-handed-hitting Hal King was sent up to hit for Bill Plummer. King was a chunky, little-used, third-string catcher. He had been to bat just ten times the whole year, with one hit. He ran the count to 2–2, then Don hung a change-up. King unloaded, swinging so hard he tore the bottom of his right shoe. He made solid contact, driving the ball off the facade of the first deck in right field for a three-run home run and a 4–3 win for the Reds. The big Riverfront crowd went crazy as we staggered into the clubhouse.

In the locker room we were stunned, absolutely devastated. That game killed us for the season. We lost another heartbreaker in the nightcap, dropping a 3–2 decision in the tenth on Perez's single. From that time on the Reds caught fire. They swept the series from us, and we lost six in a row. The Reds made up six games in six days and eventually overtook us.

The other knockout punch to our pennant hopes was delivered by our own front office when they released George Culver, the team's tenth pitcher. George didn't get into a lot of games, but he held a vital role as team comic. His antics kept guys loose and kept us in a good frame of mind. When they released him in early September, it upset the chemistry of the team. We couldn't believe it. It was like cutting out our heart. The Dodgers ended up finishing second, 3½ games behind the Reds.

I won my last five decisions in 1973 to finish at 16–7, leading the league with a .696 percentage. Sutton paced us with his 18 wins, with Claude Osteen chipping in with 14. Andy Messersmith (14–10) and Al

Downing (9–9) rounded out the rotation. I recorded a personal milestone on June 8, when I beat the Mets at Shea Stadium for my 100th win.

During the winter Campanis and I reached quick agreement on a new one-year deal for $78,000. In camp in 1974 there was an undefinable spirit, a quiet confidence, a belief among the players that this would be our year. I felt that way myself. We just *knew* we could play championship baseball. The club was nice and loose.

The Dodgers got off to another fast start, and this time we held on. The Reds gave us a furious challenge, playing .605 baseball, but we put it all together, winning 102 games to come out four games on top. Campanis had made a great trade, getting relief closer Mike Marshall from the Expos for Willie Davis. Davis was still a fine player, but his skills were on the decline. Marshall went on to appear in a major league record 106 games, winning 15, saving 21, and copping the Cy Young Award.

Another factor in our success was the emergence of Steve Garvey. Garvey did not change from the day I first met him in 1972, when he was a nobody, through his superstar years. He was Mr. Perfect, always the polite, courteous gentleman. Garv's .312 average, 21 HRs, and 111 RBIs won him a Most Valuable Player award in 1974, and he became the center of the Dodgers's well-oiled P.R. machine.

This bothered some players, however, because of what that did to the Toy Cannon, Jimmy Wynn. Jimmy also had a great season, poling 32 HRs and driving in 108 runs. But he might have done it on the moon, because the publicity was all Garvey. This brought about the beginning of a polarization on the team that took four years to fully blossom.

From my first appearance in the spring, I could do anything I wanted with the baseball. Wherever Yeager or Ferguson put their mitt, I hit it, though don't ask me to explain it. I won my first six starts, giving me eleven consecutive wins over two seasons, one short of Sandy Koufax's club record.

Going for my seventh win, the one to tie Koufax, I had the Phillies beat 2–1 in the bottom of the ninth at Veterans Stadium in Philadelphia. Mike Schmidt led off with a single, then Greg Luzinski bunted, which is in the "Garbo Speaks!" category of unlikelihood. I fielded the bunt, but Lopes and Russell got confused over coverage, and Schmidt beat my throw to second. Alston came out with the hook and brought in Marshall. Mike walked three batters, and I lost 3–2.

I won my next four games, leaving me at 9–1, and everything I touched was gold. If I didn't have my best stuff, the team scored a lot of runs. If they could give me only one run, I pitched a shutout. I was in one of those mysterious zones where you do your pitching from another plane.

I was on top of the world, on a first-place team and holding the best pitching record in baseball. The year, however, was building up to a totally unforeseen and extremely ironic ending.

Ross Newhan wrote a piece on me in *The Sporting News* on June 22. There were two interesting quotes. The first, from Newhan, stated: "It seems certain that one place John will pitch this year is Pittsburgh on July 23, the date of the All-Star game." The second, attributed to me, was: "I kind of feel as if my career is starting all over again. I feel great. *Barring injuries* [my emphasis], I should be able to pitch five or six more years."

Why were these ironic? Regarding the All-Star game, the "certainty" Newhan referred to never happened. Mets manager Yogi Berra left me off the team. First, there were three Dodger pitchers having outstanding years: me, Marshall, and Messersmith—who would finish at 20–6. It's inconceivable that three pitchers from the same staff would be named. Each team had to have at least one representative. The Expos didn't have a position player close to All-Star caliber, so Berra selected pitcher Steve Rogers, who lost 22 games that year. I was upset at Berra, dumbfounded, and disappointed, because I thought I had earned my spot. I was 13–3, and led the league in wins.

My last start before the All-Star game came on July 17 against the Montreal Expos.

That was the nightmare game where the world as I knew it came to a crashing halt.

# 7.
# THE PITCH

fter my first appearance in spring training for the '89 season, Moss Klein wrote in the Newark *Star-Ledger* that it's "almost as though the manager can't accept that John should still be pitching effectively . . . Green's last pro season was 22 years ago. John, pitching at age 45 last year, was 9–8, two more victories than Green had in his best year."

The frosty wall got thicker between Dallas and me. My second outing came on March 8 against Montreal at West Palm Beach. It was pouring rain, with the field wet and muddy. I went another two innings, giving up an unearned run and striking out two. The sinker was working again, and I got my ground balls. But after I finished, no one said anything to me. The Great Silence. When I was done pitching, I was done pitching. Period.

In my third appearance, at Fort Lauderdale on March 12 against the White Sox, Dallas let me go four innings. Pitching in front of the home fans for the first time pumped me up, and in my four innings I allowed no runs, five hits, no walks, and two strikeouts. Once more my sinker was in midseason form.

The press started to notice my pitching, which was beginning to complicate things for Dallas. If I had gone out and gotten hammered three times, it would have taken him off the hook, with his pride intact and people calling for my release. My first three outings, however, gummed up that plan. I was getting to be a pain in the butt for Dallas.

As far as the running of camp, Dallas was excellent. His schedules were efficient and well organized, and things ran smoothly. It was Dallas's show, his Big Top, but his attitude ruined it. Players wondered: "Who does this guy think he is? What did he do to make himself the sage of baseball?" I can't recall one meeting where Dallas didn't talk down to the players.

He even got on Mattingly, like he was a nobody. Donny's a quiet man from Indiana, tough but sensitive. He wants to do his job on the field and be left alone. I think if Dallas had had his way, he would have traded Mattingly. He didn't like Donny's style of play. He liked scrappers like second baseman Steve Sax and shortstop Alvaro Espinoza, the holler guys. He didn't think Mattingly could play that way. I got that impression from observation and from listening to clubhouse conversation. You could figure out where Dallas stood by listening to his coaches.

John Stearns, for example, told me Mattingly couldn't play "situational baseball." Dallas harped on that same thing all spring, so it's obvious Stearns was just repeating what Green had said. I thought it was ridiculous to think about your best hitter as a "situation" player.

"Why would you want your third-place batter, one of the game's great hitters, playing situational baseball?" I asked Stearns. "Your banjo guys play situation baseball: hit and run, bunt people over, get on base, hit to the right side to advance the runners. But not your three–four–five hitters. Those guys have to hit the ball and drive in the runs."

I've never liked the phrase "situational baseball" to begin with, often finding it a euphemism that mediocre ball clubs use to describe their style of play. Billy Connors joined the debate. He said two statistics hold true for championship teams: (1) they are at or near the top in home runs and runs scored, and (2) 70 to 75 percent of the time, the winning team in any given game scores more runs, or as many runs, in just one of their innings as the other team scores in all nine.

It's the old Earl Weaver theory on three-run home runs. Weaver wouldn't bunt. If you bunt three times in a game, that's the equivalent of your team batting one less time. You don't win games by playing situational baseball, you win them with good pitching, good defense, and on offense, home runs.

I don't care if you're making $3 million a year, the negative approach gets to you. Maybe Green's way of motivating Mattingly was to knock him down to try to get him to fight back. I don't know. But if you say to somebody long enough that they can't play, it becomes a mindwash. Donny was exasperated that Dallas would find fault with his play and find it so loudly.

That was Dallas's general approach. His favorite targets in particular were Mattingly, me, Richard Dotson, Don Slaught, whom Dallas seemed to think was the dumbest person that ever came down the road, and Pagliarulo, whom he wanted off the team.

Dallas hated Pagliarulo in the worst way. That was puzzling, because Pags's batting stroke was made for the short porch in right field at Yankee Stadium.

Pags could relate to my problems with Dallas, and he became, along with Mattingly and Righetti, my biggest backer on the team.

"Show that S.O.B. what you can do," he'd say.

Most of the team was pulling for me also, and that made a huge difference. Whenever I'd have a good outing, guys would come over to me and say things like: "You showed that bastard you can still pitch. Wonder how he liked it?"

"I'm not trying to show him up," I'd say. "I'm just trying to make the ball club."

But I can see what I meant to the rest of the ball club, a club that was learning to hate its manager. I became a rallying point, a symbol against his condescension. They loved it when I did well.

Fans don't really know what goes on with the Yankees. The common perception is that the Yankees are a team always in turmoil, with players fighting among themselves. But for all the perceived dissension, through all the managerial firings, the team got along pretty well as a group. It was a loose ball club. It used to be even looser, when they had Piniella, Catfish, Munson, Rivers, Reggie, and Nettles. Nettles was one of the funniest guys I've ever been around. But Yankee ball players are no more insecure, or unhappy, or disgruntled, than players on any other ball club. The only difference is coverage. In Kansas City, controversies stay pretty much in the clubhouse. In New York City, the media capital of the world, controversy becomes headline news. Any disagreement, however slight, becomes disaster on the unrestrained battlefields of headline warfare.

George Steinbrenner is a perfect example. His every word is scrutinized for any hint of controversy. George is not shy, and the coverage he gets results in a misperception in New York not only of George, but also of the team. They think the atmosphere is constantly combative, a war zone. That's not a knock on the fans, because New York fans are among the most astute and loyal in baseball. It's simply a reflection of the state of media relations with the New York press and the Yankees.

Steinbrenner's sports background is football. He played the game in college at Culver Military Academy and at Williams College. He later served as an assistant coach at Northwestern for Lou Saban and at Purdue for Stu Holcomb in the Big Ten. To understand George, you need to be aware of that background. In football, you yell and scream at guys to fire them up. That makes them better football players. But that approach doesn't translate well to baseball, something that George doesn't grasp. George's approach is basically: "If you can't get the job done, I'll get someone who can." That line of attack may work in football, business, and war, but not baseball, and it has cost him enormous P.R. problems, as in the case of Bucky Dent's firing in June 1990 in Boston.

The thing that fascinated George about Dallas was his reputation as a tough guy, a General Patton type, who could come in and restore discipline. Green would tell us: "If you do it my way, you'll be better." I remember somebody asking: "Well, what is his way?" No one quite knew. Except he had a habit of starting off sentences with: "When I was with the Phillies . . ."

He kept bringing up the Phillies. He won there, true, but look at the team he had. Pete Rose, Joe Morgan, Larry Bowa, Mike Schmidt, Bob Boone, Greg Luzinski, Gary Maddox, Bake McBride, Steve Carlton, Tug McGraw, Ron Reed, John Denny, and Charles Hudson. That team was stuffed with talent. They won in 1977 and '78 under Danny Ozark, and they won in '80 and '81 under Dallas. He walked into that situation. The '80 and '81 Phillies weren't a project. The 1989 Yankees, however, were. We hadn't won anything since 1981. We had some good individual players, but hadn't put the whole team together. We were in disarray, lousy on fundamentals, and I don't think Dallas was prepared for that. You could tell that from the way he vented his frustrations in the press.

"We stink. We can't field. Our pitchers can't throw a strike to save their lives . . ." Dallas would tell the press. Day in, day out, that kind of rhetoric had a numbing effect on the players.

My dad came down to Fort Lauderdale to stay with us for ten days around the middle of camp. He felt the way Sally and I did when we first came down, that he wasn't a part of it anymore. In other years he'd come into the clubhouse and talk to the players. But with Dallas around, Dad wasn't allowed to go inside, so he stayed away. The new clubhouse security policy stated that "all playing fields, dugouts, clubhouses, and related facilities and areas remain off-limits to all but essential personnel." Fathers, wives, and children were not "essential personnel." The policy also meant I could no longer bring my sons Tommy, Travis, and Taylor on the field after practice and play ball with them, as we had in previous years.

After watching his first practice, Dad came back to the house befuddled.

"Whatever happened between those two [me and Dallas]?" he asked Sally. "Did Tommy ever do anything or say anything to provoke Dallas? Because it looks as if Dallas just hates him."

Dad, who was seventy-nine and had been there every step of the way throughout my career, had a hard time observing the workout.

"Sally, I couldn't watch it. I've never seen Tommy working so hard. He was hurting. I felt all the pain he was going through. It just tears my heart out. It wouldn't be bad if only he was getting a fair deal."

"But Dallas is giving him the chance to pitch," Sally said.

"Tommy may make it through spring training," Dad answered, "but Dallas is going to get him in the end."

I had pitched well all spring, but my heels were killing me. That's what bothered Dad. Though I tried to hide it, he could see my pain. I was fooling other people, but I couldn't fool my dad, who knew me almost better than I knew myself. He felt bad for me, that all my work might be in vain. I had no choice, though. Older ball players do not have the luxury of nursing, or showing, their injuries.

In 1987 in a game at West Palm Beach, for example, a batter hit a routine ground ball to the right side. It came up nice for Dan Pasqua, the first baseman. It looked like he'd make the play, unassisted. A pitcher automatically breaks to the right side on a ball like that. It's instinctive. When Pasqua fielded it, I slowed down, thinking he'd take the play himself. Pasqua had not played much first base, however, and for some reason he hesitated going to the bag. He took the ball out of his glove, looking to toss it to me. Now I had to start up again, into a sprint. When I did that, boom, I pulled my right quadricep muscle. I kept running to the bag and bobbled the throw for an error.

The leg went into a spasm, with a stabbing pain. Pasqua came running over. I got down into a catcher's crouch, trying to hide the fact that I was seriously hurt.

"Tommy, are you okay?" Pasqua asked. "It was my fault. I should have taken that ball myself."

I laughed and lied: "Don't worry about it. The ball just hit me in the solar plexus and knocked the wind out of me. I'll be okay."

The trainer came out and I repeated the fib about the wind getting knocked out of me. I went behind the mound and doubled over, pretending to catch my breath but actually trying to stretch the leg out. The main thing on my mind was not to let anyone know I was hurt, because if I'm hurt, I'm done. You can't be forty-three and hurt. So I faked working with my stomach, all the while trying to stretch the leg. It's the old magician's decoy. Let the audience look at something else, while you perform sleight of hand, or in this case, sleight of leg.

I finished the inning, and as I came off the field, every time I picked up my leg, it killed me. But I couldn't show it or say anything. To make matters worse, I batted in the next inning and singled. Now I had to run to first base. Somebody bunted me over to second, but I couldn't run. So I jogged, hoping I'd get thrown out. It didn't happen. The play was made at first. I got as far as third base, and was stranded there as the inning ended. I walked back to the dugout and my teammates were all over me for my lack of speed on the basepaths.

"You looked like Amos McCoy out there," someone ragged, and guys started doing impersonations of a hobbling Walter Brennan. I played along with the joke, ignoring my pain.

"I need baserunning help. I'm going to report early tomorrow morning for baserunning instruction."

Everybody's laughing, and I couldn't tell the truth: the reason I couldn't run was because I had blown out my right quad.

I somehow completed my five innings. Fortunately, I had missed the team bus that morning and had driven myself to the park. So I was able to drive, unseen, to nearest 7-Eleven, where I bought a bag of ice. I mashed the ice out in the parking lot by beating it into the ground, and then strapped the ice to my quad with a big Ace bandage that I had in the car. One thought raced through my mind: don't let anyone on the team see you like this.

The ball club couldn't know about the injury, because that would have been the end of me, so I sought treatment on the sly with a physical therapist I knew, Dana Van Pelt. Each morning for the next several days I'd visit Dana at seven A.M., and he'd put me through these torturous exercises. He'd stretch and bend my leg to the point where I'd be screaming in pain. Then I'd leave, get to the park, do my workouts, and at the end of the day head back to Dana's for more treatment. I got well enough to bluff my way through camp, and when the season started, I never missed a turn. And to this day nobody ever knew there was something wrong with my leg in the spring of '87.

But there are some injuries you can't hide.

On July 17, 1974, I threw what I now call "The Pitch."

The Dodgers were at home against Montreal. We built up a 4–0 lead through three innings, and I was cruising to my fourteenth win. In the top of the fourth Willie Davis led off and beat out a bunt single. I walked Bob Bailey on a borderline, inside 3–2 pitch. I thought I had Bailey struck out, but home plate ump Harry Wendlestedt didn't. Harry would give you pitches an inch or two outside the plate, but on the inside you had to be right on the black. That brought up Hal Breeden, a good pull hitter. I was looking to get a ground ball for a double-play.

My first pitch to Breeden was . . . strange. As I came forward and released the ball, I felt a kind of nothingness, as if my arm weren't there, then I heard a "pop" from inside my arm, and the ball just blooped up to the plate.

I didn't feel soreness or pain at this point, but just the strange sensation that my arm wasn't there. It was the oddest thing I'd ever felt while pitching. I shook my left arm, more baffled than concerned. My next pitch would be the last one I threw in a big league game for the next twenty-one months.

I released the ball, and this time I heard a slamming sound, like a collision coming from inside my elbow. It felt as if my arm had come off. I immediately called time and started walking off the mound. Walt Alston came running out in that tippy-toe run of his. I just walked past him, saying, "Walter, you'd better get somebody in there, because I hurt my arm."

I walked into the dugout, got my jacket, and went right upstairs into the clubhouse. I took my uniform off, stripped down to my shorts, put a dry sweatshirt on, and waited for Dr. Frank Jobe, who was there in two minutes.

The Dodgers clubhouse is not off limits to the press. They can go anywhere except the food room where the players eat, and in the doctor's office. Dr. Jobe examined my arm in the trainer's room, and there was a crush of media pushing and jockeying for position, yelling out questions such as "How does it feel?" "Tommy, what's happening?"

All I said was: "It's a little sore. I don't know anything more."

Sally, who was in the stands, come flying into the clubhouse. She knew it was bad. Dr. Jobe told me to go home, ice it down, and come in the office the next day at two P.M. The arm was in a spasm, and he wanted to calm it down so he could get a better look. The arm didn't hurt, so I had no unusual concerns that night when I went to sleep. The next morning the phone didn't stop ringing. In L.A. this was a big story, since the Dodgers were in first place by 6½ games, and their best pitcher had walked off the mound injured. I told the press it was a cramp, and not expected to be serious.

One TV story angered me. The reporter said I had hurt my arm overthrowing, trying to show up Yogi Berra for leaving me off the All-Star team. The ignorant story was dreamed up by someone who obviously knew nothing about pitching in general and knew even less about me in particular. True, I was furious with Berra's decision to leave me off the team, but that was the last thing on my mind when I went out to face the Expos in my next start.

The next day, Dr. Jobe examined me, took some X rays, studied them, shook his head, and then said he thought I had torn some ligaments in the elbow. He sent me to see Dr. Herb Stark, a well-respected colleague, for a second opinion. Dr. Stark, from Tennessee, had a disarming "country doctor" manner. He examined me, looked at the X rays, and let out a sigh.

"Boy, I tell you what," Dr. Stark drawled. "You sure did it this time, didn't you? I sure wouldn't want to be in your spot right now. Shoot . . . tell you what. Why don't you go on down to the ball park, and I'll call up Frank and we'll talk it over and let you know what's going to happen."

When I got to the park, Dr. Jobe called me into his office.

"We think you've torn the ligament in your elbow, but we're not certain. The elbow is really unstable. Without surgery, we can't tell if you've just strained the ligament, if you've torn it completely off the bone, if you've torn it in the middle, or what. Why don't you rest it for two or three weeks. That will give the tissue plenty of time to calm down. Then you start back slowly. If it's torn, we'll know."

# The Pitch

I assumed the best, that it was a slight strain. Three weeks put me on target for a late August/early September return, in time for the stretch drive. After three weeks of rest I joined the ball club on the road at Shea Stadium. I was scheduled to throw batting practice, so I lightly warmed up on the side for about twenty minutes and my arm felt pretty good. But when I got on the mound for b.p., I couldn't throw a strike; in fact, I had trouble even reaching the plate. The high surface of the mound creates a drag on your arm that you don't get throwing on flat ground, and my pitches were coming into the vicinity of home plate from a dozen different directions. Even more troubling was the fact that the elbow started throbbing with pain.

In the clubhouse, trainer Bill Buhler taped up the elbow like you would a sprained ankle and I did the rest of my throwing out in the bullpen. With the support of the arm bandage, I could reach the plate, but with no pop on the ball whatsoever, and no control. I threw overhand, three-quarters, sidearm, everything I could think of, and nothing worked. It was incredibly frustrating.

On our next stop, right around Labor Day in Atlanta, I called Sally from my hotel room and we had a long talk. We agreed that it might be time for an operation. I called Dr. Jobe at home, reporting on my lack of progress.

"What do you think?" I asked him.

"I think you need an operation," the doctor said, "but it's not important what I think. *You* have to be the one who wants the operation, because if you don't think you need it, your chances of coming back are shot. You won't be in the right frame of mind for rehabilitation. And I won't kid you. It's going to be a long rehab." Sally and I decided do it now and concentrate on next year.

In orthopedic surgery, rehab is the most important factor in determining success. You can have two identical surgeries done on two identical arm or knee injuries by the same doctor, and in *every* case, the guy who makes it back is the one who can handle rehab in a positive, enthusiastic way. The guy who goes into it halfheartedly will not make it back.

I thought about it, and said I would do anything, no matter how arduous, no matter how tedious, to get my arm back in shape.

"Then I think you're ready for an operation," Dr. Jobe said.

"Okay. Let's get it done."

I called Sally back from my Atlanta hotel room.

"It's time. I need an operation."

She agreed. The team flew from Atlanta to San Francisco. From there I flew into Orange County Airport, where Sally picked me up.

Dr. Jobe told me he didn't want to operate on my arm without assistance. If he found a tear in the middle of the ligament and he had to do the transplant, he wanted Herb Stark and other respected colleagues on hand to help him.

"I want as many good minds in that room with me as I can get," Dr. Jobe told me. "I've never done anything like this."

Nor had anyone else. A similar operation had been done on polio patients, but never on a pitcher's arm. He said he didn't want to go in the operating room alone. That told me that he was a brilliant surgeon —much in the same way Red Adams proved his intelligence by admitting to me he made a mistake about my pitching motion. Here was a human being, I thought . . . not a superdoctor, but a human being who happens to be a doctor.

Before the operation, Dr. Jobe told Sally what he expected to find if he cut into the arm.

"If there's only a slight tear, I'll surgically repair it and the rehab will be a short one. He'll be pitching soon. If the ligament's torn off at both ends of the bone, it's easy to simply staple the ligament to the bone, it will grow back, and he'll be pitching next year. But if it's torn in the middle, that's the worst-case scenario, because the ligament would be unrepairable. We'd have to transplant ligament from the wrist area of his right hand in the elbow or use a teflon ligament. It's an operation that's never been done before, and we don't even know if it will work."

"What would his chances be of coming back if you had to transplant ligaments?" she asked, holding her breath.

"Well, the chances of him pitching again would be slim."

"How slim?"

"I'd say a fair guesstimate is he'd have a one in a hundred chance. Maybe."

"What are his chances if he doesn't have the operation?"

"None."

"None at all?" Sally asked.

"Zero chances in a hundred."

Dr. Jobe found a date when the assisting doctors would be free— September 25. To make things more interesting, Sally was pregnant with our first child, and the baby was due September 27. Accompanied

146

# The Pitch

by Sally and her mom Opal, I checked into the Centinela Hospital in Inglewood the evening of September 24. As I slept that night, I knew that if I woke up after the operation and found my right forearm bandaged, the worst had happened. That meant that the ligament was torn in the middle and the doctors had to do a transplant. Dr. Jobe had not given me the "one chance in a hundred" prognosis, but he didn't have to. I knew if he had to transplant I'd be in deep trouble. I prayed that night with the raw, unadorned power of despair.

The next morning, at seven A.M., with the anesthetic kicking in, Sally kissed my cheek:

"We'll be praying for you, Tommy."

I was wheeled into the operating room. At seven-twenty the doctors laid back the skin and underlying tissue. The only thing holding my elbow together was the skin and the nerve running through the joint. The ligament was torn in two. The muscles on the inside of the arm were ripped loose also and were sitting two inches out of place, toward my wrist. The ulnar nerve was badly bruised. One of the assisting doctors said he had never seen anything like it, saying it looked like "a bunch of spaghetti in there."

The operation took three hours. They took the six-inch-long palmaris longus tendon from my right forearm and threaded it through holes drilled above and below the elbow. The tendon was woven back and forth across the joint, and the muscles were repositioned.

When I came out of sleep in the recovery room, I coughed loose a throat tube and—my head in a cottony fog—tried to reach over to my right forearm. The left arm was heavily bandaged, but I managed to run my fingers on my right inside forearm to the wrist. It was bandaged too.

A dark chill went down my spine and my stomach sank. They did the transplant. I thought for sure my career was over.

Dr. Jobe came by later and talked to me: "You know what we had to do?"

"Yeah. You had to transplant."

"That's right, Tommy. I just want you to know what's in store for you. You've got an extremely long and hard rehabilitation ahead of you. We aren't sure what to expect."

"But will I pitch again?"

Dr. Jobe's face darkened. "The chances of you pitching again are about one in a hundred. I've told the O'Malleys, and they're willing to

147

see you through to next year, to see what you can do. But if I were speaking to you not as your doctor but as a friend, I would strongly advise you to start making other plans, looking for another line of work."

"One in a hundred, huh?" I asked him. "I'll take it." Oddly enough, my spirits were much better after hearing the odds. Fine, I thought. If I've got one chance in a hundred, that's all I need. It's not as good as two chances in a hundred, but it's better than no chance at all. All I want is a chance.

Of course, I didn't fully realize how serious the operation was and just how grueling the rehab actually would be. Sometimes, only a little knowledge is a good thing, because if I had known all the facts, I'm sure I couldn't have reacted so positively, or should I say, so naively. That naiveté saved me.

Following the operation, I had to be fed, dressed, and bathed . . . just like my new infant daughter, Tamara, who was born two days after my operation. I managed to be there in the delivery room to witness the miracle.

Sally called me from home at six in the morning on September 27.

"Tommy, I'm starting labor. If you want to see your baby born, you've gotta get out of the hospital."

Dr. Jobe discharged me, ordering me to come back and see him later in the day after the baby was born. He had to look under my cast.

My neighbor, Ed Varvello, picked me up at the hospital and drove me home. Sally was slouched in a chair, having contractions every four or five minutes. We packed her suitcase, and by the afternoon it was time to get her to the hospital. Ed wasn't there, so I had to drive Sally and her mom myself. I drove one-handed, and managed pretty well. All the anesthetic was out of me and my head was clear. When we pulled up to the hospital, they ran up with a wheelchair—for me! I was unshaven, in rumpled clothes, all bandaged up, and they had assumed I was the patient.

"No, it's for my wife!"

They wheeled Sally into the labor room. Since I could barely hold a pen, I dictated the responses to the nurse at the admitting desk for the paperwork, then eked out a scrawl that passed for a signature. When I got to the delivery room, they put me in a surgical gown, and I watched our first child being born.

# The Pitch

The sight made me forget my own troubles; I was almost dizzy with joy. It was like being present for the Creation itself. I couldn't get over how perfect the baby was, a fully formed person in miniature. To me, it was miraculous and the greatest thing I'd ever experienced in my life.

Soon after my operation, I lost all feeling in the little finger of my left hand. In the weeks after, the whole hand went dead and clawed up. The ulnar nerve had been bruised and twisted, and when the doctors put it back in its channel, scar tissue grew over the nerve. I lost complete use of my arm almost up to the elbow, leaving me with what they call a simian monkey hand. Monkeys don't have an ulnar nerve and that's why their hands and fingers curl. My hand looked like an ugly claw.

The Dodgers, meanwhile, had continued their winning ways and wrapped up the divisional flag. At the end of the season, Peter O'Malley called me and thanked me for my contributions to the team. He said that without my pitching, the team wouldn't have made it to the playoffs. He then invited me to throw out the first ball of Game Three of the playoffs, at Dodger Stadium.

As a nonroster player, I had to get Pirates manager Danny Murtaugh's permission to sit in uniform on the Dodger bench. I asked Danny about it.

"No, I can't do that, Tommy. I can't let you."

I looked at him, surprised, thinking, What the heck?

"Well," Danny said, his eyes twinkling, "maybe on one condition."

"What's that?"

"You have to let me sign your cast," he said with a wide grin.

The team won twice in Pittsburgh, 3–0 behind Don Sutton and 5–2 behind Andy Messersmith and Mike Marshall. The pregame atmosphere at Dodger Stadium for Game Three on October 8 was festive. P.A. announcer John Ramsey intoned to the capacity crowd: "Here's a man who helped make this moment possible . . . Tommy John."

I took the mound to a loud cheer. My mom and dad were in the stands with Sally, and they were crying, because they thought that would be my last time on the Dodger Stadium mound. I threw the ball in right-handed. As I walked off, I received a tremendous standing ovation, and I wondered if this was my last hurrah.

The Dodgers lost that night, but wrapped up the series the next night, with Sutton taking a 12–1 laugher. In the series, however, the Oakland A's took us in five games. It was a weird series, in that three of our four losses, and our only win, were by identical 3–2 scores. It was wonderful for the team to be in the Series, but having been out of action for so long, I felt like I wasn't part of it.

After the season my cast was changed weekly. Dr. Jobe looked at me over the weeks, and with no improvement in my clawed hand, told me I needed another operation to unknot the ulnar nerve and reroute it on the inside of the elbow, through the fatty tissue, where there would be no scar tissue formations. He was straight with me: if the operation wasn't successful, I'd have a clawed hand the rest of my life. Not only would my pitching career be over, but I'd also have a permanent deformity.

The second operation was scheduled for December 15. The Dodgers kept it hush-hush. They even kept Sally and me away from the team's annual Christmas party so I wouldn't have to answer any questions from the press. Dr. Jobe went back into my elbow a second time, in a secret operation. He scraped the scar tissue off the ulnar nerve and repositioned the nerve out of the way of the new tendon.

Before we left Yorba Linda to spend Christmas in Indiana, Dr. Jobe examined me and declared the second operation a success. He told me the nerve would have to regenerate before I regained full use of my left hand. If things went well, the nerve would grow at the rate of about an inch a month. The nerve was damaged for about eighteen inches, so he told me to figure on eighteen months before it came back fully.

Since no pitcher had ever had this kind of operation, no pitcher had ever come back from it. No one knew what to expect. We were making medical history. Even if Dr. Jobe said I had no chance, I probably would have tried to come back anyway, until I proved to *myself* that I couldn't do it. Until *I* knew it couldn't be done, no one could tell me.

In January, after sixteen weeks, they took the cast off for the last time. The arm was thin, with the muscles atrophied. The skin hung down, all loose and white, and my clawed hand looked positively skeletal. Dr. Jobe told me not to worry about appearances. If all continued well, I might be able to throw from a mound by midsummer, he said. I settled in for the long rehab.

For me, 1975 would be a rebuilding year, pure and simple. I worked hard, seven days a week, on exercises Dr. Jobe gave me to strengthen the arm. I even threw lightly, with Sally as my catcher. I still couldn't use my fingers, so I had to shove the baseball into my left claw with

Author's Collection

My first team in organized ball was Art Compton Cleaners in Terre Haute, Ind. My father, Tommy Sr., back row left, coached. I'm in the second row, far right, wearing my game face. This would be in 1954.

Gerstmeyer celebrates the sectional championship win that propelled the team into the 1954 state finals. I'm kneeling in the front row, holding the trophy. I was the team's mascot. No. 35 in the back row is Arley Andrews. Arley later signed as a pitcher with the Phillies, and taught me how to throw a curve.

Author's Collection

Author's Collection

My Babe Ruth League team was state champ in 1957. I'm in the back row, second from right, looking wicked in my flattop. I played first base and pitched. My dad is in the middle row, far left.

Author's Collection

A buzz cut and a senior's smile. In the 1960-61 basketball season at Gerstmeyer, I was all-city, all-Wabash Valley, all-Western Indiana Conference. Some 35 colleges offered me full scholarships, setting up my first big career decision: basketball or baseball.

Tommy John

Courtesy of Ken Coleman

Two hard-throwing leftys. Well, one, anyway. With Sam McDowell in Tucson, Ariz., 1962, my first spring camp after signing with the Indians.

I was traded to the White Sox in 1965. Later, Eddie Stanky became our manager. I learned more about baseball from Eddie than from any other manager. I wish I could have played for him another ten years.

Courtesy of the Chicago White Sox

Courtesy of the Chicago White Sox

Warming up at Comiskey Park in the summer of love, 1967. We got into one of baseball's all-time great pennant races that year.

Courtesy of the National Baseball Library, Cooperstown, NY

Your typical spring training shot, this taken at Arthur Allyn Field in Sarasota, 1968. "Let me see your follow through" the photographer would yell, and you'd oblige, trying not to look too befuddled.

Courtesy of the Los Angeles Dodgers

/Wide World

AP/Wide World

LEFT: After I blew out my arm in July, 1974, almost everyone thought I'd never pitch again. And I didn't . . . until the 1976 season. My first win since the devastating arm injury came in this game, when I downed the Pirates at Dodger Stadium on April 28. I never worked harder at anything in my life than I did on my comeback.

RIGHT: Here it is, the instant of my greatest moment as a ballplayer. I've just recorded the final out of my complete-game victory over the Phillies in the rain, giving the Dodgers the 1977 National League pennant and a trip to the World Series.

OPPOSITE: La-La Land. In 1972, I joined the Dodgers and learned how a winning organization did things. This picture was taken that spring, at Al Lang Field in St. Petersburg, Fla.

Courtesy of the National Baseball Library, Cooperstown, N

I found a home in the Big Apple. In my first two years with the Yankees, I posted a 43-18 mark, making me the majors' winningest pitcher in that time.

Courtesy of Bob Olen/New York Post

On Oct. 9, 1981, Reggie Jackson took my son Travis to the mound to throw out the first pitch of the third game of the 1981 divisional playoffs at Yankee Stadium. The night capped a miraculous recovery for Travis, who was critically injured after falling out a three-story window nearly two months earlier.

Courtesy of the California Angels

Family day at Anaheim in the summer of 1984. That's Tami and Tommy III in front. I'm holding Travis. Sally's got an armful of Taylor. Family days were always part of the John household.

The A's gave me a chance after the Angels released me in 1985. In Oakland, I got my head together after a numbing series of professional and personal setbacks. By the way, I think I ran faster in white shoes.

Courtesy of Barton Silverman

When I rode west to join Gene Autry's Angels late in the 1982 season, I thought it would be my final hitching post. It didn't work out that way, though.

Author's Collection

I had to go down to Ft. Lauderdale in a rehab assignment in 1986. Hard work's always a little easier when my family is there supporting me. Here, Travis and I share a moment in the dugout.

Courtesy of the New York Yankees

Another family day, this one at Yankee Stadium in 1987. We looked good in pinstripes.

thor's Collection

I get a lot of enjoyment from coaching my son's Little League team, the way my dad did with me when I was a boy. Here, I evaluate talent while young Tommy, right, warms up.

Author's Collection

The Mick and I. Mick helped me celebrate my birthday on May 22, 1989 at his restaurant in Manhattan. Mantle was the Bo Jackson of his time, a man with brute power and blinding speed. I was the last active pitcher to give up a homer to Mickey.

Enjoying Columbus Day, 1989, at Warren "Bud" Haggerty's farm in Wallingford, VT.

Courtesy of Nancy Thayer-Haggerty

What do you say about someone who means so much to you? Sally's unwavering support and strength have made the difference to me more than once. We were at Caesar's in Lake Tahoe, summer 1990, when a roving photographer came by to snap this picture. Believe me, we didn't have to paste on the smiles.

Courtesy of the New York Yankees

Fit and ready to start spring training, February 1989. I was facing the long-est odds of my career.

my right hand. The index and middle fingers were hooked, with the ring finger and pinky finger completely folded back into my palm. It wasn't a pretty sight.

I worked as hard as I possibly could on my rehabilitation. I never wanted to look back and say: "Son of a gun, maybe if I'd worked a little harder in 1975, I might have come back." That goes back to something Eddie Stanky used to tell me.

"When you don't give it your all and it loses you a game, you can lie and blame it on someone else. But when you look in the mirror at night, your reflection says: 'That wasn't true. It was *your* fault. You didn't do all that you could.' But when you walk off the field knowing you did everything you possibly could do, you can accept defeat."

That's one of the things Stanky said that really hit home with me. Always give a hundred percent, and you'll never have to second-guess yourself. I never, ever, wanted to look back on my rehabilitation and think: "If only . . ."

As spring training arrived in 1975, I was determined to make the best possible effort. I did all the work the other pitchers did, except throwing. I could move my arm through a normal pitching motion, but with the nerve not fully grown, I could only throw the ball by placing it in the shriveled claw and pulling the fingers over the ball with my right hand.

Then I worked out a way to throw where I taped my first two fingers together to keep them from spreading. I would set the ball in my glove, then place my hand on the ball. There was no feeling or control in the fingers of my left hand, but I was actually able to throw a ball that way.

After team exercises and drills, when the pitchers hurled batting practice, I went by myself to throw the ball against a concrete practice wall. This was similar to a return wall in tennis, where the infielders could work on fielding techniques by themselves. The wall was about twenty feet long and eight feet high. Day after day, for six weeks, I threw against this wall. It took on an almost symbolic aspect, representing the "wall" that I was trying to break through. I'd take four or five balls, throw them against the wall, pick them up again, and continue until I felt tired.

I started out throwing pathetic little bloopers from about twenty feet away. Gradually, and with much effort, I got to forty and sometimes even fifty feet away. It made for a sorry picture, the once and former major leaguer, tossing feeble bleeders against a concrete wall, looking as polished as a little boy throwing a ball against the steps of his back porch.

One piece of scripture sustained me, and became like a mantra to me, and that was Phil. 4:13.

"For with God, nothing shall be impossible."

Miracles happened thousands of years ago. But could a miracle happen today? Why not? What was faith, if not for moving mountains? And what was a miracle? To me, it didn't mean the impossible happening, but rather, the achieving of all that is possible.

One day when I was going through my lonely wall drill, Ben Wade, the head of scouting, ambled by. Ben was the only man in the entire camp, besides Tommy John, who believed my comeback work might not be in vain. Ben had been watching me every day as I went through my workout.

"How's your arm feel?" he asked me.

Everyone was asking me this question, but in virtually every case, the "concern" was forced—even robotic, as if it were simply something they *had* to ask to be polite—belying the questioner's unexpressed belief that I was wasting my time. I've always been pretty good at reading faces and intuitively feeling out situations. Ben asked me the question in a different way, in a sincere, honest, even touching way.

"The arm feels good, Ben, other than my fingers."

"You don't have any soreness?"

"No, Ben. None."

"Are you telling me the truth?"

"Yes, I am," I answered. "My arm doesn't hurt a bit. It just feels stiff from not being used."

"Then I'll tell you this. I've had my eye on you, and you're improving. You're throwing nice and loose. You're not holding anything back. If you can project that six to eight months down the road, you're gonna pitch again."

"Well, you're the only one who thinks that."

"Tommy, I've been around a long time. Believe me. From my knowledge of scouting and watching kids, you're gonna pitch again."

Those last words had a magic effect on me, almost like medicine.

When the Dodgers broke camp, I stayed at Vero Beach and continued my daily workouts, following a hot-and-cold therapy devised by Dr. Jobe where we alternated ice baths with hot packs as hot as I could stand it. Trainer Jack Homel and head trainer Bill Buhler also gave me massages and ultrasound treatment.

I rejoined the club in Los Angeles shortly after the season began. Buhler then came up with a classically simple, yet extremely effective exercise that I could do whenever and wherever I wanted: the Silly-Putty therapy. He had me buy several eggs of Silly-Putty, combine them into a big ball, and told me to knead the ball constantly, trying to get strength and mobility back into the fingers. That Silly-Putty went everywhere with me. Dr. Jobe had a variation of the exercise. He had me cut the shaft of one of my golf clubs just below the grip. I'd keep the grip in my hand, squeezing it constantly.

We were living in Yorba Linda, right on the golf course, and golf was part of my therapy. A typical day would be golf before breakfast, a run—anywhere from one to six miles—breakfast, followed by more golf. About four in the afternoon I'd drive into the ball park for workouts with the team and therapy with the trainers.

Then came the first major milestone in my comeback.

On the way to the ball park one June day I absentmindedly took my left hand off the wheel to stretch it. Both the ring finger and the pinky finger uncurled. That was the first time they had done that since the operation. They curled back again into their paralyzed position, and I consciously tried to uncurl them. The hand opened and closed, like a *normal hand*!

I was ecstatic and let out a shout of glee. The nerve had grown far enough to permit movement. I couldn't wait to get home that night and show Sally.

"Close your eyes, I've got something to show you."

The left hand was behind my back.

"Okay, now open them."

I began to open and close the hand. She let out a scream. We were like kids with a new toy. We jumped up and down in joy, laughing and hugging each other. That was the turning point in my recovery, because after that I could really start into serious throwing. It was a long, slow process, and I worked at it every day, pushing myself to the limit. I started throwing on the sidelines for twenty minutes each day to Mark Cresse, our bullpen catcher.

The first true indication I would actually make it back came just before the All-Star break. We were in Pittsburgh on a hot, muggy night.

Pitching to Cresse, I worked up a good sweat, got nice and loose, started feeling really good, and just kept throwing the ball harder and harder for about forty minutes. At the end, I let go with a few good *major league* pitches.

When we were done, Cresse said that was by far the best I had thrown yet.

"Tommy! That ball had some pop!" he said, amazed. "Before, the ball was just plopping into my glove. But that ball tonight came in— boom! boom!—with explosiveness. That was great!"

I threw hard the next night in Pittsburgh, then the next day in St. Louis, where I pitched batting practice for the first time, spinning off fastballs and even curves. I could feel my arm getting stronger and stronger. Counting throwing on the side, batting practice, and bullpen pitching, my throwing amounted to about an hour each day.

After the All-Star break Ben Wade came out to the bullpen to watch me pitch.

"Boy, that's a long way from Vero Beach," he said.

Cresse added: "He could probably win with what he's throwing right now."

In batting practice one August night I whistled a sinking fastball past Jimmy Wynn, who swung and badly missed. Wynn stepped out of the box with a big grin on his face.

"Damn, T.J. You've got it back, man."

I was getting better each time out. But after a certain point, you can only do so much in batting practice and pitching in the bullpen. The next test would be against live opposition in a game situation, against actual batters trying their hardest to hit me.

The Dodgers wanted me to go to the Instructional League in Arizona and pitch a few games. I couldn't wait.

On September 29, I pitched my first game at Mesa, at old Rendez-vous Park against a California Angels instructional team. Sally and Tami were there, as well as Campanis. It was a blazing, early autumn day, with temperatures in the high 90s, low 100s. They had me on a fifty-pitch limit.

Warming up in the bullpen, I felt edgy, like I was making my first major league appearance. My mind was a blank. All I was thinking about was throwing strikes. On the bench before my appearance on the mound in the bottom of the first, I wiped my brow with a towel, keeping it over my head. My young teammates nervously avoided me, I think in part awed by the veteran pitcher, in part wanting to leave me alone with my thoughts. They were basically college kids, in their first year or two of professional ball.

The first batter I faced was the Angels' number-one draft choice, Danny Goodwin. My first two pitches were balls. One thing I hate, bad arm or good arm, is not throwing strikes. If you haven't faced batters in a while and you get into a game, it feels completely different. There's no batting cage, no screen in front of you, and behind the plate you see the grandstands, the fans, the umpire. You aren't focused; everything's a distraction.

Catcher Brad Gulden called for a curveball, a surprise pitch on a 2–0 count.

What the heck, I thought, why not?

The breaking ball snapped in for a called strike, straightening Goodwin up. I came back with a sinking fastball, and Goodwin beat it into the ground at short for an easy 6–3 putout. My old friend the grounder had reintroduced itself. I went through three perfect innings, with four strikeouts, 39 pitches, and a slew of ground balls. I wanted to pitch another inning or two, but the coaches stuck to the preset limit: either three innings or fifty pitches, whichever came first.

When I left the mound after the third, I felt as if I had won the seventh game of the World Series. Sally, with Tami in her arms, gave me the thumbs-up sign from the stands. The fans gave me a nice round of applause. In the dugout my young teammates congratulated me. I shook each hand with an easy smile. I started four more games in the Instructional League, working myself up to seven innings. The arm felt better after each outing. My curveball was snapping and the fastball had a good tail. It was "pitching," as opposed to "throwing." There was no doubt in my mind now: I was ready to take my turn in 1976 and come back from the pitching dead.

# 8.

# LAZARUS

A veteran ball player running out of chances has to be perfect. In spring 1989, I was like Wallenda on the high wire, in the wind without a safety net. I couldn't afford one slip-up, one injury, one bad outing. I had to be absolutely dead solid perfect every time out. So when my heels flared up, I couldn't go into trainer Gene Monahan's office for treatment. I did my own therapy, alternating ice wraps with hot water baths and ignoring the pain.

In my fourth appearance, on March 17, we played the White Sox in a night game at the new Ed Smith Stadium in Sarasota. The sinker worked fine and I felt strong, giving up two unearned runs in five innings. The radar gun caught my fastball consistently at 84 mph. In my best years with the Dodgers and the Yankees, I threw between 85 and 87 mph. The fans were calling out for me, cheering me. They wanted me to make it. When I walked off the mound after the bottom of the fifth inning, the fans behind the Yankee dugout gave me a standing ovation. Believe me, I noticed.

One or two good outings may be a coincidence, but not four in a row. I had now pitched thirteen innings without giving up an earned run, walking just two and striking out nine. Even Dallas had to admit I was throwing well. Still, in his postgame comments, he qualified his praise:

"[Tommy] knows how to pitch. He's amazing in that he gets the ball where he wants it all the time. The way our pitching staff is going . . . well, T.J. is still here, isn't he? It's probably not what he does, but what the other guys do [that will determine whether he makes the team]."

My fine pitching wasn't a fluke, and my spirits were rising. Pitchers are more dependent on attitude than position players. Confidence often makes the difference between throwing strikes and balls, between winning and losing, between making the team or not. There's a big difference between a pitching slump and a batting slump. For a starting pitcher, four starts is about a month's time. If you have four bad games in a row, you haven't had a slump, you've had a bad month. For a batter, four games is four days. He can have seven bad games, and only a week's gone by. He always has tomorrow. A starting pitcher may have one day a week.

My fifth appearance came during a split-squad game against the Mets at Port St. Lucie on March 21. I was sent to pitch the afternoon game against the Mets with the scrubs; the regulars were to play that night against the Orioles at Fort Lauderdale. The whole team, including me, consisted of marginal players or young guys without a chance. Jamie Quirk played third, Randy Velarde was at second, Bernie Williams patrolled center, with Kevin Maas in right. My catcher was Don Slaught. Dave Johnson, meanwhile, employed his regular lineup, including Lenny Dykstra, Keith Hernandez, Darryl Strawberry, Gary Carter, and Kevin McReynolds—their big lineup.

It was a blazing hot Florida day. I kept as still as I could in the dugout, trying to conserve my energy. The Mets worked me for solo runs in the first and second, the latter coming on a home run by McReynolds. But over the next four, with my sinker working, it was a different story. I had the batters digging worms, and the Mets managed only two other hits. With each pitch I made that day I felt a rising, almost tangible sense of mastery. No one said anything to me about it on the bench, but I could sense a change in the way the players, as well as the coaching staff, felt about the way I was pitching. The ball was doing exactly what I wanted. Everyone noticed. Mets batters were making outs and shaking their heads going back to the dugout.

In one of our at bats there was a controversial play that shed some light on Dallas. One of our players was called out at second base for sliding in too hard. The umpire, a minor league substitute ump, said the runner went out of his way to hit the second baseman, and ruled a double-play that ended the inning. Dallas went absolutely crazy. He bolted out of the dugout, ran on the field, and was in the young ump's face. I came out to the mound to begin my warm-ups and there was Dallas, behind me, all over this guy.

"What are we bleepin' playing here?" he screamed. "What the bleep do you think this is, a girls' league? This is the big leagues. That's part of the bleepin' game. You're supposed to slide like that. That's what I teach my ball players."

I asked home plate umpire Jerry Davis for a new ball, and he came out to the mound.

"You don't often see a manager get that violent in spring training," I told Davis.

"Maybe he's doing that for his team. Maybe he just wants to make a point with you guys."

The more I thought about it, the more it made sense. He did it for our benefit, showing us he would stand up for his team.

My pitching line showed six innings, four hits, two earned runs, three walks, and no strikeouts. I even hit a double off the wall against Mets starter Bobby Ojeda. When my pitching was over, I walked into the dugout, accepting the kudos of my teammates. One by one they came over with a slap on the back or a high five. John Stearns told me he had never seen me throw that well, even when he batted against me when he was with the Mets in the late seventies.

I got a drink at the water cooler and began getting my gear together. Dallas was standing at the opposite end of the dugout with his arms folded. He turned, stuffed his hands in his back pockets and walked over to me. He stuck out his hand and smiled.

"That was a helluva job," he told me, shaking my hand. "Just a helluva job. Now go and get your running in."

It was the first time all spring Dallas gave me a compliment to my face.

Son of a gun, I thought, the guy actually acknowledged that I did a good job.

At that specific moment, in the dugout at Port St. Lucie near the water cooler, I felt the corner had been turned.

What impressed Dallas most was that my performance had come against a National League team. For some reason, National League guys look down their noses at the American League. Dallas was a National League guy; he played there and managed there. If someone had a good outing against the White Sox or the Orioles, Dallas would say:

"He pitched well, but it was against an American League team."

But if you pitched well against a National League ball club, especially a good one, then you had done something outstanding.

After the game Dallas gave me some substantial public support, also for the first time. He appeared to be thawing.

"Tommy's a unique guy, and maybe I didn't take that into consideration. He's busted his tail to prove a point. He's done everything we've asked of him. He certainly hasn't pitched himself off the ball club. . . ."

The last sentence was revealing. I wasn't pitching to make the club, but rather, pitching *not* to make it. In a manager's mind, that makes a huge difference. He wasn't expecting me to pitch well to make the team, but *not* pitch well for my release.

In 1976, I was set for my comeback, but baseball wasn't. The owners locked the players out of spring training for three weeks because of disagreements pertaining to the Basic Agreement. We worked out on our own as best we could, throwing, hitting, running, doing exercises, and when camp opened on St. Patrick's Day, Grapefruit League games started right away.

The lockout hurt me particularly because in the team's mind I was very much suspect. No amount of talking or practicing would alleviate this doubt; I needed some game action to prove myself. As it turned out, I received only three assignments during the shortened spring training season, pitching just fifteen innings.

I was throwing fairly well, but after my second outing, against the Astros, coach Dixie Walker said to me in his high-pitched voice:

"Hey, buddy, for what it's worth to you, they had the gun on you and you came in at 85 mph. You better start throwing the ball harder. They want you to throw harder."

The irony is that's what I was throwing *before* I got hurt, but Dixie didn't know that and neither, apparently, did anyone else. That made Dixie's statement silly: the Dodgers wanted me to throw harder, but they had nothing to base it against.

"Throw harder?" I asked Dixie. "Harder than what?"

My last tune-up before the season began came in the Freeway Series, three games the Angels and the Dodgers play each year in California before the regular season gets under way. I pitched in the rain against Nolan Ryan, who was also coming off elbow surgery, and went six strong innings. My performance earned me the Lefty Phillips Award for the outstanding pitcher of the series.

The season began with further delays for me. My first regular season start was rained out, and Alston skipped over me in the rotation. Finally, on April 16, I started against Atlanta. I was charged, pumped up, ready to go—too much so. A sinkerballer can't go out there and pitch "angry." You've got to slow it down. As a consequence, I felt out of sync, and the Braves touched me up for three runs in five innings and handed me the 3–1 loss. After the game Walt Alston said, "[Tommy's] fastball didn't sink, and that bothered me a little." The next day Alston called me into his office.

"We're giving you one more shot, then we've got to decide what we're going to do with you."

"What do you mean?" I asked.

"We've got to see if you can pitch. You still haven't shown us."

"Walt, I haven't pitched in eighteen months, and you're going to make a decision on two starts [counting my next one]? What kind of test is that?"

"Tommy, I've got the team to consider. We can't mess around. We've got a chance to win this year, but the Reds got a good ball club and we can't afford to fall behind."

"Do me a favor, then. If my next game is my last game, let [Joe] Ferguson catch me."

Walt agreed to that. Fergy, who caught second string behind Steve Yeager, knew how to catch me; that is, what pitches to call, what locations on what batters, and knew when to slow me down. He was good at instinctively being on my wavelength.

I asked Red Adams why they wanted to make a decision on me so early. He told me that during a meeting of the front-office brass, they doubted my ability to come back. Red stood up for me, saying "the guy hadn't pitched in almost two years. You can't judge him this fast. It's not fair to him and it's not fair to the ball club." Red said he thought ten starts would be a fair test. But he was in the minority and was overruled.

"Tommy," Red Dog told me, "I don't know what to tell you. I only have one vote, and it wasn't enough. They won out. I can only wish you luck."

The Dodgers had made their decision. The next game would decide my fate. If I stumbled, they were going to release me because they didn't think I could pitch.

# Lazarus

Walt let Ferguson catch me against the Houston Astros. It seems like whenever you want good things to happen, the opposite occurs. The game certainly started that way. Houston's leadoff batter Wilbur Howard hit a chopper over my head and Bill Russell had no play at first. Enos Cabell then executed a perfect hit-and-run, sending Howard to second. It was a lazy ground ball that got through the hole vacated by second baseman Davey Lopes, who had broken to cover the bag. Then I caught a break. Cesar Cedeno hit a ground ball that was turned into a fluke double-play.

Cabell was forced at second, but the relay to first went wild. Steve Garvey tracked it down quickly and threw to the plate to nail Howard, who had taken third on the fielder's choice. That left Cedeno at second with two outs and dangerous Bob Watson up. Alston had a man loosening up in earnest in the bullpen. Ferguson came out to the mound.

"He's got the bullpen up. This might be your last hitter. Let's go."

"Let's go" meant that I quickly fell behind Watson 3–0.

Ferguson came back out to the mound again and told me that one more ball probably meant the hook. He didn't have to say the rest: it could very well mean my release from the Dodgers. That's a lot riding on one pitch.

"Forget about trying to hit the corners," Fergy told me. "Just throw a strike. When you get strike one, throw the next pitch as hard as you can right down the middle of the plate. If he hits it out of the ball park, so be it, you'll go out in a blaze of glory. At least you'll know you didn't walk yourself out of the big leagues. Let me have your best three fastballs."

Watson took on 3–0, and the first pitch came in for a strike. He took a tremendous cut at my next pitch, but being a bit overanxious, fouled it off. I gave the 3–2 pitch everything I had. Watson, looking like the mighty Casey, swung and missed. That got us out of the inning and probably saved my career.

I settled down to throw six more shutout frames. J. R. Richard of the Astros was throwing a shutout as well, so I left the game with a no-decision. But the seven shutout innings earned me a reprieve. It was like one of those old prison movies, where the governor signs a stay of execution at the last minute.

In my next start, against the Pirates, my control was much better and my ball was really moving. I pitched into the eighth inning, winning 7–1. It was my first win since July 7, 1974. The normally laid-back crowd at Dodger Stadium was really into the game, and the 40,000-plus gave me a standing ovation as I walked off the mound in the eighth inning. Sally had decided not to sit with the wives, but in the box seats with my agent Bob Cohen and Nancy and Bill Hefley (now the Dodger organist) so she wouldn't be noticed by the fans. She wanted to yell and cheer like an ordinary fan. As I walked off the mound, I tipped my cap, then glanced over at Sally, who was on her feet, crying.

Baseball's tough on marriage. Life in general is tough enough on couples, with one out of two marriages ending in divorce. Throw baseball into the mix, and the figure is closer to 85 percent. The travel takes it toll, friendships break up when someone is traded or released, and many times, you see players whose wives vie with their husbands to be recognized, to be celebrities. It doesn't work, and they split.

Fortunately for me, Sally put family interests ahead of her career ambitions. She had worked at WTHI-TV in Terre Haute, cohosting a children's show, and had written advertising promotional copy for the station. She majored in physical education in college, and also had considered a teaching career. But when we married, she put the family first. Sally was brought up that way, and we both shared that notion of marriage and family. She had a hard time dealing with my arm injury at first, questioning why it had to happen. But she found her strength in God, and was with me every step of the way on the long road back. Without her support, I'm not sure I could have done it. Having her in the ballpark, sharing my first comeback win with me, has remained one of my greatest thrills in baseball.

The headlines the next day proclaimed TOMMY JOHN IS BACK, but it took me a few more outings to really get fine-tuned. Those first few times out I learned it was possible to forget how to get batters out. Now, how can an experienced pitcher forget that? And what does that mean?

Well, it means that getting hitters out with your good stuff is easy. Good pitching will always stop good hitting. That's why when a batter succeeds three times out of ten, he's a success. The trick to effective pitching, however, is winning when you *don't* have your good stuff. That's when you have to "know" how to get batters out: know when to throw certain pitches, know how to set up hitters, know where to put the ball, know when to change speeds. It's like having a sixth sense for what to throw. For example, when you get a certain batter 2–0, you throw him a fastball down the middle of the plate, but with something off of it. The guy's geared for your hard fastball, but when it comes in off-speed, he's out in front, and you get him out with what is actually a mediocre pitch.

That's exactly the thing I had forgotten how to do. I wasn't pitching with my head. There wasn't the full confidence that I could throw whatever pitch I needed over the plate. But with each succeeding start, the easier it became to get hitters out. The "feel" came back.

The story of the 1976 season was the Cincinnati Reds. The Reds had won the pennant the year before and squeaked by the Red Sox in a World Series remembered more for Carlton Fisk's dramatic home run to win Game Six. But in '76 Sparky Anderson's Big Red Machine got even better.

The Dodgers hung around the race for the first half, starting out well, as we seemed to do every year. By the end of May we were 27–15, holding a slim two-game edge over the Reds. Garvey, Cey, and Buckner were hitting, and our pitching—perhaps the only advantage we had over the Reds—was paced by Sutton, Doug Rau, and Rick Rhoden. By the All-Star break, however, we started our slide. At the break we were six games out, losing a lot of tough ball games.

Though my record by mid-July was only 5–6, my ERA was around 3.00. It was about this time that Campanis came out with a statement that almost blew my roof off. During the All-Star break Ross Newhan of the *Los Angeles Times* asked me for a reaction to Al's "announcement."

Campanis told the press the team was going with a four-man rotation for the second half, "because we want to get more consistent in our pitching. We're thinking about dropping T.J. from the rotation."

I had no comment, but asked Ross what he thought. He said he couldn't figure it out, since in his words, I was "one of the best starters on the team." I asked Ross if he thought incentive payments for the number of starts had anything to do with it. My new contract called for a $20,000 bonus if I made twenty starts, $35,000 for thirty starts.

"You have that in your contract?" he asked.

"Yeah. It kicks in at twenty and thirty starts."

"Then that explains it," he said.

Campanis's decision could cost me my bonus money. I was angry and went in to see Alston. He reassured me about my spot in the rotation.

"Tommy," he said quietly, "I really don't pay any attention to what Al says. I don't let the guy in my office here. He can come in the clubhouse, but not in here. He can't tell me how to manage. I'll do what's best for the team, and right now, you're one of my top starters and you're gonna start, simple as that. I can't take you out of my rotation. That'd be foolish."

Walt was true to his word to me, and I stayed in the rotation all year, with my record hovering around .500. My thirtieth start came on a late September Sunday against the Braves. When I threw the first pitch, I took the ball out of the game. The umpire asked me if that was a milestone ball.

"Yeah," I said. "That pitch just earned me an extra $35,000."

What killed the 1976 Dodgers was a four-game sweep in early August, pinned on us by the Reds. With those four victories, Cincinnati went up by 13 games. The race was over then and there. It's easy to explain the Reds dominance in one word: hitting. Paced by MVP Joe Morgan, Pete Rose, George Foster, and Tony Perez, the Reds led the major leagues in team batting, doubles, triples, home runs, runs scored, RBIs, total bases, and slugging percentage. For good measure, they led baseball in fielding percentage, and topped the league in stolen bases. The Reds won 102 games, finished ahead of us by ten games, and never lost in postseason, sweeping the Phillies in the playoffs and the Yankees in the Series. It was an awesome display.

The Dodgers also were dragging some extra baggage around with them—tension. Players, Ron Cey and Dave Lopes in particular, were starting to publicly criticize Steve Garvey. Others would not go on the record, but were nonetheless talking in the clubhouse. Losing only aggravated the situation. There were no confrontations, just an underlying, ever-present static.

It stemmed from the huge amount of publicity Steve was getting. Steve would talk to the writers after a good game or after a bad game. He'd patiently sign autograph after autograph. He always made himself available, like a politician glad-handing a crowd. He was the cover boy, and the Dodgers P.R. machine worked overtime pushing the Mr. Clean image. Garv's detractors accused him and his wife Cyndy—who were called "the Ken and Barbie of baseball" behind their backs—of being phonies, of carefully grooming this all-American image to self-promote their way into money-making endorsement opportunities. It was the bicentennial year; one magazine even had Steve on the cover holding an apple pie with American flags sticking out of it.

An article came out in mid-June in the *San Bernadino Sun-Telegram* in which Lopes and Cey, plus an unnamed player, criticized Steve and his wife Cyndy. The article caused a rift, and Alston suggested we call a team meeting. At the meeting, Garvey stood up.

"If anyone has anything to say about me, I want it said to my face, here and now."

No one said anything. The meeting resolved nothing, and Alston slowly lost control of the ball club.

As far as I was concerned, Steve was the same polite, courteous person he'd been since I first met him in '72. There had been no change in him, and I had no basis to make a character judgment about him. Our relationship as teammates was a good one. Only one thing mattered to me—what a guy did on the field. Even his detractors would admit that when he was on the field, Steve always gave the Dodgers 110 percent. That's where I left it.

The season ended with a bang: on September 28 Walt Alston announced his retirement after twenty-three seasons as Dodger manager. In his place the Dodgers named third base coach Tommy Lasorda as Walt's successor. Broadcaster Vin Scully asked Tommy if he felt any pressure in replacing a man like Alston, who had won more than 2000 games, seven pennants, and four World Series.

"No, Vin, I'm worried about the guy who's gonna replace me. That's the guy who's gonna have it tough."

The Lasorda era had begun.

I finished my comeback year at 10–10, with a 3.09 ERA in 207 innings. My two best games came on July 23, when I shut out San Diego on four hits, and on September 14, blanking Cincinnati 9–0. That's when pitching was more than fun; that's when it was ecstasy. The interesting thing about my complete games is that of the six, five came in my last eight starts, an unheard of total pitching for Alston. Maybe he knew he was resigning and said what the heck, let him go the distance.

After the season the awards started coming in: *The Sporting News* Comeback Player of the Year Award, the Fred Hutchinson Award for Outstanding Character and Courage, as well as numerous awards, trophies, and certificates. The Hutch award meant a lot to me. Hutchinson was a former Tiger pitcher and manager of the Tigers, Reds, and Cardinals who died in November 1964. I never met him, but people who knew him said he was an outstanding person. Other winners had included Sandy Koufax, Carl Yastrzemski, Pete Rose, Al Kaline, and Tony Conigliaro.

During the off-season many civic organizations, church groups, Little Leagues, business organizations, and schools asked me to speak about my comeback, and it gave me the opportunity to relate how God helped me conquer overwhelming odds. One man remarked that God didn't do the pitching, Tommy John did. True. God (as near as I can tell) has never taken the mound in a big league game . . . but He gave me the strength to attempt what virtually no one else thought I could do. Without him, I would have been lost.

After the 1976 season two significant things happened to affect my baseball life.

The first was the court decision involving the Andy Messersmith–Dave McNally challenge of the reserve rule. Under the old reserve clause, the ball club could renew your contract each year at its discretion. If you signed a one-year deal, the team had you for that year, plus a perpetual option year. Baseball had always operated that way. Under the reserve system, a contract was automatically renewed each year until the team decided to release you. Once you signed with a team, they had you for life.

It was a bad rule, and McNally and Messersmith challenged it. The arbitrator begged the owners and the players to negotiate a settlement, but the owners wouldn't move. They had withstood these challenges before and were confident . . . overly confident. The ruling decided in favor of McNally and Messersmith, holding that a one-year contract is a one-year contract. The decision ended the reserve system and sent baseball into chaos. It was the baseball player's equivalent of the Emancipation Proclamation. For me, it meant that when I completed my one-year contract with the Dodgers in 1977, I could become a free agent.

Many players did just that in the off-season of 1976. That's when the salaries started their rapid escalation and the entire financial structure of the game began to unravel. For so long, owners had it all their way when dealing with the players. Now, the backlash was set. Owners became their own victims, often driven by short-sighted self-interest. They got caught up in a feeding frenzy, like a shark attack, when it came to signing players. Today's multimillion deals were just a matter of time.

When you see big-money deals in sports, remember that in an open marketplace the value of a commodity is intrinsic, that is, it's "worth" only what someone else is willing to pay for it. Also, baseball's TV and broadcast revenues are enormous, and if teams didn't have the money, they wouldn't pay those huge salaries. Baseball is run by business people now. The days of the sportsman-owner—Tom Yawkey was a classic example—are over.

The other significant move that affected me came when Alston stepped down. The game had passed him by. Walt just wanted to get away and enjoy a quiet, relaxing retirement. He didn't want to deal with clubhouse turmoil or with the new breed of ball player, who would just as soon question an order as obey it.

Baseball was changing. There was more individuality. The Dodgers who had graduated to the team after playing for Lasorda in the minors were used to a back-slapping, enthusiastic, warm, emotional, affectionate, hugging manager—an equal. They never got used to Walt's reserved, aloof manner or the conservative way he ran a game. Walt's basic game strategy was "sit back and don't do anything." Lasorda, on the other hand, believed in aggressive play and wasn't afraid to try anything. Needless to say, the players were ecstatic over Tommy's promotion.

Lasorda was the opposite of Alston. He literally tore down the walls of Walt's broom-closet-sized office, made a huge office, paneled the walls, hung up portraits of his Hollywood pals, put in a plush sofa and air-conditioning. Where Alston would have a hot dog and Coke after a game, Tommy had catered meals, supervising the wine list himself. He went on talk shows. One minute he'd be kidding with the clubhouse boy, the next minute he'd be on the phone with Frank Sinatra or Gregory Peck.

Lasorda was a winner throughout his years in the farm system at Pocatello, Ogden, Spokane, and Albuquerque. In his eight years as a minor league manager, Tommy finished in first place five times, second place twice, and third once. And he won with the players who were now on the team. No fewer than eighteen Dodgers on the '77 roster had played for Tommy in the minors or in winter baseball. They knew him and he knew them. It wasn't just a new manager taking over, it was the start of a love-in.

Tommy is perhaps the greatest motivational manager ever to pilot in the big leagues. He created a winning atmosphere. For example, one of the first things he did in the off-season was write to each of the players, basically saying he was proud to be the manager and how each player would be counted on to play a major role in the success of the Dodgers. He also visited or phoned each and every man, without exception.

Lasorda has that rare ability of blending the various personalities on the roster into an effective whole. Look at the infield on the 1977–78 Dodgers. You had Steve Garvey, Mr. Perfect, at first; the opinionated Dave Lopes at second; the laid-back, almost neutral Bill Russell at short; and the gruff Ron Cey at third.

Cey, called Penguin for his peculiar way of running, was a grumpy little guy. If you came into the locker room and said "Hi, how you doing, Penguin," and he gave you a grunt, you knew he liked you. We called him Mr. Personality. As a defensive player, his range was limited and so was his arm, but he was accurate. If he caught the ball, it was an out. Offensively, he was capable of outbursts of slugging that could carry the team.

It was a volatile mixture that, given the Garvey situation, could have blown up in Tommy's face. But Lasorda wouldn't let it. He got every one of his guys to perform on the field. He wasn't stupid. He knew of the internal problems. But he was able to unite the team by becoming its focal point. That was the context that explained Lasorda's quick success.

Tommy had been a pitcher himself—with Brooklyn and Kansas City—which I thought would help me. Walt was afraid to let me pitch nine innings. Tommy might have different ideas about that. The first thing Lasorda did when we met was take me aside, put his arm around my shoulder and say: "We're gonna win this thing. We're gonna win it because you're gonna pitch well for me. There are a lot of wins left in that arm of yours."

It felt good to hear that, but I was skeptical. I had heard all the thousand-and-one Lasorda stories about the things he would pull to motivate players, and when he tells you something like that and you don't know him that well, you just go along with it just to humor him.

In his first team meeting Tommy addressed the team with one of the most inspired pieces of clubhouse oratory I'd ever heard. "Guys, I'm going to tell you right now," he started out in a subdued tone. "We've got a good ball club and we're going to win. We're going to win because we're gonna play together. You may hate the guy next to you. Off the field, fine. I don't care. But when you come in here and put that uniform on, it's got 'Dodgers' on the front of it."

Tommy's voice got louder, his body more animated.

"If a guy gets in a fight on the field, I want to see everybody out there backing him up. We're gonna win together and lose together, laugh together and cry together. But we'll do it as a team. When you put that uniform on that says 'Dodgers' on it, that transcends every bit of animosity you may feel for anyone in this room."

He was just warming up. When Tommy gets going like that, he gets emotional, because he believes what he says. And that's how Tommy neutralized the team's residual ill-feelings: through the sheer force of his personality. It wasn't that the tension was gone. It's just that, on the field, we honestly felt it no longer mattered. That was a major difference between 1976 and 1977.

The 1977 Dodgers hit the field running. In Grapefruit play we went 17–7. We went 17–3 in April and began the regular season winning 22 of our first 26 games for the third fastest start in baseball history. On our first road trip we won 10 of 11, and by the middle of May we were up by 11 games over the Reds. Cey set a record by driving in 29 runs in April.

The fast start set up one of the classic lines of that, or any, season. Someone asked Sparky Anderson about our record.

"We've given them a good lead," the Reds manager said, "but it doesn't bother us. They always come back to us in July. Don't ask me why, but they always come back to us."

"Sparky's entitled to his opinions," Lasorda replied. "Opinions are like rear ends. Everybody's got one."

The year, however, began slowly for me. I dropped four of my first six decisions, with the capper being a game I pitched in May against the Braves. We scored ten runs in the first three innings, but I gave up five home runs and didn't get out of the fourth. Tommy lifted me and I was devastated—not at being taken out, but for pitching so badly. I was angry at myself. I didn't know whether to scream, yell, throw some bats, kick a water cooler, or jump off a building.

Lasorda called me into his office after the game. He pulled out his season's schedule.

"You remember in spring training, when I told you we were going to win? Well, we *are* going to win."

He then started circling every fifth day from May until the end of the season. He'd count them off, "one-two-three-four-five," then draw a big black circle around the date. When he was done, he handed me the schedule.

"Here, you take this. These are the games you're gonna start for me this year. I don't care if you're 20–4 or 4–20. You are gonna start those games, and that's all there is to say about it. As long as I'm here managing, those are the games you're gonna start. Because if we're gonna win this thing, I need you. I don't care what happens. I've got confidence in you."

That's when I knew all those Lasorda stories *were* true. Tommy Lasorda is the best motivator I've ever seen.

From that game on, my record the rest of the way was 18–3. It took a huge load off my shoulders, hearing Tommy back me like that. The man believed in me without qualifications. Time after time he stayed with me, in situations where Alston wouldn't have. In a game against the Reds at Cincinnati, we were nursing a one-run lead going into the bottom of the seventh. The Reds loaded the bases with one out. My wife was in the stands with my mom and dad, sitting one row behind Alston, who was puffing away nervously on his cigarette looking toward the bullpen. Sally nudged him:

"Relax Walt. Tommy will get out of this."

"It wouldn't be a bad idea to bring in a reliever," Walt answered.

"But that's not you managing," she needled. "That's Lasorda managing."

Lasorda came out of the dugout, and I thought he was going to pull me.

"You want out of here?" he asked me.

"No."

"All right, then. What do we need? We need a ground ball. Now look down in that bullpen. Who do you see out there? Charlie Hough, a knuckleballer. Now who's the greatest ground ball pitcher in the whole bleeping world? You!" he said, his voice rising with excitement. "If my life depended on it, and they had a gun to my head, and I needed a ground ball, I'd want you out there on the mound throwing it!" He was now shouting. "Now get me a ground ball and let's get the bleep out of here!"

With that, he went back into the dugout. On my next pitch Ken Griffey hit a comebacker on one hop. I threw home for the force-out, and Yeager threw to Garvey at first for a double-play. I came off the field, and in the dugout Lasorda had a big grin on his face. The side went in order in the eighth and ninth, and I ended up with a 3–2, complete-game win.

That's Lasorda. He instills confidence in you. He has his ways, and some people think his act is phony. It's not. It's genuine. He's an absolute genius in terms of getting the most out of every guy on the team, from the twenty-fifth man to the superstar.

When he had to, Tommy could really ream a guy out, up one side and down the other in words that would curl the hair of even the saltiest Marine Corps drill instructor. But the thing that made Lasorda different from most managers who were screamers and intimidators was psychology. He would come in, yell and curse at a player or the whole team, but—it's a big "but"—he'd then quickly get the player or the team back up. He wouldn't leave you down. He was a master at building you back up.

Tom Lasorda is an American original. They broke the mold when they made him, and you could fill an encyclopedia with Lasorda stories.

He was infamous for calling up, looking for a ride to the park. A bunch of guys lived in Orange County, within fifteen minutes of each other, and we'd take turns driving to Dodger Stadium in a car pool. Invariably, one of our pickups would be Tommy, at his Fullerton home. One day he surprised us by picking *us* up. I got a call from Bill Russell one Sunday saying that Tommy was coming over, and about nine-thirty A.M. he pulls up with Charlie Hough, Russell, Joe Ferguson, and Burt Hooten in the car. He came in and started playing with our daughter Tami, who was dressed up in her cute Sunday church outfit.

"Oh, little Tami, come here and see your Uncle Tommy," he said, gushing all over her. "What a pretty dress! Have you got a kiss for your Uncle Tommy?"

Sally made him coffee and they visited. The guys in the car started to get impatient and were yelling for him. Finally, we got in the car. On the way in, Tommy said he was hungry, so we stopped at a roadside stand for doughnuts, sweet rolls, coffee, and milk. We're pigging out on the freeway during our forty-five-minute ride to the park. On Sundays we were supposed to be at the stadium by ten-thirty A.M., two and a half hours before the one P.M. start. Lasorda got us there at eleven-fifteen. We hurried into the clubhouse and started dressing. Tommy came out of his office.

"Oh, by the way," he yelled. "Russell, Ferguson, Hooten, Hough, John: you guys have a hundred dollars each on my desk. You were late."

"But Tommy," Hooten implored, "you drove us in."

"I don't care who drives you in!" Tommy screamed. "You guys are responsible for being here on time. You can't depend on the driver to get you here—even if it's me!"

He fined me another time for missing the team plane to Philadelphia, but he didn't take my money. I got caught in freeway traffic and arrived at the airport in time to see the plane with the big Dodgers logo pulling out of the gate. Fortunately, the airport had a regularly scheduled commercial flight leaving in a few minutes and they saved a seat for me. I gave them my credit card and they ticketed me on the plane as we were taxiing out. As it turned out, my plane passed the Dodger plane in mid-flight and I got into Philadelphia first. I got to the hotel and waited outside for the team bus to pull up. As the players got off, I snuck in line. When they walked into the hotel lobby, I was with them.

"T.J., where've you been?" Lasorda asked, surprised, as if he were doubting his own eyes. "Y-You missed the plane."

"What do you mean, Tommy?" I said innocently.

"I know you missed that plane. Why didn't I see you?"

"Maybe I was in the bathroom."

"No. You weren't on that plane."

"Tommy," I said, "if I missed the plane, how could I be here?"

He looked at me, puzzled, and then figured out what happened. He started laughing.

"I've got to fine you," he said between chuckles. "How much was your plane ticket?" I told him. "Well, make the fine payable to American Airlines."

There was only one time I saw Lasorda at a loss for words. We were driving into the ball park, and he was recounting another of his hilarious stories, telling us of the time he almost killed his shortstop. Tommy had pitched his heart out in the first game of a doubleheader, but lost because his shortstop, Chico Fernandez, didn't go after a ball as hard as he could have. Between games Tommy got on Fernandez, who said he didn't hustle because he didn't want to risk getting hurt.

"I started choking him," Tommy said. "In those days, they had soda and beer in big wooden tubs filled with ice and water to keep the drinks cold. I had Fernandez by the throat, and then I pushed his head down in the tub, trying to drown him . . ."

He went on and on, and he had us cracking up, in stitches. After the story was over, I asked him:

"Tommy, you keep telling us these stories of all the stuff you did. The fights. Screaming at umps. Now you consider yourself a top-notch motivator, right? Okay—what happens if you get a young Tom Lasorda on your team? How would you handle him?"

The guys were laughing and egging him on: "Yeah, Lasorda. What about that?"

Tommy had this serious look on his face.

"I've never thought about that," he answered.

After a long pause he looked at us and said: "I wouldn't have any idea."

After another long silence and some deep thought, he just shook his head and said: "God, I hope there's never another Tom Lasorda in this game. I wouldn't have a clue on how to deal with him."

Lasorda used to love to throw batting practice. He could throw it by the hour. One day several of the guys got on him, telling him he was going to kill himself throwing so much b.p. He stopped and yelled in:

"Okay, you guys are such know-it-alls. You see guys my age die from shoveling snow, cutting grass, things like that. But how many guys have you heard of dying from throwing too much b.p.? None! And how many women do you hear of that die from shoveling snow or mowing grass? None! That's why I have my wife shovel the snow and cut the grass, and why I pitch b.p. We like playing the odds."

With that, he went on and threw another thirty minutes of b.p.

Lasorda was like Eddie Stanky in that he never had a lot of natural talent. He had to scratch to get by, and he got as far as he did through intimidation, scrapping, battling, and knocking guys down with his curveball. Like Stanky, all he wanted from you was the same kind of effort.

It was this expectation, coupled with his innate genius for handling his men, that enabled Tommy to step in as the Dodgers manager and win immediately.

# 9.
# SINGIN' IN
# THE RAIN

The 1977 Dodgers took the lead from Houston on April 14 and were never out of first place after that. We completely turned the tables on the Reds. In '76 they beat us by ten games. We had the ten-game bulge when '77 came to a close. Lasorda had found us twenty games.

As he predicted, it was a team effort. Reggie Smith, acquired the year before from St. Louis, hit 32 home runs and batted .307. Dusty Baker, an outfielder we had picked up from Atlanta, chipped in 32 round-trippers and a .291 average. Garvey had MVP-type numbers: .297, 33 HRs, 115 RBIs. Cey lit up the scoreboard for 30 HRs and 110 RBIs. We had five pitchers who won in double figures and pitched more than 200 innings: Rick Rhoden (16–10, 216 innings); Sutton (14–8, 240); Doug Rau (14–8, 212), Burt Hooten (12–7, 223), and myself (20–7, 225).

The 1977 season was a storybook year for me, after my talk with Lasorda. For the first time, I won twenty games, including an eight-game winning streak from June 18 to August 13. My 2.78 ERA was fifth best in the league. Under Lasorda, I was even able to complete eleven games.

On September 19, against the Giants at Candlestick Park, I pitched the biggest game of my life, the game that would clinch the divisional flag. I always pitched well in Candlestick. In fact, I don't think I ever lost there. Candlestick was a miserable, cold, damp, windy place to pitch, especially at night. Guys hated to play there, and I used that as my edge. I kept in mind that I only had to be out there for fifteen or so pitches an inning.

Rick Monday got us on the board with a two-run home run in the top of the second. We added another run to take a 3–0 lead into the ninth. With one out, Jack Clark tripled, and he scored on a single by Gary Alexander. I wasn't even thinking about the shutout; the run didn't matter. The important thing was the game. Giants manager Joe Altobelli sent up Gary Thomasson to pinch hit for pitcher Dave Heaverlo. I called Lasorda to the mound.

I told Tommy I was tiring. My pitches were starting to come up. Thomasson, the tying run, hit me well in the past. Getting that one hitter was the only thing that mattered. The complete game was trivial in comparison. We had a capable bullpen. Lasorda thanked me for being honest, and congratulated me for the 8⅔ innings.

"Great job, T.J. Just one fantastic job of pitching."

Tommy summoned young lefty Lance Rautzhan. Rautzhan ran the count to 2–2 before whiffing Thomasson. We all ran out of the dugout and embraced in a team hug near the mound. The celebration carried into the clubhouse. We popped the champagne, and a dozen of us, each with a bottle, stood around Lasorda, dousing him. Tommy stood in the middle of the circle, yelling:

"How sweet it is, how sweet it is! Let it come, let it come! I want to drown in it!"

Lasorda went around the room, hugging each of the players, prompting this line the next day from writer Jim Murray:

"Tom Lasorda hugged more people than a dance hall girl when the fleet is in."

When he got to me, Tommy ended his bear hug by awarding me the highest of honors: I would be the starting pitcher when the playoffs began in L.A. Lasorda then addressed the team, after which he was carried into the showers by Reggie Smith and Dave Lopes. The victory party lasted in Tommy's hotel suite until five A.M. The next day, the woozy regulars were given the day off, and the jayvees were in there, guys like Rafael Landestoy, Ron Washington, Ed Goodson, and Lee Lacey. Garvey, who had a 338 consecutive-game streak going, remained in the lineup.

A footnote to the regular season came on September 25, when I got my twentieth victory, three years to the day of my arm operation. Twenty-five has been a good number for me.

There's more pressure on you in the playoffs than in the World Series. If you lose in the playoffs, that's all they remember about your season, no matter how good it was. The World Series is the gravy you enjoy after getting by the playoffs. There's more press, more attention, and every pitch gets magnified. No matter how much you try to prepare yourself for it, you can't fully appreciate what it's like pitching for the first time in your first playoffs.

The Phillies had given us some bulletin board material. Greg Luzinski was quoted as saying the Dodgers didn't belong on the same field with the Phils. Even their manager, Danny Ozark, predicted his team would beat us in three or four games.

Three hours before the first pitch, Lasorda's office at Dodger Sta-dium was a collection of actors, writers, broadcasters, golfers, a clown, a priest, a rabbi, a minister, clubhouse boys, and politicians. People were going in and out as Tommy held court. I tried to quiet myself down in the locker room, but I never got comfortable out on the mound. I was nervous, and I pitched poorly, leaving in the fifth trailing 4–1.

After getting knocked out of the box, I went into Lasorda's office and watched the rest of the game on TV. I started thinking about what I might have done better, and it occurred to me: I didn't challenge enough hitters. I got behind on the count and pitched defensively. I was over-striding, out of anxiety. I vowed it would be different in my next start. We rallied back to tie it at 5–5 off of Steve Carlton, taking me off the hook as far as the decision was concerned, but we eventually lost in the ninth, 7–5.

Before Game Two Lasorda had comedian Don Rickles come into the clubhouse and loosen up the guys. Again, that was Tommy. Instead of getting uptight after the tough loss, he came back the next day ready to laugh. Mr. Warmth spared no one.

"Look at him," he said, as he went over to Lasorda. "Look at that stomach. You think he's worried about you guys? No way. If you guys lose, he's gonna tie a cord around his neck and get work as a balloon."

He came over to me, where I was sitting down in front of my locker in an old baseball sweatshirt and my shorts.

"Look at T.J. He makes a million dollars a year, and he wears trick-or-treat underwear."

On and on he went, on a roll. Rickles really loosened us up, which was like chicken soup: it couldn't do any harm.

We took the next game 7–1 behind Don Sutton, and traveled to Philly for Game Three. Philadelphia had us down, out, and beaten in that game. They were about to go up 2–1 and take control of the series, before the utterly bizarre happened.

With a 2–0 lead in the second inning, Hooten walked Ted Sizemore with two outs to load the bases. On a 1–2 pitch to pitcher Larry Christenson, home plate ump Harry Wendlestedt hesitated on a close pitch and called a ball. Truthfully, he blew the call. Hooten stormed off the mound in disgust and the fans went crazy, screaming at him at fever pitch. Hooten missed with his next two pitches for ball four, forcing in a run. The fans now believed they were the reason for forcing the walk. Hooten then walked Bake McBride and Larry Bowa to force in two more runs. He had walked four straight on 21 pitches. With each base on balls, the fans got louder. Lasorda had to get Hooten out of there. He brought in Rick Rhoden, and Rick got the third out.

The Phils broke up a 3–3 tie in the bottom of the eighth with two runs, and it looked like we were dead. In the top of the ninth things got bleaker when Dusty Baker and Rick Monday grounded out against Gene Garber. The 63,719 fans were screaming. Garber had gotten eight straight ground-ball outs. The situation looked utterly hopeless.

Lasorda sent up ancient Vic Davalillo to hit, and the crafty veteran, with two strikes and two outs, beat out a bunt to the right side. An even more ancient pinch hitter, Manny Mota, then skied one to left. It should have been the third out. For some reason, though, Phillies manager Danny Ozark hadn't replaced Greg Luzinski with Jerry Martin, a strong defensive outfielder. Luzinski lined the ball up, but it came down off his glove and into the left field screen behind him. Luzinski hastily retrieved the ball, and his throw to the infield got away from Sizemore, allowing Davalillo to score and Mota to move to third.

Lopes hit a sizzler to Mike Schmidt at third. The ball, however, hit a seam in the artificial surface and bounced off Schmidt's glove to Bowa. Bowa fired to first. It was an extremely close play that could have gone either way. First base ump Bruce Froemming ruled safe. Mota scored to tie the game, and the Phillies bench exploded, cursing at Froemming for his call. Garber then became unglued. He tried to pick Lopes off at first, but threw the ball away, allowing Dave to advance to second. Russell, a great clutch hitter, then singled up the middle, driving in Lopes for the winner. It was a weird, wild victory.

That set us up for the next night, October 8, when I got my second chance in the playoffs. When people ask me if there's one game that stands out over my long career, this is the one that comes to mind, the "rain game" in Philadelphia.

The weather looked ominous from the moment Sally and I got up. A bunch of the players walked to Veterans Stadium from our hotel, right across the street. It started to rain lightly. When we got to the stadium, I immediately walked down to the dugout and looked out at the field. The rain was coming down pretty good now. We were told that there'd be no batting practice or infield, and that the game, if it was played, would be delayed.

On the days that I pitched, I usually took a pregame nap on the trainer's table. That's what I did this early evening. I slept for an hour, from about five to six P.M. Guys were coming in and out of the room, getting taped up. I slept through it all. We felt sure there wouldn't be a game, so I wasn't nervous. The players hung around the clubhouse, watching the USC–Alabama game on TV. At about seven-thirty a clubhouse kid came over to me.

"They're going to try to get the game in, Tommy."

I got dressed and got an arm rubdown from the trainer, who loaded up my arm with analgesic balm. The adrenaline started coursing through my body. It was show time. I had half an hour to warm up. Red Adams walked me to the bullpen in a light but steady rain, and we waited out there until Steve Carlton got out to the home bullpen to begin his warm-ups. Red Dog had some advice as I began my warm-ups:

"Don't go fast out there, Tommy. Don't worry about how you're throwing the ball, because it's hard to throw the ball in this kind of weather. Just worry about keeping your tempo."

"You know, Red Dog, this isn't a good night for a sinkerball pitcher."

"Well," Red answered, "this kind of weather isn't good for any kind of pitcher. Won't be good for Carlton either."

As I finished my warm-ups and walked into the dugout, Red gave me his last reminder: "Remember tempo. Don't rush yourself. Tempo is the key to this game."

In the back of my mind was yesterday's game, and how the fans rattled Burt Hooten. I had one thought: keep the fans out of it. Dusty Baker took care of that temporarily by belting a two-run homer in the top of the second. The turning point, however, came in the bottom of the inning. The Phillies loaded the bases with two outs, and Carlton, a good-hitting pitcher, up. He worked the count to 3–2, and the fans went into their act. As soon as I got on the rubber, the fans came to life. The noise was unbelievable. They were trying to do to me what they did to Hooten. I stepped back off the rubber, turned around, looked at second base umpire Paul Runge and gave him a quick smile.

"What are you going to do?" Runge asked me.

"Watch this," I said. "I'm going to play the fans."

I got back on the mound. The noise started again, louder, louder. I put one foot on the rubber, came set, then stepped back off. When I stepped off, they calmed down. When I got back on, the din rose again. When I stepped off, I turned around to Runge.

"This is what it's all about, isn't it, Paul?"

He had his head down, shaking his head, laughing. When I got back on the mound, I had made up my mind that this time I'd pitch. But the fans weren't sure. I wound up and delivered. Carlton swung and missed. The 64,000-plus got quiet in a hurry. As I walked off the field, I looked back at Runge, who was still laughing.

"You're crazy," he yelled over.

At the end of the inning the rain came down harder and the umps ordered a halt in play. The grounds crew started to scramble to get the tarp ready, but the umps changed their minds and the game continued. In the bottom of the fourth Luzinski singled to right, and he was doubled to third by Richie Hebner. Gary Maddox bounced out, Russell to Garvey, with Luzinski scoring, making it a 2–1 game with the tying run in scoring position. I struck out McCarver for the second out before walking Ted Sizemore. With runners on first and second I whiffed Carlton again. That seemed to give us a lift, because I noticed the guys really talking it up on the bench when we came back in the dugout.

In the top of the fifth we picked up two insurance runs. Baker walked, and with one out Steve Yeager singled to center. After I struck out, Lopes took a wild pitch for ball four, on which Baker scored. With Yeager on third, Russell laid down a bunt, and the rain became a factor for the first time. Carlton broke off the mound to make the play, but he slipped on the wet grass. Russell was safe at first and Yeager plated the run, giving us a 4–1 edge.

Meanwhile, the rain continued to fall harder. I did my best to ignore it, which wasn't easy to do. Drops of water kept falling off the bill of my cap, my uniform was soaked, and my shoes were full of mud. The mound was slick and gummy. Players were starting to skid when going for balls. They had treated the infield with a ton of absorbent material. The mud at home plate must have been two inches thick. In the ninth inning I got a base hit against Tug McGraw, and I thought they were going to throw me out at first because I couldn't get out of the mud around home plate.

Incredibly, the baseballs never got wet until the ninth inning. But in the ninth it started pouring. By that time, however, they would have let us finish the game in a deluge. With two outs in the bottom of the ninth, the Dodgers leading 4–1, I threw a third strike past Bake McBride to end the game and win the pennant.

Lasorda led the troops out to the dugout. Yeager was the first to reach me on the mound. Soon we were one bobbing, hugging mass of Dodger blue. I could hear Lasorda from somewhere in the middle of the pack, yelling louder than anyone: "We did it! We did it!" As we made our way into the riotous clubhouse, the heavens opened and a torrential downpour fell. What we didn't celebrate in San Francisco, we did in Philadelphia, with champagne, horseplay, jokes, and laughter, woven around a slew of print, radio, and TV interviews. The celebration continued at Lasorda's family restaurant about forty minutes outside Philly. We had three buses go out, with players, front office, scouting people, and staff. We were there until four A.M.

The World Series against the Yankees opened in New York. The Dodgers hated going into New York because of the fans, who were obnoxious. They were always yelling at you, when you got off the team bus, when you came in and out of the hotel, when you arrived at and left the park. But as I came to find out later, that's the way it is for anybody wearing the gray uniforms. If, however, you wore the Yankee pinstripes, they were the greatest fans in the world. They were loyal.

The Series probably turned in the first game. Don Sutton and Don Gullett hooked up, and we ended up losing a twelve-inning heartbreaker, 4–3. But we earned a split in Game Two, coming back behind Burt Hooten, 6–1. The split put us in good shape with the next three at home. I lost my only start, going six innings in Game Three. The Yanks scored three times in the first. We tied it in the third, but Mike Torrez went the distance in the 6–3 New York win. Ron Guidry and Graig

Nettles beat us in the fourth game, 4–2, but Sutton staved off elimination the next game, a 10–4 Dodger rout. Game Six was spelled R-e-g-g-i-e, as Jackson poled three home runs—one each off Hooten, Elias Sosa, and Charlie Hough—sending us down the tubes, 8–4. Reggie's outburst was one of the greatest displays of long ball in the history of the game.

Before the final inning of that last game, we emptied the bullpen so guys wouldn't have to fight their way through the wild New York crowd, which was soon to explode onto the field. After the final out, the Yankees had to scramble frantically to get off the field in the middle of the mob. Reggie Jackson had to bowl fans over like Bronco Nagurski to get safely in the clubhouse.

The Series loss hurt me, because I honestly thought we had the better ball club. We were a team built on power, with four men with thirty or more home runs, and another three in double figures. But the Yankees had something that was intangible. They were the epitome of the cliché "they knew how to win." The Yankees simply made all the big plays when they needed to make them. They were a veteran team that would not beat itself.

The loss was tough—it always is—but not devastating. I liked the way Lasorda put it. He told the team that the best possible thing that could have happened to us this season was winning the World Series. The second best possible thing was to lose the World Series. There were twenty-four other teams in baseball who would have loved being in our shoes. My most satisfying year in baseball was 1977, and I have to think that without Tommy Lasorda, it would have been a far different year.

That year was marked by another honor: the birth of my first son, Thomas Edward John III, who was born on August 31. Sally had a frightening delivery. She was given an epidural injection. The idea was to numb her legs and hips so she could witness the birth. I was there to see my son born, and was having a soda with the doctor outside the delivery room. All of a sudden there was a commotion inside the room and I heard someone yell, "Oxygen, now!" The obstetrician bolted inside the room, yelling at me to stay where I was and telling me not to come into the room.

Something had gone wrong, and the injection was made directly into Sally's spine. A scalding, searing pain shot up her spine, paralyzing her body. The baby was delivered with no problem, but Sally started to panic, not knowing what was happening. She could not talk or move, and felt as if she were dying. She lapsed into unconsciousness. Outside, my heart was racing, almost near panic.

Three hours later the doctor came out, told me the baby was fine, but explained what had happened to Sally. She came out of her coma when the anesthetic wore off, but was in horrible pain for several days after. She had to remain perfectly still and on her back for two days, and for some time after, she experienced agonizing pain in her right arm and shoulder. To this day Sally still has problems with her right arm because of that botched injection. I never knew the depth of my love for her until that day, when I saw her slipping away.

The next spring my agent Bob Cohen and Al Campanis went through a series of fruitless and frustrating negotiations on a new deal. We wanted three years at $800,000; the Dodgers were offering two years at $500,000. Neither side budged, and we made no progress throughout the 1978 season.

I tried not to let the contract become a distraction for me during the season, but no matter who you are, a protracted contract hassle will drain some energy and cost you some concentration. Lasorda, to his credit, stayed out of it. He supported me where it counted—on the field.

It was a tough year emotionally. A pulled leg muscle kept me out of action for seventeen days, and after that I pitched with the leg taped from ankle to knee. Sally was pregnant with our third child, and as the year wore on, the contract talks became nastier. Both sides were playing hardball.

After another of our typical hot starts, the team cooled off around mid-May. We weren't hitting or pitching well as a team, and by the end of June we trailed San Francisco by six games. But that month the front office made a key move: they brought up twenty-three-year-old fireballer Bob Welch from Albuquerque. The move gave us a spark, as Welch contributed a 7–4 record in 111 innings. His ERA was a glittering 2.03, with three shutouts.

In late August an incident occurred that brought the Garvey matter to a head. In hindsight, it was probably the best thing that could have happened as we entered the stretch drive. Sutton was having a hard time dealing with the publicity and attention Garvey was getting. The two had this feud going. When Sutton signed a four-year contract for $1 million, four weeks later Garvey signed a five-year deal for $1.8

million. When Sutton bought a beautiful home in the San Fernando Valley, Garvey bought one three houses down the street. We could see this thing building the whole year. Lasorda knew about it, but he was hoping it would just blow over. You have problems like that on every ball club.

The boiling point came when Sutton blasted Garvey in a newspaper article for being the only guy on the team to get any publicity. Sutton said Reggie Smith, not Garvey, was the best player on the team and also the Dodger leader. But he added that because Reggie didn't engage in self-promotion or kiss up to the right people, people ignored him.

I actually agreed that Reggie was more of a leader. He was a Don Baylor type, an outspoken enforcer, a guy who played his fanny off for us. Steve was not outgoing with his teammates, not a man we could rally around. But I didn't pick sides in the Garvey-Sutton feud. I thought they were both wrong. Or maybe they were both right.

We were on the road, playing the Mets. The day after the article appeared, Garvey walked up to Sutton in the Shea Stadium locker room with a copy of the newspaper article and asked him if the quotes were accurate. Sutton said yes.

They went back and forth at each other, the talking became yelling, and you could tell something was brewing. I was sitting in front of my locker, about four stalls away, signing eight dozen All-Star baseballs. I could hear them arguing.

"Yes she did!" and "No she didn't!"

I didn't hear specifics, but Sutton was ripping Garvey's wife Cyndy, who was not well liked by most of the players or the wives. Sutton poked Garvey in the chest, they jostled, and the next thing you knew the two of them were on the floor, fists flying. We let them fight.

Somebody yelled: "Stop the fight!"

"No," Ferguson answered, "let 'em go. Maybe they'll kill each other."

Garvey picked Sutton up and threw him into my locker. Sutton landed with a crash, spilling the 96 baseballs I had been signing.

Campanis and Lasorda came running out of Tommy's office.

"What the hell's going on?" Tommy shouted.

Finally, Lopes, Smith, Russell, and Rick Monday got the combatants pulled apart. Amazingly, no one was seriously hurt. Garvey ended up with a red eye from a thumb poke. That was about it. Lasorda called them into his office. He didn't fine either man and didn't demand any apologies. Instead, he addressed the team.

"I don't care if you like each other or not. I can't make you do that. All I'm asking is that this doesn't carry onto the field. We must play as a team. We've got twenty-five guys here. We can't have thirteen pulling from one end of the rope and twelve from the other. That won't get us anywhere. We have to pull together."

It happened just that way after that. If Sutton pitched a good game, Garv was the first one to shake his hand. If Garvey hit a home run, Sutton would be the first one there to pat him on the back. They were pros: they didn't let their feud carry onto the field.

The fight was cathartic in that it finally got the hostility out in the open, and we played extremely well after that for the stretch run. But the fight ticked me off. Teammates aren't supposed to behave like that. There are better ways to solve differences. I went onto the field right after the fight, and coach Monty Basgall asked me what had happened. I filled him in.

"I'll be a son of a bitch," he said, scratching his head. "What's going on with this ball club, anyway?" he asked.

Fueling my reaction to the fight was my contract situation, which was still totally up in the air. The Dodgers were hardballing me at two years, and I wanted three. I started seriously thinking about declaring for free agency after the season.

"I'll tell you right now, Monty. They don't have enough money to get me to come back here with all this stuff going on. Why can't guys just live and let live? Play the darn game. That's all we're supposed to do."

"I don't blame you a bit," Monty said.

Near the end of the season Lasorda made his pitch for me, asking Campanis to give me the extra year. I had won 37 games for Lasorda in the last two seasons. He told Al the team wouldn't lose anything by giving me that third year.

"Even if he can't start for us in that third year, we'll use him out of the bullpen," Lasorda told Campanis. "He's got that kind of arm. You'll be covered no matter what."

Tommy even went out of his way to try and cheer me up and take my mind off things. One day he called me into his office.

"Close the door," he said, grim-faced, "and sit down."

He made like he was about to deliver bad news. Tommy reached into his desk drawer and started pulling out little plastic cartons and putting them on the desk. It was Chinese food.

"Let's wait for Ferguson," he said, suddenly smiling. "We're gonna have us a feast."

Joe came in, and the three of us devoured a delicious six-course Chinese dinner. What other manager would do something like that?

The Dodgers bandied back and forth with the Reds, finally outlasting them in the stretch to take our second straight divisional title by 2½ games. Garvey led the hitters with a .316 average and 113 RBIs, with key offensive contributions from Smith, Cey, and Lopes. Hooten led the staff with 19 wins, with Rau and Sutton adding 15 apiece. I slipped to 17–10, with a 3.30 ERA, not as good as last year, but still a solid season.

Once more we faced the Phillies in the playoffs, with similar results. We swept the first two games at Veterans Stadium, Welch taking the first game. In Game Two I shut out the Phils on four hits, 4–0. Having a year of playoff experience made a crucial difference for me. Carlton bested Sutton in Game Three at L.A., 9–4, but we made it two pennants in two years for Lasorda by squeezing out a 4–3, tenth-inning decision in the clincher. Terry Forster got the win in relief.

We got our second chance against the Yankees in the '78 World Series. It started off well, for both the team and me personally. I walked away with an 11–5 win in Game One at home. I really pitched just well enough to win, but the offensive barrage didn't require much more. We followed that with a 4–3 win in Game Two, Hooten over Hunter.

That second game provided a great moment of high drama, as Mr. October, Reggie Jackson, came up against young Bob Welch with two outs in the ninth, the tying run on second, the lead run on first. It was a classic confrontation: fastball pitcher versus fastball hitter. On the 1–1 pitch, Welch got a fastball up and Jackson took a mammoth swing. He missed the ball and nearly screwed himself into the ground on his follow through. The crowd let out an audible gasp. Reggie fouled off two tough, blistering fastballs before Welch missed outside for a 2–2 count. After another fastball and another foul, Welch missed to run the count full. There were then three more great fastballs that Reggie spoiled.

Neither man was giving an inch, but someone was going to lose. On the bench Lasorda paced back and forth like an expectant father, clapping his hands and yelling out encouragement. Welch checked the runners, rocked into his motion, and blew a third strike by Reggie. We exploded out of the dugout to congratulate the kid. Welch had given the Fall Classic one of its great individual moments, and more important, we took a 2–0 lead in games.

Yankees third baseman Graig Nettles owned Game Three. He threw leather at us all night, making a series of fantastic plays, each time with runners aboard. He robbed Lopes on a diving stab of a line drive. He stopped a bullet off the bat of Reggie Smith on his knees and threw him out. He robbed Smith and Garvey of doubles, and later came up big against Lopes again. He took away at least three runs and possibly as many as seven, and the Yanks won, 5–1. If not for Graig Nettles's glove, we might have taken a 3–0 lead.

The turning point in Game Four was Reggie Jackson's famous "hip volley" on the basepaths. I was cruising into the bottom of the sixth with a 3–0 lead. Jackson singled in Roy White to make it 3–1. With Jackson on first and Thurman Munson on second, Lou Piniella hit a sinker off the end of his bat to shortstop Bill Russell, who scooped it up and made an unassisted force of Reggie at second, who had stopped running. With Piniella, a slow runner, moving down the line, Russell took his time and lobbed his throw to first base. Reggie then angled his hip into the ball. It ricocheted away from Garvey, allowing Munson to score. Instead of an inning-ending double-play, our lead was cut to 3–2. Lasorda argued the call like crazy, claiming interference, but the play stood, and we ended up losing 4–3 in ten innings. I told Ed Vargo, the senior umpire and crew chief:

"You know where we screwed up on that play? Russell should have taken that ball and thrown it with all his might at Reggie's head, and then see if he wanted to stand in front of the ball."

Vargo looked at me and said: "You're absolutely right."

We were now even in games, but the extra-inning loss was a back breaker. The Yankees came out smoking in Game Five, routing Hooten, 12–2. We flew back to L.A. for Game Six, but the home cooking didn't matter. Catfish Hunter and Goose Gossage combined to shut us down, 7–2, with Sutton taking the loss. Once again we had come up short. That's when you start thinking, just how many more chances will I get to win one?

After the game, I went to the Yankee locker room to congratulate the guys. Thurman Munson and Dick Howser asked if I was going the free agent route. I said probably. Thurman said, "With your great sinker and style of pitching and our fielding, Yankee Stadium is made for you."

Dick Howser, then third base coach, said, "T.J., the Yankees would love to have you if you leave L.A." Dick told me to think about it and stared at me.

Just after the Series ended, my contract problems really got nasty. Campanis kept harping on my "ingratitude" for what the team had done for me during my rehab from the arm injury. There were stories about how the Dodgers had paid my hospital bills; raised my salary for 1975, a year in which I could not pitch; and stuck by me when I was all but washed up. And how does Tommy John show his thanks? He holds a gun to the team's head on the three-year deal.

The truth was that my hospitalization didn't cost the Dodgers a dime; the insurance company paid the bills. As far as paying me for doing nothing in 1975, they *had* to offer me a contract, or else lose me without compensation to some other team. Paying me for the 1975 season was the only way of holding their option for my services in 1976. The Dodgers did only what they were legally bound to do, based solely on the terms of my contract and those in baseball's Basic Agreement. Business was business. Peter O'Malley admitted as much.

In October, in an attempt to move things along, Campanis made his final two-year offer and told Cohen that we had twenty-four hours to decide on it, "take it or leave it." Sally and I talked it over all night. We weighed the two-year security blanket and the guaranteed half-million dollars. Was my stubborn insistence on a three-year deal worth losing the two-year, $500,000 "bird in hand"?

The Dodgers were counting on the fact that I didn't want to leave. Playing for the Dodgers is probably the best baseball job in the world. You're playing before three million fans a year in a beautiful ball park in great weather. Playing for Lasorda was fun. Never, before or since, have I had so much fun playing baseball in the major leagues. Could I walk away from all that?

The next morning we turned the Dodgers down. They couldn't believe that a player would decide to leave the team. That had never happened before. Everyone who had ever left the Dodgers had done so via a trade or a release or retirement; in other words, they left because the team didn't want them any longer. On November 1, the night before I was declared a free agent, Campanis called my agent with one last ploy. He said if I would call Al and tell him I wanted to remain a Dodger, the team would draft me. A player could be drafted by a dozen or so clubs, and whichever teams drafted you could negotiate with you on a contract. Al's request sounded like asking me to cry "uncle." If the Dodgers were interested in me, they'd draft me anyway. I told Cohen I wouldn't make that call. And with that decision, my days as a Dodger came to a close.

Campanis was stunned, hurt. But this was baseball in a new atmosphere. As a ball player no longer bound by the reserve clause, I had options. I was in a good position from which to deal. I'm a stubborn Welshman. The simple fact of the matter is this: if the Dodgers had offered me three years, I would have stayed.

With my ties to the Dodgers severed, it was time to look ahead into the uncharted waters of free agency.

I was selected by a dozen teams in the draft, and we had serious offers from several teams, including the Angels, Cardinals, Royals, Yankees, Braves, Rangers, Reds, and Brewers.

Ted Turner of the Braves was the first to call. He was a no-nonsense kind of guy, and immediately put a five-year, $1.8 million offer on the table. When Bob Cohen started to negotiate with him, Turner told him:

"Cut the bull! What's this going to cost me in hard dollars? And don't be telling me how nice it is out in L.A. I don't want to hear any of that crap. Just tell me, what's it going to cost me in hard dollars?" By hard dollars he meant immediate dollars, not deferred payments or annuities.

I turned down Ted Turner because the Braves needed more than me. I wanted to go with a team that had a chance of winning, not with one trying to rebuild. One by one the offers weeded themselves out. Bing Devine was fired as general manager in St. Louis, and Pete Peterson rescinded the Cardinal offer. The Angels got bogged down in the bureaucracy of Golden West, the holding company that controls the team plus other Gene Autry interests. An accounting quagmire took the Angels out of it.

It came down to the Brewers, the Royals, and the Yankees. Each team made good offers, but no one pursues his quarry more relentlessly than George Steinbrenner. When George wants somebody, he puts on the full-court press.

I had heard a lot about the Bronx Zoo. People were saying that when you went to New York, it was like walking into the belly of a beast. They were right. And they were wrong.

# 10.

# THE APPLE

B y the third week of March 1989 the Yankees pitching corps started thinning out. Kids were sent down, other guys were released. There also was a rash of injuries, including Candelaria (knee), La Point (shoulder), Dotson (shoulder), Righetti (shoulder), and Guidry (elbow). Our position players were dropping as well. Dave Winfield underwent back surgery and was lost for the year. Rafael Santana, our regular shortstop, had elbow surgery. In light of these developments, my pitching took on an added importance. Dallas Green was desperate for healthy bodies, especially on his pitching staff.

With so many injuries, the Yankees were trying to make some moves, especially to find a shortstop and pitching, but not much happened except in the front office. George Steinbrenner bypassed general manager Bob Quinn in favor of Syd Thrift, who had an excellent trade record in Pittsburgh. Syd, who had come out of semiretirement, was in the locker room every day, but rarely said a word to me except to hint that he wanted me out of New York. Thrift made no secret of the fact that he liked power pitchers, as opposed to finesse pitchers such as myself.

What remained of the pitching staff was having its problems. In one four-game stretch, opponents scored 41 runs; Andy Hawkins was the only healthy starter, and opening day was less than three weeks away.

My next start came for Columbus, the Yankee Triple A entry in the International League, on Sunday, March 26, in Tampa. The Yankees were the only team in baseball that had their minor league teams train at a location separate from the major league team. The farmhands trained at the Yankee Complex on North Himes Avenue in Tampa, near the corporate headquarters of George's shipbuilding company. Tampa is two hundred miles away from Fort Lauderdale, five hours by car. On other teams, when you pitch in a minor league game, you just go down the road behind the main stadium. Not with the Yankees. So early that morning I found myself in a small commuter plane, heading to the St. Louis Cardinals' minor league complex, also in Tampa.

I started against Louisville Cardinals and went seven innings, giving up seven hits and one earned run, with one walk and two strikeouts. My control was exceptional, and that pleased me the most.

When I got back to Fort Lauderdale, Dallas called me into his office and asked to see my stats from the Columbus game. It felt a little like getting called into the principal's office. He looked at the stat sheet with a poker face. But then I saw a dawning awareness in his eyes. He didn't gush about it, but it was written on his face: I had a chance to make this ball club.

"I said a forty-five-year-old shouldn't be playing major league baseball," Dallas began. "I still believe it. He shouldn't be. But you are, and you're pitching very well. I was wrong. There's more in you than I thought. When George offered me the job last year, I had the chance to see you pitch a couple of games, and also look at some tapes. I didn't like what I saw."

"My pitching can do that to you, Dallas, because when I'm off, I look like I've totally lost it."

"I made a mistake on you," he added.

I just about floated out of his office. He had finally admitted he was wrong. This was my payoff for months of back-breaking work. Dallas hadn't come out and said in so many words that I had made the club, but he didn't need to.

One of the writers asked Dallas if he was "tormented" by my strong performance.

"Tormented? That's not even close . . . Can Tommy be our opening day starter? Very conceivable. Absolutely. And I didn't even think he'd be on our staff in December."

That's when the press started really picking up on my story, saying it looked like Tommy's going to pull off another miracle resurrection. In the clubhouse Bill Connors asked me a question that sounded like a joke.

"What would you say if you found out you were going to be the opening day pitcher?"

"By default, or what?" I asked, thinking he was pulling my leg.

"No, really," he said, laughing. "You're throwing the shit out of the ball. You're pitching well, better than anybody down here right now."

"Bill," I countered, not wanting to count chickens, "there's still a long road left. I still have to climb the mountain."

George Steinbrenner wasn't gloating, but he was obviously proud of me.

"You can never count Tommy John out," he said. "He was on a winter exercise program like he'd never done before, and I knew that Dallas had never been around him much. But Dallas is the one who gave him the chance. Dallas should get the credit too."

George was playing senior diplomat with that last comment, because the fact remained that I got the chance to pitch myself *off* the ball club, not on it. I just didn't cooperate.

The next day, Easter Sunday, March 27, Dallas made it official. I made the team.

"Choosing Tommy was easy. He's pitched better than most; he deserved it. But I told him that I still think I'm right—that forty-five-year-olds can't pitch in the major leagues. . . . He's unique, one in a million. He changed my mind when I saw he could get people out. He used his stuff and his knowledge, and he's a professional."

I told the press it was the biggest upset since Hickory beat South Bend Central in the movie *Hoosiers*.

"When I came in here," I told the writers, "I don't think anybody would have given two hoots in the wind that I'd stay around as long as I have. I mean, if I'm the opening day starter, it'll be the biggest upset in sports history."

My story got national attention, in part because the Yankees are a national team, but also because of the Pete Rose and Wade Boggs scandals. Boggs's affair with Margo Adams was the big story over at the Red Sox camp in Winter Haven, and in Plant City, Pete's gambling received saturation coverage. Both stories were bad for baseball, and I think my struggle to make the Yankees gave the media a positive alternative to the Boggs-Rose affairs.

I was shocked by the Pete Rose revelations. Almost everyone who knew Pete knew he liked to bet on the horses, but we never suspected his problem went as far as it did. When the reports came out that baseball was investigating his gambling activities, I didn't believe them; I didn't want to believe them. As it turned out, it was a serious matter.

Baseball was Pete's life. He loved the game. That's why the charges he bet on baseball came as such a shock. People who weren't in his shoes can say he handled it wrong and that by being combative, he put baseball through the wringer and only aggravated the scandal. Only Pete knows what actually happened and why he acted the way he did, but I think Pete should have gone to Commissioner A. Bartlett Giamatti at the very beginning, when the stories were first coming out. He should have admitted his problems and stepped down for the good of the game. I believe Giamatti would have accepted that. People plea bargain for murder. Surely, they could have worked out a deal for Pete and kept him in baseball.

But Pete's a battler, which explains his actions. He came from a tough area of Cincinnati and had to fight all his life. That's why he chose to fight Giamatti and baseball. Ironically, it was that same aggressiveness that made Pete the player he became. Whatever Pete got into, he did it whole hog. He wanted to be the best. That's how he played baseball, and, apparently, that's how he gambled.

As a ball player, no one played with more combativeness and desire. Pete listed me as one of the three toughest pitchers he ever faced, the others being Jim Brewer and Randy Jones. When Pete came to the plate, I could tell if he was going to try to hit the ball up the middle, pull it, or go the opposite way, just by the way his feet were placed. Generally, I never looked at a batter's feet, only where the man stood in relation to the plate. With Pete, however, I could tell by his feet what he was trying to do. When he was looking to hit the ball to right, his feet were slightly closed. When he was going to pull or go up the middle, he stood even or slightly open.

Pete once hit a line drive back up the middle against me. I mean, he really nailed it. The ball was headed for center field, a sure base hit, but it hit the side of the mound and caromed right to shortstop Bill Russell, who picked it up and threw Pete out at first. As he trotted past the mound going back to the Reds dugout, Pete was shaking his head:

"Even when I hit the ball hard, I can't get a base hit off of you."

## The Apple

"You've got to keep it away from the mound," I told him. "That's why the mound is shaped the way it is. For guys who hit like you."

He laughed his way back into the dugout. Pete was a friend, and I was sorry to see his banishment from the game.

My philosophy has always been "believe in yourself." But I even surprised myself by how well I was pitching in the spring of 1989. Normally, a sinkerballer starts out slowly. It takes a while to get your mechanics together. But I didn't have any time to waste. One bad outing would have sealed my fate with Dallas. When I was a twenty-game winner and my ball wasn't sinking, I wouldn't worry. You can get hammered three in a row and nothing's said. The manager will alibi for you: "Well, there's nothing wrong with Tommy. He's working on a third pitch, that's all." In my position in 1989, I couldn't have a bad outing.

Part of my secret was visualization, where you pause and picture in your mind's eye the things you want to happen. The practical benefit was that it made me consciously aware of the pitching process. When you picture yourself on the mound, you must make the same decisions you make in the actual game. It's like a dress rehearsal. I spent a lot of time that spring just thinking about pitching.

For example, I knew I couldn't afford to pitch high, not with my fastball. Pitching low was a win-win proposition for me. If the batter didn't like the ball low, he'd lay off and I could get the low strikes. If he did like it low, I would come just out of the strike zone, and get guys to fish for balls.

I wanted my catcher setting up low, right over the middle of the plate. The sinker would start in the middle, then would dip or tail away. When the ball approaches the hitter in the middle of the plate, he thinks the ball is hittable . . . until it's too late. He'll swing and miss, or get on top of the ball. That's how you get 18 and 19 ground balls a game; by starting that sinker in the middle of the plate.

I also talked to the umpires.

"The pitch to Harold Baines . . . was that ball low?"

"Yeah," the ump would reply.

"Okay," I'd answer. "I thought it might have been a strike."

What you're doing is creating doubt in the umpire's mind. He starts thinking: "Maybe that ball wasn't low. Maybe it was a good pitch. I'll look at it a little closer the next time." Then the next time you throw it, you may get the call. That's another aspect of pitching with your head.

Each umpire has a different strike zone. The rule book defines what a strike is, but the umps have their own interpretations. The pitcher's job is to know what a particular umpire will and won't give you. Some umpires have a tight strike zone. With them, you've got to throw good strikes. You can't get behind on the count, because you won't catch a break on tight calls. Pitching down in the count is like carrying over a credit card bill month to month by paying the minimum amount. Eventually, the total bill comes due, with interest.

I liked to throw a lot of first-pitch curveballs, because most batters go up there looking for the fastball on the first pitch. On the first pitch you have some leeway; you don't have to make a perfect pitch, so I liked the curve. If you miss, you're only down 1–0. And even if you don't throw it for a strike, the batter has a little more to think about. He knows if you come in with a curve on the first pitch, you're liable to do anything at any time in the count. Pitching's a mind game in which you try not to out*think* the batter but out*psych* him.

Sometimes a first-pitch curve will make the batter change his eye levels from high to low. That was Gene Mauch's theory of pitching: make the batter change eye levels. It means if you throw a pitch low, throw the next one high, then low again. A lot of pitching coaches believe in the "eye-level" theory, and I like it . . . for power pitchers like Bob Gibson, Sandy Koufax, or Roger Clemens. But pitchers like me have to stay low. Period. If I came up in the strike zone with my mediocre fastball, that would be one fat, juicy pitch.

These were some of the things I'd go over in my mind in the spring of 1989, when I lay in bed at night before going to sleep, or when I sat in the locker room before I went out to pitch. Just visualizing myself doing well. It's a variant of the notion: Beware of what you think, for what you think will come true.

I had no idea what to think about my free-agent negotiations in 1979. In 1977 I made $100,000 in baseball for the first time. That sounded like big money, but little more than a year later we were talking in multiples of that.

George Steinbrenner pulled out all the stops. He presented the advantages of playing in New York: the fans, the city, the endorsement opportunities, the money, Yankee tradition. He left the actual deal up to Al Rosen, his general manager.

Rosen, a great player and the American League's MVP in 1953 when he played third for the Indians, never forgot the player's viewpoint. He also was an honorable man, warm and outgoing, pleasant to talk to, and I thought the negotiations would be a breeze. Al did an outstanding job of selling me on New York. Al and the Yankees even sent Sally a beautiful Steuben glass apple as a gift, at Howard Cosell's suggestion. But I didn't know Steinbrenner. I was about to find out what "hardball" meant.

We met Howard Cosell at a "Joe Louis" dinner in Las Vegas. Howard was really great. He was friendly, polite, and very adamant about me coming to New York. He caught Sally's ear and she was really impressed. She was scared to come to New York from all she had heard about "the cold, cruel, unsafe" town. Howard capitalized on all the positives and won us over. He's been a friend and loyal supporter ever since. He and Emmy are very special people.

When we flew out to meet with the Yankees, I was thinking about what Munson and Houser had said. Sally was one week shy of nine months pregnant. She was wary about flying out, but the doctor said it was okay and she wanted to be with me. George solved the problem: he had a hospital room and an ambulance ready, if needed. Sally was due in five days, but nature isn't that precise. We could see it now: she has a baby on the plane, and our third child comes into the world named "TWA John." Fortunately for everyone, little Travis cooperated nicely and didn't make his debut in the world until December 6. He was a beaming, bright little boy, and Sally and I were overjoyed by the new addition to the growing John clan.

George and Al Rosen met us at the airport, and we sat down to talk in the TWA Ambassador Club lounge. My first impression of George was "Businessman" with a capital "B"—a tough, no-nonsense guy with a large ego, a man accustomed to snapping his fingers and watching people jump. He talked in quick, choppy, emphatic sentences. He wore a nicely tailored, conservative business suit, white shirt and tie, and had the hurried, darting manner of a deal maker. George didn't stay for dinner, since he had to get back to Tampa on other business.

"You and Al finish up this business," he told us. "Get the contract worked out and get it signed."

Bob Cohen then mentioned that we needed to talk first.

"What are you talking about?" George asked, incredulously. "You didn't come to sign?" He paused, then turned to Rosen: "Right! You've got work to do. Better get busy. I have to fly to Florida."

With that, George wheeled and made a dramatic exit.

Bob and I talked about the general parameters of what we were after, and Al explained what the Yankees were thinking. We continued our talks over dinner that evening at the 21 Club, and afterward we all went back to the Plaza Hotel, where we had a two-bedroom suite. Sally and Bob's wife Joanie went into one of the bedrooms, while Cohen, Rosen, and I stayed in the main drawing room. We talked about salary, bonus money, deferred payments, and the myriad other things that go into a baseball contract. Finally, at about four in the morning, Al came up with an offer. We stumbled a bit on the deferred payment arrangements, and Al had to call George, who approved the figure and the structure of the deal. We all shook hands and slated a press conference for the next day. We would actually sign in a week to ten days later, after the lawyers drew up the actual contract.

The deferred payments were not included in the reported contract amount. The deferred money was not with the Yankees at all, but came from two other companies, including one owned by George, in two separate contracts. The Yankees, however, guaranteed the money. Cohen checked all the contract language and had no problem with the arrangement. It was perfectly legal.

When you sign a baseball contract, it goes to the league office, and all the other teams get to see the amount. By not including the deferred money in the Yankee contract, George didn't have to report it to the league. Theoretically, that could help him keep costs down for future contracts with other players.

So what the league saw on the Tommy John contract was a three-year deal at $1.6 million. The actual amount was $2.8 million for three years. The other teams who had talked to us were upset, because they had offered me more money and wanted to know why I signed with the Yankees for "less." The agreement, however, prevented me from saying anything about it.

Buzzie Bavasi, the general manager of the Angels, blasted me for another reason. He called me deceitful, mercenary, and dishonest. He said we had used the Angels as a bargaining tool to drive my price up with the Yankees, which wasn't true. He even sent a letter calling me "a Phony with a capital P."

We had the press conference, and when the contract actually came back days later for my signature, we stumbled badly. The contract we agreed to had no strike language in it. When George saw that, he told Rosen there had to be standard strike language, to the effect that if the players went out on strike, I wouldn't get paid. We said fine, but if they put in strike language, we wanted lockout language. If the owners locked us out, as they had done in 1976, the Yankees had to pay me. Al had no problem with that, and it went into the contract. If there was a strike, I wouldn't get paid; if there was a lockout, I would.

When George read the new contract, he refused it.

"There's no way we can have lockout language in there, dammit! It'll be the only contract in baseball that will have it. That won't happen!"

Rosen called back, saying that we had to take the lockout clause out. Cohen agreed, but only if they took the strike language out. Bob called me:

"Tommy, we got problems. George won't accept that contract."

"What are we going to do?"

"I don't know," he answered. "Maybe we don't have a deal anymore."

Finally, after days of going back and forth, everyone got together on a marathon telephone conference call: Steinbrenner, Rosen, Yankee attorney Peter Alkalay, Cohen, and me. Poor Al. He was roused out of a vacation down in the Virgin Islands or Barbados, some remote paradise where they had only one phone. Leave it to George to find the number.

Bob and I had agreed to toss them a bone, a sign of good faith, and we compromised on a life insurance clause in the team's favor. The Yankees happily accepted that. Then we came to the lockout-strike thorn. We repeated our wish, that if the lockout language were removed, the strike clause had to go.

"Dammit," George exploded. "That's not the way I remember our conversation! I can't drop the strike clause. That's in the contract of every player on our ball club," he screamed. "I'll be damned if you're going to be any different. If you won't agree to that, the deal's off!"

Bob stayed cool and reported that if the deal was off, "I suggest you call another press conference saying you have backed out of the deal. Tommy will then be free to negotiate with other ball clubs."

Silence.

"Okay," George huffed. "Put it on paper and I'll sign it. No lockout clause and no strike clause."

After the conference call ended, Rosen and Alkalay hung up, leaving George on the line with us.

"Glad we got it done, Tommy," he snapped. "Welcome aboard. And Cohen, listen. You should be working for me. You're a damn sight better than what I've got working for me now!"

Welcome to New York.

I realized just how good a negotiator George was. Look at what he did with the lockout-strike matter. The first agreement, which he approved, didn't mention the issue at all. Then he raised it himself at the eleventh hour, and finally ended up giving us what he had okayed in the first place . . . while making it look to us like he had conceded something. He drove us down on the life insurance policy in the bargain, and won a point.

When George is looking at you from the other side of the table, he'll look for any edge he can get. Ironically, that led to George's undoing more than a decade later, in the summer of 1990. When he paid money to a confessed gambler for information on Dave Winfield, George opened himself up to an investigation by Commissioner Fay Vincent. The probe led to his removal from managing the day-to-day field operations of the Yankees.

George is a complex man, difficult to understand. But one thing was clear. With the Yankees, nobody could make any deal—trades, money transactions, the traveling secretary wanting to change hotels on the road, a secretary buying office supplies—without George's approval. That's the way the team was run. He was an extremely tough boss who paid top dollar and demanded excellence. He figured if you're paying someone top dollar, they owe you top performance. That equation may work in business, but not in baseball.

When the negotiations were done, I told him: "I can't tell you how many games I'm going to win. That depends on the days I pitch, injuries, things like that. The only thing I can guarantee you is that every time out, I will give you a hundred percent."

"Tommy," he said, "that's all I've ever wanted from anyone."

Going from spring training in Vero Beach to the Yankees camp in Fort Lauderdale was culture shock. Vero is a small hamlet in the Indian River area. The ball park was ten minutes from the beach. In Fort

# The Apple

Lauderdale it takes you forty-five minutes just to get from one end of town to the other. Lauderdale's a metropolitan area, jammed with traffic and city clutter, with all the problems of a big city—drugs, crime, prostitution. The city doesn't have a great freeway system, and when you get around, it's mostly stop-and-go street traffic. It's a wild place at night in the strip area, where the college kids go, totally crazy.

But the action on the field was pretty much the same. A field is a field. I adjusted easily. I knew most of the Yankees from the previous two World Series, plus I had played against almost everyone at one point or another in my career.

My new manager was Bob Lemon, with Tom Morgan as the pitching coach. Both were good men and coaches. Lemon was an outstanding manager who never got the credit he deserved. He was like Al Lopez; he let you alone and treated you like an adult. I responded better to managers like that. Give me a chore. Tell me what you want, then leave me alone and let me do it.

Lemon had suffered a tragic loss in late October when his son Jerry died in a motor vehicle accident, something that Bob was trying to overcome as spring training and later the regular season began. But he was having trouble focusing on baseball.

One thing I noticed right away was the difference between the Dodgers and Yankees. The Yankees weren't as good fundamentally, and they had a way of walking through drills. Some players took advantage of Lemon by not working as hard as they could, skipping a lap here and there, dogging it through exercises. When we had a long bus ride, some players would come down with convenient injuries to miss the trip. This was a veteran ball club that had just won three consecutive pennants and two World Series. They were not hungry, and as a result, were not prepared for the regular season.

I was third in the rotation behind Ron Guidry and Ed Figueroa. The Yankees opened at home against the Brewers, one of the contenders in the American League East. Guidry and Figueroa both got beat, and I didn't realize how bad 0–2 starts were with the Yankees. The fans got noisy and loud. What a difference from laid-back Los Angeles, where baseball was more a social thing, a place to be seen. They didn't live and die on each game, as the fans did in New York. Every game was like a playoff game.

That made me nervous and apprehensive in my first start as a Yankee. I led off the game with four straight balls to Paul Molitor. The fans started booing. Welcome to Yankee Stadium. Robin Yount was up next, and he took my first pitch for ball one. The boos started to cascade down from the upper decks. People were yelling stuff like: "Get this stiff back to L.A." and "You got gypped, George."

Tom Morgan came running out of the dugout.

"Dammit, John, start throwing the bleeping ball over the plate. Listen to these fans. You're gonna get me fired!"

"Morg, what's my problem?" I asked.

"I don't know," he replied. "You tell me."

"I think I'm just overthrowing a bit."

"Yeah, probably," he said, then trotted back to the dugout.

The Brewers nicked me for a run in the first, but—making a conscious effort to slow my motion down—I shut them out over the next six innings. Mickey Rivers made a couple of great plays in center. I left the game in Goose Gossage's hands with a 2–1 lead. Goose got six outs in a row, and I had a win. The fans quickly forgot those first five balls.

Then I got into one of those hot streaks—similar to the first halves of 1968 and 1974—ripping off nine wins in a row. My pitching earned me Pitcher of the Month honors for April, a month in which I logged a 4–0 mark and a 1.12 ERA. From May 2 to 20 there were four straight complete games, with my best coming over Boston on May 20, a two-hit shutout.

I lost my first game on a Saturday in Cleveland, the town where it all began for me. I was supposed to pitch Thursday night, but that game and Friday's game were rained out. On Saturday it was still pouring rain, but they were determined to squeeze in the game since there was a big advance sale. The field was in horrible shape. I gave up a ton of runs in four innings, and when Lem came to take me out, he had a sympathetic look on his face.

"Well, meat," he said, using his favorite nickname for players, "games like this drove me to drink a lot of V.O. in my time."

Despite my hot start, the ball club floundered near or below the .500 mark. Steinbrenner lashed out at us in the press, trying to light a fire under his lethargic club, but it didn't work. The Yankees were under a dark cloud, it seemed: first, the death of Lemon's son; next, the listless camp. It didn't improve.

On April 19 a clubhouse incident drastically affected any chance we had of shaking our slump. Jim Palmer and the Orioles had beaten us in Yankee Stadium. In the clubhouse after the game, Reggie Jackson started riding Cliff Johnson, our designated hitter-catcher, about not playing that day. Heathcliff, as he was nicknamed, was one of Jackson's favorite targets. Reggie ragged Cliff about his inability to hit Goose Gossage when they were both in the National League.

"Heathcliff, bet you're glad you don't have to face Goose anymore."

"You kidding?" he answered. "I hit him pretty good. He's lucky he doesn't have to face me anymore."

Lou Piniella and Thurman Munson started hollering, trying to fan the flames. Johnson got up and went to the showers. While he was in there, Gossage said he used to strike Johnson out all the time. Guys were just laughing and having a good time with the joke, until Cliff came out from the shower.

"Hey, Cliff," Reggie instigated. "Goose says you couldn't touch him."

"He couldn't hit what he couldn't see," Goose said, to much laughter. Johnson threw a roll of trainer's tape at Gossage.

"Do you really believe that I couldn't hit you?" Cliff asked Goose. Soon, the two men were face to face, shouting. Everything happened so quickly. Someone threw a punch, and the two heavyweights—Johnson at six-four, 225, Goose at six-three, 215—were duking it out. It sounded like a stampede. When it was over, Gossage was holding his pitching hand. He had torn ligaments in his thumbs and would miss three months. We had no other closer out of the bullpen who could come close to Gossage. It was a demoralizing blow to the team.

In early June, Reggie tore a calf muscle and we lost his bat for a month. Shortly after, on a plane ride to Texas, several of the players got out of hand. The raucous bunch were partying, with music blaring from tape players. This came right after a loss to Minnesota. Lemon, however, said nothing, and I think that was Steinbrenner's signal to act. After 65 games we were 34–31, and George fired Lemon, bringing back Billy Martin for the second time. I think Lem had some idea he would be gone. With the Yankees, if you don't win, you're history.

Billy came in and told us we were going to play "hard-nosed base-ball." Billy liked to mix it up offensively, much more than Lemon. Bob didn't like to hit-and-run or anything like that. Billy, on the other hand, loved the wide-open game, and believed in creating runs.

Off the field, Billy had a stormy life, as we all know. But between the white lines he was able to channel his aggression. He felt comfortable being back as manager, and had his favorites, guys who had won for him in '76 and '77: Graig Nettles, Munson, Guidry, Piniella, Chris Chambliss, Roy White. He didn't care a lot for Reggie, and Reggie didn't like Billy. That stemmed back to the fight they had in the dugout at Fenway Park in Boston on national TV two years earlier.

Billy's clubhouse was great. He'd let ballplayers bring their children in before and after the game. It probably surprises fans to hear this, but Billy created a relaxed, homey atmosphere on the team and in the locker room. I think that's because, to Billy, the ball park *was* home. He didn't mind guys leaving the bench during the game to go to the clubhouse. Before games, he let us watch TV. *Jeopardy* was the clubhouse favorite, and each night before game-time we'd have it on, playing along. Billy ran a loose ball club and let guys do what they wanted, just as long as they were ready to go hard when the game started.

There was no evidence of his personal problems when he was at the game. He used the ball park as an insulation against his problems. It was almost as if Billy believed that once he left the park, trouble was out there waiting, ready to find him. On the field, though, Billy was as good a bench manager as there was in baseball. Baseball was his love. He'd be the first one to the park and the last one to leave.

About a month after Lemon was fired, Al Rosen quit. He and Lemon were friends, and I think the move bothered Rosen. He had had enough of working for George, and decided to walk away of his own accord, on his own terms; one of the few in George's stable who managed to do so.

The team started playing better under Billy, but it was too little, too late. That, however, paled compared to the tragedy that lay ahead.

On August 1 we beat the White Sox at Comiskey Park, leaving us 14 games out of first place. The team caught a charter back to New York . . . everyone but Thurman Munson. Munson flew his private jet back to his home in Canton, Ohio, to spend the off-day with his family. Thurm had recently purchased the Cessna Citation, and was getting a feel for flying it. On August 2, the off-day, he took off at 2:45 P.M. from the Akron-Canton Airport to practice touch-and-go landings. In the plane with him were two friends, both licensed pilots. Just past three P.M. Thurman tried to land the plane but came in too slowly. He tried to throttle up, but it was too late. The Cessna "NY 15"—after his uniform number—hit some trees about a thousand feet short of the runway, then crashed into an embankment leading to runway 19. The jet burst into flames. The two passengers kicked out the side door and made their way out. Thurman was motionless, harnessed into the seat. The two men frantically tried to get him out, but the fuel ignited, enveloping the fuselage in flames. The medical examiner's report said Thurman died of smoke inhalation.

I was home relaxing with my family when the phone rang. It was George. His voice didn't sound right.

"Tommy, I'm calling you and some of the veterans before you hear about this in the press. Thurman's dead."

I was staggered and dazed. As I sat there and looked at my children—so innocent, so oblivious to a thing like death—I thought of Thurman's three children and his wife Diane, and couldn't get him out of my mind.

As a ball player, Thurman wanted to give you the impression of being gruff, with that snarl he wore on the field. But as a teammate, he was anything but that. He was a giving, dedicated family man. Ironically, that was the reason why he took up flying. So he could fly to Ohio after games and spend more time with them. Thurm was a clubhouse leader. Guys looked up to him. Reggie did a lot of the outward leading, with his bat and with his talking. But in the locker room we looked to Munson. He was the main reason I came to New York.

He was an excellent catcher who called an outstanding game. In early May at California we were down to one pitcher, so I volunteered to go to the bullpen to be the "in caser"—the guy a manager can go to in case the last pitcher gets in trouble. Lemon brought me in to face Rod Carew with runners on second and third and two outs. Munson called curveball after curveball after curveball. I couldn't figure it out, but didn't shake him off. Finally, on a 3–2 pitch, I got Carew on yet another curve. I pitched two more innings, and Thurm started calling for some fastballs. We scored four runs in the top of the eleventh; I finished up, and got the win out of the bullpen. After the game, while icing my arm in the clubhouse, I asked Thurman why he called all those curveballs in the ninth.

"Well," he answered, "when you warmed up, you had nothing. Your fastball was straight as a string. You throw one fastball, and the game's over. We had a chance with you throwing curveballs, so what the heck. In the last two innings you found your rhythm, and it was safe to throw the fastball."

After Thurman died, the team had a hard time focusing on baseball. A tragedy of that proportion makes the game seem insignificant. As players, we gave it our best effort, of course, but subconsciously I think you tell yourself that there are more serious things in life to set straight. They could have cancelled the rest of the season. That's how bad we felt.

We played our weekend games, with me pitching on Sunday. The funeral was on Monday. The Orioles, in a magnanimous gesture, offered to cancel Monday's game, to be made up later in the year if necessary. Most of the guys felt that Thurman would want baseball played. We agreed to fly into Ohio for the services, then fly back to play that same night. We left Yankee Stadium at eight in the morning and flew on a chartered jet to Ohio for the funeral and burial. It was gut wrenching, and easily the worst day I've ever spent in baseball.

Nettles and Munson were very close; part of the way Graig deals with things is with humor. As we were leaving the cemetery in the bus, Graig said: "When I looked down the hill [from the graveside], I saw a Dunkin' Donuts and a Burger King. Thurm was buried in the right place." Thurman was a junk-food junkie, and we laughed. It was good medicine, the kind of joke Thurm loved.

When the charter got us back home, Gossage came over to my house and we just flopped down on the floor and fell asleep until it was time to go to the Stadium. That night we played one of our most inspired games of the season: we trailed the Orioles 4–0 at one point, but came back to win in the ninth, 5–4. Bobby Murcer drove in all five runs.

As a silent tribute, Thurman's locker was left empty the rest of the year, his Yankee uniform shirt facing outward in remembrance.

We limped home to a fourth-place finish, trailing Baltimore by 13½ games. Personally, it was my most successful season to date, with a 21–9 record and a 2.78 ERA. My 276 innings and 17 complete games were career highs that I never topped. But teamwise, 1979 was just one bad incident after another. That's not what I expected in coming over to the twice-running world champs.

Shortly after the season was over, the club's bad luck continued. On October 29 Billy Martin got into a brawl with a marshmallow salesman in a hotel lobby. Five days later George dismissed Billy. As his successor, he appointed my old Cleveland teammate, Dick Howser.

Dick had an immediate impact. He had been a coach in 1979, and he was determined that spring training would have none of the laxness that plagued us the year before. In his first team meeting he told us that he would not tolerate rules infractions. When he issued an order, he expected it to be carried out. He didn't bluster. He just said it in a firm, no-nonsense way. There's a huge difference. The players took heed and the camp was great. We were ready to answer the bell on opening day.

Dick was his own man, something I think took George by surprise. As a coach, Dick had been a quiet guy. But as manager, he ran his team his way. Sometimes, if he were talking to the writers after a game and George would call, Dick wouldn't take it. Or he'd just pick up the phone and say "Can you call back? I'm busy." Other times, when George would make one of his "suggestions," Dick would say something like: "I'll pass along what you say" or "I think that's the wrong move, George." He did it sedately, but he made his point.

With a year in New York under my belt, and with my 21 wins giving me some status on the team, I felt totally at home. We had a fun bunch of guys on that team, a charismatic mix of men that made the Yankees "the Yankees."

First there was Reggie, who was easily the most flamboyant person I ever played with. He had a genius for capturing the moment; off the field, by saying or doing something to which the press could gravitate; on the field, with a big hit. As important as his big bat was, Reggie served an even more crucial clubhouse role: he took a lot of the heat —the press attention, the controversy—away from the rest of the team, and he loved it. He was a two-way buffer between the team and Steinbrenner, and between us and the press. That allowed other guys to go about their business in relative peace. George made a huge mistake when he let Reggie go, and he knew it. Reggie was great to my children. They loved him.

Willie Randolph provided the stabilizing influence. Willie was the club's quiet leader. You couldn't believe how good Willie was until you were on the same team and saw him play every day. He liked to stay in the background, and off the field was a devoted family man, a man interested in the community.

Bucky Dent, our shortstop, didn't have a lot of range or a strong arm, but whatever he got to, you were out at first base. He knew how to position himself, and he got to balls that were missed by other shortstops with better range. I don't think I ever saw Bucky make a bad throw to first. Not one. He was a reticent, shy man who was catapulted to reluctant fame with his home run in the 1978 playoff game against the Red Sox, and his great postseason play. He became a teen idol, a poster boy, but it never changed his shy ways. Bucky didn't want the spotlight; it was thrust upon him.

Graig Nettles was great with the one-liners, the zingers. He was always cutting up, needling someone. He was the team's pressure valve. He had a knack of defusing a tense situation with humor. Every clubhouse needs a guy like that, the guy with the acerbic wit who can take your mind off a bad situation. If Steinbrenner blasted the team, Graig would have just the right retort. Nettles also was a defensive artist, as I knew from the World Series, and could hurt you with the bat. He had a left-handed swing tailored for the short porch in right. Graig battled hepatitis all year, which limited him to 89 games in 1980.

Howser gave the team some fresh air. There was new life in the locker room, constant needling and laughter. I had a ringside seat to some great performances, with Nettles, Reggie, Gossage, Piniella, and Mickey Rivers going at each other. Then you had guys like Jim Spencer, who would stir it up then sit back and watch.

Reggie liked getting on Rivers, Mick the Quick. When he felt like playing, Mick was a brilliant center fielder. But when he was down or something was bothering him, he wasn't the same player. One day on the bus Reggie saw a truck driver.

"Hey Mick, there's you about four years after you quit playing ball, driving that truck," he said as the bus laughed.

"Might be, Reg," Mick replied. "But you know what? I'd be happy doing it."

Not that it was all smooth sailing. It never is, on any ball club. You just notice it more in New York. Dick liked to platoon, and when guys had to sit, they grumbled. Piniella, Murcer, and others had a hard time dealing with the bench, but actually, that's the kind of reaction you want. You want competitive athletes who want to get back in the lineup and prove you wrong. Dick understood that.

We dropped our first two games in Texas, but it wasn't the same as last year. We won the next two, got a little winning streak going, and finally took over first place on May 14. We stumbled a little in August as the Orioles tried to make their move, but we regrouped and ended up winning 103 games, three games ahead of second-place Baltimore.

The Yankees had some lumber on that team, with Reggie leading the way, hitting 41 of our 189 home runs. The Big Four of the rotation—me, Guidry, Rudy May, and Tom Underwood—won 68 games, with

# The Apple

Goose Gossage backing us with 33 saves and 103 strikeouts in 99 innings. I turned in a 22–9 mark in 1980, giving me a two-year record of 43–18, making me the winningest pitcher in the majors over that time. My 200th career win came on June 6 against Seattle.

What accounted for that record? Pitching is getting into a rhythm, a rhythm of self-confidence. When you have it, you go out and expect to pitch well. And you know that even if you're throwing only so-so, you'll still win. The only way you're going to lose is if you have nothing at all.

The odd thing about my performance in 1980 was that I achieved it under Stan Williams, a pitching coach who was not that good for me. Stan had been a power pitcher during his career, and he didn't understand sinkerballers. That's not a knock against Stan, who was a hard worker and was great with a guy like Guidry.

I had one brief down period in 1980, where I got out of sync. But Stan couldn't diagnose my problem. Not knowing what else to do, I called up my ex-coach Tom Morgan, who was now scouting in Palos Verdes, California. He had watched me on TV and spotted one little thing regarding my motion—I wasn't getting on top of the ball and driving down. The next time I went out, I made a small adjustment and the ball acted entirely different. It probably took Morgan a minute to explain the mechanical correction I needed to make, yet that minute got me back on track.

People forget how good that 1980 Yankees team really was. We won 103 games, but we had a bad playoffs, a controversial playoffs, and that's all anyone remembers. We were facing a strong Kansas City Royals team, led by George Brett and his .390 average. It would be a stiff challenge, since the Royals gave us trouble in the regular season.

Guidry got beat in the first game at Kansas City, 7–2, and it was one of the few times anyone could remember when he didn't respond in a big game. After the game Steinbrenner stormed into the clubhouse. His face was flushed and he appeared out of breath. He chewed us out, asking how we could lose the game. I sat there thinking, This isn't L.A., Toto, remembering how Lasorda responded after we lost Game One of the '77 playoffs to Philly. He brought in Don Rickles. Tommy was ready to laugh. George was ready to lambaste.

Rudy May went all the way in the second game, had one bad inning in which he gave up the only three Royals runs, but it wasn't enough.

We lost 3–2, a game that featured an extremely controversial baserunning play involving Willie Randolph and our third base coach Mike Ferraro.

It was a fluke play. Randolph was the tying run on second with two outs. Bob Watson rifled a ball to the corner in left. The ball rattled off the wall, but bounced nicely to Willie Wilson. Randolph didn't get a good jump off second. As he rounded third, Ferraro was windmilling Randolph home. Wilson, not noted for his throwing arm, overthrew shortstop U. L. Washington, the cutoff man, and it looked like a sure run. But as luck would have it, the ball came flukishly to third baseman Brett. Brett wheeled and threw a strike to catcher Darrell Porter, nailing the sliding Randolph. Brett later claimed he was the double cutoff man on the play, but that was ridiculous. If that had been the case, he would have been lined up with the left fielder, in between the shortstop and home plate. As it was, he was standing in back of third base. Brett got the errant throw by accident.

The play would have been forgotten, but the network TV cameras immediately focused in on George's reaction, and he was animated in his displeasure. He shot out of his chair, shouting and shaking his head. TV viewers coast to coast watched George fume over the play. He was reacting as a fan, but being George Steinbrenner, owner, he was not allowed that luxury. George wanted Ferraro fired on the spot, but Dick stood up for his man. By refusing to fire Ferraro, Howser sealed his fate as Yankee manager.

I pitched the third game, and there was controversy there. I was ahead 2–1 at Yankee Stadium with two out in the seventh when Willie Wilson doubled. Howser took me out and brought in Goose Gossage to face U. L. Washington, the absolutely correct move. But U. L. beat out a chop hit over the mound, putting runners on first and third. That brought up George Brett, who crushed a Gossage fastball for a three-run homer to win the game.

Steinbrenner blasted Howser for bringing Gossage in, but it was the ultimate second guess. Howser had Gossage, one of baseball's best relief pitchers, ready in the bullpen. He had to bring him in the game.

The playoffs ruined a great season, and it meant the end of Howser. George brought Gene "Stick" Michael in to manage in 1981.

Who knows why George selected Gene Michael? But hearing the rumors and shop talk in the clubhouse made me realize that some of the

# The Apple

veteran Yankee players thought they knew: Michael would not be independent, like Howser, but basically follow Steinbrenner's lead. When
George phoned, Gene would answer. When George sent down a new
lineup, Gene would use it. I hadn't played with Michael on the Yankees,
so I viewed it as an "outsider." From my perspective, Stick had managed
well at Columbus in the International League, and I thought he rated a
shot.

We had a good team that year, but not a championship team; strong,
but not as strong as the year before. Fortunately, we got off to a good
start, playing .600 ball. My won-lost record wasn't all that great, but
the ERA was under 3.00. I was pitching in hard luck. Then on June 6,
the day we took over first place, a freak accident happened. I was
standing in front of our sink in our bathroom preparing to shave. I reached
into my shaving kit to get my razor and heard a ripping noise. I pulled
my hand out of the bag and saw blood cascading down; the index finger
on my pitching hand was sliced wide open. The protective cap had fallen
off the razor and I was bleeding like a stuck pig.

I was scheduled to pitch that night. I went immediately to see trainer
Gene Monahan and Michael. Gene was angry.

"Why didn't you tell me earlier?" he asked.

"I didn't cut it earlier. I cut it just now."

"We just sent Gene Nelson down and can't get him back for seventy-
two hours. I'm stuck now, two pitchers short for three days," he said,
annoyed. "If you would have called us in the morning—"

"Stick," I interrupted, "if I had known I was going to cut my finger
later in the day, I would have told you: 'I'm thinking about cutting my
pitching hand later, so have somebody ready to take my place.' That's
not logical, Stick. Think about it."

He was still upset. I couldn't understand Michael's reaction at the
time, but knowing what I know now, Gene was probably under George's
gun about something. George wasn't fully satisfied with Gene's managing
or with the team's play, and he was letting his manager know, loudly.

The Yankees put me on the disabled list. I packed my baseball bag
and went home to New Jersey. Sally and the kids had flown to Indiana,
so I threw some clothes together, got my golf clubs, put everything in
the car, and drove all night to Indiana. Two days later I learned the
players had gone on strike.

It wasn't a bad summer. If you're going to be on strike, that's the
time to do it. For three weeks we just spent every day lazing around,

watching TV, swimming, going on picnics, going to the lake. Truthfully, it was nice being home with the kids and doing the things you don't have a chance to do when you play baseball for a living. We spent a lovely Father's Day together, and enjoyed a family outing to Vermont. I was also getting paid. Since we had no strike language in my contract, the matter was ambiguous, and the team kept paying me. Later, the team protested the payments, but the court ruled in my favor.

After the third week I started to throw some batting practice to the kids who played amateur ball in our town. I liked doing that, because it forced me not to overthrow. All you're doing in batting practice, especially throwing to juniors, is working on getting your arm up and throwing the ball properly.

The strike lasted forty-nine days. The teams that were in first place when the strike began were declared first-half winners. The second half would be played as a separate miniseason, with the divisional winner of that race meeting the divisional winner of the first half—the Yankees. With an automatic playoff berth in hand, the team sat back on its laurels in the second half.

I beat the Rangers at home in the first game of the second half. That made me the only pitcher in baseball history to win two opening day games in the same season. I had won the April opener, also against Texas. After that series, we flew into Detroit to play the Tigers. On the morning of April 13, I played golf at Oakland Hills C.C. with Bob Zankl, a friend. That played an important part in the terrible events that were soon to unfold.

I was out in the bullpen at Tiger Stadium, working out. The batboy came out and told me I had a call. I told him to get a number and I'd call back. A moment later Jeff Torborg, one of our coaches, came running out. Sally was on the phone, Jeff told me, and she sounded really upset. I threw my glove down, sprinted into the clubhouse and picked up the phone.

"Tommy," Sally said hysterically, "Travis fell and he's dying."

The people, the clubhouse—everything seemed to recede, as if I were seeing them through the wrong end of a telescope. My heart was pounding. I felt as if someone had just slugged me in the gut.

When the team went on the road trip to begin the second half of the season, Sally took the kids down to Bay Head, on the New Jersey shore, to visit our friends, Chuck and Carol Schaefer. Sally's sister Judy

**210**

# The Apple

went along as well, bringing her two children. They had just arrived that afternoon, and were staying in this big, three-story house. Travis, then two and a half years old, and Tommy, four, had bedrooms on the third floor. Sally's bedroom was on the second floor. The happy group was getting ready to go out that night to dinner, then take in an evening of fun on the boardwalk and at the amusement park.

Sally had taken a baby-sitter with her, with explicit instructions: "One of us will not take our eyes off the boys for one second." She made it clear that at no time were the boys to be left alone. The baby-sitter, a fifteen-year-old girl, was with the two boys in their bedroom, but left the room for an instant, to get a sweater. That's all it took. One instant.

The house had low windowsills, low enough for a two-and-a-half-year-old to climb. Travis was sitting in the window, rocking back and forth against the screen. The next thing anyone knew, he crashed through the screen and fell out the window. His brother Tommy was on the floor playing. He looked up and saw Travis's feet leave the window.

Tommy ran next door to his sister's room, telling her that Travis had just fallen out the window. Tami, almost eight at the time, screamed: "Mommy, Mommy. Travis fell!"

Sally went tearing out of her room, down the stairs, and saw Travis lying unconscious, his head propped up against the bottom step leading to the front door. His face was turning blue, with blood coming out of his ear. He had hit his head on the front end of Sally's car, then slammed head first into the concrete sidewalk, near the steps. His heart was beating, but he wasn't breathing. Travis had swallowed his tongue and his mouth was locked.

"He's dying!" Sally screamed.

Somehow she had the presence of mind to try to pry open his mouth and free the tongue. But his jaws were locked tight. It's strange how seemingly insignificant things can come to mean so much. Just as she heard Tami's scream, Sally had been holding a bottle of nail polish, which she was going to drop in her purse. When she came flying downstairs to Travis, she still held the bottle in her hand. It had one of those long, translucent stemlike handles on it, like a steeple.

Sally worked the stem of the bottle into Travis's mouth and with all her strength pried his teeth apart just enough to stick one finger in his mouth. She ran her finger back down his throat, and as soon as she got it back there, the tongue rolled forward. When she did that, Travis gasped for air, and then started breathing on his own.

Sally was shrieking. A policeman who was in the neighborhood heard her, came running over. As they loaded Travis into the police car, he started moaning and his body shook with spasms. Sally rode in the front seat, trying as best she could to comfort Travis.

"Mommy's here," she kept saying frantically. "God loves you and He will help you. Please God, help him! Oh, help him!"

On the way to the hospital the police car got caught in traffic.

"Drive up on the sidewalk," Sally pleaded with the driver. "For God's sake, keep going."

The driver speeded up on the pavement, past the long line of cars. After they got Travis to Point Pleasant Hospital and took him to the Emergency Room. she put in her call to me.

Torborg and the trainers came running into the clubhouse. They had seen my mad dash from the bullpen and knew something was wrong. When I hung up the phone, they could see the color drain from my face.

"What's wrong, Tommy?" Torborg asked.

"Travis fell out a window and broke his neck. He's dying. I'm leaving. I'm going back to New Jersey."

They asked me if I needed help.

"Let me have Dr. Bonamo's phone number [the Yankees orthopedic surgeon]."

My logistical problem was how to get back to New Jersey quickly. The air controllers were on strike, and there were no flights going from Detroit to New York. I thought of driving. My mind was racing a thousand miles an hour. Then it hit me. Bob Zankl. I had played golf with Bob that morning, and during the game we chatted about flying and his private plane. I called Bob at his car dealership, explaining my emergency.

"Tommy, my airplane isn't here, it's being used. But I have a friend who might have a plane available."

I sped over to Pontiac, where the plane was ready and gassed up. We had called ahead to the hospital, and they gave us the location of the nearest airport, in Monmouth County. They made arrangements to have a police car meet me upon landing to rush me to the hospital. We had to wait a while for clearance to take off, and finally we were in the air.

All during the flight I tried to get myself ready to accept the unacceptable. I steeled myself for this scenario: when I got to the hospital, I would find Travis dead. I prayed for strength.

Give me strength to handle what's in front of me, I prayed. If Travis is dead, give me strength to handle that. But if he's alive, give me the wisdom to make the right decisions that could weigh the outcome of his life.

I prayed he was going to be okay, but I kept visualizing walking into the hospital, with a doctor coming out and saying "Your boy's dead, Mr. John." I played that scene over and over.

We landed at the airport at about two A.M., and a squad car whisked me to the hospital, past the waiting reporters. Sally was in hysterics. She ran to meet me, then collapsed in my arms.

"Travis is going to be all right," I told her. "Sally, listen to me. Be strong. He's going to be all right."

She recovered and told me Travis had undergone brain surgery. The doctors let us visit him in the recovery room. His neck wasn't broken, but the doctors said there was serious danger of brain damage. They had drilled four holes in his skull to ease pressure from his traumatized brain. The recovery room was cold, almost frigid, to reduce brain swelling.

How can I describe what it was like, seeing our little boy lying there, unconscious, his head shaved, and all connected up with wires? Travis was bound to his bed, to keep him from moving about or thrashing with spasms. His eyes were open, but he saw nothing. It was scary and heart-wrenching.

"We've got to make some decisions," I told Sally.

# 11.

# RECLAMATION

As the 1989 camp went on and my pitching started to attract attention, some of the pitchers cooled off toward me. Not Righetti, who was just about my campaign manager that spring, but others on the staff. That didn't bother me, because pitching staffs have been like that ever since I've been in baseball, and probably since baseball began.

My making the ball club meant someone was going to lose his job. These "threatened" pitchers were like mini versions of Dallas Green: unfriendly and cold. They thought old T.J. belonged somewhere else, doing something else . . . like serving on the local school board, or rocking in a chair eating strained oatmeal. It was professional jealousy.

If you have ten pitchers on a staff, there are probably seven who hope you fall flat on your face. It's human nature that you take care of yourself first. Competition didn't bother me; if somebody was good enough to beat me out of a job, then so be it. But some pitchers will try most anything to boost themselves at a teammate's expense.

In 1971, my last year with the White Sox, there was a young left-handed pitcher named Don Eddy. He used to keep his own personal depth chart taped on the inside of his locker. All the pitchers on Don's chart were left-handers, guys like me, Wilbur Wood, Jim Magnuson, Rich Hinton, and Terry Forster. When Eddy thought he passed someone, he would cross out the guy's name. It was a big joke in the clubhouse: Who did Don Eddy cross out this week? One day, Wood came up to me.

"Don got you this week," he said with a mock laugh.

"Good for him," I told Wilbur. "If that makes him happy, that's great. But I tell you what. I'll be playing ball long after he's gone."

Don Eddy ended his career with major league totals of 0–2 and 35 innings in 29 total appearances.

I relished competition because it forced me to work hard. And that's one of the things that Dallas Green appreciated: my work ethic. I threw a lot; Dallas also believed a pitcher should throw as much as possible. That's something we talked about several times that spring. On one of my off-days I went out to get in some extra throwing. He came over.

"You like to throw a lot, don't you?" he asked.

"Yeah, Dallas. I've got to do it to be effective. Because if I don't throw often, then I don't improve."

"Tommy," he said, "that's something you can't get across to young pitchers today. Nobody wants to work hard anymore."

He made an excellent point. Today's players are better physically, but for the most part, they don't have that burning desire that was so prevalent when I first came up to the majors. How do you change that? It starts in the minor leagues. You tell your minor league managers to get their pitchers to throw more. Today, organizations overprotect their minor league pitchers. Ball clubs are afraid of hurting their young arms because they have so much money invested. To prevent sore arms they tell young pitchers to throw less. The problem with that is they don't learn to pitch.

That's why I'd love to manage in the lower minor leagues, to teach this to kids. You improve by pitching often. During games, let them pitch out of trouble. How else do you expect pitchers to learn how to close out a game? But at the first sign of trouble, there's the manager with the hook. The complete game is an endangered species in baseball today.

One thing I'd consider if I ever managed would be a four-man rotation. Today, the five-man staff is dogma. But why? Is it written in stone somewhere? No. Baseball went with four-man rotations for generations. Look at what George Bamberger did as pitching coach of the Orioles in the late 1960s, early seventies. George had his guys throwing on the side the day after they pitched. All of a sudden the Orioles had a great staff: Jim Palmer, Mike Cuellar, Dave McNally, and Pat Dobson, a quartet that in 1971 won 81 games and pitched 70 complete games.

A four-man rotation makes sense because of a simple fact: most teams do not have five, or even four, solid starters. The New York Mets and Oakland A's in the late eighties were exceptions. Most staffs have three good starters and two average or below. Would you rather have your top three starters pitching 75 percent of your games, as in a four-man rotation, or 60 percent, as in a five-man cycle? The four-man rotation also frees up another pitcher for the bullpen without losing a roster spot for an additional position player.

As spring training wore on, my legs felt tired, but a sinkerballer can pitch with "dead" legs. Most pitchers must learn to do that at some point during the long season because the legs take such a beating. That's why pitchers run so much, to keep the legs in shape. But I don't think the legs play as much a part in pitching as the experts say. Some pitching coaches talk about leg drive as if it's *the* sole determinant in a pitcher's success. But leg drive is overrated. Legs are not driving tools as much as they are balancing tools. The main function of a pitcher's legs is to act as shock absorbers, to keep him stabilized. That's why I was so religious about my leg exercises, not just in the spring of 1989, but throughout my whole career.

My son Travis was near death. Any mistakes—any wrong choices— in this early stage of treatment could have had devastating consequences. *That's* pressure. Pitching the seventh game of the World Series is like playing in the sandbox compared to that.

Sally and I talked it over, and I called Dr. Jack Bonamo, the team orthopedic doctor. Jack had heard about the injury on the radio. We asked him for the name of the best doctor for a case like this. He referred us to Fred Epstein, a doctor on staff at NYU Medical Center in New York.

In the meantime, several hours earlier, Dr. Stu Siegal was driving on one of the freeways in L.A. and heard a news report about Travis. Stu was head of hematology and oncology at Children's Hospital in Los Angeles, the beneficiary of the annual golf tournament I host in December out in L.A. Stu tracked down our hospital by calling the newspapers. When he called, the hospital wouldn't put him through, so he left his number for Sally, with a message to call.

# Reclamation

When they told Sally, she cried out "Stu!" We had a lot of confidence in him. She called him, and he told her: "Sally, you've got to get him to a qualified hospital. That's a fine hospital where you are for emergencies, but Travis is going to need specialized help. Get him to a medical center where they have a CAT scanner on the premises. If they try to tell you not to move him, don't take no for an answer. You must get Travis either to New York or Philadelphia. He's got to be moved in the morning. You can't waste any time."

"But who . . . where can we move him?" Sally asked.

"Let me check and find who's the best pediatric neurosurgeon."

He called back later and said that his people "tell me that one of the best in the world is in New York at NYU. His name is Fred Epstein."

That sewed it up, for now we had two different people, independent of each other, tell us that Epstein was the best.

It was five in the morning. I got Dr. Epstein's number from information and gave his answering service our message. At 7:45 A.M. Dr. Epstein returned our call. He asked some preliminary questions. We explained the situation, and he immediately took the case. He asked for Travis's vital signs, and we got them from the chart. When he heard the numbers, he said: "He's got to be moved. You've got to get him up here [to NYU Medical Center]."

"How do we do that?" I asked.

"You just tell the doctors. Insist. The state has a helicopter service that will move patients like that."

"What if the doctors won't let us move him?"

"They'll do it," Dr. Epstein reassured me.

"But what if they won't listen to us? Would you mind calling them?" I asked. He agreed.

Dr. Epstein called the doctors at Point Pleasant Hospital and explained what he wanted done. The Point Pleasant doctors cautioned us that the move would be dangerous and Travis might not survive the flight. The decision was ours. Do we leave him at Point Pleasant, where they lacked the proper equipment, or do we take him by helicopter to NYU and risk having him die? We said a prayer, then decided to place our faith in Dr. Epstein.

We flew to NYU in two helicopters, one for Travis, the medical personnel, and equipment, the second one for me, Sally, and Carol, who stayed by our side. In the helicopter we prayed that Travis would survive the flight.

NYU is at Thirty-fourth Street and First Avenue in New York, with a helipad in back at Thirty-fourth and the river. We landed, brushed past a throng of waiting reporters and TV cameras, and followed the ambulance around the corner into the emergency room. Travis weathered the stress of the flight as well as could be expected. Dr. Bonamo and a pediatric surgeon were in the emergency room, along with nurses and aides. They conducted a preliminary examination to make sure there were no internal problems or other conditions that needed emergency attention. Dr. Epstein performed a more thorough exam soon afterward, then patiently answered our waterfall of questions. There was really only one question, however.

"What are Travis's chances of full recovery?"

Dr. Epstein paused. "It's hard to say right now. But I'm encouraged. I see no signs of irreversible brain damage."

Despite the ambiguous answer, his manner and his confidence gave us the reassurance that we had indeed found the best doctor.

Dr. Epstein increased Travis's medication to put him in a deeper, medically induced coma. His brain was active, and the only way to quiet it was to take him into a deeper coma. As Dr. Epstein explained, that would reduce the swelling of the brain.

Calls were pouring into the hospital from celebrities, baseball people, politicians, presidents, fans, friends, and those unknown to us but who wanted to offer their support. People sent cards, flowers, gifts, toys, rosaries, and prayer cards. That support had an incalculable effect on Sally and me as we tried to hold up under the strain. Tragedy opens up closed hearts, and often becomes the bridge that enables people to offer each other support, kindness, and even love.

During the first few days, Travis would open his eyes, but with no recognition. He would then drift away. It was incredibly upsetting to see. At the end of the second day he started having trouble breathing on his own, and they hooked him up to a respirator. The way the doctors explained it, the machine would breathe for him, to take some of the strain off his body. The respirator was a frightening machine, with beeping monitors, wires, and a chilling mechanical wheeze.

Dr. Epstein told us the next few days would be rough. If Travis was going to get well, he would have to bottom out first then start his way slowly back up. But if he didn't bottom out—if he sank deeper and deeper—he'd be in trouble. That's when patients become either dysfunctional—vegetables—or they just die in their coma. We stayed by Travis's bedside constantly, talking to him, telling him of our love, of God's love, and urging him not to give up.

"Please be strong, honey. Mommy and Daddy love you and want you to get all better. We are here, darling. We are here."

The doctors put a pressure monitor in Travis's head. They drilled into his skull and screwed it in, much like you would screw a bolt into a plasterboard wall. The device measured brain pressure. If the pressure exceeded safe limits, they could then take rapid corrective measures, such as cutting the scalp open and drilling directly into the brain cavity.

We took rooms at a nearby hotel, about five minutes away by car. The Yankees arranged for limousine service to and from the hospital. We spent practically all our time those first few days at the hospital, coming back to the hotel only to sleep. Or I should say, to try to sleep. We knew little peace, especially Sally, who would call the hospital frequently for any update.

Sally's a questioner. The doctor would come in and give us a brief word, and she'd have forty questions about details, specific things. She was relentless, and wouldn't let up until she understood the answers. I was the opposite of her. I basically listened a lot. When the doctor told me they thought there was no irreversible brain damage, and that through long and hard therapy our boy could possibly get back to normal, that's all I needed to hear.

"We'll do whatever it takes," I said. "If it takes a year, if it takes two years, whatever, that's how long we'll work with Trav. We won't give up and we won't quit until they say there's absolutely no more that we can do."

One of our worst nights came on Sunday, August 15. When we entered the intensive care unit on the pediatric ward, we knew something was wrong. We couldn't put our finger on it at first. The atmosphere was uneasy, almost crackling with subdued, unexpressed, unresolved tension. Or hurt. Something we couldn't quite identify hung ominously in the air.

Then we found out.

The four-year-old girl who had occupied a bed near Travis's had died. Her body was shrouded in white, mummylike coverings. The gravity of our ordeal then slammed into our hearts, cutting jaggedly into the soul. Until then we were operating solely on nervous energy, but this tragedy really woke us up to the awful potential consequences of Travis's injury. Tears welled up and we just held each other in silence, there being no words to say.

At that moment we knew what it meant to place ourselves utterly, *unconditionally,* in the hands of God. Because He was our only hope.

Dr. Epstein said it was too early for a definitive prognosis. Brain scans confirmed brain injury, but there was no evidence of irreversible brain damage. He said the recovery was going to be long and tedious. The way he explained it, when you go into a coma, you go back in time to your birth. You then have to work your way back and relearn everything, motor skills, physical things, and the like. That's why adults with brain injuries have a much harder time than kids. There's so much farther to come back. But fortunately, Travis was only two and a half, and he had very little to relearn.

The press kept a vigil of their own, wanting updates and exclusives. In the emotion of the situation, Sally wanted to shut everybody off, but we couldn't do that. As a public figure, that was one responsibility I couldn't avoid. So I held what amounted to a press conference, making a plea for prayers. The papers played it up big and we got over ten thousand letters and prayer cards, plus uncounted prayers we never knew about except for their effect on us and on Travis.

One visit we'll never forget was from Terrence Cardinal Cooke. He had come to NYU to say Sunday mass, and dropped by unannounced at the pediatric intensive care ward. He blessed Travis and the four other children on the ward, and gave us counsel.

"Just shower him with love," the cardinal advised. "Because he's going to get strength through your love. All the prayers that are being said out there are going to enter Travis through you. Just keep telling Travis day after day how much you love him and how much the people out there love him, and how much God loves him. I'm sure he can hear you. Travis will get better through these prayers."

The visit of this holy man was a tremendous lift to our spirits, and we followed his advice. We always talked to him, telling him about our love, and reading to him from his favorite book, *Good Night Moon.* The doctors told us that sometimes in a coma the mind is still awake and it can understand things. The person may not be able to bring it to the surface, but when they come out of it, they'll remember things that happened.

Poor Sally. She spent day after eighteen-hour day at the hospital, with little respite, plus she was seven months pregnant with Taylor, our fourth child. At least I had the ball park for mental and emotional release. I resumed my workouts with a fever, pouring everything I had into my running, stretching, and throwing.

The first game I pitched after Travis's injury was against the White Sox at Yankee Stadium on the night of August 19. I left the hospital, went to the locker room, and tried to concentrate on the game. But I was totally unprepared mentally. Usually, I go through the opposing lineup and visualize how to pitch to each batter, but this time it was useless. I couldn't get Travis out of my mind.

On the mound my mind kept wandering back to the hospital. The Yankees took a 2–0 lead off Richard Dotson, but in the third our infield unraveled. After singles by Greg Luzinski, Wayne Nordhagen, and Chet Lemon, Dent and Nettles made errors. Graig misplayed a grounder by Bill Almon that was ruled a hit, and no one handled a bunt single by Mike Squires. Four runs scored. We tied it in the bottom of the fourth, but ended up losing 6–5, the team's fifth loss in six games. I felt like a sleepwalker in the unreality of a baseball game. George came into the clubhouse after the game and said, "We played awful. You gave one hell of an effort. I know it was hard for you to concentrate and I appreciate what you did."

My emotions were wound up tight like piano wire. It took a little thing to break them. The Yankees had an elaborate "eye-in-the-sky" system of upstairs coaching. George had Doug Melvin up there with a walkie-talkie, communicating with Yogi Berra in the dugout by phone. Melvin would tell Yogi how to position the outfielders. But someone hit a gapper in an area in right-center that I had specifically asked to have covered. The hit opened the floodgates and led to my early shower. When I came off the field, I grabbed my jacket and saw Yogi on the phone, talking to Melvin. I grabbed the phone and ripped it off the wall.

"Here," I said to Yogi, handing him the receiver. "For all those guys are doing moving outfielders around, you can stand here with a dead phone, because it's not working."

Yogi sat there for the rest of the game with the dead headset up to his ear, pretending to talk into it. He didn't dare put it down, for fear that Steinbrenner would see it and get mad. The next day I apologized to Yogi for losing my head.

In my 3⅓ innings, the Sox touched me up for ten hits and five runs.

Steinbrenner was in the clubhouse after the game and he came over to my locker.

"Tommy, that was a gutsy performance out there," he told me. "It wasn't your fault we lost. You did a helluva job, and I admire your strength. Not many guys could go out there and do what you just did tonight."

The game provoked Steinbrenner. After Reggie singled to lead off the eighth and Nettles walked, Bob Watson failed to bunt the runners over and struck out. There had been several such lapses in recent games, and George had had enough.

"I'm not getting my money's worth," George complained to the press, and then ordered a workout on the next day's slated off-day. "We're going to practice and practice and practice until we get it right. These guys are the highest paid team in baseball, and they're ripping me off."

George was very accommodating when it came to my schedule. When the team went on the road, he allowed me to stay behind to be at the hospital. When I was scheduled to pitch, I would fly in the night before, check in at the hotel, pitch the next night, then catch the first plane back to New York the next day.

It's strange, but after getting to the ball park, I realized what a refuge it was. The atmosphere of being around my teammates, of losing myself in the familiar routines of baseball, helped more than I realized. For the first time I truly understood why Billy Martin practically lived at the park: it was a safe port in a swirling storm. I was able to achieve an almost unreal focus, and it showed in my performance. I won my next three starts. Probably the best games I pitched all year came in those four or five starts when Travis was in the hospital. From September 3 to 25 I threw five straight complete games.

Day after day we watched, waited, and prayed. Travis's eyes were open, but unfocused. We talked to him, read to him, sang songs, played with toys, trying to get some small recognition from him. We were spending sixteen to eighteen hours a day at the hospital, by his bedside. We had enormous support from family and friends, who took care of Tami and Tommy and ran errands. George's wife Joan came by and take Sally out for lunch, just to get her out of the hospital. She had gone through a similar experience with her son Hal and she was very comforting for Sally to talk to. And for the thirty days of Travis's hospitalization, we heard from Al Campanis and the Dodgers just about every day. The Dodgers never forgot us, and our son's injury became the way to smooth over any differences left over after I declared free agency at the end of the 1978 season.

The first voluntary movement Travis made came about two weeks into his coma. We were at his bedside. Sally was stroking him and talking gently into his ear. Slowly, his left arm moved. Sally looked at me. I caught her eye. Was it just a spasm? Travis's arm continued up to his face. He curled his little fingers into a light fist and rubbed his eye, as if he were waking up in the morning. We watched in amazement. A silent tear trickled down Sally's cheek. We hugged each other in excitement.

"Did you see that?" I asked. "He moved his arm. He did it all on his own."

Prior to that, Travis had been moving spasmodically. This was different. This was movement with a purpose. Our hopes shot up. The next day he did it again. We had covered Travis with his favorite blanket. Travis loved that blanket, and used to poke his finger through a particular small hole. There he was, in his coma, when his right arm came out from under the blanket and started searching for the hole. His tiny hand crept across the tattered surface and finally came to rest in the hole. Our son was returning to us.

After that, the signs were continually more hopeful. We were secretly terrified that the waking-up process would halt, but he made rapid progress, regaining more and more movement. We would stand him up in bed, support him, and try to move his feet back and forth on the bed, to simulate walking. Travis would have to relearn these movements. We also exercised his muscles, since his body had shriveled up from inactivity.

Travis woke up by degrees. One of the crowning moments came when I wasn't there, but at the ball park pitching. Sally and Carol Schaefer were watching the game on TV. The ump called me for a balk, and I went over to talk to the umpire about it. The camera had a tight close-up of my face. Travis, who was looking at the set, broke out with a smile of recognition. There was Dad.

I brought some brightly colored orange Tommy Armour golf balls to the hospital so we could roll them to him. Travis would almost be able to catch the ball, but he couldn't figure out how to move his body. We'd put a ball in his hand, and his hand would start shaking, and you could tell he just wanted to throw that ball, but couldn't figure out how to do it. This was the relearning process that Dr. Epstein talked about. But he got better at it and soon was able to catch and return the ball. Only a few days later, a doctor walked by and Travis picked up one of the balls and smoked it at the doctor's feet.

He eventually starting walking and talking again and was moved out of intensive care on August 31, a joyous day for us. In all, Travis was comatose for seventeen days and was in the hospital for thirty. We continued his therapy, and, though he was on the regular pediatric ward, we hired a nurse to be with him all night. We had come too far to take anything for granted. The miraculous aspect of his recovery is that the doctors couldn't really explain its rapidity. Once Travis came out of the coma, he got "normal" with lightning speed. He went from comatose to walking in thirteen days. One of the doctors said he couldn't explain that, and added that "whatever avenues you people used have got to be good ones, because it's just not probable for anyone to get well that fast."

The ball-tossing sessions were one example. One minute Travis couldn't figure out how to throw, but then, in the next session—boom!—he could fire the ball hard. He needed to do something just once to open up the brain passages controlling particular movements.

My explanation for his recovery lies with God. Take the series of "coincidences" that happened, Sally's car, for example. When Travis fell, he hit the hood of the car first, which broke his fall before he slammed into the concrete. Sally originally had parked the car farther back in the parking space. She got out of the car, but then had second thoughts. She went back inside and pulled it closer to make it easier for her sister and the kids to get in the driveway with her car. If she hadn't done that, the fall would have killed Travis because he would have landed on solid concrete.

My golf date with Bob Zankl; the policeman who was in the neighborhood; the stem of the nail polish bottle that enabled Sally to force open Travis's mouth; Stu Siegal's hearing the report of the accident on the radio as he was driving—these were just a few of a multitude of "coincidences" that occurred, each one of which played a major role in Travis's recovery. I saw them as divine intervention. As a wise man once put it, coincidence is God's way of remaining anonymous.

As Travis's discharge drew closer, Sally grew extremely anxious. The hospital had become a secure environment for her. She knew that if there was any setback, the best doctors and equipment were seconds away. But what if Travis had a seizure at home, or had some other setback when we were sleeping? These thoughts haunted her.

The release date came quickly, and looking back on it, those thirty days of hospitalization went by like a blur, like a VCR put on fast forward. When Travis got his final blood test, he screamed when the needle went in but bravely told Sally:

"I was a good boy, Mommy."

He certainly was.

The doctors reassured us that Travis could recover well at home. They said the protective tissue had grown over the four holes in his skull and would not be opened if he bumped his head. They tried to answer all of Sally's questions, and gave her the assurance that leaving the hospital was now the necessary step in his recovery. We had to let go.

On Thursday, September 10, Travis was released. We said our good-byes to everyone: the parents and patients, the nurses and doctors, the staff and volunteers. We were leaving friends and felt both happy and sad. We took the elevator down to the door, and an assembled group of hospital people broke out in applause.

Travis smiled broadly, and at our urging, blew everyone a big kiss. The cameras caught him, and the next day the photo of his kiss ran on the wires across the country. On the drive home we played a cassette containing his favorite song, "The Rainbow Connection," a Muppets song. As we pulled into the driveway of our Franklin Lakes home, Travis saw his tricycle in the garage.

"Bicycle, Mommy! Bicycle!"

He remembered! A great sign.

We went in the house; Travis went immediately to the toy box in his room and started playing with some balls. That night we put *The Muppet Movie* in the VCR and viewed it with him three times. Watching the TV news later that night, Travis saw the film of us leaving the hospital.

"That's me! That's me!"

Travis's recovery went as smoothly as possible, though after we returned home, the impact of the ordeal hit us in a different way. We were emotionally exhausted, and I think Sally had her hardest time after we got Travis home. At the hospital she ran simply on adrenaline.

But at home she had time to think. She'd wake up screaming in the middle of the night, with nightmares that Travis was leaving her or wasn't breathing. She kept seeing him walking out a door. She was afraid to wake up and find his recovery was all a dream, that he didn't survive, that he had died in the fall.

She also had to deal with the residual guilt from the accident. She had taken every precaution, yet the baby-sitter's momentary lapse was enough to undo the most careful plans. As Sally put it, motherhood comes with a built-in feeling of *total* responsibility, and a mother will always feel some blame when one of her children suffers. Her feelings were normal, and—with faith—she was able to work through them. But it wasn't easy.

After the accident she took Travis everywhere she went. She literally would not let him out of her sight. People would want to touch him, hug him, hold him, as if he were some sort of religious relic, and you can't tell me that he didn't absorb some of that love. Travis was a little boy who had come into direct contact with something larger than all of us.

Today, Travis is a happy, healthy, and loving boy and perfectly normal. He enjoys playing baseball, football, wrestling, and other sports. People still ask us about him. He's special to us, naturally, but *all* of our children are special. Travis's injury made us better realize that. What happens in my career doesn't matter, because we have four of the most beautiful, happy, healthy children any parents could want: Tami, Tommy, Travis, and Taylor. Each has their own talents, and each gives and receives love in their own way.

We're so lucky. We saw other parents at the hospital who had to deal with a child's death. We came so close ourselves with Travis. He easily could have gone the other way, and there's not a day that goes by where Sally and I don't thank God for sparing his life, and thank God for the health of all our children.

I learned something else from Travis's accident, namely, that tragedy offers you a different perspective on your life. It allows you to grasp that there are far more important things in life than wins and losses. You don't appreciate water until the well runs dry, and you don't appreciate how much you love your children until one of them is taken or nearly taken from you.

A rabbi told us in the hospital that God had a very special plan for Travis, and that's why he was saved.

"That plan is out of your hands," he told us, "and it's out of the boy's hands. You can't control what it is. You have to love him and guide him, but God will steer him toward the purpose He has in mind for the boy."

It will be exciting to watch as it unfolds. I don't know where God will lead him, but it's a fact that Travis has more compassion and love in his body than any kid I've ever been around. It happened the way Cardinal Cooke said it would happen. We became channels through which Travis received all that love. It's really incredible.

He knows about the accident now, through reading about it and watching videotape. He understands he was seriously hurt, and that he recovered. As he grows older, he will have a greater appreciation of the miracle that God worked for him.

After the strike, as I mentioned, the Yankees played uninspired baseball. With the first-half divisional "title" wrapped up, we lost our intensity, playing one game under .500, finishing in sixth place at 25–26. Even though we had secured a spot in the divisional playoffs, Steinbrenner became incensed by our listless play.

Soon after we resumed play in the second half, Goose Gossage came down with a sore arm, nothing serious, but normal for what was essentially a second spring training. That upset George. He called a meeting of the coaches and trainers and raked them over the coals.

There was another incident in late August, when George caught his designated hitters, Lou Piniella and Oscar Gamble, in the clubhouse lounge, lying down on the couches, watching the game on TV. George was furious. He kicked them out of the lounge and declared the area off limits during games. Steinbrenner blamed Michael for allowing the incident to occur. George ordered a workout for the next day, a scheduled off-day.

George also was feuding with Reggie over Reggie's hitting, and who knows what else. He told Michael to bench Reggie, then ordered his angry superstar to submit to a physical examination. Reggie took the exam, but not before he told The Boss where he could go.

Rumors surfaced that Michael was on shaky ground. Gene got on us, coaxed us, lectured us, pleaded with us, but nothing could make us play better. The last straw came when George blasted Gene for not having his team ready for the upcoming playoffs. Stick told the press in Chicago: "If he wants to fire me, let him get it over with." With twenty-five games left to play, the ax came down on Michael. He was handed his head, and Bob Lemon came back for another go-round.

Gene had notebooks full of data that he and his coaches studied. Lemon was the exact opposite. He wanted to uncomplicate everything, which I liked, since baseball is a simple (though subtle) game.

We had a pitchers' meeting right after Lemon came back that showed the difference between Michael and Lemon. Pitching coach Stan Williams took out this thick notebook and started giving us detailed rundowns on the opposing batters. I forget what team we were preparing for, but Stan was saying things like:

". . . this hitter's six feet, three inches tall, weighs two hundred pounds, with blue eyes and blond hair. He likes to eat steak during the day, and enjoys following it up with two beers . . ."

He had every conceivable bit of information on the guy. Finally, Lemon stood up and broke in:

"Hey, meat! Wait, wait!" he told Williams. "You're baffling me with all this. Where's his power?"

"He likes the ball over the plate," Stan said.

"Okay. Does he like it up or down?"

"Likes it up."

"Okay, he likes it up and out over the plate. You pitchers—pitch away from his power. Next hitter. Let's go."

We just sat there looking at each other, trying to hide our snickers. That was pure Lem. He believed baseball was a game, not a science. You pitch, catch, throw, run, and field. The guys that do it better win. That's it. He was a pleasure.

We limped to the end of the schedule, finding ourselves in sixth place, five games behind the Milwaukee Brewers. The divisional playoffs opened in Milwaukee, and we took the first two games, 5–3 (Guidry) and 3–0 (Righetti) respectively. Game Three switched to Yankee Stadium on October 9, and there was a special moment before the game began.

George requested that Travis be on hand to throw out the first ball. It was a great gesture on George's part, one I will never forget. I was pitching that night and couldn't escort Travis and Sally—who was weeks away from delivery of Taylor, our fourth child—to the mound. So in the clubhouse I asked Reggie Jackson to do it. Reggie had visited

# Reclamation

Travis numerous times in the hospital, and he really had a way with Trav.

Reggie looked at me, and his eyes teared up.

"Tom, I would love to. But why me?"

"Because you're a friend and Travis loves you."

"This is one of the greatest honors of my career," he told me, wiping his eyes.

A regulation-sized baseball was too big and heavy for Travis. We bought a little white rubber ball, and Sally painted stitches on it with red fingernail polish. Reggie, Travis, and Sally walked out to the mound to a thunderous ovation. Travis threw a strike to Rick Cerone. The crowd erupted again.

Afterward, some players accused Reggie of using the moment to hog the spotlight. That wasn't the case, and I got angry:

"It wasn't Reggie's idea. The idea was Sally's and mine."

It was unbelievably petty for anyone to think ill of Reggie in that situation, and it bothered me.

The Brewers beat us 5–3 in Game Three to stay alive. I went seven-plus innings, and actually had a 1–0 lead through six. The next night they beat us again, 2–1, to tie up the series. We made some bad plays on the bases and left a lot of guys on base. It was a sloppy performance in a game we should have won. Immediately after the game the clubhouse was closed to reporters and the clubhouse guy shouted there would be a meeting. Soon after, George marched in, dressed in a blue suit, white shirt, and a Yankee tie. He got on the team for not playing well, and accused us of embarrassing not only him, but the fans of New York. Rick Cerone, who had struck out with the tying and winning runs on base at the end of the game, stood up in front of his locker, yelled, "Bleep you!" and continued into the lounge.

There was dead silence.

"You're gone next year," George countered. "Nobody talks to me that way."

Rick came back to his locker, and George was still speaking.

"What do you know about it? You never played this game!" Cerone shouted.

George glared, continued the "there's no tomorrow" part of his speech, and the meeting ended. When the reporters were finally let in, they knew something had happened. Cerone was too upset to talk. Bobby

Murcer asked the press to leave him alone. Reggie filled the void by talking to the press for two hours. It was a perfect example of what he meant to the Yankees. He took the heat off the rest of us, who really didn't want to say anything about what had gone on behind closed doors.

The series was deadlocked, with the deciding game on October 11 at the Stadium. Through three innings the Brewers held a 2–0 edge, but a four-run fourth inning gave us a 4–2 lead we never relinquished. Reggie, Gamble, and—ironically—Cerone hit home runs, and Gossage saved it for Righetti, 7–3.

The Yankees moved on to the league playoffs against Billy Martin's Oakland A's. The way the rotation went, I opened up the series, matched against Billy's ace, Mike Norris. Billy tried to psych me out in the papers.

"We can beat Tommy John," Billy told the writers. "The Yankees better pray for rain."

He said I had no chance against Norris, that I wasn't the pitcher I once was, and that I probably should just stay home and phone my pitches in—coming to the park would be a waste of time. I knew Billy well, of course, liked him, and just laughed at his comments. Billy was a friend, and he absolutely adored our daughter Tami, who had earlier that year baked him some cookies.

If anything, Billy's pregame comments put all the pressure on Norris.

The tabloids made the most of Billy's return.

GEORGE'S GALL VS. BILLY BALL read the *Daily News.* The New York *Post* ran a picture of George and Billy, toasting each other, with the caption: "Who are they kidding?"

Most ball clubs are reflections of the manager's personality, and the A's were no exception. They played aggressive baseball, always looking for any edge, and forcing situations on offense. Billy tried to upset me in the game by having his hitters request the umpires examine my ball for scuffmarks, but that was just Billy. We played well, and with relief help from Ron Davis and Gossage, I was credited with a 3–1 win. We easily swept the next two games, 13–3 and 4–0, to win a trip to Los Angeles for the 1981 World Series. But true to our tumultuous second half, even our playoff victory brought strife and turmoil.

George invited the players and families to an Oakland restaurant called Vince's to celebrate. I was sitting at a table with Sally, Howard Cosell, and Raider boss Al Davis. Graig Nettles and his family took a table, then got up to go to the buffet. Ginger Nettles left her coat and pocketbook on her chair. Reggie then came in, with a huge entourage.

# Reclamation

Ginger got back to the table first, to find that Reggie's party had taken their seats. Her purse was missing—actually, it was on the floor.

"We were sitting here. Will you please move?" Ginger asked. Then she noticed the missing purse. "Where's my purse? My purse is gone!"

Someone in Reggie's party said something to Ginger, and she told Graig. Graig, who was holding a beer, went over to Reggie.

"Your people took my family's seats."

Reggie slapped the beer out of Graig's hand, and—in a second—Nettles decked him with one punch. Reggie got back up, ready to mix, but everybody grabbed him. That was the end of the fight. George came in, said something to Reggie, and Reggie left.

Never a dull moment. Guidry won the World Series opener at Yankee Stadium, 5–3. Ron Davis set up Gossage for the save. I followed it up in game two with a four-hit, 3–0 shutout. Our first run, scored in the fifth, was unearned, and that was the winner. Randolph reached on Lopes's error, I sacrificed Willie to second, and he scored on Larry Milbourne's double. Just as in 1978, my team got up 2–0 in games, and it seemed destined that I would finally get a world's championship ring.

Out in L.A. we had Fernando Valenzuela on the ropes in Game Three and were one base hit from busting the game open. But Valenzuela escaped, trailing only 4–3 after three innings. That's where we lost not just the chance to K.O. Valenzuela, not just the game, but actually the Series itself. Fernando shut us out the rest of the way and the Dodgers eked out a 5–4 win.

Game Four was a heartbreaker, an 8–7 loss in which we blew a 6–3 lead. We left twelve men on base, botched two fly balls, and made two baserunning blunders. George Frazier, our long man, became the first pitcher in forty years to lose two straight Series games. In the fifth game the agony continued. Guidry dueled Jerry Reuss, with the Yankees leading 1–0 through six innings. But in the bottom of the seventh Pedro Guerrero and Steve Yeager connected for circuit clouts, giving the Dodgers a 2–1 lead that stood up. We were now down in games, 3–2, when the Series came back to New York for my start in Game Six.

I pitched well, hooking up with my former roommate, Burt Hooten. After 3½ innings, the score was tied 1–1. We had two on, two out, in the bottom of the fourth when Lemon sent Bobby Murcer up to hit for me.

I was flabbergasted. The Dodgers had scored just one run off me in thirteen innings, and our bullpen had had trouble holding them the entire Series. It was only the fourth inning of a tie game. Besides, I could handle the bat. In fact, I had been used as a pinch hitter when I was with the White Sox.

"You got to be kidding me," I told Lemon.

"Nope. I'm going to the bullpen," he responded.

"Who're you gonna bring in?"

"I'm bringing in [George] Frazier."

"Frazier? I can't believe it. He's lost two games already."

"Damn it," Lemon said, getting mad, "I'm going to the bullpen. That's what I'm going to do. End of discussion."

"That's the worst move I've ever seen in my life."

I walked to the end of the bench and stood against the wall, shaking my head for a hundred million TV viewers across the country and the world.

The move wasn't consistent with the way Lemon usually managed. First, he was taking out his best pitcher in the series (0.69 ERA), and second, he was putting Frazier in there instead of Gossage. Gossage was the closer, but when you face elimination, you bring him in, no matter what inning. In that situation, you simply can't let the other team score any more runs. In a deciding game, you don't save your closer for the ninth inning, because he may never get the chance. That's just what happened. Murcer flied out to end the bottom of the fourth, and the Dodgers rattled Frazier for three runs in the fifth. They tacked on four more against Ron Davis and Rick Reuschel in the top of the sixth, and Gossage never got in the game. Frazier lost a record third Series game, and the Yankees lost the Series.

I found out later why Lemon made the move. He made it covered by the long, dark shadow of George Steinbrenner. Before big games George would sit down with the coaching staff and go over the "game plan." Well, in baseball, there is no game plan. The game dictates the plan. But George, coming from a football background, talked about the "game plan." And part of George's plan for Game Six was to try to get a lead early, then go to the bullpen to hold the lead. So when we got the two guys on in the bottom of the fourth, Lemon felt he had to try to get the lead by sending Murcer to the plate. It was not sound strategy, but it was sound politics. Lemon was a good soldier.

That made four times—1974, 1977, 1979, and 1981—that my teams made the World Series, and four times we came up short. Naturally, I would have liked winning just one, but it didn't happen. I didn't get that ring; it bothers me, but it doesn't haunt me. There were too many good things that happened in my career for me to worry about that ring.

In 1982 it unraveled for me in New York. The team went through managerial paroxysms that were unsettling and disruptive, even by Yankee standards. Lemon was dismissed fourteen games into the season; a 6–8 record. Steinbrenner had been relentless in his criticism of Bob, and Lemon was fed up. He almost resigned the week before, but coach Mike Ferraro talked him out of it. When George made the move, I think Lemon was relieved.

George brought back Gene Michael for his second tour, which lasted all of 86 games (44–42), and finished out the string with Clyde King (29–33). The troika managed the Yankees to a 79–83 record, good for fifth place, 16 games behind the Brewers.

In 1982 George became fascinated with speed, and we went from power to a running game. It was an ill-advised move. We got Dave Collins as a free agent and Ken Griffey in a trade. But both were Astroturf players. When they played on grass, they weren't the same. Two moves killed us. The first might have been the biggest mistake of George's reign. He let Reggie Jackson slip away to the Angels. Reggie was irreplaceable. George looked to Dave Winfield to fill the gap. Dave's an outstanding all-round player, but nobody but Reggie will ever be Reggie Jackson. The other bad move was when they unloaded Bucky Dent and got Roy Smalley to play shortstop. Roy was a better hitter, but in my mind he was exclusively a DH. He had no range at short. No range at all. He was bad news for a pitching staff. Dent was kind of taken for granted, until the Yankees unloaded him and discovered what he meant to the infield.

After that, the team obtained several players who were past their prime. John Mayberry came over from Toronto during the season and hit .209. Lee Mazzilli, Butch Hobson, Barry Foote, Lynn McGlothen, and Roger Erickson weren't much better. Suddenly, we didn't resemble the Yankees anymore. Jerry Mumphrey was a decent player, but not the kind of guy who could carry you. We had no starter win more than Guidry's 14 games, and Ron was the only one who totaled more than 200 innings. We went through eighteen pitchers during the year.

Things were just as bad for me personally. I got into one of my pitching slumps, a deep funk that got worse the more I tried to get out of it. Off-the-field pressures weren't helping my frame of mind either.

First, in early April we had to take the Yankees to arbitration at the Federal Mediation Office in New York City, where the mediators upheld my payments during the strike of 1981. I won the arbitration and that didn't sit well with Steinbrenner.

Another problem was my contract. During the off-season we had grudgingly worked out a two-year deal with George. Part of the agreement was a $200,000 loan that we were going to use for a down payment on a new house. Sally, still getting over the effects of Travis's fall, wanted badly to get out of our three-story home. The loan was to be used to purchase a new house, a one-level ranch home.

In June I went to the front office to get the loan. The finance people looked at my contract and confirmed that indeed the loan was forthcoming. It was there in black and white. They told me they couldn't give me a check on the spot. It needed paperwork, approvals, things like that. They told me to come back in a couple of days and they'd cut me a check. But two days later, when I came in for my money, they refused to pay. George would not release the funds.

Bob Cohen called George to try to find out what the problem was, and came away with an answer. The problem was that I had a losing record. I was something like 3–7. If I had been 8–2, the money would have been there instantly. Sally begged me to go in and see George face to face to get it straightened out, but I didn't. I should have listened to her. George was taking me to the woodshed.

My days as a Yankee were numbered. I didn't need an Indian guide to read the signs. The first indication was my banishment to the bullpen. The second was the realization that the only way I was going to get the money, short of a drawn-out and expensive legal battle, was to go to another club. When you go to a new team, they pick up the terms of your existing contract. In this case, that would include the loan.

During my stint in the bullpen, Michael only used me in mop-up situations. I'd go five, six, eight, ten days without pitching. When the score was lopsided, he had me warming up. When the game got close, he sat me down. It was clear: I had to get out of New York.

Things came to an ugly head in Texas. Jane Gross of the *New York Times* asked me if I had seen the comment made by team vice president Bill Bergesch.

Bergesch, reacting to my statements about the bullpen banishment, said I should just shut up and do what the Yankees wanted me to do because of all that George did for me when Travis was in the hospital.

# Reclamation

I asked Jane if she was sure he said it, and she said yes. Three other writers got the same quote and the same words. There was no doubt what Bergesch said.

The game went on, and I sat out in the bullpen, seething over Bergesch's statement. After the game I saw Bergesch in the clubhouse. I'm not a violent person, but the pot had boiled over.

"Bill, I want to talk to you in private."

We went back to the laundry room. There's probably a plaque today over the doorway to the laundry room of the visitors' clubhouse in Texas, commemorating the "Tommy John Memorial Outburst."

I asked Bergesch if he made the remark. He said he was misquoted. I told him four reporters got the same quote in the exact same words.

"What was your reasoning in making such a stupid remark?"

"Well, George let you pitch on your own schedule while your son was in the hospital. You didn't have to join the ball club on the road."

"Bill, let me tell you. With my son in the hospital, I would have quit baseball just to be with him. I appreciate what George did, but don't go telling me I've got to be subservient to somebody the rest of my life because of what happened last year. Because what you say happened didn't happen that way."

"It most certainly did."

Something snapped. I got in his face, screaming at the top of my lungs. I called the guy every name in the book, using language that would wrinkle your clothes. I was hoping he'd make a move to shove me or something, because I was ready to flatten him. He had this New York Yankee tie on; all the executives had to wear them. I thought of choking him with it. But he didn't make a move. The whole ball club heard the outburst. When I got done, I was shaking. I could not calm down.

Yogi Berra, who was sitting next to the laundry room and saw the whole thing by peeking around the corner, came over to me and said in the understatement of the century: "Boy, you were mad."

The reporters descended on me, asking me what that was all about. I told them as best I could, as composed as I could, then took a cold shower. The cold water poured down on me like an accusation. I tried to calm myself down and stop my shaking. I've never been like that in my life, ever. The strange thing is that Bill is a nice guy, a fine man. When I see him now, we're friendly to each other. But he was George's yes man, and issued his statement at George's "request." With my mental state, it was more than I could take.

In the meantime, Michael had been fired again, a hundred games into the season. George was hounding him pretty good, holding Gene to blame for our .500 record. Stick, fed up with the abuse, made a public statement criticizing George's interference. You don't take on George in the press and win, so George fired him and brought in Clyde King. That was a break for me, because Clyde understood pitchers. He also brought in Sammy Ellis to replace Stan Williams as pitching coach. Clyde immediately put me back in the rotation.

Ellis came up to me and asked me if my arm was okay.

"Sam, something may be wrong with my head, but there's nothing wrong with my arm."

"Well, then let's go out to the bullpen and go back to work," he said, patting me on the back.

Sammy worked with me day after day, watching me throw in the bullpen for forty and fifty minutes at a time. Then one day he made an astute observation.

"You know, I always recall seeing you pitch with your hand laid back like you're gonna throw a pie."

"You know, Sam, Bill Singer used to say that same thing," I answered.

Sammy had me make the corresponding hand adjustment. I looked like Moe Howard in the middle of a Three Stooges pie fight, and all of a sudden the spin on the ball was different. My ball started sinking again. I was like a kid with a new toy.

"Sam, watch this!"

I'd throw, and the ball would whoosh in, sinking nastily. We repeated this over and over, until my problems were straightened out. You might wonder, if the hand adjustment was so simple, how come I couldn't figure it out myself? That's just the point. With a finesse pitcher, especially a sinkerballer, the difference between good mechanics and poor mechanics is often so subtle that you aren't aware of it on your own. Because when you throw, it all feels the same. You absolutely can't tell what the problem is. Coaches who weren't familiar with my style of pitching—a Stan Williams or an Art Fowler, who was Billy's pitching coach—couldn't help me. But give me a Sammy Ellis, a Red Adams, a Ray Berres, or a Mark Connor, and they knew what to look for.

Once back in the rotation, my pitching improved. But George was still stonewalling me about the loan. It was on my mind when I went on national TV with Howard Cosell on ABC's *Monday Night Baseball.* Howard and George are close, and Cosell had sniffed out my loan problem.

I made a horse's ass out of myself during the interview, but the only way of dealing with George at that point was to call his bluff. I recalled a statement he had made in a team meeting. He said anyone who didn't want to be a Yankee just had to say so, and they would be accommodated. Cosell, in his stacatto inflections, asked me:

"So, T.J., what's the solution?"

"The solution is that I don't want to be a Yankee anymore. I've got to go elsewhere, because my stay here has ended."

It was a totally unrehearsed comment. It just came out. Sally, watching at home, went bananas. When I came home, she kept asking me: "What did you do? Do you know what you're doing?"

I shouldn't have made the remark. Rather, I should have followed Sally's advice: see George privately about it. But the damage was done, and from that day on Bob Cohen and I called Bill Bergesch every day, pestering him, asking if they had traded me yet.

Near the end of August, Reggie Jackson called Sally at home.

"Does Tommy think he can still pitch?" Reggie asked her.

"Yes," she answered.

"Well, we need help out here with the Angels," Reggie said. California was in a close race with the Royals for the Western Division title.

"Reggie," Sally said, "use your influence with [Manager Gene] Mauch, [owner Gene] Autry, and [General Manager] Buzzie [Bavasi] and see if you can help get Tommy on your team. Because the Yankees will trade him for just about anything."

On August 31, I got my wish. Reggie apparently got to the right ears and a trade was announced with California: Tommy John for a player to be named later—Dennis Rasmussen, who came to the Yankees on November 24 to complete the deal.

We were back in the L.A. area, back with a clean slate, and back in a pennant race.

As all pitchers must do, I had landed on my feet.

# 12.
# KING OF THE HILL

**M**y final appearance of spring training came on March 30, 1989, a start against the Orioles at Miami. It was the bookend to my very first appearance against the Birds on March 3. My final tune-up went seven innings, good for two runs, six hits, three walks, and four strikeouts.

There were media types swarming all over me, wanting the story about how I had turned from Sayonara to Cy Young. Even while I was warming up, people were requesting interviews. It was chaotic, but I had fun with it.

"Look what you've created," I kidded Dallas. "I can't even work."

Generally, the media weren't a distraction, because at the Yankee camp they couldn't follow you everywhere, like they could at Dodgertown. The press could only be in the Fort Lauderdale clubhouse at specified times. Also, the New York beat writers, guys like Moss Klein, Bill Madden, Mike Martinez, and Murray Chass, were friends, and almost did as much as I did to get me on the ball club. In their stories they created a Robin Hood underdog figure out of me.

New Yorkers love underdogs, and the fans were captivated by this old pitcher who just wouldn't give up. The fans who followed me through spring training felt special when I made the club; it was almost as if *they* had made it. The New York fans and I have a very special feeling for each other, stemming from their tremendous support in seeing us through Travis's ordeal in 1981. That special relationship with the fans of New York shall remain intact for the rest of my life.

The theme of the fans was "Tommy showed Dallas, didn't he?" But I didn't feel that way at all. As camp started to wind down, my feeling was one of joy over having made the team, not one of satisfaction for having "shown" Dallas. I just wanted to pitch. I felt light as a rookie. I was enjoying myself. Baseball was fun again.

And then Dallas made his bold decision: forty-five-year-old Tommy John would start on opening day when the New York Yankees faced the Minnesota Twins at the Hubert H. Humphrey Metrodome in Minneapolis on April 4 against Frank Viola, the previous year's Cy Young winner.

Logically speaking, the move was understandable. The other four starters were Andy Hawkins, Al Leiter, Dave La Point, and John Candelaria. All but Hawkins were left-handers, so Dallas wanted to use Hawkins in the middle, with two lefties on either side. La Point and I were similar pitchers. It was clear Dallas wouldn't start us one-two, and with Dave's injury problems, he would not be the opener. That left either Candelaria, Leiter, or me. Leiter was twenty-three and too young. If they had named him to start on opening day, he wouldn't have slept for a week. That's how high-strung he was. He was a rookie bouncing off the walls. But there was no choice between Candelaria or me, either, since Candy was recovering from a knee injury, and Dallas wanted to give him extra rest.

But logic or not, it was still incredible to find myself in position as the opener. What were the odds?

I had come into camp with "no chance" of making the team; I would be given no help from the manager or his coaches. Yet here I was, accorded the honor reserved for a team's best pitcher. Upon hearing the news, I didn't feel surprise as much as validation. I never stopped believing in myself, never stopped hoping and working for the best. Those feelings were proven out. Now, even the doubters had faith.

Dallas's postmortem to my final spring outing against the Orioles: "He can pitch, can't he?"

Apparently, the California Angels thought the same thing on August 31, 1982, when they traded for me. I found myself back in a pennant race, with a contribution to make. Angels manager Gene Mauch said he wanted to get me ten starts in the last month of the season. Under

Sammy Ellis's guidance, I had straightened myself out with the Yankees, winning four of my last five decisions, and Mauch wanted to use me as much as possible.

"Gene," I said, "pitch me however you want to. Start me, use me out of the bullpen between starts, pitch me every four days, every three days. Whatever you think I can do to help this ball club, pitch me that way. I'd kinda like to play in the World Series again."

Gene knew the baseball rule book better than anyone in baseball. He was a brilliant strategist and one of the most astute bench managers I ever saw. He had been managing since 1960, but he never won a pennant because he didn't understand pitching. That's what killed him in 1964 with the Phillies, and with the Angels in '82 and '86.

Shortly after I reported to the Angels, Gene called a "players' meeting" in the lunchroom. When I reported for the meeting, Don Baylor met me at the door.

"T.J., we like you, buddy, but this meeting's just for hitters."

I went back outside, and Geoff Zahn and Bruce Kison were laughing.

"You can't go in there," Bruce said. "That's just for 'players.'"

"Well, what am I?"

"T.J., you're a *pitcher,* and over here, a pitcher is not a player."

Mauch said you could play the game of baseball with a pitching machine as easily as you could a live pitcher. The game doesn't begin, he'd say, until the ball is thrown to the plate. Thus, a pitcher is an initiator of action. That's the only thing he does, and a machine could easily do that job.

Gene got me into seven games in September, all starts. I went 4–2, and the Angels edged out the Royals by three games to take the division. My Angels stats gave me an overall 14–12 mark, with a 3.69 ERA, not too bad, considering everything I went through in 1982. More important than this, however, was the fact that I was able to make a contribution in the stretch drive.

Mauch had enough confidence to start me in the first game of the playoffs against the Brewers on October 5, but without Don Baylor, it might have been a disaster. In the second inning, leading 1–0, I gave up a two-run homer to Gorman Thomas. The Brewers touched me for another run in the top of the third. Coming back to the bench, we trailed 3–1. I felt terrible, and sat with my head down, dejected.

I had heard about Don Baylor's leadership abilities, and now was about to find out firsthand just what people meant when they called him one of the game's great motivators. Baylor came up to me and tapped me on the head.

"Hey, T.J., get your head up," he told me. "If you hold them at three runs, I'm personally good for four runs against [Milwaukee starter Mike] Caldwell. So if you hold them there, you win, 4–3. I guarantee it."

Baylor wasn't good for his word. He was better. He drove in five runs, not four, and we won 8–3. In Game Two Bruce Kison beat Pete Vucovich, giving us a 2–0 lead in the five-game series. All we had to do was win one of the next three games to get into the World Series and give Mauch his first pennant ever. But the Brewers came back at home to beat Geoff Zahn, narrowing our series lead, 2–1.

Mauch then decided to pitch me on three days rest. The move caused a furor in the press.

Going into the series, Mauch planned to use four starters: me, Kison, Zahn, and either Mike Witt or Steve Renko. But his sudden change of plans brought the writers' wrath down on him. To understand the press's reaction, you had to go back to 1964 and the fabled "Phillies Phold."

Gene was managing Philadelphia to the pennant, holding a 6½-game lead with two weeks left. But then he panicked, and started Jim Bunning and Chris Short on two days rest the remainder of the season. The team lost ten straight to finish in a second-place tie with Cincinnati, one game behind the St. Louis Cardinals. It was the worst swoon in baseball history, one Mauch never lived down. So when he announced he was bringing me back on three days rest for Game Four, the ghosts were resurrected and the media inquisition began.

I must have been in front of my locker for two hours answering questions about the move. Even at night at the hotel, writers kept calling. Gene was a good guy and a good manager, and I thought he took a lot of unfair heat because of that decision. The move itself wasn't that bad, but his timing was horrible. He announced the move immediately after we lost Game Three. It *did* look like panic. The press collectively went: "Uh-oh. Here he goes again."

Mauch could have avoided the controversy simply by announcing a three-man rotation *before the playoffs began.* He could have then calmly explained why he was doing it, thus avoiding the appearance of panic. I wanted badly to win Game Four, just to take the heat off Gene. I knew that if I didn't do well, he'd be crucified. I didn't, and he was.

I tried my best, but it was nowhere good enough. The Brewers knocked me out of the box in the fourth inning, and we lost 9–5. The next night Milwaukee wrapped the pennant up by edging us 4–3. Gene had another "folly" on his hands. He resigned soon after. It was the best team talentwise I ever played on. We were one player short.

The footnote to this is the 1986 playoffs, when Mauch's Angels were leading the Boston Red Sox three games to one. Gene lifted Mike Witt with two outs in the ninth inning of Game Five, and the Red Sox rallied back from the dead, not only winning the game, but taking the next two for the American League championship. Gene never did win a pennant, and he will forever be remembered for those three failures.

I wanted to close out my career with Gene Autry and the Angels, but it didn't happen.

Autry was a fine gentleman, a singer from Oklahoma who hit the big time. It was funny playing for an owner that you used to see in the movies at Saturday matinees and listen to each Sunday night on *The Golden Ranch Theater.* Gene's burning desire was to get his team into the World Series, and I felt comfortable in that atmosphere. Plus, we enjoyed living in southern California again. We had built our dream house with a tennis court. We absolutely loved it. But it just wasn't to be. I pitched for the Angels in 1983 and '84, before they let me go in June of 1985.

The seed of my eventual dismissal was planted just after my trade, when General Manager Buzzie Bavasi unilaterally and unexpectedly extended my contract for three years through the 1986 season. Buzzie had made the request, not us, and we gladly accepted. The first inkling that something was wrong, however, came just after I signed the extension. As we walked out of the office, Mike Port, the assistant general manager, came up to me.

"If that were me," he said, "I would have never given you three more years."

That jolted me, but I shrugged it off.

"Well, that wasn't you, was it Mike?"

But I knew then if Port ever became general manager, I'd be gone. That's how baseball works. When a guy says something like that, it's not a passing remark. He's sending a message. The question is, why would Buzzie want to extend me for three years at $1.8 million, on his own initiative? After all, he was the guy who in 1979 called me a "Phony with a capital P" when I signed with the Yankees.

First, when the Angels obtained me and got a look at my contractual arrangements, they saw the deferred money Steinbrenner had paid me. Buzzie then realized he hadn't offered more than the Yankees, and could now understand why I went to New York.

In 1983 John McNamara replaced Gene Mauch as manager. I had known Mac since 1963, when he managed in the minors. Mac was a quiet guy and I didn't expect any problems working for him. Tom Morgan was his pitching coach; we worked well together, and I was looking forward to a fine year. The pitching rotation that spring included Ken Forsche, Geoff Zahn, Bruce Kison, myself, and Mike Witt. I had a good spring under the watchful eye of Morgan. The young pitchers didn't like him because he was abrasive. He was tough on young pitchers. But he could look at me and pick up when I was out of sync. That's what I needed above all from a pitching coach.

The '83 Angels had a world of talent, with Rod Carew, Doug DeCinces, Fred Lynn, Brian Downing, Reggie Jackson, Bobby Grich, Rick Burleson, and Bob Boone. But we had two major holes.

The first was losing Don Baylor in the off-season to the Yankees. Baylor was the catalyst of that team, and when we lost him, we lost our guts. Pitchers *feared* Don Baylor. I was one of them. Even if he were hitting .190, you hated to see him come up with the game on the line. Moreover, his effect in the clubhouse was incalculable. He wouldn't tolerate any griping and backstabbing. If a player persisted in being a jerk, he had to physically take on Baylor, and there wasn't anyone dumb enough to do that.

The second problem was that we had no bullpen. Our relief corps had the fewest saves in the league, with Luis Sanchez topping the club with only seven. When your "closer" has just seven saves and a 3.66 ERA, you know you're in deep trouble.

It was as if the Angels had been left behind by the rapid change that swept baseball in the eighties, namely, the development of setup men and closers in the bullpen. Under the old "rules," starting pitchers went a lot of innings. Now, the starter was supposed to get you into the sixth inning with what was called a "quality start," defined as at least six innings with no more than three runs scored. In the seventh and eighth the setup man would come in and hold the lead, giving way to the closer in the ninth, usually a big flamethrower who would come in and blow batters away to nail down the win. The Angels didn't have such a bullpen, and it burned us game after game. I know I lost at least sixteen games in '83 and '84—wins—because the bullpen came in and blew leads. The Angels were late in catching on to this new concept in baseball, and it cost them dearly. Gene Mauch got the blame when he didn't have the stopper that was necessary.

We also lost Don Aase and later Rick Burleson to injuries, and we just didn't play well as a team. The Angels finished a pathetic 70–92, 29 games behind the White Sox.

My stats reflected an uneven year: 11–13, 4.33, in 234⅔ innings. I pitched well at home (8–6, 2.64) but stunk on the road (3–7, 7.13), and to this day I have no idea why. It wasn't the park. Pitching in Anaheim Stadium was like pitching in a bandbox, a shooting gallery, especially after they enclosed it to accommodate the Rams. Most hitters love to go in there and play. Logically speaking, I should have had more trouble at home than on the road.

In 1984 my problems continued. I just never got untracked. I started well, holding opponents to three or less runs in my first 11 games (3–3, 2.48). Career win number 250 came on May 1, a two-hitter against Oakland. But around midseason I got out of sync, losing five of seven decisions before McNamara lost all confidence in me and banished me to the bullpen.

Physically, I felt fine, but had developed the nasty habit of making the bad pitch at the wrong time. You can't do that and win on the big league level. It puts too much pressure on you, because the fans know you're going bad, the players know it, the press knows it, the front office knows it, and each time you go out there, you think your next game has to be your best game to silence your critics. That's when it never happens.

To add to this difficulty, my communication with John McNamara deteriorated rapidly. Mac prided himself on the way he handled a pitching staff, but that was a joke. In one game against the Yankees at Yankee Stadium, we were leading 3–1. I told Mac after the eighth inning I had nothing left and was losing my stuff. He ignored that and asked me to go back out in the ninth. Remember, the guy had no bullpen to go to. After getting two quick outs, DeCinces booted a ground ball off the bat of Baylor. Piniella followed with a ringing hit, bringing up Mattingly. I was tiring, and didn't want to pitch to Donny, because if you make a mistake with a hitter like that, he pops it out of the park and the game's over, 4–3. Mac came out and asked me how I felt.

"Mac, I told you last inning. I've had it. I'm tired. I've lost my stuff."

"Well," he answered, "go after Mattingly."

I couldn't believe it, but he was the manager. I pitched carefully to Donny and walked him, loading the bases. Mac came out with the hook and brought in Sanchez, who promptly gave up a two-run single on the second pitch to Butch Wynegar to tie the game. We eventually won the game in the tenth on a home run by DeCinces, but after the game I was mad that Mac hadn't listened to me. Managers usually listen to you.

Soon after that game we had another run-in. Pitching against Milwaukee at Anaheim Stadium on a blazing hot Sunday afternoon, I got through the seventh inning with a 5–2 lead. In the dugout Mac asked me how I felt, and I told him I had a hump in my fastball. When I lost too much on my fastball, it slowed to the point where it didn't sink, but "humped," with the ball just hanging dangerously in the strike zone.

" 'Hump'?" Mac asked. "What does that mean?"

"It means I've lost my fastball, Mac."

He nodded his head. I went upstairs to the clubhouse to change out of my uniform, when the batboy came running in: "Tommy, you're back in the game!"

"What?" I asked.

"Yeah," he said, out of breath, "you better get down there."

I put my uniform top back on and asked the pitching coach, Marcel Lachemann, what was going on.

"Mac wants you back in there," he said.

Having no other choice, I went out in the top of the eighth with no stuff at all, gave up two ground-ball base hits, then a three-run, game-tying home run. Mac then came out to get me. I looked at him and flipped him the ball.

"Thank you very much, Mac," I said with all the irony I could muster. "I sure do appreciate it."

I walked off, leaving Mac on the mound. He was livid. The next day in the press he blasted me, saying there was no communication between us. He was right about that, but he put the blame all on me. After reading his quotes, I went into his office.

"Mac, did I read you right in the papers today, or were you misquoted?"

"No, they quoted me right."

"Weren't you there when I came in and told you that I had a hump on my fastball?"

"Yes, but I thought you were kidding," he said.

"You can't be serious," I answered.

"Well, Tommy, you know, veteran pitchers are supposed to tell me when they pitch and when they come out—"

"Mac, whoah," I interrupted. "I get paid to pitch. You get paid to manage. If you give me one fifth of your salary every time I pitch, I'll manage for you. But until then, you're the manager. It's up to you to make the moves. If you ask me if I'm tired, I'll tell you how I physically feel and be honest with you. Then it's up to you to make the decision to remove me. If I tell you that I'm tired, like I did yesterday, and you keep me out there, you're dumber than anyone gives you credit for. I can't believe you did that. Besides, I did tell you!"

"Well that's the way I did it with Seaver," he shot back, starting to boil. Mac had managed Tom Seaver in Cincinnati. "When he wanted out, he took himself out."

"Fine. Then go bring Tom in here."

Mac sat behind his desk, seething, his face all purple and red. He didn't understand me and wouldn't listen.

A couple games later I was pitching against the Tigers in the third inning. Marty Castillo lined a ball right back at me, heading toward my face. At the last possible second I threw my glove up, deflecting the ball away. My glove hand instantly started killing me. I went down on the ground, rolling around. I was sure my hand was broken. It felt like there was a knife stuck in there, or hot coals. I tried to shake it off, took a few warm-ups, and continued. Mac didn't take me out. Twenty-two of my next 25 pitches were balls. By the time the inning was over, the Tigers had scored something like ten runs. Mac left me in there to die.

Later, the doctors checked the hand, which was black and blue, swollen about twice the size of normal. X rays showed no breaks, just a very bad bruise with a lot of blood in it.

Mac came out the next day in the papers, saying that I'd "lost it," that is, my effectiveness. He said a big league pitcher should be able to throw the ball over the plate, and—since it was clear that Tommy John couldn't do that anymore—announced my demotion to the bullpen.

Again, it struck me as incredible. I hadn't had trouble throwing strikes before being hit, but after the line drive, all of a sudden I lost my pitching ability. Did Mac ever think that maybe—just maybe—the pain from the line drive could have caused me to miss the plate? Could a swollen and nearly broken hand have had anything to do with my sudden ineffectiveness?

I hadn't been pitching well, so I took my removal from the rotation positively. Sometimes, the bullpen is where you work your way out of problems, and I looked forward to throwing as much as possible. With nothing broken, my hand recovered quickly and I asked Mac if I could throw batting practice. He said no. I asked him why. He said he might need me in the game that night. It was a flimsy excuse, since pitching batting practice would not affect my availability later that night. I have that kind of arm, and you need to pitch off the mound.

"Well, when can I throw?" I asked him.

"In the ninth inning of the game," he said, "when I know I'm not going to use you."

There was to be no pitching batting practice and no throwing out in the bullpen during the game before the ninth inning, unless he called for me to warm up.

How much can you pitch in half an inning? That's what Mac reduced my throwing to—despite the fact that I was totally lost and needed a lot of work to find out what was wrong. Instead, he force-fed me a steady diet of baseball politics.

"Mac, you mean to say you're gonna send me to the bullpen to try to get me straightened out, yet you're not gonna let me throw, or let me work with Marcel? He won't be out there in the ninth inning, you know."

"I can't let you throw. I might need you."

"Wait a minute. The pitching coach is here to help people get untracked. That's his job. When can he work with me?"

Mac had a terse reply: "He can't."

"That's totally unfair."

"Well, Tommy, sometimes baseball is unfair."

My first relief appearance came on September 5, and Mac used me in mop-up roles on the road a couple of times. I was lousy and totally frustrated, a pitcher who had no idea what he was doing wrong. Marcel Lachemann wasn't available for me, so in desperation I called up Tom

Morgan for help. He was doing some scouting for Atlanta since his dismissal as pitching coach. We went out to a park in Long Beach on the sly and he suggested a couple things that helped me right away.

But my main problem was that Mac wouldn't let me pitch: in the bullpen, or, more important, to batters, either in batting practice or in simulated games. He just wouldn't let me throw. Nowadays an agent would not allow this to happen. Frank Pastore said the same thing happened to him while he was pitching for Mac in Cincinnati. Frank got out of the groove and was demoted to the bullpen. Mac wouldn't let him throw at all. He sat. He agreed with me that it was very frustratng not to be able to work out your pitching problem like a golfer would work on a swing inconsistency.

We were in Kansas City and the situation was reaching ridiculous proportions.

Mac's killing me, I thought. I've got to do something on my own, or it's all over.

I took a cab to Royals Stadium and got there at eleven A.M. The balls were locked up, but I managed to scrounge up twenty-five old, beat-up practice baseballs. I put them into a bucket and carried them out to the bullpen. Kansas City grounds keeper George Toma gave me permission to use the bullpen. I took a tarp and folded it up to serve as a screen about three feet in back of the plate. I threw 200 pitches, or eight rounds of 25 balls. I'd throw until the bucket was empty, then gather up the balls and do it again, eight times. I was trying to throw the ball in the dirt. Sometimes that's the way to get over the top of the ball, which—instinctual self-diagnosis told me—was my problem. After my 200 pitches I started to get a little better feel for things. When I was done, I gathered the balls, raked the bullpen, put the tarp back, showered, changed, and cabbed it back to the hotel without anyone knowing about it.

Before the game that night I risked heresy by asking Jerry Narron to catch me in the bullpen.

"What about Mac and Lachemann? They don't want you throwing," Narron observed cautiously. Clearly, he didn't want to get in trouble.

"I hate to say it, Jerry, but there comes a time when you've got to take the bull by the horns. If they say anything to you, just tell them I made you do it. I'll take full responsibility."

With that, I ambled to the dugout.

"Mac, can I throw before the game tonight?" He looked at me with a bored expression, and gave me the same old story about needing me during the game.

"Okay, Mac. Then don't get upset by what you're about to see."

With that, I trotted out to the bullpen to join Narron, where I threw and threw and threw. I could see Mac and Latch in the dugout, watching me, but no one came out to tell me to stop. Mac has a ruddy complexion anyway, but now his face was crimson, with all the veins in his nose sticking out. He looked like he was going to have a heart attack.

We worked for forty minutes and Narron said my throwing wasn't bad. There were more good ones than bad ones, he told me. That was on a Tuesday. Mac had told me that I'd be starting Friday in Texas, to fill in for an Bruce Kison. We had an off-day Thursday. On Wednesday I went down to the bullpen again with Narron before the game and threw for another forty minutes. We worked in Kansas City's bullpen because ours was in use. Narron said that was the best I'd thrown in nearly two months. Gradually I started to feel better.

When I got back to the dugout, Mac was a volcano ready to erupt.

"Now I can't use you tonight!" he screamed.

"You were going to use me tonight?" I asked.

"Yes!" he shouted.

"You mean you thought we were going to be down by that many runs that you could risk putting me in the game?"

He looked at me and growled, muttering invectives. I could feel myself getting worked up, and the emotion of the moment took over.

"Mac, I only want to say one more thing. What you're doing is absolutely the most unfair thing I've ever seen in baseball. I don't know what your problem is, but I can't pitch like this. You're sending me out on a big-game hunt, and you're giving me a BB gun. I'm sorry I went out to the bullpen without your permission, but I had to do it. If you don't like it, fine. If you like it, that's fine too. But if you managed like this with your other ball clubs, I can see now why you didn't win."

I turned around and walked away. He cursed me, and his face was an indistinguishable mass of blue contortion. I never understood him. You can't let a personal conflict affect the ballclub. To this day, if you ask John McNamara about Tommy John, probably the best thing he'll say is: "Did he die?"

In my start in Texas I threw pretty good baseball, something like two runs in 6⅔ innings. When we were going back to the hotel, Preston Gomez, one of our coaches, told me: "T.J., that's the best stuff you've had in six weeks."

If the season had four or five weeks left, I could have salvaged something, but we were now into late September, and mentally, I was whipped, totally beaten and defeated. My totals were pathetic: 7–13, 4.52 ERA in 181⅓ innings.

Despite hovering around the .500 mark, the team was in the hunt for the divisional flag all year. Kansas City won the title playing six games over .500. We finished exactly at .500, and were only three games back. Mac wasn't sending his best people out on the field, and it might have cost us a shot at the playoffs. It was an "if only" year: if only Mac had let me work out my troubles in the bullpen, if only my removal from the rotation hadn't been a sham, I have to believe my recovery would have been swift, maybe in time to make a difference down the stretch.

There was another continuing psychodrama playing itself out concurrently with my running feud with McNamara, and this one involved Jackie Autry and Sally. They had become good friends. Gene Autry would go to bed each night at about nine P.M., and Jackie, with nothing to do and no one to talk to, would call up Sally and they'd have nice, friendly chats. Sally had even organized a wives' softball team, which Jackie joined. The two had developed a warm relationship.

Jackie was a great lady, a lot of fun, but she had no understanding of baseball. She was a banker. During a particularly bad stretch of games for me, Jackie called up Sally, practically begging her to talk me into retiring, because, in her words, "Tommy's embarrassing Gene and the organization. He's not worth the money he's being paid." And I admit, I wasn't. She was absolutely right about that. But "worth" is established in baseball not by truth, but by the legalisms of a contract. I was "worth" what the Angels agreed to pay me in my contract.

Sally was a nervous wreck from Jackie's phone calls. Jackie told her if I would just quit, she and Gene would take care of me, maybe put me in the TV or radio booth. She wanted me to "go out with pride" by quitting and walking away from a big contract. She would get a lot of positive attention for me. Sure she would. I had $1.1 million left on my contract. By walking out, I would forfeit the money and end up in the radio booth at $60,000 a year. Of course she'd take care of me. By taking care of me, the Autrys would save $1 million. Don't get me wrong, Jackie's a fine lady; but if a person has something to say to Tommy John, don't say it to Sally. That's what bothered me the most about the phone calls.

Over the winter, the club fired John McNamara and brought back Gene Mauch for 1985. I felt good about that. I called up Gene for a golf date. We played eighteen holes, had some lunch, and talked about the upcoming season. I asked him where I stood.

"You didn't pitch well last year, Tom," he told me.

"That's fair because it's true. But would I be wasting my time coming to spring training? Are you going to evaluate me? Do you plan to start me or use me out of the bullpen?"

"Where do you think you can help me the most?"

"I honestly think I could help you anyplace, Gene. I could pitch every day out of the bullpen or I could start. I'll do whatever you want me to do."

"I think there are some bullets left in your gun, and I think I can get them out of you."

Mauch's statements had me feeling better about things than I had in a long time. But in January the optimism was quickly replaced by a shroud of gloom. My mother was operated on for cancer and was very ill. It happened all of a sudden; one day she was fine, the next day they found her loaded with cancer. To make matters worse, my dad was shaken up in a head-on car crash after he left from visiting mom in the hospital. My parents needed me at home, and when spring training opened on February 17, I wasn't in Arizona with the Angels. I was in Indiana with my mom and dad. Sally and I had been rushing to get things done, flying back and forth between L.A. and Indiana. It was exhausting.

The very day we were packing the car to drive to Mesa, Arizona, for spring training, the phone rang. It was Jackie Autry, wanting to talk to Sally. I just happened to answer the phone. Jackie jumped on me, asking what I was doing home.

"You're supposed to be in spring training."

"Jackie," I replied, "I'm sorry I'm late. What more can I tell you?"

She then reamed me out about how I had to be in Mesa with the ball club. I had been under a great deal of emotional strain, and Jackie didn't realize how much. I said some things I shouldn't have said. The conversation degenerated into an argument.

"Gene wants a championship, and by hanging on, you're holding the team back from that goal," she said.

We argued about why the Angels had never been to the World

Series. The more I talked, the more sarcastic I got. I should have held my tongue, but I blasted her, really aired her out.

"I've never been talked to like that in my life," she huffed.

"Welcome to the big leagues," I retorted. "You invited this by badgering Sally last year to get me to retire. Now you get on my back, and because I speak up, you're crying. Well that's tough."

My mother's illness was really troubling me. Jackie called at the worst possible time and started on me in the worst possible way. It wasn't the first time I had stuck my foot in my mouth, and it probably won't be the last.

When I reported to Mesa, more trouble awaited. Bavasi had quit as general manager and Mike Port was promoted as his successor. This is the same Mike Port who told me minutes after I signed my contract extension with Bavasi that he never would have done what Buzzie had done. When I got into camp, I asked Port what he had planned for me. He said the Angels were going to "evaluate" me.

Evaluate? Nobody worked with me all spring.

Whenever I went to the mound to throw, Marcel Lachemann would immediately walk over to another diamond to work with the other pitchers. I ended up throwing totally on my own. But I kept my mouth shut, pouring myself into my work to keep my problems—especially Mom's deteriorating health—away from me.

Finally, needing to turn to someone for help, I asked the Triple A pitching coach, Frank Rieberger, to work with me.

"Frank, I know Marcel's been told to avoid me. I'm Peck's bad boy around here. But can you just watch me and make sure I'm getting my elbow up, my hand up, and that I'm driving over the ball?"

"Sure, Tommy, I'll help you."

"You won't get in trouble?" I asked.

"Don't worry about it."

Rieberger was the only coach who gave me the time of day all spring. So you see, when I received the cold shoulder early in camp during 1989 from Dallas, my skin had long before been thickened.

My mental state wasn't good at all, with Mom's illness and all the insane baseball politics driving me crazy. At a team party in Mesa, Jackie and I got into another verbal battle. We were talking, and she started berating the Players' Association and "greedy ball players." Then she brought up my retiring again. She told me I was too old to jog, and that's why I wasn't pitching well. She set me off like a rocket on the Fourth of July. I flipped, and said a bunch of regrettable things. That pretty much branded me in the eyes of the Angels as an unredeemable renegade.

When the Cactus League season began, Mauch used me regularly in the rotation, but only in B games. One of my best games was against the Cubs. That's when I impressed their general manager, Dallas Green, who tried to get me in a trade, according to Bob Verdi of the *Chicago Tribune.*

I was pitching to make the ball club, and kept every stat on myself: how many balls, strikes, first-pitch strikes, ground balls. I shut out the Brewers in my last spring stint, and in the Freeway Series against the Dodgers, pitched six innings of two-hit, shutout ball to win the Lefty Phillips Award for the outstanding pitcher of the series.

So here's old T.J., the sixth finger, the guy they're trying to bury, winning the award for best pitcher. They were forced to keep me on the roster. When the regular season roster was finalized, however, nobody had the courtesy to tell me I had made the team. I had to read about it in the newspaper.

Gene used me in the rotation as the fifth starter, but after four games I was only 1–3, 4.26. Gene decided to send me to the bullpen, but again nobody bothered to tell me; I had to read about it in the papers.

I was standing out in the outfield during batting practice when Marcel Lachemann came up to me.

"Is this about not pitching Thursday night?" I asked him.

"Yes. Did Gene say anything to you about it?"

"No."

"Oh shit," Lachemann answered. "Gene was supposed to tell you before the press got it. That's my fault. I should have told you. But Gene said he was going to do it, and I guess he forgot. I apologize."

"Why should you do that?" I asked. "You only apologize to people you respect."

Marcel looked surprised. "You're taking it all wrong."

"Well, how would you like it? You wouldn't do that to the rawest rookie, let him go four days and not tell him he's not starting. Yet you did it to me. What have I done?"

"I don't know what to say, Tommy. I thought Gene was going to do it and he didn't."

I made two more spot starts and six other appearances in relief, with terrible results. It was odd. Of the thirteen runners I inherited in relief, none scored. But when I started fresh the next inning, I couldn't get anybody out. The bottom dropped out in Boston, when I gave up five runs in one third of an inning. It doesn't take many outings like that before your ERA skyrockets.

I was in lousy spirits. Mom wasn't doing well. I tried to visit her whenever I could. When the club played back east and we had an off-day, I'd fly in to Terre Haute to visit her, then join the team the next day. I had told Mauch about my mom's problems and said I'd be leaving the team periodically. He had a problem with that.

"As your manager, I can't let you do that. But," he added enigmatically, "as a father and a son, my advice to you is leave whenever you want."

"As my manager, you won't let me go to see my mom, who's dying of cancer? What will you do? Fine me?"

"That's to be determined."

"Fine me whatever you want, Gene. I don't think it will hold on a grievance. How would it look, you fining me for seeing my dying mother? I'm not even an integral part of the team. You're pitching me every ten, twelve days. You won't miss me."

"You do what you have to do," he said.

"I fully intend to. Because I only have one mom, and I intend to see her."

I was torn. A professional ball player has work obligations, just as any employee does, but I wanted so badly to be with my mom and dad in Indiana.

"I'll get you," he said, grinning.

When it rains, it pours, and as 1985 headed into June, it deluged. Sally was having stomach problems. She got violently ill. We took her to the doctors and they found an ovarial growth. We were scared to death it was cancerous, and when she went into surgery on the morning of June 19, I was there with her. Baseball didn't matter at all at this point. My wife's health did. I sat in the waiting room like a man in a daze, feeling the world crushing me from all sides. I called the ball park to tell Mike Port that Sally was being operated on and that she wouldn't be through it until late that afternoon. Leslie Wilson, Port's secretary, told me that Port was in a meeting.

"Oh yes," I said, cracking a serious joke. "He's probably meeting to decide about my release."

Leslie went completely silent, and then she started stammering. At that moment I knew I was history.

"Leslie, it's okay. Here's the number where Mike can reach me at the hospital when he has some news. I'm at the UCI Hospital in the surgery waiting room, at this extension. Have him call me here."

About an hour later the phone rang. It was Port, telling me the ball club had put me on waivers with the intention of handing me my outright release. He offered to delay making an announcement, but I wanted it done immediately. The sooner I made a clean break from the Angels, the quicker I could try to line up something else.

Sally came out of surgery. Fortunately, the growth wasn't cancerous; the doctors removed it, and also her appendix. The first thing I told her when she woke up was that the Angels released me.

"We've got to look for another ball club."

Actually, I was pleased by the team's decision. The Angels had become devils to me, and I couldn't leave fast enough. What sense of relief that gave me, however, was destroyed by the continuing deterioration of Mom's health.

I flew back to Indianapolis to play in a charity golf tournament for the Heart Fund, then drove home to Terre Haute. I hadn't seen Mom in about six weeks. When I got in the house, she was lying down on the couch. I almost didn't recognize her; that's how bad she looked, just wasted from the disease. Later I joined Sally for a visit to her sister's house in Covington, about fifty miles north of Terre Haute.

We got a call from Dad, telling us to get home fast. Mom had passed blood, he said, and they had her in the hospital in Terre Haute. We left the kids with Sally's sister and rushed back to Terre Haute. We checked into a hotel, went to the hospital, and there I saw my mom, clinging to life. We stayed there all evening and into the night, sitting with Mom and Dad. Sally left about eleven P.M. to go back to the hotel. I stayed for a little while more, until exhaustion set in.

"Pop, I think I'm going back to the hotel. If there's any change, let me know."

At six A.M. Sunday, June 30, the nurse called. Mom had another bad spell. The nurse said she was dying. Sally and I threw our clothes on, got there, walked into her room, and the nurse met us: "Your mother just had her last breath."

She died as we walked into the room.

It was emotionally devastating. It all hit me at once, everything about the last month. Mom's death; its effect on Dad; Sally's operation; the clubhouse politics; my release. It's hard to understand my grief unless you've been really close to your parents, as I was. They had lived their whole lives for me, sacrificing everything to help me. Then this happened, and so suddenly. I felt helpless and alone. I was totally sick of baseball, fed up. I thought my career was over. Without doubt, that was the lowest point of my life.

After several days my head was more together, and we had to start thinking about what was next. ABC television called and asked if I'd like to do color commentary on the backup Monday night game with Tim McCarver in Oakland. I was happy to do it, to get my mind off things. That broadcast led to a meeting with Oakland's general manager, Sandy Alderson.

"Are you thinking of playing again?" Sandy asked.

"I would like to. I think I can still pitch."

"The A's might be interested, Tommy. We'll see what we can work out."

Sandy got together with my attorney, Bob Cohen, and they worked out a contract where I would sign with Modesto, Oakland's A-level minor league team. I would work out there for a couple of weeks, then join the A's. I hadn't pitched since the second week of June, and this was July 12. The A's were in the process of turning their franchise around. José Canseco was less than a year away from the big leagues, and a championship club was just on the horizon.

At Modesto I started two games, pitching badly, but my arm felt good, and I signed a contract with Oakland on July 26. The A's gave me one more tune-up, with their team in Madison, Wisconsin. I joined the A's on the road in Boston and got my first start in the next series, on July 26 at Milwaukee, going six innings of shutout ball for a win. My next win came in Oakland a month later, against the Yankees on August 27, when I pitched seven three-hit shutout innings. But true to form for the entire year, there was another setback.

While pitching against Seattle with two outs in the bottom of the third, I picked Phil Bradley off first base. But we blew the rundown and I had to cover first. Bradley came back into the bag clean but hard, trying to knock the ball out of my glove. In doing so, he crashed into my left side and I ended up with two dislocations in the little finger of my pitching hand.

The team traveled to Seattle, and I used the off-day to see Herb Stark, the hand specialist in L.A. who helped Dr. Jobe with my elbow surgery in 1974.

"Tommy, how old are you?" Stark asked.

"Forty-two."

"If you were younger, I'd advise you to rest it for the remainder of the season, to make sure it gets well. But in your case, if you can stand the pain, go ahead and pitch."

I started working again, but couldn't throw well. My finger was all taped up, and every time I would snap my wrist, the finger would painfully curl under.

Yet eight days after dislocating the finger, I was pitching again. It was a mistake to come back so soon. To keep the finger from hurting, I subconsciously changed my motion. I pitched one decent game, then went downhill from there, losing my final five starts. In those five games I gave up 21 earned runs in 20⅔ innings for an astronomical 9.14 ERA. I started eleven games for the A's, winning two and losing six, leaving me with an overall 1985 mark of 4–10, 5.53 ERA in 86⅓ innings. The sad statistics neatly summed up my dark year.

But my brief stay in Oakland turned out to be one of the most pleasant times I ever spent in baseball. It came at a time when I needed it the most. The organization never put any pressure on me, and the kids were always welcome on the field and in the clubhouse. Young Tommy had a great time helping Mike Heath with his fan mail. Moreover, the Bay area is beautiful and the fans were great. The unfortunate thing is that I didn't pitch well, and the A's front office, the players, and the fans get a huge apology from Tommy John. They didn't get to see the real Tommy John on the field, and I deeply regret that.

# 13.

# WINDUP

**M**aking the team.

The feeling was similar to that long-ago spring in Tucson, when I made my first trip north with the Indians. Imagine, feeling like a rookie at forty-five years old.

The 1989 Yankees broke camp flat and listless. I didn't sense that rah-rah, let's-get-'em attitude that's common when a team finally ends spring training. It made quite an interesting dichotomy: my elation played against the team's weariness. That was the silver lining to the cloud of having to come into camp with no chance: it forced me into a high state of motivation, so that I didn't burn out. Most of the rest of the team didn't have that advantage, if I can call it one. Dallas's main strategic mistake was running us full tilt from Day One. He tried to build off of that level of performance and he couldn't. We had peaked too soon. Normally, you start slowly with your conditioning, then build to full tilt as the camp winds down.

The Yankees broke camp and flew to the Metrodome in Minnesota. Usually, the day before opening day, you put your new uniforms on, see if they fit, go out on the field, pose for the photographers, and enjoy a light, even token, workout. Not Dallas. He had us out there for a rigorous two-and-a-half-hour spring-training-type workout. After we got through it, the team was wondering: "When do we get a break?" That last run-through knocked the guys down mentally.

# Windup

Sally, young Tommy and Sally's friend May Kohan joined me in Minnesota. We settled into our hotel room, enjoyed a nice dinner and relished every moment of my being the starting pitcher the next day.

Though I had my friends on the team—particularly Mattingly, Pagliarulo, and Righetti—I usually stayed to myself on the road. When the team was at home, I was with the family. It's difficult when you're twenty years older than your teammates; you don't have a lot in common. So on the road I'd read a lot and watched TV. I'd call Sally every night for our chats, to learn what happened that day with her and the kids.

This trip was special, of course, and fortunately, Sally and Tommy were there to share it with me. We watched the TV news that night, and during the sports segment, they did an interview with Minnesota's Gary Gaetti. Gaetti said that the Twins were hoping I'd be anxious, pumped up, and wanting to overthrow, so that my ball would get up high in the strike zone. I made a mental note to consciously do things slower the next night. We closed the light for sleep, and in my mind there I was, on the mound of the Metrodome, slowing my motion down and throwing a nasty sinker . . .

Those happy thoughts were a long way from the nightmare 1985 season. Being in Oakland in the second half helped a lot with my mental recovery. In our short time there we came to love the area and the team. The A's were an enlightened organization. They treated players and their families with dignity.

We spent October 1985 trying to recover emotionally. I had one more year on my contract, but after that, everything was fuzzy. We sat down with the A's to feel them out on a contract extension. We proposed an extension to 1987, with an option for 1988. They weren't interested in that, so we came back with an option for 1987. Again it was no dice. The A's were only interested in the 1986 season and didn't want to go beyond that.

My contract status with the A's was complicated. I never understood it. The A's didn't really own my contract; the Angels were obligated for my final year. To keep me for the 1986 season, the A's had to sign me by a certain date. When that date passed with no agreement, I became a free agent, on November 12.

Sally and I weren't sure about the future. We hoped I would be playing baseball somewhere in 1986, but after that, we had no idea. That's when I first entertained thoughts about coaching college baseball.

It seemed natural: I loved baseball, enjoyed working with kids, and had knowledge to share.

We made several inquiries, and one of them was at the University of North Carolina at Chapel Hill. I had met UNC's head baseball coach, Mike Roberts, a couple of times when George Steinbrenner took the Yankees there to play spring exhibition games. George's daughter went to school at UNC, and the exhibitions were George's gift to the school. To our surprise and excitement, UNC got back to us saying the athletic department had funded a third coaching position. The school asked if I was interested in the job.

In December 1985 we went down to the campus to meet the people and look around. Sally, Tami, and Travis flew down with me. We left Tommy and Taylor back in Anaheim. From the start Sally had bad vibes, mostly little things.

One thing that bothered her was Mike Roberts's behavior when he met us at the plane. We were loaded with baggage. After he introduced himself, he walked away through the terminal about ten paces ahead of us. It was strange. Sally told me it struck her as egotistical; Roberts never offered to help the kids or Sally with their bags and didn't walk with us to his car. We followed him. Sally said that showed Roberts didn't think highly of us. But I was looking beyond the 1986 season and my life after baseball, and I didn't listen to her. If I did, it would have saved us a giant hassle.

During our interview, Roberts made promises and boasts, telling us everything he would do for us. He promised us two cars, one for Sally and one for me. Plus, there would be six season tickets for UNC basketball games, one for each member of the family. In the Chapel Hill area, UNC basketball tickets are like gold.

Mike was talking of a starting salary of $30,000, relatively high for an assistant's job. It wasn't enough to make me jump for joy, but Roberts ran a baseball camp and said he would split the profits of the camp with me in exchange for my appearances. He said it was one month's work that would "at least" double my salary. So now, he said, we're looking at something a bit higher. Add the value of six UNC basketball tickets and the cars, and it's closer to $70,000. Moreover, Roberts's assistant coach had quit to take a scouting job with the Boston Red Sox. That meant an elevation in title to assistant head coach and pitching coach. The UNC offer started to look better.

We were looking forward to meeting Dean Smith, the legendary basketball coach who in effect ran the athletic department at UNC, though they had a titular A.D. We immediately liked Dean, who had a national reputation as one of sport's gentlemen, and also a man highly visible in Christian circles. But as our interview with him wore on, again, something didn't feel right. It was like an itch you couldn't scratch. Sally picked up on the same feeling. If Dean told us once, he told us ten times what a great Christian he was, a man of virtue and high moral standards. He said he had but one vice: he smoked.

When we were alone, Sally brought it up first: "I don't trust him, Tommy. I know about his reputation and all that, but I don't trust the guy."

"Sally, why?" I asked, feeling it myself, but again blinded by my desire to set up a situation after the 1986 season.

"Anytime anybody has to tell you how good they are, how great they are, how clean they are, how honest they are, how they only have one vice, how this, how that, something's wrong."

"But Sally, this is Dean Smith," I replied.

"Tommy," Sally answered, "I know that. But how many genuine Christians blow their own horn like that? Does Billy Graham go around telling you how virtuous he is? No. Or when people meet [the Reverend] O.S. [Hawkins, pastor of Fort Lauderdale's First Baptist Church] for the first time, does he tell them what a great Christian he is? No. Because they live it and show it."

Sally was right. I guarantee you, and I've found this to be true a hundred percent of the time in baseball: the good ball players never tell you how good they are. They don't have to. It's only the mediocre ones who tell you that, because they want you to put them on that level. They need to build themselves up artificially. As many times as I've talked to Pete Rose, he never told me how good he was. The same with Sandy Koufax, or Ted Williams, or Mickey Mantle. Yet Dean Smith was telling us what a great Christian he was. I should have known better. Beware of Christians who carry the Bible under their arm or wear it on their sleeve, because they're hiding something. A truly good Christian lives his faith, acts it, does it, twenty-four hours a day. He doesn't have to tell people. They can see it for themselves.

Our conversations with UNC went on all winter. Nobody was knocking down my door as far as baseball was concerned, so we talked about a late-summer starting time, if I didn't hook on with a team.

Shortly after Christmas, Sally asked me: "Tommy, you want to play one more year. Where would you play if you had a choice?"

"Probably the Yankees."

"Well, why don't you call George?"

I called Clyde King, who was now the general manager, and asked him if there was any chance for me with the Yankees.

"Well, Tommy, we can use pitching, that's for sure, but I don't know about Mr. Steinbrenner."

He was referring to my stormy exit in 1982. But the truth is, I've never felt badly about George in my life. I've always thought of George as a friend, and any problems we had were strictly business, not personal. If anybody understood that, it was George. So I told Clyde to ask around.

"Tommy," he said, "it may take a while. You can't ask Mr. Steinbrenner things at certain times. As you know, you have to wait for the optimum time. But I'll bring it up. All we can do is go from there. I can't promise anything."

About two weeks later Clyde called back.

"I talked to Mr. Steinbrenner, and he told me 'Clyde, you do what you think is best for the ball club.' "

Clyde explained that I'd be invited to spring training as a walk-on, with no guarantees.

"How much do you want to come down here?"

"Nothing. All I want is expenses, same as any ballplayer."

"Let me run that by Mr. Steinbrenner."

George agreed to that arrangement, and when spring training opened up, I walked in as a nonroster player, assigned a scrub's number 65 uniform top. The players needled me about that, saying it was close to my age. They were surprised, but glad, to see me again in Yankee pinstripes. So was I.

George welcomed me back in his own unique way. When the Yankee team photo was taken, he asked me and Phil Niekro, another nonroster veteran, to be in it. Normally, invitees do not make the team photo. It was his way of saying all was forgiven.

"I couldn't leave you out, Tommy," he said with a wink. "There's seven hundred big league wins between the two of you."

Sam Ellis and Mark Connor were the pitching coaches that year, Sam with the Yanks and Mark on the minor league level. Sam had helped me immeasurably in 1982, just after Clyde took over as manager. I was meeting Connor for the first time. He turned out to be a brilliant coach.

## Windup

He knew what to look for in my motion, and had an intuitive understanding of the way I threw the baseball. Every time I pitched that spring, in games or on the side, one of those guys was there, watching, working with me, pushing me, encouraging me.

Lou Piniella, the new manager, promised to work me into his schedule as much as he could. The point is, the coaches went out of their way to make me feel welcome and give me a chance.

I pitched well in grapefruit games and started rising on Lou's depth chart. Even when rain washed me out of a start, it helped me, because other guys weren't doing so well. I rose on the chart without actually pitching. With each succeeding appearance, Ellis, Connor, and Piniella restored my confidence, and I got back into that zone where you think you can never throw another bad pitch.

Lou used me in three games—nine innings, two runs, eight strikeouts—before an injury slammed the door on what had been an idyllic spring. The day before my scheduled start in Fort Myers against the Royals, I stepped into a small depression while running in the outfield grass at Fort Lauderdale Stadium. It threw me off balance, and as I tried to right myself, my upper back went into spasms around the shoulder blades—to the point where I almost couldn't breathe. They took me into the clubhouse and checked me out. The spasms didn't respond to treatment, and Dennis Rasmussen—ironically, the player to be named later in my trade to the Angels in 1982—got my start in Fort Myers. He had been scheduled for demotion to Columbus, but he pitched seven innings of two-hit ball against Kansas City and ended up making the team. Now, all of a sudden, he's back in the picture, and I'm the eleventh pitcher on a ten-man staff. Funny how things work out. My injury was Rasmussen's ticket to making the club.

As camp broke, Clyde King asked me if I had a problem with staying down in Florida to continue working out with the minor leaguers. I said no, provided the team took care of my expenses. I worked out those arrangements, and for the next month Sally and I lived at the Howard Johnson's hotel on the beach. Every fourth day I'd go to the ball park and pitch a simulated game with Mark Connor watching my every pitch.

Late in April they flew me into New York to pitch a simulated game at Yankee Stadium on the off-day, and a few days later the Yankees told me they were going to make some roster moves. John Montefusco had hurt his hip and could hardly walk. Ed Whitson had pulled rib muscles. Both were put on the disabled list, and the team needed pitchers. Clyde called me, and we signed a contract on May 2, and that same day I made my first appearance in Yankee Stadium as a Yankee since August 24, 1982.

Lou got me into eight games by June 12, and my record was 3–1. But my left heel started hurting me. It didn't bother me during games if I had it taped up, but one day Lou ran out of pitchers in a lopsided contest in which we trailed the Orioles. That was the game where Larry Sheets showed me up by bunting. Lou offered to send in a position player to pitch a couple innings, but I told him I could mop up. It was a mistake, a foolish show of overenthusiasm and bravado. I had pitched six innings the day before, and the strain was too much for my left heel.

Immediately after the game the Yankees flew to Detroit. When I got off the plane, my heel was absolutely killing me. The next day I tried to throw on the side, but to my dismay, the injury prevented me from getting up on my toe during delivery. Jack Bonamo, the team doctor, looked at the heel and said rest was the only cure. The Yankees put me on the disabled list on June 12. I rested it for six weeks, but the heel never got better. It would reach a certain point of recovery and improve no further. To this day the heel still bothers me.

On July 25 the Yanks assigned me to Fort Lauderdale of the Florida State League under baseball's injury rehabilitation program, and I stayed there through August 7, pitching in three games.

In the meantime, Mike Roberts and UNC kept in touch on the coaching position, pressuring me to commit to them. He flew into New York during the season on a recruiting trip and we had lunch. Mike asked me if I was coming down to Chapel Hill. I told him if the job was open as he had outlined it to me and Sally, yes. We agreed that I'd report in October, after the season ended. On July 24, I announced my retirement from baseball following the 1986 season and the acceptance of the coaching job at UNC. It appeared that my future after baseball would be at Chapel Hill. Little did I know.

The Yankees activated me from the disabled list on August 8, and in my first two games back I felt great, winning against the Royals on August 8 and the Indians five days later. In those games, I threw 15 shutout innings. In my next start, against Seattle, I survived a close call when Alvin Davis hit a line drive up the middle that caught me on the ankle; it stiffened up, but X rays were negative. One bullet had been dodged, but the next one had my name on it. On August 30, I pitched my first complete game in more than two years, losing 1–0 at Seattle. That dropped my record to 5–3, but the game itself was encouraging. That old "feel" was coming back. Besides, the team was playing good ball for Lou, in the thick of the hunt for a good part of the season, before the Red Sox ended up winning it.

The pattern for the last couple of years had been one step forward, two steps back. It seemed whenever I got into a good groove, something would happen to knock me down. After our series in Seattle, we traveled to Oakland. On September 3, I went out to the park to do my between-game throwing.

My son Tommy had come with me on the road trip, and we went out to the park early, where I hit him ground balls and fly balls. The ground and grass at Oakland at that time of day gets wet from dew, and my spikes got soaked. The wet dirt kept building up on the bottom of my spikes, almost covering the cleats. I went to the bullpen with Don Mattingly to do some throwing. Donnie was standing in the batter's box, taking balls.

I've never heard of anybody falling off the mound, but that's exactly what I did. Near the end of my throwing, on one of the last pitches, my mud-clogged spikes didn't grab the dirt and my feet went straight out from under me, like doing the splits. I stuck my hand out to break the fall and ran my left thumb straight into the ground. I heard a sickening "pop" noise, and an intense wave of nausea immediately swept over me. I almost tossed my cookies right there. Never in my life have I felt pain as intense. It was an indescribably unreal pain. Mattingly ran over as I writhed on the ground, and he and Mark Connor walked me back into the clubhouse. Trainer Gene Monahan saw me.

"What the heck happened to you?"

"I jammed my thumb, Gene."

The trainer looked at it and said: "I'm not qualified to make a diagnosis, but I think you've got more than a jammed thumb. Looks like you tore a ligament."

Dr. Herb Stark checked me out the next day in L.A. and confirmed a torn ligament. The operation was done in New York. That ended my season and my career, since I had announced my retirement from baseball. What a way to go out—falling off the mound in the Oakland bullpen. I told Sally. She called George and said I had a broken thumb. George said, "He can't retire from baseball and a great career with a broken thumb!"

In mid-October we packed our stuff, loaded it into the car, and drove south. The John family said good-bye to the hectic life of baseball and hello to the serene academe of Chapel Hill. I started my coaching position on October 20. It would come to an angry halt just one month later.

I was at the school every day, and we had the kids on a Monday-Wednesday-Friday workout schedule. Tuesdays and Thursdays were their lifting days. If the weather was nice, we'd go out and throw. If it wasn't, we'd drill inside, run, and call it a day. It was a lot of fun, and we were enjoying ourselves.

The first inkling that something was wrong came one night early in my tenure when Mike Roberts invited us to his house for dinner. The two cars he had promised were now one car, he said, and to get that, we had to forfeit our six basketball tickets. That was incredible since at the time the University provided a ticket for each employee, and each member of the employee's family. Roberts was trying to take away a "perk" that was actually an automatic part of my job. The school had never intended to provide me with even one car, let alone two. Roberts had lied to me about it, although he was quick to deny making any promises. He said he could get me a Toyota through a friend of his, but to do so he'd need the six basketball tickets. Six basketball tickets at North Carolina can buy a heck of a lot more than a Toyota.

When we went home that night, Sally said: "It's starting. It's starting."

"What's starting?" I asked.

"I guarantee you," she said, "that this guy will renege on three quarters of everything he's promised."

Roberts had a way of patronizing people through his boasting. He kept telling me how big he was with the Converse shoe company and how he could get me extra money making appearances for them. Little did he know I was on the Converse staff. But he'd always talk about how he could do this for you and that for you, bragging about his "big connections."

As part of my agreement with UNC, I could run my Tommy John Baseball Schools in New Jersey. Once a month, one week a month, we operated youth baseball academies in New Jersey throughout late fall and winter. In early November I went up to Jersey to make a weekend appearance at the clinic. One of my instructors came up to me.

"Tommy, I thought you were only appearing at your own baseball schools?"

"That's right, I am."

"Well, I've got a brochure at home that says you're in some schools in South Jersey, down by New Brunswick."

"Really? That can't be. Can you bring it in?"

The next night he brought in a brochure advertising baseball schools in the New Brunswick–Toms River area. There on the cover of the brochure was a picture of me in a Yankee uniform, with a cutline reading: "FEATURING New York Yankees' Tommy John."

Featuring? I had never heard of these guys.

Small world. On the inside was a mug shot of none other than my boss at UNC, Mike Roberts. Then I put two and two together. Roberts did a lot of recruiting in the Toms River area; not so coincidentally, the two high school coaches who ran these schools were from the same area.

Something was strange. I only knew one thing for a fact: I had never given permission to anyone to use my name or photo, and I certainly hadn't committed to appearing at these schools, as the brochure advertised. The next day, I called my attorney. He wrote a letter to the school directors, saying that I had never contracted for these appearances, that I had no intention of showing up, and ordering them to withdraw the brochures. The school's director replied that "Tommy John had better make his appearances. I've got a signed contract with his name on it."

I was incredulous. How could they have a signed contract? We got a copy of the agreement. The signature wasn't mine. Mike Roberts had signed for me. In fact, he'd signed "Tommy John by Mike Roberts," falsely implying that I'd given him my power of attorney. Soon after all this broke, I was in my office doing some work and Roberts came in.

"I need to talk to you," he said.

"I would think so," I answered, wanting to get to the bottom of the mess. He came in and closed the door.

"I got a call from my friends in Jersey," Roberts said, somber-faced. "What's this about your attorney?"

"You got it, pal," I answered. He then started pulling this southern "dumb poor boy" act on me.

"Lawyers? Why, we can't have lawyers and all that down here. We don't know nothing about lawyers down here."

"I just want to ask you one thing, Mike. Why did you do what you did? What gives you the right to sign my name on any document you deem fit? How many more of these things do you have out there?"

"I've got a couple; two or three."

"Did you sign my name to them?"

"Yeah."

"I'll tell you, pal. You'd better get them back real quick, because there's going to be no Tommy John showing up at those schools."

"Well, I knew you were looking for extra income. They're going to pay you a hundred dollars."

"Mike, I wouldn't let these people watch me brush my teeth for a hundred dollars. If they would have called me up and asked me, I probably would have done it for nothing. You know what my normal fee is for a two-day event like that? Five thousand dollars. Where do you get off doing this? You don't own me."

His reply was like something out of a B movie: "When you work for me down here, I can do about anything I want with your name."

"Maybe they don't teach this down here, but the Emancipation Proclamation ended slavery in 1865. You've heard of Abraham Lincoln? Now get this straight. You don't own me. You don't own my likeness. You don't own my name. I'm going to have to get the lock on this office changed. I can't trust you. What if I leave my checkbook out on my desk? Would you help yourself to a check?"

"No," he answered, "that's against the law."

"Signing someone's name on a contract is also against the law."

"I don't know anything about that."

"Mike, you better get yourself an attorney and find out. You've got a lot of problems."

"Yeah? Well as long as you work for me, I can do just about anything I want to do," he repeated.

"Mike, let me tell you something. I've just worked my last minute for you."

"You don't want to do that."

"People told me about you. They told me you lie. They told me all sorts of things. I didn't believe them. I gave you the benefit of the doubt. I didn't think you'd do it to me because I didn't think you were dumb enough. You've left me no other choice but to quit."

In the meantime I had gone in to inform Dean Smith about the matter. UNC had a new athletic director, a guy by the name of John Swofford, who had about as much backbone as an eel. He was handpicked by Dean. He was in Dean's pocket. Dean ran the show at UNC, no ands, ifs, or buts.

# Windup

"Dean, I've got a problem. Mike Roberts has signed my name on contracts."

He couldn't believe it.

"This is terrible. I don't know what to tell you, Tommy," Dean said, "but let's try to get it worked out. I don't want word of this to get out. I'm sure we can work something out like gentlemen."

Dean was concerned with one thing and one thing only: keeping it out of the media. He didn't want adverse publicity connected with the hallowed UNC athletic program. He wanted to keep UNC's nose clean. He didn't care that I had been ripped off.

When I told Swofford about the problem, he said we should "work on the situation internally. Let's see if we can make Mike repent." There seemed to be unusual interest in keeping the whole thing quiet and not doing anything to come down on Roberts.

I also told Swofford about a couple possible irregularities that made me extremely nervous. There was a high school kid from the Virgin Islands who lived with Mike. His first name was Glen. I don't even know his last name. Glen worked out with the baseball team every day. In fact, some of the guys told me that Glen may have even played in a fall practice game for UNC. If that were true, having that kid work out with, much less play for, the UNC baseball team would have been a violation of NCAA rules. Another potential problem concerned a tennis court Mike said he had built; he bragged to me about using players from the baseball team to help him build it to cut down on the cost. I didn't know if the story was true or not, but it had me concerned. The irony is that when I first got down to the school, Mike threw the NCAA rule book down on my desk. He told me to learn the rules, because he didn't want me doing anything "to screw up the school."

What was going on down there? I wanted to know. How could I stay there? I asked Swofford what kind of program were they running.

"You've got a coach that doesn't go by the rules. He lies. He cheats. He signs names on contracts. I can't stay here. I've got to go."

"I don't believe it," Swofford replied. "But what do you think we can do to make Mike a better guy?"

Swofford was talking about making Roberts "a better guy." I found out later why UNC was reluctant to reprimand their baseball coach. His dad, a wealthy lumber dealer from Kingsport, Tennessee, was a large benefactor of the school. My sources told me he donated large amounts every year to the UNC program. He was also a factor in landing the baseball coaching job for his son. A quarter of a million dollars buys a lot of protection.

Dean Smith and the UNC basketball team had left to play in the Rainbow Classic tournament in Hawaii for the weekend. They departed on a Thursday and were back in Chapel Hill on Monday or Tuesday. At the end of that week, on November 21, I handed in my resignation letter to Swofford.

"Are you sure this is what you want?" he asked.

"Yes. When you lose trust in a person, you can't work for him. That gap can never be bridged. People told me about Roberts. Jeff Torborg told me Mike had promised scholarship aid for Jeff's son, but when they went to get it, there wasn't any money there. Other people told me things as well."

"Well, then," Swofford said, "we've got to make sure it's done in a quiet way."

That's all everybody down there was concerned about. The late Orville Campbell, editor of the local paper, had lunch with me and Sally, and he kept telling me to "Keep your powder dry. Don't go off half cocked and say things you'll regret. Don't say anything that's going to hurt the school. Keep your powder dry."

In Chapel Hill the school means everything. UNC and Dean Smith come before God, Mom and Dad, apple pie, the U.S. government, and the flag. Chapel Hill looks down upon every school that is not UNC. We had some friends at Duke over in Durham. When we'd mention the name Durham to the people of Chapel Hill, they'd say it with contempt.

"Durham? That's a tobacco city," they'd say. "That's a dirty, filthy tobacco city."

At my final meeting with the team I told the kids that "Coach Roberts and I had a falling out." I told them to keep working hard on the things we talked about and that I had enjoyed our time together.

"I'll see you somewhere down the line, someplace."

Shortly after that, Roberts fired my assistant, Dwight Shellman, apparently because he knew too much about what had happened, and it wouldn't be good for him to be with the players.

When Dean Smith returned from Hawaii with the basketball team, he called me up at home.

"I see where you've resigned, Tommy. Do you really want to go through with it?"

"Dean, I can't trust the guy."

"I'm sorry about that, because you would have been a big plus for the program. But I just want you to do one thing."

"What's that?"

"When the press asks you why you left North Carolina, don't tell them the real reason. Just tell them you want to play baseball again. Say you left to resume your big league career."

"But Dean, that's not the truth."

"Yeah," Dean added, "but it will just look better for the school if it's not brought out, because of the problems you've had with Mike. It'll look bad for the school if the truth comes out."

I sat there, holding the phone to my ear, flabbergasted at what I was hearing from the legendary, the virtuous, the squeaky-clean Dean Smith.

"Dean, all you people down here seem to have a horror of telling the truth. Mike lied to us about the cars, about the basketball tickets. He may have broken NCAA rules. He signs my name to several contracts, then tells me he can do whatever he wants, since he's my boss. Your athletic director doesn't do anything about it. And now you want me to lie for the school, because if any of this comes out, it'll make the school look bad. Where do you guys come off with all of this?"

"That's the way it should be, Tommy," Dean replied. "We have to think of the reputation of the school."

"You know who gets hurt in this? Me. Pure and simple."

"What can I say? Best of luck to you, Tommy. If you need tickets to a ball game, call me up."

"What are they, hush tickets?"

"No," he said with a laugh, "just a way to make it up."

Dean later told a friend of mine we'd never had that conversation, and the story of what happened to me in North Carolina never came out in the press. Sources at the school planted the story that I quit my job to pitch for the Yankees in 1987. Giving my side of it to the press would have simply ended in a mud-slinging contest, so we let it drop. Sally and I wanted to end it as quickly as possible. The state eventually agreed to pay me one month's salary for my work there, my moving expenses, and some other incidental expenses, and we washed our hands of it.

The experience opened up my eyes to the corruption of big-time college athletics. Because if UNC, one of the country's class institutions, is doing this in a non-revenue sport, what's going on at the other places, in the big-money sports? I shudder even to think about it.

Ironically, the debacle freed me up for another year in baseball. When all of this broke, George Steinbrenner—who had heard rumors—called me up.

"What the hell's going on down there?" he asked.

I told George the whole story, and he offered me support:

"You shouldn't have been down there anyway, dammit. You're my best pitcher. What are you going to do now?"

"I don't know, George. I've got to clear my head first."

"Why don't you and Sally come down to see me after Christmas."

We flew down to Tampa the first week of January and met with George at his hotel.

"You can still pitch, Tommy, and I want you doing it for the Yankees. I'm selfish, you see," he said with a smile.

Yankee general manager Woody Woodward worked out a contract with me, and on January 8, 1987, I signed for one year.

In 1987 it felt great to be playing baseball again. Overall, I had a good spring, but my first two outings were disastrous. I didn't throw that winter because I didn't think I was going to play anymore. My arm hadn't been built up, but I worked hard to catch up, trying to do in six weeks what I usually got done in three months. Lou Piniella was patient with me, however, and ended up using me as the fourth starter.

The Yankees couldn't sign Ron Guidry until May 1 that year. Ronnie didn't sign his contract by the January 8 deadline, and so became a free agent. By the time May came around, rumors started circulating that with the impending return of Guidry, my job was in jeopardy. It was the newspapers trying to stir things up, but still, you never like to hear or read about it when it's you they're talking about. Lou came in with some gratefully received reassurance:

"Don't worry about what the papers say. You're going to be pitching here. It may be out of the bullpen, but you're going to pitch. You can still get batters out."

Lou's confidence in me, fortunately, was justified. My 13–6 mark was good for fifth in the league in winning percentage (.684). My ERA was high, 4.03, mostly because of two godawful back-to-back starts against Boston, the first on June 20 at Fenway Park, the second a week later at the Stadium. Take away those 14 earned runs in six innings and my record becomes 13–4, 3.47. I was most pleased with staying healthy the whole year; my 33 starts and 187⅔ innings led the ball club. I was also a good-luck charm for Lou. In my starts, the Yankees were 22–11.

The team never really put it together in '87. Lou managed the whole year, an accomplishment in itself when you manage for George, but we didn't have the right mix. We were like mixing mortar with too much sand. It looks good for a while, but when it dries, it crumbles.

We were solid at first base (Mattingly), second (Randolph) and third (Pagliarulo), but we needed a shortstop. Winfield (right) and Henderson (left) held down the outfield, but we didn't really have a true center fielder. A major blow came when Rickey lost two months to a leg injury. Losing Henderson from the leadoff spot took a whole dimension out of our attack. Behind the plate, Cerone and Joel Skinner weren't enough. Eight years after his death, the Yankees still had not found anyone to fill Thurman's shoes. The fabulous tradition of Yankee catchers—a grand legacy that went from Bill Dickey, to Yogi Berra, to Elston Howard, to Thurman—was clearly over.

In 1987 another Yankee tradition died as well: left-handed power. The last time we won anything, in 1981, we had Reggie, Nettles, Murcer, Jim Spencer, Oscar Gamble, Dave Revering, and Bobby Brown (a switch hitter). Left-handed thunder had been a Yankee trademark for so long, starting with Ruth and Gehrig, and continuing with guys like Johnny Mize, Charlie Keller, Cliff Mapes, Berra, Mantle, Maris, John Blanchard, and so on.

Injuries took their toll as well, and not just with Rickey. Randolph, Cerone, and Rick Rhoden—our top starter—were out for long stretches. Lou did a fine job keeping us in the race, however, until a well-publicized run-in with Steinbrenner in early August.

Lou was supposed to be in his Cleveland hotel room to wait for one of George's calls. But there was some miscommunication, and when George called, Lou wasn't there. George blew his top and he and Lou had words. Soon after, George issued a press release blasting Piniella. Ironically, in the middle of all the fuss, I pitched my best game of the year, a two-hit shutout of Detroit at Tiger Stadium on August 8 for TV's *Game of the Week*—my forty-sixth career shutout and seventh career two-hitter.

Before the game, Lou called a team meeting and he read us the text of Steinbrenner's statement. It was a scathing indictment of Lou. The timing couldn't have been worse on George's part. It took the starch right out of us. Players were sitting in the clubhouse, shaking their heads, saying things like: "Here we go again" and "Doesn't it ever stop?" I just laughed at it. What else can you do?

People pointed to the press release as the reason why we fell out of sank. It's a fact. We sank like a stone after George issued his statement. George had every right to be upset at Lou for missing the call, but I think he was wrong for going public in a press release, especially when he did, with the team still in contention. George's action poured gasoline on what should have been a dying ember. The papers had a field day with it. Steinbrenner has got to be the best copy the New York press has ever had, except for maybe Babe Ruth. It must be a joy covering George, because you know you'll always have a story.

It takes a certain kind of individual not to be distracted by the media circus that follows the Yankees, or be swallowed by the ensuing swirls of controversy. Guys who come in from other teams have no idea what it's like. And it's not just George's forceful presence—it's the media crush and the pressure from the fans to win all the time. When you come to the Yankees from a team like San Diego or Kansas City, you think you've walked into a meat grinder.

The New York press was never a problem for me, but certain guys couldn't play in that atmosphere. Ed Whitson and Bill Gullickson were two. I think Mark Langston would have had a hard time playing in New York, and also Bruce Hurst. The secret to surviving in New York is to be like a reed in the wind: you bend but don't break. You take the abuse, the heat, and all the stuff that goes with it, and just go out and do your job. If you can't do that, if you can't just laugh it off, you'll go through hell. It'll eat you alive.

Another example is Andy Hawkins in 1989. The fans and the press really got on Hawkins. The pressure started when he accepted George's big money, and it increased when Dallas came out and said Andy would be the "anchor" of the pitching staff.

They built up expectations that were too high for Hawkins. He was a .500 pitcher in 1989. He held up fairly well, winning 15 games, but I think he would have been much better coming in not as a savior but simply as just another starting pitcher.

In 1988 pitching coach Mark Connor wasn't around, nor was Lou Piniella. George fired Lou after the season. I've played with Lou, against him, and for him. As a player, all he ever cared about was hitting. But as a manager, I thought he really came into his own. He certainly proved himself by the outstanding job he did with the Reds in 1990, guiding them to a World Series victory over Oakland. He understood he had to take care of his pitching staff, players' egos, and their feelings. Lou had an excellent grasp of the interpersonal aspects of managing a baseball team. He silenced his critics by demonstrating that he understood there was more to the game of baseball than offense—though as a hitting instructor, he ranks with Charlie Lau and Walt Hriniak. Lou also was secure enough when he managed the Yankees to name a strong coaching staff: Gene Michael, Mike Ferarro, Stump Merrill, and Connor.

George brought Billy Martin back for the fifth time—"Billy V," as the press dubbed it. As sure as spring follows winter, Billy named Art Fowler as his pitching coach.

In the off-season George asked me if I wanted to keep playing in '88. When I said yes, he told me "as long as you can keep doing the job, I'll sign you. What do you want for a salary, Tommy?"

"George, I never thought I would say this, but you've been too good to me. What figure would you like to see next to my name in the papers? Just fill it in. I know you'll be fair."

Down in Fort Lauderdale Billy pitched me six times, five as a starter. In 26 innings the opposition scored nine earned runs, a performance good enough to earn me a spot in the rotation. One day, I was standing out in the outfield, shagging flies during batting practice, and it struck me how hitters had changed from my first few spring trainings. Hitting is much more scientific and technical today. Batters study it in an almost academic way, making videotapes and analyzing data. But great hitting transcends eras.

People often ask me who was the toughest batter I faced. There are so many! But a few stand out. Joe Morgan, Cincinnati's great second baseman, has to be near the top of the list. Joe was tough because he had the smallest strike zone in the world. The umpires gave him every-thing. If he didn't swing at the pitch, it was a ball. Tony Perez was extremely tough on me because of his good power to right-center field. He waited on the ball well and I couldn't throw hard enough to get it by him inside.

Roberto Clemente was a killer because he hit the same way I pitched: with his head, outthinking you. Carl Yastrzemski was like that too, a smart, intelligent hitter. It surprised me to hear Yaz say he considered me one of the toughest pitchers he faced. In my early years in the

American League, through 1971, Yaz hit me pretty good. But when I came back to the league in '79 and Yaz was in his last few years, I had some success against him. I think that's what he remembers.

Wade Boggs was another outstanding hitter who always seemed to know what was coming next. Mattingly's the better all-around ball player, but for pure hitting, Boggs is the best I've ever seen. He's a phenomenon, a pure hitting machine. I've never seen anything like him. He lit me up. What would I do if I faced Boggs again? I'd have my catcher tell him exactly what was coming in. I'm serious. I first heard that from Birdie Tebbetts. He told us if we ever faced a guy who owned us, who we couldn't get out, just tell him what's coming in and don't lie about it. Because the batter will always think: "He's setting me up." What you're doing is creating doubt in the hitter's mind.

I did pretty well against Mickey Mantle. He hit a home run off me in 1964 the first time I ever faced him, but overall, my luck held up with Mick. Speaking of Mick, there's one hit I'll never forget. It came in 1967, when I was pitching for the White Sox. Mantle rocketed a ball by my head, and into centerfield for a single. I swear I felt the wind of the ball and heard it "buzzzz" as it whizzed by my ear. That's the only time that ever happened to me, where a ball was hit so hard and so close that I *felt* it and *heard* it but didn't see it. When Mick got to first, I looked over, and he gave me that laugh of his. Then it occurred to me: another fraction of an inch, and . . . visions of Herb Score flashed into my mind. Score was the brilliant Cleveland lefty whose career was shattered by a line drive off the bat of New York's Gil McDougald on May 7, 1957. It took me a couple of minutes to get ready to pitch to the next batter. Mantle was the Bo Jackson of his time; when he first came up, he could run like blazes and was impossibly strong.

A hitter like Mantle would have benefited greatly by the DH rule. To me, the DH is like saccharin. It's artificial. It's good for the offensive part of the game, but that's about it. Part of being a well-rounded pitcher meant being able to take care of the bat. I'm not talking about hitting for average, but just being able to bunt and move runners along.

The DH rule also makes a big difference because, in the American League, you never face that easy part of the batting order: 7–8–pitcher. In a typical game, the ninth spot bats three times. That's a full inning. In the National League, if you pitch 250 innings, and take away all the pitchers' at bats, that brings you down to about 215 innings. That's 35 innings, or almost four full games, of facing nothing but pitchers at bat.

# Windup

Managing without the DH is a lot different too. It's tougher to manage in the National League because you have to know when to pinch hit, when to leave the pitcher in the game, when to double switch.

The beauty of the 162-game season is that its sheer length usually weeds out the pretenders from the contenders. Many teams start off fine but have trouble sustaining it, especially down the stretch. That was the 1988 Yankees. We took over first place on May 3 and stayed there until June 19. We hung close, and as late as July 27 we were still in first. But the schedule caught up with us. We lost a crucial mid-September series at Fenway Park in Boston, which was really our last shot at catching the Red Sox. Boston took a flag, and we dropped to fifth, 3½ games out.

In 1988 I had trouble getting untracked. After my first four games my ERA was 8.18. I fell into one doozy of a slump, and Fowler was incapable of helping me out of it. He gave me the "throw strikes" treatment. I was at wits' end trying to figure out what I was doing on my own, and Sally suggested that I call Mark Connor, who was now the baseball coach at Tennessee. I did just that, and on an off-day, flew down to see him. Mark was able to give me some helpful mechanical adjustments. Sally suggested I call George just to let him know what I had done. He appreciated it and said do whatever is necessary to get straightened out.

When Billy heard about what I had done, he was furious. He perceived my action as an end-run, wherein I'd bypassed his pitching coach. Billy took it as a slap in the face, but I never meant it that way. All I was trying to do was figure out my problem. Anyway, it worked. Almost immediately my ball was sinking again. By the end of the first half I was 8–3, 3.65, and Billy's best pitcher.

The staff was depleted by injuries, and Billy used me a lot. There was one eight-day period, from June 8 to 15, when Billy used me four times—two starts and two relief appearances. He was criticized in the press for using me this way, and that was a major factor in Steinbrenner's decision to fire him for the last time. When I saw Billy at the old-timers' game in 1989, he was still angry about it.

"I read in the papers that you thought I was using you too much [in that eight-game stretch] last year. Why did you say that?"

"Bill, what are you talking about?"

"I read the stories," he said.

"Did you ever read a quote from me criticizing you?"

"No."

"You read it from [Mike] Lupica [of the *Daily News*], didn't you? Bill, think about it. How many times did I ever refuse the baseball from you?"

"None."

"Doesn't that tell you anything?"

I wasn't surprised when I heard about Billy's death. You always expected something like that. If someone came up to you and said: "Hey, did you hear about Billy?" you expected the next words to be something like: "He got knifed in a bar," or "He got shot in a fight," or "He got busted up in a scuffle." And it's a shame. Billy was an excellent manager, but he was eaten up by his problems off the field.

The thing I liked about Billy as a manager was that he never followed a game plan. He played the game by the seat of his pants. He would do things, and you'd ask him about it, and he'd explain his strategy by saying: "I felt the other guy was gonna do such-and-such . . ."

He "felt"—I loved that. When it came to managing, Billy had the depth of feeling of a poet.

Billy was the product of his childhood. He came from a broken home, a tough childhood; and Billy was an extremely tough guy. His record as a manager speaks for itself. He won every place he went. He didn't win for long in any one place, but he won. Yet he was self-destructive. Billy did it *his* way. Unfortunately, when you work for owners, you've got to listen to *their* way. You just can't butt heads with your boss time and time again. But that was Billy. That's the way he played, that's the way he managed, and that's the way he lived. I liked Billy. He was a unique guy. My family loved him.

The second half of '88 was almost a reverse image of my first half. After July 27, I made 12 starts, going 1–5 with a 6.00 ERA. My inconsistencies were baffling. There was a game against Kansas City that typified my problems. In the first inning they went out three up/three down, all easy outs. In the second inning I pitched as if I had never touched a baseball in my life. Total inability—there was no explanation.

In the second half lots of people were saying that "Tommy's all done. He's losing it." When you're forty-five years old, you can't afford any bad stretches. Lou Piniella, back again as manager in relief of Martin, hung with me as much as he could.

When I was 8–3, I didn't have one complete game, but when the bullpen came in, they shut the door. In those games, I left the game with 23 runners on base, and only three scored. In the second half the bullpen caved in. Of the 16 runners left on base when I left the game, 13 scored.

With the mirror halves, my 1988 totals went into the record books this way: 9–8, 4.49, 32 starts (first on the team), 176⅓ innings (second), and 81 strikeouts (third). Statistics are essentially meaningless, since you can prove anything you want with them. By manipulating the stats, you can make yourself better than you were, or the ball club can make you look worse than you pitched. But there was one statistic that told me that I could still pitch, age be damned, and that was my ratio of ground balls to fly balls. It was 2.6 to 1, second in the major leagues to Orel Hershiser. The ratio proved my ball was still sinking.

Those final twelve games, though, were enough to seal my fate. When Dallas Green came in as manager, my second half is what he looked at, and hence his judgment: Tommy John is too old to pitch. It appeared my days as a big league pitcher, certainly my days as a New York Yankee, were over.

But God closes some doors only to open up others.

# 14.

# THE BEGINNING

On Tuesday morning, April 4, 1989, the writers kept calling my hotel room at the Radisson Plaza in Minneapolis for quotes about my imminent start. After taking a few calls, we had a quick breakfast, and then young Tommy and I went on an errand. Tommy, then twelve years old and a Little Leaguer, wanted a new bat. We drove around the night before, trying unsuccessfully to find someplace open that had the kind of bat he wanted. In suburban Brooklyn Park the next day we found a sporting goods store with a nice selection of bats. The store employees were surprised to find the Yankees starting pitcher for that night's game walk in.

"Aren't you Tommy John?" an employee asked. "Hey, this is great."

"Are you the opening pitcher tonight?" the store manager asked me. "Well, for crying out loud."

Tommy checked out the bats, found one he liked, and I signed a few autographs. I've always enjoyed signing; to me, it's a compliment, an honor. On the way out of the store we noticed a poster advertising a body-building contest. The photo showed a strongman flexing his muscles.

"That," I said to Murray Chass of the *New York Times*, who had accompanied us to the store, "is what Sally thought I'd look like when I got finished working out this winter—Mr. America."

## The Beginning

The writers found it amusing that I would take my son shopping on the day of the big game. But if we were home in Cresskill, I'd have been doing the same thing: trying to find my son a bat. Why should it be any different because we're on the road? The family's important wherever we are.

Sally and I try to be friends with our children, but also set limits for them. Managing a family is a lot like managing a baseball team. You've got to know how far to let them go; you have to be in control, yet foster a comfortable and relaxed atmosphere. In baseball, you do it with openness and communication. In the family, you do it with love. Sally and I have made a conscious effort to spend time with each of the four kids; it's a matter of priorities. If you are serious about making the family work, you develop relationships with your children. You find the time. You *make* the time. That's something my dad did. He worked hard for 46 years at the power company as a line serviceman. But whenever his kids needed something, he was always there for us.

The atmosphere back at the hotel was electric, like a World Series game. Hordes of people were coming up to wish us good luck for the game, including Tom Seaver, who was broadcasting for the Yanks. After a light lunch, Sally, Tommy, me, and May Kohan—one of Sally's best friends from New Jersey, who accompanied Sally for the trip—went shopping in the mall attached to the hotel. We were in a good mood, anticipating the game.

Game time was at 8:05 P.M., and I got to the Metrodome a little after five. I always liked getting to the park early, about three hours before game time (I never forgot, Jim Piersall). Bill Madden of the *Daily News* and Moss Klein of the Newark *Star-Ledger* rode to the park with me in a cab. I got to my locker, undressed, and took a hot whirlpool bath for about ten minutes to loosen up my muscles, as was my habit on the day I pitched. The bath also gave me time to collect my thoughts and quiet my mind.

The players started filing in, and when everyone was there, Dallas called his pregame meeting, right before we went out for batting practice. He gave us a five-minute talk. It was interesting. His tone changed. There was none of the pomposity we saw day after day in spring training. This was more like, "Hey, I'm just one of the guys."

"We've had a long, tough spring training," Dallas began. "But it all starts in earnest now. We're back to square one, and we're back here together. That's how we're going to do it this year: together. This is a good ball club. This is the ball club that my staff and I have picked. You were the best of the group down in Florida, and that's why you're here. We're going to win with you guys. We're going to go out there and break out fast."

It was hard to take what Dallas said as gospel, because of the way he worked the camp. In Florida he was abrasive and distanced himself from his players. Now, all of a sudden, it's "We're all in this together." The team didn't respond. There was something lacking about the team. I don't know exactly what the word is to describe what I mean. Maybe it's "cohesiveness." There just wasn't any. The team was mentally exhausted. Guys weren't looking forward to the start of the season. That's a dangerous attitude for a ball club to have. The blame for that lies with the manager.

After Dallas's speech we broke up into groups with our respective coaches: pitchers, infielders, and outfielders. The position players reviewed defensive alignments, the pitchers went over the hitters. Pitching coach Billy Connors asked me at the meeting if I needed help going over the Twins lineup or if I wanted the charts. I said no. Having faced the Twins quite a few times, I knew what to expect.

Pitching charts were never useful to me. The important thing for me was knowing the hitter's preferences. Is he a fastball hitter? A breaking ball hitter? How does he hit with men on base? When you know this, you know how to "work" a batter. For example, when some guys come up with men on base, they become breaking ball hitters. Brooks Robinson was like that. You could throw Brooks a diet of curveballs . . . until you got men on base. Then you had to throw him fastballs, because he would just sit on the breaking ball. His logic was this: What do they teach pitchers when they want a double-play? They tell you to throw the curve, because when the ball breaks down, the batter often hits the top of the ball, giving you a grounder that will start a double-play and get you out of an inning. Brooks would look for that particular pitch: a breaking ball down. That's being a smart hitter. A smart pitcher won't give him that pitch. Steve Garvey was another good breaking ball hitter. Pitchers would get two quick strikes on him, throw him a curveball, and Garvey would just hammer it.

The Metrodome—one of baseball's most synthetic stadiums—was known as the Homerdome because of the short fences and the way the ball carried, but I had won my last four starts there. Which leads to a point about pitching on Astroturf. When a sinkerballer is pitching well, when he has his good stuff, it's easier to pitch on Astroturf than it is on grass infields. People are surprised to hear that. The reason is that you don't get any bad hops. You're throwing ground ball after ground ball, and all of the bounces are true. There may be balls that sneak through for hits that otherwise would be slowed down on grass infields, but those are made up for by the plays infielders make by playing deeper on turf. They can get to balls they otherwise couldn't reach. Obviously, you need a strong infield behind you. Also, the turf must be in good shape, not like the broken stuff they used to have in Seattle. That was horrible turf, hard and slick, full of seams. I liked plastic grass for one other reason—it was easier on my heels when I ran.

I went on the field early to stretch, then did my running with the team. We threw the ball a little bit, playing long toss to loosen up our arms. We went back in, showered, changed into our game uniforms, and started our individual pregame mental preparations. With the long, 162-game schedule, baseball players don't—can't—prepare with the same intensity of, say, football players. But opening day is special. Everyone feels the butterflies, no matter how long you've played. It's not like you're back in spring training. Now, if you slip up, it goes on your record. There's a special feeling about opening day that's hard to describe; it's like a combination of anticipation and urgency. You're optimistic and on edge, confident and nervous, at the same time.

As far as the usual opening-day media distractions, I caught a break. Frank Viola, my opponent for the game, was having some well-publicized contract problems. He had issued a statement saying that once the game began tonight—that is, once the season began—he would refuse further contract talks with the Twins. He had taken out an ad in the paper, thanking the fans of Minnesota for their support. He was saying goodbye. Frank put a lot of pressure on himself, and almost all the writers in the park were over in the Twins locker room, staying on the story. He was the previous year's Cy Young Award winner and he was big news. That left me in relative peace, with just a few writers.

I joked with Ross Newhan, who was covering the game for the *Los Angeles Times*. Ross asked me how I spent the afternoon.

"I watched the movie of my life on HBO. George Burns in *18 Again!*" In fact Ross wrote about that and I got a great letter from Jonathan Prince, the producer. He even sent me a copy of the movie.

Then the topic of my age came up.

"I'm old. It's a fact. I'd like to say I've lost fifteen or twenty miles off my fastball, but I don't know if I ever had it to lose. They didn't have radar guns when I started."

In my pregame preparations, I visualized pitching against the Twins lineup, and also remembered the Gary Gaetti interview from the night before, where he said the Twins were hoping I'd be pumped up so much that I'd overthrow. So I made a conscious effort to slow everything down. I dressed slower, walked slower, even talked slower than usual.

I walked out to the bullpen almost in slow motion, deliberately, looking straight ahead, focusing my thoughts. The stands of the Metrodome cascaded around me, giving me the mental effect of walking through a tunnel. John Stearns warmed me up, then the bullpen catcher Mike Fennel took over. We didn't talk much. We just got down to work. I got into a repetition of motion, the way I liked to do while warming up: slow windup—extension—explode into ball—ball hits mitt—return of ball—slow windup—extension—explode into ball—ball hits mitt—return of ball—slow windup . . .

Slow down, Tommy, I kept repeating to myself. Slow down.

I usually could get a pretty good idea of my stuff by the way I was throwing in the bullpen. My rhythm felt good, and I liked the way the ball was moving.

Before the game, nobody said much to me. But I knew that the team had faith in me. If there were skeptics, they kept quiet. I could tell they were for me by the way the guys were coming up before the game began, wishing me good luck. They were saying things like:

"You pitched better than anybody in camp. You deserve this, T.J. Let's go out there and have some fun."

What a transformation. When I walked on the field for the first time in February, the only guy that had any faith in me was George Steinbrenner. George stuck by me from start to finish, as he had done the previous three years. They asked George about it in the papers that day, and he said he "just had a hunch that Tommy was going to be effective." Of course, if I didn't make the team, I don't know what George would have said.

I was extra aware of the need to have an easy first inning, which is usually the toughest for a sinkerballer, since the tendency is to overthrow. If you can get through the first inning okay, it makes everything easier for you. But if a pitcher expends too much energy in the first, he usually doesn't recover. Somewhere down the line, it catches up to you.

We fielded a lineup that just a few weeks before would have been listed as a million-to-one against. Gary Ward was in right field replacing the injured Dave Winfield. Roberto Kelly, our center fielder, had all of 61 games and 129 career at bats under his belt. Steve Balboni, who started spring training with the Seattle Mariners, was our first baseman, relieving Don Mattingly and his ailing back. Alvaro Espinoza, a nonroster nine-year minor leaguer, was at short for Raphael Santana. Tom Brookens, a recent Detroit castoff, was the designated hitter, and forty-five-year-old Tommy John was on the mound.

The lineups went like this:

| | |
|---|---|
| Henderson, lf | Gladden, lf |
| Sax, 2b | Backman, 2b |
| Brookens, dh | Puckett, cf |
| Balboni, 1b | Gaetti, 3b |
| Ward, rf | Hrbek, 1b |
| Pagliarulo, 3b | Laudner, c |
| Slaught, c | Castillo, rf |
| Espinoza, ss | Larkin, dh |
| Kelly, cf | Gagne, ss |

By starting the game, I tied Deacon McGuire, a catcher who played from 1884 to 1912, for most seasons in a career: 26. I became the second oldest pitcher to start an opener—Phil Niekro was forty-six when he started the Yankees opener in 1985.

Sally, our son Tommy, and May Kohan were sitting in the wives section of the Metrodome, which was way back at the top in the nose-bleed seats, thirty-six rows above first base. During my warmups, Sally came down by the railing with her video camera to tape my throwing, but when she went to film, she discovered she had left the blank tape at the hotel. Her camera was running on empty. Sally had wanted to tape some of the incidental pregame stuff, such as my warm-ups, to fully document the evening. Fortunately, WPIX-TV in New York later gave us a tape of the entire game.

The Yankees went down quietly in the top of the first, and before I went out to the mound for my first inning, Dallas clapped his hands and said: "Go get 'em, T.J."

Viola and I hooked up for a scoreless first three innings. Frank was almost unbeatable in the Dome, compiling a 23–3 record there going back to May 22, 1987.

In the first inning the Twins gave me a scare. Dan Gladden led off with a base hit. Wally Backman was up next. Backman was a pesky hitter, ideal in the number-two spot, and he worked me to a full count. Catcher Don Slaught called a fastball, down, and Backman swung over the sinker. Twins manager Tom Kelly had Gladden running, but Slaught made a fine play and threw him out at second. That was a crucial pitch and play. If I had missed with ball four, we would have faced runners on first and second and no outs, with the 3–4–5 hitters coming up. But Slaught's play cleared the bases with two outs. Kirby Puckett followed with a routine ground out to end the inning.

In the second inning the Twins put a runner on second with two out, and Carmen Castillo, the number-seven batter, up. I quickly got ahead, 0–2, and then went right at him. I threw one of my best sinkers of the night, and Castillo swung and missed. That pitch caused a minor controversy. Twins manager Kelly claimed I was scuffing the balls.

"Man, that ball dropped that much," Kelly said the next day, holding his hands a foot apart.

For years managers made claims about my alleged scuffing, and also about my alleged spitter. For me to have done all the things to a ball that I was accused of doing, I would have needed a carpenter's belt out on the mound. Of course, I didn't mind having opponents *think* I doctored the baseball. That gave me an edge. Let me set the record straight about the spitball. I can't throw one. The spitter, where the pitcher moistens the ball with saliva or vaseline, changes the aerodynamics of the ball. It's the exact same thing as a split-fingered fastball. Art Fowler and Stan Williams actually tried to teach me how to throw a spitter, with poor results. At the 1982 All-Star break Stan and I worked for about an hour on the spitter. We were out on the mound at empty Yankee Stadium with a jar of vaseline. I loaded that ball up, but with no results. I couldn't throw a spitter if my life depended on it.

In the fourth the Twins got on the board first. Backman led off and singled to left. Puckett, always a tough out, grounded into a fielder's choice to Steve Sax, who made the play unassisted. Gary Gaetti followed with a single to right, with Puckett moving to second. Puckett rode home on Kent Hrbek's single to center. After Tim Laudner struck out, a double steal and a walk loaded the bases. It was another key point in the ball game. We were down 1–0. A base hit would have made it 3–0, and might have meant an early exit for me. I reminded myself again to slow down.

Just get this guy, I told myself. All you got to do is get one out. One single out. How many times have you done that in your career? Thousands and thousands.

My little pep talk to myself paid off. I made a nice pitch to Gene Larkin and he grounded out to Sax at second base, who threw to Balboni to get us out of the inning with no further damage.

The Yankees came right back to take the lead in the top of the fifth. Slaught led off by skying to Puckett in center, but Espinoza singled to center. Kelly, the number-nine hitter, rifled a drive off the wall in left. By the time Gladden got the ball back in, Espinoza had raced home to knot the score. Rickey Henderson then topped a ball to Gagne at short, and with his blazing speed, he beat it out for a hit, with Kelly moving to third. It was a great example of what speed can do for a lineup. Rickey wasted no time with the open base, stealing second, putting two runners in scoring position. Sax then did his job by getting the ball in the air to Castillo in right, plating Kelly with the go-ahead run. It looked like we might get more when Rickey stole third and Brookens walked, but Viola toughened to get Balboni on a fly to left.

The Twins threatened again in the bottom of the sixth. They loaded the bases with two outs and Greg Gagne up. Gagne fought me pitch for pitch. After working me to a 3–2 count, he fouled off several tough pitches, refusing to go down. Sometimes when a batter does that, a pitcher loses his concentration, subconsciously lets up on a pitch and gets hurt. The longer you go in a particular sequence, the more likely your chances of making a mistake. But the effect of Gagne's tough at bat was just the opposite on me. Our little mini-drama pumped me up. I didn't want to walk him. I remember thinking, Let him hit it. Put the ball in play. No walks.

Up in her nosebleed seat thirty-six rows above first base, Sally was screaming: "C'mon. You can do it. You know you can do it."

Gagne swung at the next pitch and hit a little blooper down the right field line. As it came off the bat, it looked like trouble. It was like a dying quail, sinking fast. If it fell, it would have cleared the bases. Gary Ward came charging in and made a great running catch for the third out. When Ward made the play, I gave out with a small, almost unnoticeable skip and hop.

"All right," I said quietly.

"He caught it?" Sally screamed in disbelief. "He caught it! He caught it!" She was jumping up and down, pumping her fist in the air. My quiet son, Tommy, had a big smile on his face.

When we got back in the dugout, I went over and shook Ward's hand. The team was now infused with emotion. The bench was alive. The guys were walking up and down, clapping their hands, talking it up.

The top of the seventh started out promising for us. Espinoza and Kelly, the bottom hitters who combined for six hits and all of our runs in the game, both singled to center, putting runners on the corners. Manager Kelly got the bullpen up. Roberto Kelly stole second, and Henderson walked to load the bases with no outs. That 2–1 lead in the Metrodome was awfully thin, and we were on the bench, hoping for the hit that would bust it open. With Sax up, Kelly pulled Viola in favor of Juan Berenguer. Berenguer induced Sax to ground to Gagne, who flipped to Backman for the force of Henderson. But the Twins could not complete the double-play, and Espinoza scored to make it 3–1. The Twins right-hander avoided further damage, fanning Brookens and getting Balboni on a pop up to second. It was a nice bit of pitching by Berenguer.

In the bottom of the seventh the Twins made their last run at me. Gladden, who just about owned me in our times facing each other, singled to left. Gladden was one of those guys who, if we played him to pull, hit up the middle. If we played him up the middle, he pulled to left. Backman followed with an infield hit off my glove. The capacity crowd in the Metrodome came alive as Puckett stepped in. I backed off the mound, to slow myself down and also take the crowd out of it a little. I made doubly sure to remind myself to keep the ball down. With one swing of Kirby's bat, I could be on the short end of a 4–3 game. I threw a biting sinker. Puckett topped the ball back to the box. My only play was to first. We got the out, but the runners moved up to second and third, one out. With Gaetti up, Dallas came out to the mound.

"What do you want to do, Tommy? You've got a base open. Do you want to pitch to him or face Hrbek?"

"I'll pitch to Gaetti. I can get him."

"Okay, Tommy. Go after him."

Dallas walked back to the dugout. His visit gave me a bit of a breather. Gaetti grounded to Pagliarulo at third, who made the play to Balboni at first, Gladden scoring. The score was now 3–2, with Wally Backman, the tying run, ninety feet away. I worked the lefty Hrbek tough and got him to ground to Sax to retire the side. As we trotted off the field back to the dugout, Dallas came out and shook my hand, then put his arm around me.

"That's enough, Tommy. You did a hell of a job."

It was a typical Tommy John outing: seven innings; ten hits, all singles; 16 infield outs; two runs, both earned; two walks and three strikeouts.

My teammates came up to me shouting, cheering, patting me on the back, and congratulating me. Kelly got us an insurance run in the top of the ninth with a home run to make it 4–2, and Dale Mohorcic came in to pitch two innings of perfect, shutout relief. When he got the third out in the ninth, we all ran out to the field.

I had won on opening day!

As we were out on the field celebrating, I waved to Sally up in the stands to come down and join me. She had to fight her way down against the tide of the exiting crowd like a salmon swimming upstream. Sally and Tommy came over to me and we embraced in a triple bear hug. Tommy was jumping up and down and May was screaming with excitement. We left the field through the dugout. I went into the locker room with Tommy, while Sally and May waited in the wives waiting room outside the clubhouse.

The press lined up four and five deep in front of my locker. All the New York media were there. The national press was represented, with various magazines, network TV, and the wire services. Wave after wave the press came at me, asking the same questions. I answered each one with the patience of a monk and the enjoyment of a kid. This was fun.

"What pleased you most?"

"Going seven innings . . . I think a lot of people think if I get past four, we're lucky. People have doubted me since I first started. When I was nineteen, they said I couldn't throw hard."

Someone asked me what I thought of Dallas letting me go seven, allowing me to work out of trouble.

"Dallas is a pitcher," I answered, "and I think he understands pitching and what you have to do. If you want to get innings out of your pitchers, you let them pitch. He showed confidence in me."

What was the key moment? How did you feel? Did you tire in the seventh? And so on and so on. Over on the other side, they asked Viola for an assessment.

"Tommy's phenomenal. He's been thrown out the window, and he keeps coming back."

"You have to tip your hat to Mr. John," Puckett added. "We were one hit away from winning it, and it never happened."

"Tommy does a lot of things out there," Kelly said. "He steps off the mound, fakes a throw to a base. He plays on your emotions and tries to slow you down. He's a tease out there."

Outside, Sally and Kathy Viola met and hugged. The Violas are good friends of ours, so it was bittersweet for them. Then Frank came out of the dressing room. Sally saw him and yelled for him.

"Frank! Frank! Thanks for giving up those runs!"

He shot a glance back, wondering who would be saying something like that to him. Then he saw it was Sally. He came up to her, gave her a hug, and said he was really happy for me.

Some writers came over and started interviewing Viola, who was full of praise for me. As Sally watched, she broke out in tears. When you get a compliment from a star on the opposing team, it's the ultimate compliment.

The questions continued in the locker room. Writers kept asking for my highlight of the game. The answer was: "winning." Starting on opening day didn't thrill me as much as winning the game did. The start was an individual thing, but the victory was something all of us could share as a team.

Little Tommy and I were the last ones out of the clubhouse. When I finally met up with Sally in the waiting room, she smiled and broke out in an impromptu tap dance. Rickey Henderson saw me, shook my hand, and picked Sally up and swung her around.

"We're so happy for T.J.," Rickey said. "We're so happy for the old man."

Later that night we went out to eat and enjoyed a delicious dinner. When we got back to the hotel, we couldn't get to sleep. We got telegrams and phone calls from all over the United States.

The next day we got up and went to this little jewelry store in Minneapolis that specializes in hard-to-find baseball jewelry. We were in the store browsing—Sally, Tommy, and me—when Dallas walked in with a couple of his coaches. He came over and put his arms around me.

"What do you think of that husband of yours?" he asked Sally.

"I've never been so proud of him," she answered. "And thanks for leaving him in there, for having confidence in him. That means a lot."

"Your man really proved it to me," Dallas said. "He's amazing."

"Are you going to get your wife some jewelry?" Sally asked.

## The Beginning

"No. I'm just going to look."

"You should get her some stuff to celebrate!"

Dallas laughed, and we left the store.

Over the last couple years of my career, I was miscast in the role of number-one or -two starter. To me, the veteran Tommy John is a fourth or fifth starter, the stabilizing influence on the staff. He's no ace. One of the reasons I was let go after 1988 was that I was judged as the number-two starter and I didn't pitch well for the second slot. But as a fourth or fifth starter, my performance was exactly what you were supposed to do.

In those years, the people who were supposed to be one-two-three in the Yankee rotation were hurt or ineffective, so I stepped up by default. Guys like Guidry, Candelaria, and Rhoden missed a lot of games. All of a sudden, I was the number-one or -two starter, expected to pitch into the late innings. A fifth starter, on the other hand, goes out every fifth day and gives you six strong innings. After that, the bullpen takes over.

Because of the problems Dallas had with the rest of the rotation, I was miscast once again in the role of ace. The game would move into the seventh, the eighth innings, and I'd still be pitching, with no bullpen action.

On April 9, I made my second start, this one at Yankee Stadium versus the Indians. I went seven innings, giving up four runs, only two of them earned, in taking a 4–3 loss. That defeat, our fifth straight after winning on opening day, was particularly frustrating in that we beat ourselves with a series of blunders on the bases and in the field.

Two examples. In the bottom of the third Tom Candiotti walked Rickey Henderson, who promptly stole second and scored on a single by Steve Sax. But Sax made an ill-advised dash for second base on the throw home. Pete O'Brien cut the ball off and threw Sax out by a wide margin. That took us out of the inning, and took the bat out of Don Mattingly's hands, who never got out of the on-deck circle.

In the top of the fourth I walked Joe Carter to start the inning. O'Brien then singled to right, putting runners on the corners with nobody out. It looked like I would wriggle out of this monster jam when Cory Snyder popped out and Luis Medina fanned. But Brook Jacoby lined a single to right to tie up the game. I was mad at myself for the pitch to Jacoby. Still, that's part of the game, and you just shrug it off. But then

291

our defense fell apart. Andy Allanson grounded to Pagliarulo at third, and Pags threw over Mattingly's head at first. Carter scored, giving the Indians a 2–1 lead, and Jacoby moved to third. Felix Fermin was at the plate when the Indians put on a double steal. Allanson broke for second. Slaught threw low to Espinoza, who was late covering and couldn't handle the throw. Allanson was safe and Jacoby scored the third run. In the dugout Dallas shook his head and swore in frustration. In the owner's box George Steinbrenner pounded his fist into the wall.

After the game, Dallas was clearly feeling the effects of a 1–5 start in New York.

"We didn't execute again, and we got our butt kicked. We don't have a team that can overcome [its own mistakes] . . . They're making two million dollars a year . . . they should be able to execute properly."

The frustration continued. Over my next five starts, in which I went 1–4, I pitched 35⅓ innings. That's certainly not the way you use a fourth or fifth starter, who would have gone about 30 innings. Those five extra innings made a huge difference. My statistics over the first six innings of games were excellent. In my first seven appearances for 1989 my record was 2–5, with a 4.74 ERA. But in the 40⅔ innings pitched before the seventh inning, my ERA was 2.48. In the 7⅔ innings pitched in the seventh inning or after, the ERA zoomed to 14.79. If I had been the fifth starter, as I should have been, I might have pitched the whole year.

Some people raised the question: Why wasn't Dallas using me the way one would think a forty-six-year-old starter should be used? Some speculated that he did it to hang me out to dry, to sandbag me, to finally vindicate himself by "proving" that I could no longer pitch in the big leagues. Only Dallas knows for sure, but I don't believe he did that. First, he was trying to win ball games. He was a new manager, and knowing George's nervous trigger finger, I doubt he would let a personal vendetta get in the way of doing what he thought was best to win for the team. Second, the bullpen didn't get off to a good start. Righetti was hurting, and Dallas lacked a closer or a reliable setup man. Third, that was Dallas's general way of managing. He was from the old school; he believed starters had to go a lot of innings. Fourth, his comments about me were supportive. For example, after I lost a tough 3–1 game on April 23 to the Indians, he had this to say:

"John pitched his butt off. We have an anemic offense. The guy's pitching his butt off, he's going to be in the Hall of Fame, and you'd think we could get some offense. We've got guys not even hitting their weight."

As the losses mounted, the impenetrable wall of ice that had divided Dallas and me in spring training was back up again. The team as a whole was playing badly, and he was feeling pressure from upstairs.

But on April 27 at Kansas City it came together for me one last time. My mates gave me a 3–0 lead through five innings; on the mound, the ball was doing anything I wanted it to. Going into the ninth, I was crusing with a four-hitter, leading 3–1. Kevin Seitzer led off with a high, arcing fly ball in the right field corner. It was catchable, but Stanley Jefferson overran it and misplayed it into a double. Jim Eisenreich plated Seitzer with a single to right, shaving our lead to 3–2. Danny Tartabull ripped a single up the middle, and Dallas had seen enough. I left the game—88 pitches, 65 for strikes—in Dave Righetti's hands.

When Dallas got to the mound, he took the ball from me.

"Tommy, you can't pitch any better. That was one hell of a job. We've got to nail this one down for you. We owe you."

Righetti came in; Dallas gave him the ball, explained the game situation, gave him a little pat, and then said, "Smoke 'em, baby."

Pat Tabler bunted the runners to second and third. Royals manager John Wathan sent up Bill Buckner to bat for Bob Boone. Dallas ordered an intentional pass, loading the bases and setting up a force at any base. Wathan continued the managerial chess match by countering with George Brett as a pinch hitter for Kurt Stillwell. That move surprised me, since Wathan had the right-hand-hitting Bo Jackson on the bench, recovering from a minor leg injury but available to pinch-hit. But for some reason Wathan wanted the lefty Brett matched against the lefty Righetti.

The 35,173 fans stood up on their feet in anticipation of a big hit. They roared. The three Royal baserunners took their leads. Dave paused. I paced in the dugout, silently hoping for Rags to get Brett.

"Get a pop out, Rags. Pop him up."

Dave came in with heat on his first pitch. Brett couldn't lay off the rising fastball, swung late, and lofted a fly ball to shallow left field—the proverbial "can of corn." Henderson came in, made the easy putout, and the runners held. With two outs, that brought up Frank White, a dangerous clutch hitter.

Of all the batters they had, I hated to see White up there. He was a crafty, veteran hitter who knew how to respond to pressure. White stood with one foot in the batter's box, eyeing the field, looking over the defense. He stepped in, planted the back leg. Rags went into his motion and came in with a blazing, low fastball. White hacked at the first pitch and bounced a grounder to Espinoza at short. Espy fielded the ball cleanly, then tossed to Sax covering second for the force out to end the game.

We came out on the field to congratulate Rags for saving the win for me. It was career win number 288. It would be my last.

The team continued to flounder, and some of the players publicly criticized Dallas. That was enough for George, who erupted in the papers, blasting the behavior of the team.

"They're acting like babies," he said. "I'm sorry to think they'd speak out. They're the third highest paid team in baseball. It shouldn't be them complaining, it should be me. I'm the sucker. When Dallas said they stink, he's right. They stink . . . I've watched them night after night play like Little Leaguers. Sometimes when I'm watching this team, I see things that turn my stomach and I want to turn to the hockey playoffs or the Knicks."

I lost my next four starts after the win against the Royals, and the tense atmosphere on the team didn't help matters. Rumors, speculation, and scuttlebutt began, and I wasn't oblivious to it. People were wondering how long it could go on and how long Dallas would stick with me.

"I think I'm history," I told pitching coach Billy Connors after my next-to-the-last appearance against Oakland on May 18, a 6–2 loss in which I went just 4⅓ innings.

"Nah, don't say that," he said, trying to be encouraging. "Shit, you've thrown the ball too good for that."

My problem? I wasn't staying on my side of the plate, which is outside. I could miss outside and not get hurt. The worst I'd get out of it is a ball in the count. When I missed inside, as I was doing, I got in trouble. But that was a location problem. It had nothing to do with my arm, which still felt fine.

Dallas had his own speculations. He told the press I was "hanging on" to get 300 wins, the way Early Wynn did in 1963. Dallas said George felt sorry for me and that's why I was still on the team. That was all presumptuous nonsense. The 300 wins didn't concern me. Winning 300 games was a goal to shoot for, and nothing more. Dallas had no idea of what motivated me. I just enjoyed playing baseball. *That* was my motivation.

On May 25, I made my last appearance in a big league uniform, starting against the Angels at Yankee Stadium. I went 5⅓ innings, giving up five runs in a no-decision effort. For future editions of *Trivial Pursuit,* let it be recorded that the last batter I faced in my career was Devon White, who singled. The last out I recorded was Johnny Ray, who, appropriately enough, grounded out, Pagliarulo to Mattingly.

Give credit to the New York fans, who are among the most astute in all of baseball. They sensed this could be it. As I walked into the dugout after being relieved in the sixth by Dale Mohorcic, the home fans gave me a standing ovation, a last hurrah that will stay with me the rest of my life.

I got in ten games in 1989, all starts, compiling a 2–7 mark with a 5.80 ERA. The stats didn't adequately sum up how I was actually pitching, since they didn't break down the first six innings versus the seventh inning plus. But it was clear. Dallas didn't want to use me anymore. I hung around for four more days. Finally, on May 29, Connors said Dallas wanted to see me.

"Bill," I said, sticking out my hand, "it's been a pleasure."

I walked into Dallas's office. Dallas, Syd Thrift, and Connors were there. No one could look at me and tell me point-blank that I was finished.

"Tommy, we called the White Sox. They don't want you," Thrift said.

"No kidding. Who would take me now? Would the Yankees take someone and have to give up a player in return?"

"We told George what we want to do," Thrift continued, "and George says it's time to implement Plan B."

"What's Plan B?" I asked.

Dallas started laughing, saying: "Apparently, George is the only one who knows what Plan B is."

"Plan B," Thrift relayed, "is that you're going to go down to Fort Lauderdale and coach."

"No. I don't want it. I intend to try to keep playing. I talked to George about doing some things in the minors after I'm out of baseball. I don't consider myself out of baseball now."

Judging by his next question, Thrift either didn't hear me, wouldn't listen to me, or didn't believe me.

"You want to stay here and officially announce your retirement?" he asked.

"No, Syd. Listen to me. I have no intention of announcing anything in Dallas's office. I've led my life in baseball with style and class, and if I announce anything, it will be the same way. I'll have a party for the writers at the 21 Club. When we go out, it won't be in Dallas's office. We'll go out with balloons, fireworks, and guns blazing."

"Well, what should we tell the press?" Thrift asked, puzzled.

"You tell them anything you want. I'm going home to tell my family first, then call my dad, before he hears it over the air and has a heart attack or something."

Dallas immediately informed the press.

"It was a tough call. With the class person Tommy John is and always will be on and off the field, it's a difficult time for a manager to make this kind of decision. I was tempted, very tempted [to give him another start]. I thought about that. I kept searching my soul, to see if I could see any difference, if he wouldn't continue to hurt twenty-three other guys. But I've reached the conclusion that we've got to prepare for the future, and the future is younger pitching. You can read his record as well as I can. What I was looking for from spring training on was an improved pitching performance. Tommy went the other way."

That may have been the case, but my fastball was better than it had been in spring training and my ball was still sinking. What Dallas didn't admit was that he had used me improperly. If I had been the fourth or fifth starter, the ending would have been quite different.

Don Mattingly signed a bat for the kids as a going-away present. When I got home, I walked in, gave Sally the bat, and said:

"I got released today. I'm no longer a Yankee."

Her eyes welled up and we hugged. We knew it was coming, but when it actually happens, you can't help feeling regret. I then called my dad. He was there in the very beginning for me, making my strike zone out of string and wood, and he was there at the end, comforting me.

"Pop, they released me."

"You've had your time in the sun. I'm proud of you."

There was one other call to make. To George Steinbrenner. He wasn't in, but he quickly returned my call.

"George," I told him, "I want to apologize. You stuck your neck out for me. I had the ball for a while and dropped it. I thought I pitched well, but things didn't break right. I want you to know one thing. I tried my absolute best and I appreciate everything you did for me. I will always appreciate that, because it took a lot for you to go out on the limb like that."

George wouldn't have any of it.

"Tommy, you proved me right by making the team. But what you did this year is irrelevant. You got that chance because you're a winner. You're still a winner, and in my book you'll always be a winner. If the Yankees had more guys like you, we'd be better off for it. You knew how to be a Yankee. You don't have to apologize to me. I'm the one who's thanking you."

I wasn't ready to call an end to my career, and contacted some other clubs. There was interest from several, notably the Tigers, Cardinals, and the Red Sox, but nothing happened. The end of May is one of the worst times to be released, because the pennant races haven't heated up, and most teams think that what they have will be enough to get them through the year. They don't start looking to add to the roster until the stretch drive. So I spent the summer at home, working out a little, playing with the kids, helping them with their Little League team. The chance of playing again in the big leagues just kind of faded out, like a long-playing record album coming to an end.

I'll always remember the 1989 season as one of triumph and victory.

The opening day win had been the culmination of the long, tortuous road that began in the late fall with my intensified workouts. My success was measured by the fact that, by believing in myself and through the support of my family, I was able to defy the odds one last time. In a real sense, the experience crowned a long and satisfying career in an absolutely fitting manner. Stanley Kubrick couldn't have directed a better script: here was the old left-hander, surprising everybody by making the team; by being named opening day starter; by pitching like I did; and by beating Frank Viola, the current Cy Young Award winner who was a noted Yankee killer. The only regret was that I didn't get to bow out on my own terms. The actual end should have been more of a celebration.

There's a sense of relief when I look back on my career, knowing that it's over. The only thing I would have done differently is learn the change-up much earlier, because it's such a devastating pitch. Other than that, I wouldn't change a thing. I feel things happened the way God intended.

I was blessed being able to make my living at playing baseball and also to be able to throw a ball the way I did. My style of pitching accounted for my longevity: the "here it is, hit it" approach. My pitching philosophy, if I had to sum it up in a few words, would consist of just three elements: (1) pitch quickly, (2) throw strikes, and (3) change speeds.

Despite the dramatic changes we've seen in the game from the time when I first broke in, the game itself remains essentially the same. From the mound to home plate is still sixty feet, six inches. The bases are still ninety feet apart.

It would be a shame if money ends up ruining the game. I know the fans have a hard time understanding the new financial ground rules. People think athletes are overpaid. But is Bruce Springsteen worth what he gets? Is Lee Iacocca? Is Bill Cosby? There's money in baseball. That's the reality.

Baseball has Peter Ueberroth to thank for its present financial success. Peter did a great job as commissioner. He enhanced revenues through aggressive marketing, licensing, and broadcast contracts. He went out and sold the game, just as he did for the Olympics in 1984. If a company now wants to be an official sponsor of major league baseball, it will cost them big bucks.

Bowie Kuhn was a great guy but not a forceful commissioner, so different from Peter. Bowie was laid back, a "let's see what transpires" type. Peter was a "let's make it happen" type. Bart Giamatti's brief tenure was like the presidency of John F. Kennedy. He wasn't in office long enough for one to make an informed judgment. A lot of owners liked Bowie and Bart but hated Peter, which tells me something. It tells me that Peter wasn't afraid to step on toes, or, as the owners viewed it, bite the hand that fed him. He made the owners pay up x number of dollars to the players. He was tough and forceful with the owners. That's hard to do with the people who pay your salary. Historically, baseball's commissioners have slept in the same bed with the owners. That's something I never understood about baseball. I've always thought the commissioner should be picked and paid by both the owners and the players, for the good of both sides.

I didn't know Fay Vincent, although he was reluctantly put into the spotlight by a series of bizarre events, most notably the earthquake in the 1989 World Series, and his involvement in the George Steinbrenner case in the summer of 1990. A lot of people asked me about that case.

I don't think Vincent took action against George, as much as George took action against himself. The commissioner was in favor of a two-year suspension, but George opted for a lifetime removal from his day-to-day running of the Yankees.

People couldn't figure out why George would take the lifetime ban over a two-year judgment, but what did he really give up? He was allowed to keep almost half interest in the ownership of the team, as well as retain his voice in the major financial decisions regarding the ballclub. Another factor may have been his wife, who was ill at the time. I think George wanted to spend more time with her. Besides, George had been looking to wind down his daily involvement in the team anyway. Running the Yankees, as much as George reveled in it, also had become a heavy burden.

I wasn't a part of the investigation. All I know is what I read in the papers and from that information, I don't think George got a fair shake. It's no secret that over the years, George has been a disliked person throughout baseball, but he treated me and my family fairly. So when the dam started to break, people rushed in with innuendo, speculation, and distortion. And this was New York City, media center of the world. And this was George Steinbrenner, the most controversial owner of his time. It would have been hard for Solomon himself to rule on the case objectively, or even cover it objectively.

What George did was morally wrong, no question about that. He paid $40,000 to a confessed gambler, apparently for information on Dave Winfield. George shouldn't have done this. But I personally didn't think the action was worth the notoriety it got. George really hurt himself in Vincent's eyes by changing his story about why he paid the $40,000. He first said he felt sorry for the guy. Then he said he paid it because he feared for his personal safety and that of his family. If he had just admitted: "I was in a battle with Winfield, and I thought I could use the information," I think things would have been better for him.

I felt bad for George. Shortly before the commissioner's ruling, I wrote him a note. I just told him I appreciated all he had done for me, Sally, and the family over the years, and added that regardless of what the commissioner ruled, he would always have two friends in Sally and Tommy John. I still feel that way about George. I closed with a quote from Robert Schuller: "Tough times don't last. Tough people do."

Every ballplayer in the game today should go up to George and shake his hand, because he was the man primarily responsible for today's multimillion-dollar contracts. He was the first to really open up the checkbook, along with Ted Turner and Gene Autry. Of course, the new financial realities of the game have their downside, especially for the fans, who are sick of hearing about money. They don't think guys are worth what they're getting. Besides, they'd rather hear about box scores and batting averages than the contract renegotiations and signing bonuses.

I can only hope the financial prosperity baseball now enjoys doesn't turn into a festival of greed that damages the game and totally alienates its true fans. Both owners and players alike should never forget: the fan makes this the great game it is.

Playing baseball for a living is the greatest job in the world. I loved baseball. It was fun for me, and that's why I played. The only real negative was the travel time, the time away from my family.

Baseball is a game that allows us all a chance to stay young at heart. Who knows? Maybe twenty years from now they'll discover an elixir in St. Augustine, Florida, and I'll become young again. And I'll come back again. If not, I'll come back to cherished memories, memories of my life in baseball. And I'll embrace whatever the future promises for myself and my family.

With God's help, I'll see things through. After all, I've had experience in that sort of thing. I've been coming back all my life. Each time I do, I'll remember a sign that Dallas Green hung in the Yankee clubhouse in spring training:

A GREAT PLEASURE IN
LIFE IS DOING
WHAT PEOPLE SAY YOU
CANNOT DO

Dallas, you were sure right about that.

# BIO NOTES

**Tommy John** pitched 26 years in the major leagues from 1963 to 1989 for the Cleveland Indians, Chicago White Sox, Los Angeles Dodgers, California Angels, Oakland A's, and New York Yankees. He won 288 big league games. An avid golfer, Tommy lives in Cresskill, New Jersey, with his wife Sally and their four children, Tami, Tommy III, Travis, and Taylor.

**Dan Valenti** is a writer with eleven books to his credit. He has written extensively about baseball. Other works include fiction, criticism, humor, poetry, and screen writing. Dan has a Master's degree from Syracuse University. He lives in Massachusetts.

# APPENDIX

## TOMMY JOHN'S LIFETIME RECORD

| YEAR | TEAM | G | GS | W-L | ERA | IP | H | R | ER | BB | SO | CG | Sho | SV |
|------|------|---|----|----|-----|-----|-----|-----|-----|-----|-----|----|-----|-----|
| 1961 | Dubuque | 14 | 13 | 10–4 | 3.17 | 88.0 | 74 | 47 | 31 | 59 | 99 | 4 | 1 | 0 |
| 1962 | Charleston | 21 | 20 | 6–8 | 3.87 | 128.0 | 129 | 67 | 55 | 71 | 114 | 7 | 0 | 0 |
|      | Jacksonville | 8 | 7 | 2–2 | 4.76 | 34.0 | 29 | 20 | 18 | 16 | 27 | 1 | 1 | 0 |
| 1963 | Charleston | 12 | 12 | 9–2 | 1.61 | 95.0 | 85 | 25 | 17 | 12 | 45 | 8 | 2 | 0 |
|      | Jacksonville | 18 | 14 | 6–8 | 3.53 | 102.0 | 115 | 53 | 40 | 39 | 63 | 4 | 2 | 0 |
|      | Cleveland | 6 | 3 | 0–2 | 2.21 | 20.1 | 23 | 10 | 5 | 6 | 9 | 0 | 0 | 0 |
| 1964 | Cleveland | 25 | 14 | 2–9 | 3.91 | 94.1 | 97 | 53 | 41 | 35 | 65 | 2 | 1 | 0 |
|      | Portland | 13 | 11 | 6–6 | 4.26 | 74.0 | 75 | 38 | 35 | 24 | 72 | 5 | 0 | 0 |
| 1965 | Chicago (AL) | 39 | 27 | 14–7 | 3.09 | 183.2 | 162 | 67 | 63 | 58 | 126 | 6 | 1 | 3 |
| 1966 | Chicago (AL) | 34 | 33 | 14–11 | 2.62 | 223.0 | 195 | 76 | 65 | 57 | 138 | 10 | 5* | 0 |
| 1967 | Chicago (AL) | 31 | 29 | 10–13 | 2.47 | 178.1 | 143 | 62 | 49 | 47 | 110 | 9 | 6* | 0 |
| 1968 | Chicago (AL) | 25 | 25 | 10–5 | 1.98 | 177.1 | 135 | 45 | 39 | 49 | 117 | 5 | 1 | 0 |
| 1969 | Chicago (AL) | 33 | 33 | 9–11 | 3.25 | 232.1 | 230 | 91 | 84 | 90 | 128 | 6 | 2 | 0 |
| 1970 | Chicago (AL) | 37 | 37 | 12–17 | 3.28 | 269.0 | 253 | 117 | 98 | 101 | 138 | 10 | 3 | 0 |
| 1971 | Chicago (AL) | 38 | 35 | 13–16 | 3.62 | 229.0 | 244 | 115 | 92 | 58 | 131 | 10 | 3 | 0 |
| 1972 | Los Angeles | 29 | 29 | 11–5 | 2.89 | 186.2 | 172 | 68 | 60 | 40 | 117 | 4 | 1 | 0 |
| 1973 | Los Angeles | 36 | 31 | 16–7 | 3.10 | 218.0 | 202 | 88 | 75 | 50 | 116 | 4 | 2 | 0 |
| 1974 | Los Angeles | 22 | 22 | 13–3 | 2.59 | 153.0 | 133 | 51 | 44 | 42 | 78 | 5 | 3 | 0 |
| 1975 | Los Angeles | — | — | — | — | ON DISABLED LIST | | | — | — | — | — | — | — |
| 1976 | Los Angeles | 31 | 31 | 10–10 | 3.09 | 207.0 | 207 | 76 | 71 | 61 | 91 | 6 | 2 | 0 |

# Appendix

## TOMMY JOHN'S LIFETIME RECORD

| YEAR | TEAM | G | GS | W-L | ERA | IP | H | R | ER | BB | SO | CG | Sho | SV |
|---|---|---|---|---|---|---|---|---|---|---|---|---|---|---|
| 1977 | Los Angeles | 31 | 31 | 20–7 | 2.78 | 220.0 | 225 | 82 | 68 | 50 | 123 | 11 | 3 | 0 |
| 1978 | Los Angeles | 33 | 30 | 17–10 | 3.30 | 213.0 | 230 | 95 | 78 | 53 | 124 | 7 | 0 | 1 |
| 1979 | New York (AL) | 37 | 36 | 21–9 | 2.97 | 276.0 | 268 | 109 | 91 | 65 | 111 | 17 | 3 | 0 |
| 1980 | New York (AL) | 36 | 36 | 22–9 | 3.43 | 265.0 | 270 | 115 | 101 | 56 | 78 | 16 | 6† | 0 |
| 1981 | New York (AL) | 20 | 20 | 9–8 | 2.64 | 140.0 | 135 | 50 | 41 | 39 | 50 | 7 | 0 | 0 |
| 1982 | New York (AL) | 30 | 26 | 10–10 | 3.66 | 186.2 | 190 | 84 | 76 | 34 | 54 | 9 | 2 | 0 |
|  | California | 7 | 7 | 4–2 | 3.86 | 35.0 | 49 | 18 | 15 | 5 | 14 | 0 | 0 | 0 |
| 1983 | California | 34 | 34 | 11–13 | 4.33 | 234.2 | 287 | 126 | 113 | 49 | 65 | 9 | 0 | 0 |
| 1984 | California | 32 | 29 | 7–13 | 4.52 | 181.1 | 223 | 97 | 91 | 56 | 47 | 4 | 1 | 0 |
| 1985 | California | 12 | 6 | 2–4 | 4.70 | 38.1 | 51 | 22 | 20 | 15 | 17 | 0 | 0 | 0 |
|  | Modesto | 2 | 2 | 0–0 | 5.73 | 11.0 | 12 | 8 | 7 | 6 | 11 | 0 | 0 | 0 |
|  | Madison | 1 | 1 | 0–0 | 3.00 | 6.0 | 4 | 2 | 2 | 4 | 3 | 0 | 0 | 0 |
|  | Oakland | 11 | 11 | 2–6 | 4.70 | 48.0 | 66 | 37 | 33 | 13 | 8 | 0 | 0 | 0 |
| 1986 | New York (AL) | 13 | 10 | 5–3 | 2.93 | 70.2 | 73 | 27 | 23 | 15 | 28 | 1 | 0 | 0 |
|  | Ft. Lauderdale | 3 | 3 | 2–0 | 0.00 | 13.2 | 7 | 2 | 0 | 1 | 7 | 1 | 1 | 0 |
| 1987 | New York (AL) | 33 | 33 | 13–6 | 4.03 | 187.2 | 212 | 95 | 84 | 47 | 63 | 3 | 1 | 0 |
| 1988 | New York (AL) | 35 | 32 | 9–8 | 4.49 | 176.1 | 221 | 96 | 88 | 46 | 81 | 0 | 0 | 0 |
| 1989 | New York (AL) | 10 | 10 | 2–7 | 5.80 | 63.2 | 87 | 45 | 41 | 22 | 18 | 0 | 0 | 0 |
| MAJOR LEAGUE TOTALS |  | 750 | 700 | 288–231 | 3.34 | 4708.2 | 4783 | 2017 | 1749 | 1259 | 2245 | 161 | 46 | 4 |

*Denotes tied for league
†Denotes led league

## POSTSEASON RECORD

| YEAR | TEAM | G | GS | W-L | ERA | IP | H | R | ER | BB | SO | CG | Sho | SV |
|---|---|---|---|---|---|---|---|---|---|---|---|---|---|---|
| **Division Championship Record** | | | | | | | | | | | | | | |
| 1981 | N.Y. vs. Mil. | 1 | 1 | 0–1 | 6.43 | 7.0 | 8 | 5 | 5 | 2 | 0 | 0 | 0 | 0 |
| **League Championship Record** | | | | | | | | | | | | | | |
| 1977 | L.A. vs. Phil. | 2 | 2 | 1–0 | 0.66 | 13.2 | 11 | 5 | 1 | 5 | 11 | 1 | 0 | 0 |
| 1978 | L.A. vs. Phil. | 1 | 1 | 1–0 | 0.00 | 9.0 | 4 | 0 | 0 | 2 | 4 | 1 | 1 | 0 |
| 1980 | N.Y. vs. K.C. | 1 | 1 | 0–0 | 2.70 | 6.2 | 8 | 2 | 2 | 1 | 3 | 0 | 0 | 0 |
| 1981 | N.Y. vs. Oak. | 1 | 1 | 1–0 | 1.50 | 6.0 | 6 | 1 | 1 | 1 | 3 | 0 | 0 | 0 |
| 1982 | Cal. vs. Mil. | 2 | 2 | 1–1 | 5.11 | 12.1 | 11 | 9 | 7 | 6 | 6 | 1 | 0 | 0 |

# Appendix

## World Series Record

| | | | | | | | | | | | | | | |
|---|---|---|---|---|---|---|---|---|---|---|---|---|---|---|
| 1977 | L.A. vs. N.Y. | 1 | 1 | 0–1 | 6.00 | 6.0 | 9 | 5 | 4 | 3 | 7 | 0 | 0 | 0 |
| 1978 | L.A. vs. N.Y. | 2 | 2 | 1–0 | 2.88 | 14.2 | 14 | 8 | 5 | 4 | 6 | 0 | 0 | 0 |
| 1981 | N.Y. vs. L.A. | 3 | 2 | 1–0 | 0.69 | 13.0 | 11 | 1 | 1 | 0 | 8 | 0 | 0 | 0 |

## All-Star Game Record

| | | | | | | | | | | | | | | |
|---|---|---|---|---|---|---|---|---|---|---|---|---|---|---|
| 1968 | A.L. at Hou. | 1 | 0 | 0–0 | 0.00 | 0.2 | 1 | 0 | 0 | 0 | 0 | 0 | 0 | 0 |
| 1978 | N.L. at S.D. | Did | not | play | — | — | — | — | — | — | — | — | — | — |
| 1979 | A.L. at Sea. | Did | not | play | — | — | — | — | — | — | — | — | — | — |
| 1980** | A.L. at L.A. | 1 | 0 | 0–1 | 11.57 | 2.1 | 4 | 3 | 3 | 0 | 1 | 0 | 0 | 0 |

**Named left-handed pitcher for *The Sporting News* American League All-Star team, 1980

## Major League Hitting Totals

| AB | H | HR | RBI | Avg. |
|---|---|---|---|---|
| 900 | 141 | 5 | 61 | .157 |

## Personal

Born: May 22, 1943 in Terre Haute, Indiana
Height: 6 feet 3 inches
Married: Sally Simmons July 13, 1970
Weight: 200
Children: Tamara, Thomas, Travis, and Taylor